LOCAL
FLAVORS

ALSO BY DEBORAH MADISON

THE GREENS COOKBOOK

THE SAVORY WAY

VEGETARIAN COOKING FOR EVERYONE

THIS CAN'T BE TOFU!

VEGETARIAN SUPPERS FROM DEBORAH MADISON'S KITCHEN

VEGETABLE SOUPS FROM DEBORAH MADISON'S KITCHEN

LOCAL
FLAVORS

COOKING AND EATING FROM
AMERICA'S FARMERS' MARKETS

DEBORAH MADISON

PHOTOGRAPHS BY LAURIE SMITH

ILLUSTRATIONS BY PATRICK MCFARLIN

Broadway Books | New York

A hardcover edition of this book was originally published in 2002 by Broadway Books.

BROADWAY BOOKS and its logo, a letter B bisected on the diagonal, are trademarks of Broadway Books, a division of Random House, Inc.

Visit our Web site at www.broadwaybooks.com.

All photos are © Laurie Smith 2002, except those on pages i, ii, 50, 54, 76, 97, 100, 168, 206, 212, 214, 229, 263, 266, 282, 290, 306, 311, 342, 372, 377, 380, which were taken by the author.

Library of Congress Cataloging-in-Publication Data
Madison, Deborah.
    Local flavors : cooking and eating from America's farmers' markets / Deborah Madison.—1st ed.
       p.   cm.
    Includes bibliographical references and index.
     I. Cookery, American.   2. Farmers' markets.   I. Title.
  TX715 .M1157   2002
  641.5973—dc21   2001049940

PRINTED IN CHINA

ISBN 978-0-7679-2949-3

10 9 8 7 6 5 4 3

For Michael and Dianne,

for quitting your day jobs to grow good food,

gorgeous flowers, and great girls.

And in memory of Marion Rullo,

a good farmer

and fine cheesemaker.

Contents

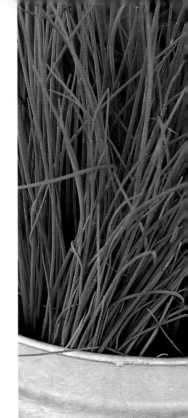

Acknowledgments

The number of people who gave me their time, advice, insights, and information is phenomenal. First, of course, are the farmers, without whom there would be no farmers' markets. In particular, I wish to express my heartfelt appreciation to those farmers from northern New Mexico, whose dedication, skill, vision, and endurance have long nurtured our community. It is your well-honed art of the field and farm that puts the true joy into cooking. It would be a dull world indeed without the treasures you bring to the market.

Farmers are essential, but markets would not happen without the numerous volunteers. Among the volunteers, managers, and market founders I met are those who fielded my many questions, especially Patty Brand, Donita Anderson, Mary Holmes, Randii MacNear, Laura Avery, Abby Mandel, Janine MacLachlan, Sarah Stegner, Cynthia Hizer, Joanne Neft, Richard McCarthy, Joel Prataker, Cecelia McCord, Dee Logan, Ann Yonkers, and Doug Warner. Thank you all for your help and your insights.

My thanks also to those of you who took me to your markets: Kitty Morse, Chris Hastings, Amelia Saltsman (and for her mushroom recipe), Dee Logan, Jeff Roberts, Russ Parsons, Ellen Ogden, Odessa Piper, Molly Stevens, Maureen Callahan, John and Emily Sutcliffe, Sue Mei Yu, Cliff Wright, Martha Rose Schulman, Dorothy Patent, Kathleen Craig, Grant Flemming, and Elizabeth Zippern. My deep thanks to my brother, Michael Madison, who cheerfully came out of the field any number of times to answer my botany-related questions, and to Dianne Madison who, in addition to visiting farms and markets with me, also found those missing phone numbers of farmers when I needed them, and so much more. I would also like to express my appreciation to cooks and writers who have offered me their valuable perspectives: Odessa Piper, Lucia Watson, Parker Bosley, Alice Waters, Gary Paul Nabhan, Stephen Facciaola, Michele Anna Jordan, Greg Patent, Fred Plotkin, Diana Kennedy, and Damon Lee Fowler.

Thank you (and kudos) to Ruth Murphy for insisting that I visit the children's farmers' market in St. Paul. To Sandy Szwarc, Joe Colanero, Tamar and Barbara Haskell, Lynn Weddach, Bill Webb, and Eliot Coleman, my gratitude for acting as my far-flung correspondents, letting me know what was ripe in your area when I couldn't be everywhere at once. Many thanks to Bruce Aidells for responding with alacrity and enthusiasm to my request for a beef recipe—no one I know could be a better provider, and to Joanne Neft, market manager par excellence, for her delicious persimmon recipes and her long friendship.

Many farmers and growers have been especially generous with their time, explaining to me how they grow their crops, raise their animals, harvest nuts, and press their oils. My deep thanks to Riley Starks and Tom Delahanty for sharing their pastured chickens expertise, to Judy Olsen for her flair with nettles, and to Tracee Canisso for explaining all about sweet potatoes. Thanks also to Robert and Ellen Lane and Rink and Jenny DaVee for that splendid lunch on the farm, Rich Collins who knows more about endive than anyone else, Dennis Donahue and Lucio Gomiero who taught me about the other chicories, Michael Abelman for the avocados and other expertise, Jan Barbo for her bushels of quince, and Rusty Hall for his extraordinary almonds and vision of what will keep small farmers going. Eremita and Margaret Campos have generously shared both their stories and their produce over the years, while Timothy Broughton finally explained what makes kiwis sweet in between bites of hot roasted chestnuts. Carol Ann Sayle and Larry Butler of Boggy Creek Farm in Austin, Texas, have been invaluable informants when it comes to the ins and outs of growing organic food and raising chickens in an urban market. They have fulfilled an outstanding vision. Thank you for teaching me, feeding me, and becoming such good friends.

Patty Karlovitz, publisher of New Mexico's *Localflavor,* in whose pages I was able to first publish some of these market stories, was gracious in allowing me to share the title of her magazine. Joan Dye Gussow, who became truly local by farming in her backyard, supplied me with certain elusive facts and figures. I would particularly like to thank Kent Whealy of The Seed Savers Exchange for his vision of diversity, his inspiring talks, and good conversation. He is, in many ways, at the heart of this book.

I would be remiss not to express my deep thanks to Les Dames d'Escoffier for choosing me to receive the MFK Fisher Mid-Career Award in 1994. The generous gift that accompanied this honor was what initially started my research on farmers and farm markets.

Thank you also to the following publications in which some of these recipes previously appeared in slightly different forms: *Fine Cooking, Kitchen Garden, Williams-Sonoma TASTE, Gourmet,* and the *Los Angeles Times.*

When it comes to making the book, my debt is also large. I wish to warmly thank Laurie Smith, whose beautiful pictures of food and markets grace these pages, not only for her art but for her cheerful willingness to change gears in midair and accommodate my enthusiasm for the unexpected image. Laurie, you're the best! Many thanks to Kathi Long who has unfailingly worked with me for many years on photo shoots and in the kitchen. To our photo sessions came bags of dishes and linens from the Clay Angel, which are as inspiring and beautiful as the foods and flowers our farmers grow. My warmest thanks to the ever-accommodating staff who has wrapped and unwrapped them all on my behalf many times, and especially to owner Judy Espinar for her unfailing generosity and support through all my various projects. My gratitude to Esther Kovari, Lynn Walters, Cheryl Jamison, Lé Adams, Pam Roy, Lynda Prim, Sarah Grant, and Sibella Kraus for your friendship, hard work, and shared commitment to local agriculture. Years of conversation with all of you are the background of this book. I am also grateful to the Slow Food community for its clear and inspiring vision of where we need to go with food.

To Doe Coover, agent par excellence, for her good cheer, friendship, and clarity, I am ever indebted. I wish also to thank Harriet Bell who began as my editor, for her enthusiasm for the subject and who has continued to share recipes and market visits. And my warm thanks to Jennifer Josephy, who gamely took it over when the publishing world shifted, and who has been supportive throughout. My gratitude to Rebecca Holland for tying up the final loose ends with dedicated grace and skill. The staff of Broadway Books has been consistently helpful and always cheerful, for which I'm ever appreciative.

And lastly, I offer my everlasting gratitude to my husband, Patrick McFarlin, for visiting more farmers' markets than he ever thought he would, and for using those visits to make the drawings that begin each chapter. He captured everyone and everything with grace and humor. While this project might have been completed without you, it was infinitely more fun, and far more meaningful, with you.

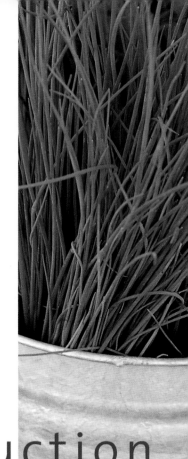

Introduction

"You know, the farmers' market is about much more than farmers selling produce." Don Bustos, the president of the Santa Fe Farmers' Market, is speaking to shoppers at the farmers' market in Santa Fe, on its twenty-fifth anniversary. Other speakers have voiced their praise of the market and hopes for its future, but Don is saying more about what the market is. "The farmers' market is about protecting our farmland and water; it's about keeping the farming traditions and cultures in northern New Mexico *alive,* and it's also about providing our communities with *good food.*" Don's New Mexican accent gives an added emphasis to the last words and there's urgency in his voice.

Don and I have talked often about the farmers' market, and we agree that, in addition to being about sales and sustenance, the market is also about culture, regionalism, and having a healthy sense of pride in one's work and one's land. It's also about joy, and it depends on—and creates—healthy rural communities. Don's experiences as a farmer and mine as a shopper have brought us to the same conclusion, that the scope of the farmers' markets is enormous. Farmers' markets are vital to our national health in the deepest sense of the word. They not only supply food that is alive and truly nutritious but are good for our state of mind, too.

Today there are over 4,000 farmers' markets across the United States, while just twenty-five years ago, there were but a handful. The farmers' market has long been my first choice for ingredients, but their growing presence suggests that they offer more than produce. They're the new village green, the plaza, the town square, the place where everyone gets to know each other.

They're friendly, and they make a small town out of a big one. "I think the main thing the farmers' market does is make us more of a community," says a market manager in Utah, echoing a thought expressed by many. It's also one of the few places where there's a healthy environment of diversity, with regard to both plants (many varieties) and people (different races, different backgrounds). "The market brings a lot of different people together who would never cross paths otherwise," one shopper tells me. "Food is a true celebration of diversity," enthuses Richard McCarthy, manager of the Crescent City farmers' market in New Orleans. "Whether you come from uptown, downtown, or back of town, your life is involved with food. If you're stuck in an elevator in New Orleans, the topics that will be discussed are fishing, football, and food."

Farmers' markets stand out from the monotonous commercial landscape that so dominates our view. No two are exactly alike. Your market may be only 2 years old, or it might be 150. It may consist of six farmers meeting in a parking lot, or there might be more than a hundred farmers under a protective roof. One vendor might harvest unusual varieties of persimmons from her backyard, while another has fifty acres of field crops in the next county. Depending on where you live, you might find heaps of Asian vegetables, farmstead cheeses, cracked hickory nuts, or organic meats. At another it may be a treasure trove of exotic citrus and subtropical fruits that catches your imagination. (The photograph of fruit on page 334 came from a twenty-dollar purchase at the Vista, California, market.) At a tiny, start-up market, there may be little else besides overgrown zucchini, tomatoes, and corn. But markets have the ability to grow, adapt, and extend their seasons.

Sandy Szwarc, a food writer who has been telling me about her market in Des Moines over the past several years, had little to report on at first, although she was immensely pleased with the local corn, peaches, and melons she found there. "But this year," she writes, "farmers are offering Yukon Gold and fingerling potatoes, little squashes instead of gigantic ones, exotic eggplants, Asian greens and bitter greens, heirloom tomatoes, and now we're seeing our first Iowa goat cheese, Iowa-grown bison, and fresh eggs!"

Farmers' markets provide a way of revitalizing local food cultures, which are ever in danger of disappearing into the lackluster sameness of the national menu. But here is where you can find those foods that truly typify a region—wild rice, native New Mexican chile, Rocky Ford cantaloupes, hazelnuts, wild huckleberries, green peanuts—the foods that have their roots in place. "For us," says Richard McCarthy in New Orleans, "food says what's best about our region, and that we have a food culture that's worth preserving. There's a regional pride here, and everywhere, that makes one place different from another." And having regional differences in our foods makes life interesting for all of us. How dull it is when everything is all the same, all the time.

My market visits have taken me around the country, to the corners, the edges, the middle, to Hawaii, and also to our neighbors, Canada and Mexico. Inevitably people will ask me, "Oh, have you been to such-and-such a market?" Usually, I haven't. "You *haven't?*" they ask, usually in tones of incredulity, for they know their market is among the best. And for them it is. While there are a lot of great markets I didn't visit and a lot of little not-so-famous ones that I did, I set out to sample, not conquer. And regardless of the nature of any particular market, after visiting more than a hundred of them, I'm convinced that *all* markets have something worth seeking out, some treasure to be discovered. Sometimes the eye must be retrained to see the value that is there, and this matter of seeing is in large part what these pages address. While I haven't referred to all the markets I've visited by name, they have all played their valuable parts in informing my experience.

Farmers' markets often look and feel simple, even when they're large, but many hidden hours of work are concealed behind that appearance. While some markets struggle to keep going and others receive support from their local governments, all markets require a lot of volunteer effort in order to take place. Some markets offer a variety of activities that have little to do with farming but which you and your children may enjoy—music, cooking demonstrations, master gardener talks, even massage!—while others are pretty bare-bones. "No espresso. No frills. Just food and lots of it," says one farmer speaking of his market. Some states, like California, certify their farmers' markets, which insures that the food sold is grown on the farm whose name hangs above it. Most don't, at least not yet. But whether certified or not, that the person selling the food grew it, or lives in the family that did, is what lies behind the spirit of a true farmers' market. Whether the selling takes place in a market setting, at a roadside farmstand, or from the back of a pickup in a parking lot doesn't matter. That the seller is also the grower does.

Even when wholesalers are present in a market—and I visited those types of markets, too, because sometimes that's all a community has at first—you can tell who the real farmers are. They're the ones who look connected to what they're selling. They are the ones who can answer your questions. And they often look tired. Most often they're older, too, for the average age of the family farmer, which is ever rising, is now around fifty-four, an age when many people are thinking about retirement.

The marketplace where food, goods, ideas, and money are exchanged is an ancient public place, and one that we respond to in a deeply intuitive way despite the omnipresence of the supermarket. "Magically and inevitably, the farmers and their food create a human space that links us back to the most ancient centers of civilization as well as to the present cycle of seasons," says Ann Yonkers, who founded the six FRESHFARM markets in Washington, D.C. Such a universal marketplace is not really new to America, although it may be new to many of us. The exposure travelers have gained to the rest of the world's colorful outdoor markets has no doubt been a factor in reconnecting many Americans to the farmers' market. How many thousands of American tourists have found themselves transfixed with delight by the bustle in Rome's lively Campo dei Fiori or the beautiful market in Nice, buying, perhaps, something to take on a picnic and vowing to do this at home?

This recent emergence of farmers' markets began in California about twenty-five years ago, with a legislative act that allowed farmers to sell directly to the consumer. What the farmer could sell was the produce that didn't conform to the industry standards—fruits and vegetables that were too small, irregularly shaped, or otherwise lacking in some measure of visual perfection. Beyond the perfect apple or potato are those perfectly edible culls that are otherwise thrown away, but which many are happy to buy. So what if a pepper is a little crooked, or an onion is on the small side? There's a use for everything, and this screening for some idea of perfection wastes a great deal of food.

Selling directly to the consumer worked well enough that it attracted farmers who started growing food expressly for the farmers' market, bypassing the wholesaler in part, if not altogether. "Today," Ann Yonkers remarks, "farmers' markets are the good news among the bad news in American agriculture. In a sector grim with stories of farm failures, consolidations, and rock-bottom farm prices, farmers' markets are growing and prospering." Here is where family farmers actually have a chance to make a living and make their small farms work. In fact, they may well be the best hope for the family farm. Quite possibly, they're the only hope.

But the idea of direct marketing has taken on other meanings, too, especially for consumers, who find almost as much value in having a direct connection with the farmer as in buying the food she grows. A shopper in New Mexico, who grew up on a farm in Wisconsin, expresses what others have told me in every market I've visited: "Although I know the value and taste of food you've raised yourself, I think I value the exchange with the growers even more." When you think about it, the farmers' market is really about the only place left in our lives where we can interact with someone who makes something we use. And it's hard to imagine what is more vital or intimate than the food we consume, for it becomes our health, our pleasure, our nourishment, who we are, in fact. Today it is farmers who are providing the fragile connection that binds us in a meaningful way to our own humanity. In this sense, they are selling far more than tomatoes.

Direct marketing. Dry words that are loaded with great possibilities mean that at the farmers' market a shopper can look the farmer in the eye, ask a question, or express appreciation for work well done. They mean we can trust our food sources, for we can come to know those who actually grew the vegetables and the fruit, raised the chicken, milked the goats, and made the cheese. And they make it possible to sit down to dinner and put a face and a name to everything we're eating— from the vegetables and meats to the honey, preserves, and sometimes even the candles, flowers, and tea. Although this didn't used to be so, knowing who produced what we eat is one of the most extraordinary experiences a diner can have today, one that allows us to discover that our lives are inextricably connected to others'. The feeling that comes from eating such a meal is better than any amount of gourmet finesse you might imagine, although that needn't be excluded. In fact, they may well be one and the same. To me they are. Eating well is about finding the source, then cooking from it, however simply, rather than relying on fine imports from afar, no matter how sublime they may be.

Many people still think that the farmers' market is where you go for cheap food, and sometimes there are bargains to be found. But we would do better to think of the farmers' market as the place where we can find food that is impeccably fresh and delicious, truly local and therefore truly seasonal, quite likely raised by sound, sustainable methods and by someone who might become your friend. This is where you can be assured that your food is not genetically modified or irradiated. The chicken, meat, and eggs you find will not have been raised in huge factory farms, treated with antibiotics, or fed hormones. This is food that tastes so good that little has to be done to it in the kitchen. The price we pay may well be higher than that in the supermarket, and it should be, for it comes closer to reflecting the true costs of growing good food, although it doesn't necessarily cover them. Most family farmers have day jobs, or a spouse who does. Parker Bosley, the chef-owner of Parker's Restaurant and Bistro in Cleveland, has worked closely with farmers and ranchers for twenty years. He once grumbled to me, "People will drive across town to shop at Saks, but they won't go to the farmers' market and pay a little more to eat well." When food is cheap, we tend to treat it carelessly and wastefully. But when it's dear, when it costs what it's actually worth, we tend to pay closer attention to it. In this sense, good food can sharply focus our world.

Farmers get a pretty small piece of each dollar you spend in your supermarket, from 7 to 25 cents, depending on whether it's wheat, corn, or tomatoes. The rest is distributed along a long chain of handlers that involve packagers, transport, and marketing. If produce were sold for the amount the farmer actually gets for it, you'd think it was an incredible steal. (Try 9 cents for a head of lettuce, as opposed to the $1.29 charged in the supermarket.) But that low price is what farmers have to live on. It's not surprising that family farms have failed so badly in the larger marketplace.

While farmers' markets may be about making a living for the farmer, for the consumer they are not only about fruits and vegetables but about slowing down and taking time to enjoy choosing our food and, later, cooking and eating it. You won't find children nagging their mothers for candy and junk food. You won't find people rushing through their shopping as if it's an odious task to be gotten through as quickly as possible. The market will smell good, not like floor wax and cleaners. You will run into friends and meet new ones. You might find yourself sharing recipes or making a plan to share a meal that evening with someone you've met at the market. I can't tell you how many impromptu dinner parties I've overheard being planned on any Saturday morning. Here you'll have an opportunity to taste foods you've never tasted before, or to ask a farmer a question you've long been meaning to ask. You might be inspired to try something new when you see a chef demonstrate how to use it. After shopping you might stash all your finds in a cooler in your car and go back to the market to have a cup of coffee with a friend. What a civilized way to spend a morning.

Children, those so-called recalcitrant consumers of vegetables, can become good eaters when they see the connection between the farmer and the food they eat. This is especially true if they have a chance to participate in some kind of farming experience, such as picking strawberries or gathering eggs at a farm stand, learning about honey at the market, visiting a farm or farmers' market. They won't know it, but they're learning good eating habits by developing a taste for truly fresh, delicious food when they're young, which will inform their food choices and affect their health over a lifetime.

Finally, other intangible benefits and delights that come from the market have to do with the food we find there. Colors, pattern, charm, fragrance, flavor, and variety conspire to fill us with ideas. I know of absolutely no one who goes to the farmers' market with a list and comes home with just what's on it, or who doesn't spend every penny she brought. Instead, we shoppers tend to get carried away. You come home and can't decide whether to put all your produce out on the table to look at it, or to cook it. You fill a vase with armloads of larkspur or sunflowers, then go back to the kitchen. Perhaps you're thrilled about a treasure you've found, some wild berries or a basket of Wolf River apples that you know will make the best pie ever, or those pretty blue and green Araucana eggs. If it's summer, there are those gorgeous eggplants, perfumed Ogen melons, the moist shelling beans, and delicate white nectarines. If it's spring, it might be wild nettles, green garlic, and thick, crisp asparagus that excites us. In late fall it is those handsome Hubbard squash and gnarly roots that start to look enticing, or the promise of a golden quince. You are incalculably rich and happy at this moment.

Although you might be tempted to cook everything you've bought as soon as you get home—a Saturday-night feast is common in our house—this food will last very well, since it hasn't traveled long distances. It is said that the average distance food travels in our country is fifteen hundred miles. I suspect it's more, now that we regularly import food from New Zealand and Chile, as well as Israel and Spain. Fewer miles from farm to market mean that food is fresher, more nutritious, and better tasting, and miles-to-market can be as few as two, ten, or a hundred at a farmers' market. Food comes from somewhere, not somewhere else. "When we turn elsewhere for our agriculture needs," one of our farmers says, "we're giving away the most precious thing we have, our independence with regard to food." Farmers' markets are helping local agriculture economies to become sound by forging strong urban-rural connections.

After experiencing the many joys and satisfactions that the farmers' market provides, we can't help but become aware of such things as land value assessment, water allocation, approval of new developments on agricultural land. As these are issues that affect us all at the table, eating is, indeed, a political act. Supporting land trusts and agricultural easements is one way to insure that farmland will exist. But making sure that farmers can enjoy financially sustainable lives is perhaps the most important way we can ensure that real farm foods remain a part of our lives. If young people are to be attracted to a life of farming, they have to be able to expect a reasonable financial return for their hard work, even if that work is fueled with passion and commitment.

We get a lot for the dollars we spend at the farmers' market. There are many threads there which, when woven together, create the fabric of a civilized life where the production of good and nourishing food coincides with healthy communities. It is where there is a give-and-take between independence and cooperation, urban and rural life. Here is a flourishing platform for diversity, a sense of security and connection to our landscape and our neighbors. And the market is also a source of joy. For me the farmers' market has been the key to becoming more deeply at home where I live, which is not the place I'm from, as is true with so many of us. When all is said and done, I can't think of a better thing to do than go to the farmers' market.

A NOTE ABOUT THE ARRANGEMENT OF CHAPTERS

Rather than letting the parts of the meal dictate the order of recipes, botanical families and regional seasons themselves have been given that guiding role. Regardless of the actual month of the year, most markets open with the same foods (greens, salad, herbs, green garlic) and end up with the same foods (roots and tubers, apples and squash), while corn, tomatoes, squash, melons all tend to arrive around the same time in summer. Quite often fruits and vegetables that are related botanically share qualities of taste and use, and when that's the case, I've grouped them together: stone fruits (peaches, apricots, cherries, and plums), for example, or the nightshades (eggplants, peppers, and tomatoes). My categories are admittedly more fluid than they are absolute—for the seasons themselves are that way. Some foods share more than one category—cabbages like cool weather, as do turnips, which are also roots, and so forth. But one thing I know for certain is that what's in season depends more than anything on where you live. Season never stands apart from location. Local and seasonal, space and time, are really the same thing.

Because I live in Santa Fe and have been an active participant in the life of our farmers' market for the past twelve years as a shopper, market manager, and board member, I have referred to our market as a touchstone throughout the book. However, this is not a book about the Santa Fe farmers' market; it's simply the market I know best. And after years of visiting other markets and talking with their managers, farmers, and shoppers, I believe they are as universal as they are particular.

MARKET TIPS

1. Plan to spend time—slow time—at the market. Start by walking around to see what's there before you start to shop, especially if you're new to the market. It's fine to buy randomly, choosing what looks good and appeals to you, but if you take a few minutes to stroll around, you may also find some menus and recipe ideas forming in your head.

2. If you don't recognize what it is you're looking at, or need a tip on how to use it, ask the growers. They don't always know, but often they do, or they have recipes available. And if you ask in a loud enough voice, invariably a nearby customer or two will chime in with a few ideas. And don't forget to consult your cookbooks.

3. Bring cash. Some farmers will accept a check, especially after they've seen you shopping at the market for a while, but many don't. If possible, try to show up with small bills.

4. If it's important to you that your food be organic, ask if it is or how it's been raised. It may be unsprayed (*pesticide free*) or on its way to becoming organic (*transitional*) or organic. Those who have been certified will most likely have their certificate on display. However, not all organic farmers choose to become certified, a process that can be prohibitively expensive and enormously time consuming. They may prefer to rest their claims as to how they farm on trust and the openness they enjoy with their customers.

5. If someone offers you a taste of something, take it! It doesn't commit you to buy. Farmers *want* you to taste their food. You might discover something new that you like, or you might find that what a farmer sells is not the same as what you find in the store. Vine-ripened kiwifruit, for example, are sweet and tropical tasting rather than sour. A taste could change your mind about a fruit or vegetable.

6. Take a feast-now approach when shopping. Unlike at the supermarket, the appearance of a particular fruit or vegetable is often short, and when something's gone, it's *gone*. When you find something you really like, ask how long it will be available. A favorite peach might be around for only two weeks, so buy accordingly and enjoy.

7. If you think it will be a while before you get home from the market, bring a cooler. It will help keep your food fresh while you stay on to visit or do other errands. And if it's berry season, you might want to have a basket or plastic bag for transferring really juicy fruit, such as mulberries, from the paper bags they're sometimes sold in.

8. Take your kids along and let them buy a few things from a farmer, too.

9. If you have a chance to take a farm tour, do. It always deepens our appreciation for and understanding of where our food really comes from to walk down the same rows the farmer does. It's also a way to get to know the farmers.

10. If you don't like shopping, but you enjoy the farm food that the farmers' market offers, consider joining a CSA—a farm that participates in Community Supported Agriculture. In a nutshell, the consumer, in exchange for buying a share early in the year when farmers are months away from receiving any income, receives a steady delivery of produce when it finally does come into season. The consumer shares the risks and enjoys the benefits, along with the farmer.

NOTES ON INGREDIENTS USED

These are the ingredients I've used throughout the book. You, of course, may have other preferences.

ALL PRODUCE is assumed to be washed.

BUTTER: I have called for unsalted butter throughout, but it is especially important in pastry and dessert making for its purity of flavor. Also, it's difficult to taste for salt when making desserts, or to add it once a batter or dough is made. For savory dishes, salted butter is fine if that's what you have. You will be using more salt in any case, and adjusting to taste is usually easy to accomplish.

CREAM: I use heavy whipping cream, which is what we have in the West. If possible, I use cream that hasn't been ultra-pasteurized, a process that robs cream of its flavor.

EGGS: Unless otherwise stated, they're large. However, eggs from the farmers' market aren't always graded for size, so you may need to be a bit more relaxed in approximating what a large egg is exactly. For the most part, I can't imagine that exact size matters terribly, at least in these recipes. What does matter is the flavor.

MILK: Unless otherwise called for, I use 2 percent. In some dishes, soy milk works fine as well, especially those with lots of other overriding flavors.

OLIVE OIL: Extra virgin olive oil is what I've used throughout the book when olive oil is called for, even if it just says "olive oil." For everyday cooking and sautéeing, this is likely to be a good-quality, reliable oil, such as Colavita. But I also have special bottles of fine olive oils gleaned on travels, such as the Barianis' or the Sciabicas' oils, that I may set aside for a special use as a finishing oil. When that's the case, I've called for extra virgin, meaning your favorite olive oil.

ONION: 1 onion = medium yellow or white onion (4 to 6 ounces). A medium onion yields about 1 cup chopped or sliced.

PARMESAN CHEESE: I usually use Parmigiano-Reggiano, but a less expensive Parmesan-type cheese will be fine, too, as long as it's freshly grated, as all grated cheeses should be. I've specified Parmigiano-Reggiano in those dishes where it seems more essential, such as a risotto, or a dish in which it is specially featured, such as a fennel salad.

PEPPER: Whatever the color, it's always freshly ground. I use white mainly in dishes that are white, where the black flecks could be off-putting.

SALT: I have used sea salt exclusively: fine salt for cooking and flaky Malden sea salt for seasoning at the table. If you prefer to use another kind, you might find yourself using a little more, since sea salt is often "saltier" than other kinds.

ROASTED PEANUT OIL: A very aromatic, tasty, full-flavored oil that smells of roasted peanuts. I use a brand called Loriva. Their website is Loriva.com if you can't find it where you live.

WINE: Unless otherwise stated, wine used in cooking is dry, which is what most people drink and tend to have sitting around on their counters.

MEAT IN THE MARKET

While many of my readers expect me never to stray from a vegetarian approach, I can't ignore the fact that meat is a growing feature in farmers' markets, and for good reasons. One has to do with its quality, which is often superb. But there are also those aspects that address a larger picture: Increasingly, people want to know that the meat they're buying is free of added hormones and antibiotics and that the animals haven't been fed foods they shouldn't be eating, such as other animals. They also want to know that the chickens, beef, buffalo, and lamb they're buying have been raised in a kind and humane way by people who consider the needs of animals as animals rather than units of production. Many of us are also concerned about the damaging effects that large-scale animal production wreak on the environment, to which small-scale animal husbandry is a proven sound alternative, while others are particularly interested in grass-fed meat both for its flavor and its beneficial nutritional profile. In case after case, those farmers and ranchers who sell at farmers' markets are meeting these concerns, and regardless of my own proclivities towards eating meat or not (and I do enjoy it occasionally), I heartily applaud their efforts. They are a part of the changing face of American farming and should be included in this portrait.

Greens Wild and Domestic

It's spring, and farmers' markets across the country are beginning to open. Greens are the vegetables that many will start out with. They're what you can count on finding early in the season. And depending on where you live, greens may flourish throughout the duration of the season, or they may disappear as soon as some real heat comes on. Greens like it cool, and some even like it cold. Salad greens are a huge challenge in Phoenix past March, which is just when they're looking great in Santa Monica. They might be diminishing in Sacramento by about June, but in Santa Fe or Londonderry, Vermont, they're with us from start to finish.

A key sign that it's spring isn't only that greens are available but that they have an irrepressible quality. They practically glow. I've picked up bunches of kale that squeak with vitality, spinach and chard that bounce with life. The arugula is nutty, not bitter; chicories have a sweet edge from the last frost of the season. Potherbs, like sorrel, nettles, and wild spinach, are tender and delicate, and the deep reds of the red lettuces, like Merlot, haven't lost their luster as long as there are those nightly temperature dips. This is also when you might find miner's lettuce, chickweed, and other edible weeds, which, if you haven't tried them, make exciting additions to salads.

This green glory will fade as the season progresses into labored production, when hot days and nights keep plants churning and growing overtime. But for now, everything leafy is at its very best. This, in fact, is one of the prime times for big green salads, now and the fall. Come midsummer, sliced tomatoes and cucumbers will better fill that role.

The Simplest Tender Greens | SERVES 2 TO 4

If your greens are tender and not too voluminous for your pan, simply wilt them in a skillet with the water that clings to their leaves after washing, or steam them. Although boiling is usually considered a less nutritious way of cooking vegetables, the more quickly they cook, the fewer nutrients they lose, and tender greens will spend only the briefest time in a big pot of boiling water.

These methods are especially well suited to those quick-cooking greens, such as spinach, young chard, and wild spinach, although tougher greens, like kale, can also be treated this way if simply cooked a bit longer. (For the more assertive greens, like mustard, see the recipe on page 6.) In general, 2 or 3 people can easily consume a pound of greens, for they shrink to nearly nothing.

1 to 2 pounds greens, coarse stems removed
sea salt and freshly ground pepper
olive oil or unsalted butter
lemon wedges or vinegar

1. Bring a large pot of water to a boil. While it's heating, wash the greens.
2. Add salt to taste to the water, then plunge in the greens all at once. Cook just until they're tender, then scoop them into a colander. Leave them to drain for 2 to 5 minutes.
3. Toss the greens with olive oil or butter to taste and season with salt and pepper. Put them in a bowl or on a platter and serve with the lemon wedges or vinegar. A bit of acid always benefits greens.

COOKING GREENS IN THE PAN: Put greens that have been washed but not dried in a wide skillet and sprinkle with salt. Cook over high heat until tender, for 3 to 5 minutes, turning them occasionally with tongs. Lift them out of the pan, leaving any liquid behind. Toss with butter or oil, taste for salt, season with pepper, and serve with the lemon wedges or vinegar.

Chard and Cilantro Soup with Noodle Nests | SERVES 4 TO 6

Cool-weather markets can count on a steady supply of chard and cilantro, which get together in this pretty soup. Diana Kennedy is responsible for the noodle nests—I never would have come up with them myself—but they're a great addition, giving texture and substance to a light soup. Consider using them in place of dumplings and croutons in other brothy soups.

THE NOODLE NESTS

2 eggs, separated

3 ounces (1¾ cups) fine egg noodles
    such as fideos or capellini,
    uncooked

⅓ cup grated Monterey Jack cheese

2 tablespoons chopped cilantro

sea salt

peanut oil for frying

1. Beat the egg whites until they hold firm peaks, then stir in the yolks, noodles, cheese, and cilantro. Season with a few pinches of salt, then really work the mixture with your hands or a wooden spoon so that it's more or less homogenous. It will look impossibly dry and stiff.

2. Heat enough oil in a medium skillet over medium-high heat to float the noodles, at least ⅓ inch. When it's hot, drop the batter into the oil, dividing it into 4 or 6 portions by eye. Fry until golden, about 1 minute, then turn and fry the second side, another minute. Set aside on paper towels. These can be made hours ahead of time.

THE SOUP

1 tablespoon olive oil

2 bunches scallions, including an inch or
    2 of the greens, finely chopped

1 celery rib, diced

1 cup finely chopped cilantro stems
    and leaves, packed

leaves from 1 bunch chard, green or
    Rainbow (Bright Lights), about
    6 cups, packed

sea salt and freshly ground pepper

6 cups Vegetable Stock, page 385,
    chicken stock, or water

cilantro sprigs for garnish

1. Warm the oil in a soup pot. Add the scallions and celery and cook over medium-high heat, stirring occasionally. After a few minutes, add the cilantro and ½ cup water so that the vegetables stew rather than fry. Add the chard leaves, sprinkle with 1 teaspoon salt, then cover and cook until the chard has wilted down. Add the stock or water.

2. Bring to a boil, lower the heat, and add the noodle nests to the pot. Simmer until the chard is tender, about 10 minutes. Taste for salt and season with pepper. Ladle the soup into soup plates, include a noodle nest in each bowl, and serve garnished with a sprig of cilantro.

Hearty Pungent Greens with Anchovies and Garlic | SERVES 4

Like salad mix, jumbles of cooking greens have become a fairly regular feature at farmers' markets across the country. These typically include mustard or turnip greens, small chard and beet greens, dandelion, different kales, tatsoi, and other Asian greens. If they're really small and tender, simply sauté the greens in olive oil flavored with garlic, pepper flakes, and anchovy. If the greens are larger and tougher and need further tempering, drop them into a big pot of boiling salted water, keep them there long enough to wilt them to near tenderness—a few minutes—then drain. Press out the bulk of the moisture, then finish them in the pan.

Four cups of hearty cooking greens, very loosely packed, weighs about ¼ pound and will cook down to a cup.

1 pound or more cooking greens

sea salt

olive oil

1 or 2 plump garlic cloves, chopped

4 anchovies, optional

good pinch red pepper flakes

red wine vinegar

1. Wash the greens well. If there are any stems or ribs that seem tough, remove them. Parboil the leaves in salted water as described in the headnote, or not, as needed.

2. Heat 2 tablespoons oil in a sauté pan over medium heat with the garlic, anchovies, and pepper flakes. Mash the anchovies with a fork until they disappear into the oil. Before the garlic colors, add the raw or cooked greens, raise the heat to high, and sauté, turning frequently, until tender. (If the greens prove tougher than you thought and need more time to cook, add water in ½-cup increments so that they steam until done.) Taste for salt—they may not need any if you've used the anchovies.

3. Pile the greens onto a platter and douse lightly with vinegar.

Green Herb Soup with Sorrel and Lovage | SERVES 4 TO 6

Sorrel fares miserably when packaged in plastic clamshells—it just falls apart. Plus sorrel is something you want to use by the bunch, not just by the leaf, and the farmers' market is one place you can often find this tart, lemony herb in abundance. Lovage is harder to find, even at the farmers' market, but ask an herb seller if she has some or would consider growing it. It's an easy herb to grow, and its bracing, dynamic flavor adds a lot of personality to all kinds of dishes. Together these herbs give this soup a mysterious flavor that's a little hard to place but definitely exciting. (A small bunch of cilantro would do the same thing, lacking the other herbs.)

Made with the lesser amount of liquid, the soup is thick and hearty. Using the full amount makes a more refined soup. Serve with small croutons crisped in olive oil or with a few tablespoons of cooked rice in each bowl.

1 tablespoon unsalted butter

1 tablespoon olive oil

1 red onion, thinly sliced

2 small potatoes, thinly sliced

1 carrot, thinly sliced

3 to 4 cups (6 to 8 ounces) sorrel, stems removed

4 cups chard leaves

1 cup lovage or cilantro leaves, finely chopped

sea salt and freshly ground pepper

4 to 6 cups Vegetable Stock, page 385, chicken stock, or water

lemon juice or white wine vinegar

⅓ cup crème fraîche

1. Warm the butter and oil in a soup pot. Add the onion, potatoes, carrot, sorrel, and chard, along with the water clinging to its leaves. Add two thirds of the lovage and sprinkle 1½ teaspoons salt over all. Cover and cook over low heat until the greens have collapsed and the potatoes are partially cooked, about 15 minutes. If the pan seems too dry at any point, add water in small increments so that nothing burns.

2. Add the stock or water, bring to a boil, and simmer, partially covered, for 15 minutes. Puree or leave the soup with some texture. Stir in the remaining lovage. Taste for salt and season with pepper and lemon juice or vinegar to taste to bring out the flavors. Sometimes several adjustments are necessary to get it right. Stir in the crème fraîche and serve.

WILD AND UNUSUAL GREENS

Aside from your own backyard or through your own foraging skills, the only place you're going to find greens such as these is a farmers' market. Keep your eye out for them and give them a try.

AMARANTH An edible carpet of soft, pink leaves was the spring result of a summer amaranth planting in my garden. Leaves like these are the ones you're most likely to find at the market—green on top and a pearly shade of pink-plum beneath. Though one variety goes by the name of Pink Cress, it has none of the hot and spicy characteristics of true cress. In fact it's exceedingly mild. Use tender amaranth leaves in a salad. If they're large, or you have them in quantity, you can cook them, as you would spinach.

CHICKWEED Just a few tufts of this sour little garden weed added to a salad will wake up the tongue!

CLAYTONIA, OR MINER'S LETTUCE Both wild and cultivated, small white flowers bloom from the tiered, circular leaves of this charming plant. Miner's lettuce is as tender as can be. Add it to salad, but keep the dressing light so that the leaves don't collapse. Or simply strew them over the top of your salad.

CORN SALAD (MÂCHE) A cultivated green that's not seen often enough, the rosettes of spoon-shaped leaves are extremely tender and particularly good with beets. To serve the pretty rosettes whole, in clumps, you'll need to ascertain how sandy they are and if they can really be cleaned with a long soak and a gentle rinse in cold water. Soil does get down into the basal leaves. Taken apart, the single leaves don't have the compelling look that they have when grouped. However, they make a great addition to other greens in the salad bowl.

UPLAND, ROCK, PEPPER, BROADLEAF, AND CURLY CRESS All of these cresses (and there are more) are hot and peppery, but the shape of their leaves, their colors, and everything else about them differs from true watercress. Nonetheless, a few sprigs can make a spicy addition to a salad or a sandwich. Taste first, though. Lively can turn aggressive, in which case a little goes a long way.

LAMB'S-QUARTERS, GOOD KING HENRY, *QUELITES*, WILD SPINACH Here's a wild plant (and a cultivar) whose greens are tender like spinach but with a slight edge of the wild in their flavor.

Lamb's-quarters taste as if they're bound to be good for you—in a good way, that is, for they're mild and quite delectable. They're always delicious steamed until tender, after just a few minutes, then treated as you would their relatives, spinach and chard. Among the various cultivars, there's one that's stunning in a salad, Magenta Spreen lamb's-quarters, available from Seeds of Change. It goes from magenta at the base to lilac and finally to green.

PURSLANE There is the wild purslane that skirts along the ground of vegetable gardens everywhere, and there are cultivars that have much larger leaves—a bit more satisfying to use. You may see both at the farmers' market. When young and small, purslane can be added to a salad with no preparation except to wash it well and pluck the clumps of thick, fleshy leaves from their stems. Later, when it's a bit more weathered, parboil it first in salted water for about 1 minute, then use it in salads. Purslane is succulent, crispy, and a bit tart. In Santa Fe, the Hispanic farmers who bring purslane, or *verdolagas* as they're called in Spanish, suggest frying them with onions (very good) or cooking them with pinto beans. You can also use them in potato salads.

RED OR RUBY ORACH OR MOUNTAIN SPINACH Because it thrives in weather that's too hot for true spinach, you might be able to find this in your market during the height of the summer. The leaves are soft and large, pointed at the tips, and magenta on the surface facing the ground. The purple turns green when cooked, but it also bleeds, staining foods like pasta pink. The flavor of orach is not unlike spinach, and it can be used in the same way. While this is something of an exotic to most people, it has been in the American garden since the early 1800s and is frequently offered at farmers' markets.

STINGING NETTLES Though weeds to most and often an annoyance as well, for their tiny hairs do sting when you brush up against them, once plunged into boiling water (pick them up with tongs), nettles become as compliant as any other green. They also produce a vibrant broth that is densely rich in vitamins and minerals. Although nettles are suddenly becoming chic in restaurants, they're still not a common find. I have, however, seen them in a few markets. It's hard to imagine a farmer who doesn't have a nettle patch somewhere on the property, so if none have appeared in your market, you might ask around. Here's a fledgling industry waiting for some enterprising weeder. Spring nettles are the best, and it's the tops, rather than the whole plant, that are preferable.

Nettle Soup | SERVES 6

One day I entered *nettles* on the Web and found information about not only *Urtica dioica* but also the Nettles Farm on Washington's Lummi Island. Intrigued, I called. A few months later I visited the farm where owners Riley Starks and Judy Olsen laughed in disbelief when I told them that some of our farmers actually plant nettles—a necessity due to our dry climate. It *would* seem strange if you were living in a moist and cool habitat that required you to clear them away on a regular basis, but Riley and Judy use their nettles, too. During my visit Judy made nettle ravioli, adding cooked pureed nettle tips—an unbelievable shade of iron-park-bench green—to her pasta dough. She also uses them for a spinach and herb filling for other ravioli. Nettles cook up easily and go beautifully with eggs. They can, after their preliminary blanching and a quick sauté in olive oil, be perched on crostini or strewn over pasta or a pizza. And you know you're doing the right thing when you dip your spoon into a bowl of soup that's as green as Ireland. A friend told me that eating this soup made her feel like an animal that had been out grazing in the wild, which is just how a spring tonic should make one feel.

6 to 8 ounces (a plastic vegetable
    bag filled) nettle leaves
2 tablespoons unsalted butter
1 cup sliced onion or scallion
1 small potato, thinly sliced
6 cups chard leaves, thinly sliced
sea salt and freshly ground pepper
6 cups Vegetable Stock, page 385,
    chicken stock, or water
½ cup cream

1. Bring 3 quarts of water to a boil. Using tongs or wearing gloves to handle them, plunge the nettles into a bowl of cold water and swish them back and forth, then drop them into the boiling water for 2 minutes. Drain and chop coarsely, discarding any large stems.

2. Melt the butter in a wide soup pot and add the onion and potato. Cook over medium heat, stirring occasionally, until translucent, about 5 minutes. Add the chard, 1½ teaspoons salt, and the stock. Bring to a boil, add the nettles, and simmer until the potato is completely soft, 15 to 20 minutes.

3. Puree the soup until smooth, then return it to the stove. (If the nettles were stemmy, pass the soup through a food mill.) Add the cream, heat until hot, then taste for salt. Season well with pepper and serve plain or with whole wheat croutons browned in butter.

Lamb's-Quarters with Sonoma Teleme Cheese | SERVES 2 TO 4

If you look closely at the little bags of greens labeled "spinach" that are sold in our market in Santa Fe, you'll see that, in fact, they're *quelites,* or wild spinach. Around the same time in Montpelier, Vermont, you might pick up some big verdant bunches of cultivated Good King Henry, or lamb's-quarters, as they're also known. Those in the know buy vast amounts. A few minutes of steaming and these greens are bright and tender. Some of the farmers tell me that they add them, once steamed, to sautéed onions, which is very good. I sometimes add a little Teleme cheese, then wrap them in a corn tortilla to make a delicious *taquito.* Or I just serve them as a vegetable. They're excellent added to a pot of beans, too.

Teleme has long been a northern California specialty, but now it's marketed nationwide. It has a pleasant acidity, as well as the most amazing ability to melt. Even when cold, Teleme is ready to run.

10 ounces *quelites,* lamb's-quarters, or spinach, stems removed
2 tablespoons unsalted butter
1 large shallot or small onion, diced
1 garlic clove, finely chopped
sea salt and freshly ground pepper
freshly grated nutmeg
½ cup Teleme or grated Monterey Jack cheese, more or less

1. Wash the greens well, then steam or plunge into boiling water just until they're wilted. Drain, then rinse under cold water. Press out the excess water (they needn't be bone-dry) and chop finely or coarsely, as you wish.
2. Melt the butter in a medium nonstick pan. Add the shallot and garlic and cook, stirring frequently, for about 2 minutes. Add the greens and cook until heated through and any water has evaporated. Season with salt to taste and scrape in just a little bit of nutmeg. Stir in half of the cheese.
3. Scrape the greens into a bowl and spoon the remaining cheese over them. Season with pepper and serve.

Collards with Potatoes | SERVES 2 TO 4

"If it tastes like collards, it will sell at our market!" Cynthia Hizer, former market manager of Atlanta's Morningside market, assures me. Bacon, made without nitrates and from wholesomely raised pigs, has recently appeared in our market, and it is superb, especially with these greens, but just leave it out if you're not a bacon eater.

2 bunches collard greens or a mixture
    of collards and kale
sea salt and freshly ground pepper
3 medium yellow-fleshed potatoes,
    scrubbed and coarsely diced
3 or 4 strips bacon, cut into small
    pieces, optional
2 tablespoons peanut or olive oil
½ onion, finely diced
2 plump garlic cloves, finely chopped
good pinch red pepper flakes
hot pepper sauce or vinegar for
    the table

1. Strip the collard leaves from the stems and wash the greens. Bring a few quarts of water to a boil. Add salt and the greens, then simmer for 10 minutes. Scoop them into a bowl. Add the potatoes to the cooking water and simmer until tender, 7 to 10 minutes.

2. Meanwhile, cook the bacon in a large nonstick skillet over medium heat until browned. Set it on paper towels to drain, discard the fat, and wipe out the pan.

3. Return the pan to the heat, add the oil, and when it's hot, add the onion. Cook over medium-high heat for 5 minutes.

4. Coarsely chop the cooked greens, then add them to the pan along with the garlic and pepper flakes. Scoop some of the potato water into the pan as well so that everything cooks in a little moisture, adding more water as needed.

5. When the potatoes are tender, scoop them out and add them to the greens. Add the bacon, then toss everything together. Taste for salt and season with pepper. Keep everything distinct or mash the potatoes into the greens. It's messy-looking this way but especially good. Season with pepper sauce or vinegar to taste.

Lasagne with Chard, Ricotta, and Walnuts | SERVES 4 TO 6

Usually lasagne has a béchamel or tomato sauce for moisture, but here I just use milk. With the moist ricotta, it's enough to keep the noodles from drying out. Dipping no-boil noodles into boiling water for 1 minute makes them more moist and pliable, closer to fresh pasta. This fall lasagne should serve 6, but if you put it on the table with only 4 people present, it will be finished in a single sitting.

1 cup freshly cracked walnuts
sea salt and freshly ground pepper
2 to 3 pounds (or bunches) chard,
    leaves only
2 tablespoons olive oil, plus extra for
    the dish
3 large garlic cloves, minced
⅓ cup white wine
1 cup sheep's milk or cow's milk
    ricotta, preferably whole-milk

1. Bring 2 gallons of water to a boil for the chard and the pasta. Preheat the oven to 400°F, then toast the walnuts in a shallow pan until pale gold and fragrant, 7 to 10 minutes. Chop finely and set aside.

2. When the water boils, add 1 tablespoon salt and the chard. Cook until tender, about 5 minutes, even if the water doesn't return to a full boil. Scoop the chard into a colander and press out most of the water. Reserve the water. Finely chop the chard.

3. Heat the oil in a wide skillet and add two thirds of the garlic, then the chard. Cook over medium-high heat, turning frequently, for several minutes, then add the wine and allow it to cook down. Turn off the heat.

1 cup freshly grated Parmesan

2 (4-ounce) balls fresh mozzarella, coarsely grated

1¼ cups milk

1 (8-ounce) box no-boil lasagne noodles

4. Combine the ricotta, Parmesan, all but ¾ cup of the mozzarella, and the remaining garlic in a bowl. Stir in ⅓ cup of the chard cooking water, then add the chard. Mix together, taste for salt, and season with pepper.

5. Bring the water back to a boil. Lightly oil an 8 x 10- or 9 x 13-inch baking dish. Drizzle ¼ cup milk over the dish. It won't go on evenly because of the oil, but this is all right.

6. Drop 3 pieces of the instant pasta into the water and boil for 1 minute. Remove them and fit them in the baking dish. Sprinkle with ¼ cup of the milk, a third of the cheese mixture, and ¼ cup of the walnuts. Repeat twice more with the pasta, milk, cheese mixture, and nuts. When you get to the last layer, add the remaining milk, mozzarella, and walnuts. Place 4 toothpicks in the pasta to make a tent, then cover with foil, and bake for 25 minutes. Remove the foil and bake for 10 minutes longer or until lightly browned on top. Let sit for 10 minutes, then cut into portions and serve.

Bright Lights
Chard Gratin | SERVES 4 AS A MAIN DISH; 6 AS A SIDE DISH

Bright Lights or Rainbow chard is the variety with multicolored stems that are often smaller and more tender than the big silver leaf or red-leafed chard. It works beautifully here because of those narrow stems, but any variety can be used, of course. Other greens can go in with the chard as well, such as *quelites,* nettles, sorrel, and spinach. Serve this gratin as a vegetarian main course or as a side dish.

2 pounds chard, including half of the stems

4 tablespoons unsalted butter

1 onion, finely chopped

sea salt and freshly ground pepper

1 cup fresh bread crumbs

1 garlic clove, minced

3 tablespoons chopped dill or parsley

1 tablespoon flour

1 cup milk or cream or a mixture of cream and stock

1 cup crumbled fresh goat cheese

1. Separate the leaves and chard stems. Wash the leaves in plenty of water, then coarsely chop them. Trim the ragged edges off the stems, wash them well, then dice them into small pieces.

2. Melt half the butter in a wide skillet over medium heat. Add the onion and chard stems and cook, stirring occasionally, until the onion has begun to brown a bit, about 20 minutes. Add the chard leaves, sprinkle with 1 teaspoon salt, and cook until they're wilted and tender, another 10 minutes.

3. Meanwhile, preheat the oven to 400°F and lightly oil a 2-quart gratin dish. Melt half the remaining butter in a small skillet and add the bread crumbs, garlic, and dill. Cook, stirring for about a minute, then scrape the crumbs into a bowl and return the pan to the heat.

4. Melt the last tablespoon of butter, stir in the flour, then whisk in the milk. Simmer for 5 minutes, season with ½ teaspoon salt, and add to the chard mixture. Add the cheese, then taste the mixture, correct for salt, and season with pepper.

5. Pour the mixture into the prepared dish and cover with the bread crumbs. Bake until heated through and golden on the surface, about 25 minutes. Let settle a few minutes before serving.

OPENING DAY AT THE SANTA FE FARMERS' MARKET
LATE APRIL

If the winter was mild, our hopes are high; and if it's been cold, our expectations are low. Because our altitude is seven thousand feet, the first farmers' market of the season is usually meager. "There was nothing there!" you'll hear people say, for the corn, chile, tomatoes, and peppers that left such a vivid impression when they were here last year are months away. Instead, on this first day, there will be the dried foods—ground chile, *chicos,* and *posole,* beans, peas, lentils. But there will also be some fresh ones: radishes, leeks that a farmer has wintered over, a mix of salad greens, sorrel and chives, maybe spinach, certainly fresh goat cheese, field-grazed chicken, and perhaps some green garlic or early chard. Every year more food is available at the start as our farmers become more adept at extending the season with structures that buy them time: greenhouses. They've also gotten better at storing food over the winter. So this year, for the first time, we began the season with fingerling potatoes and apples, the foods we usually end with, and long English cucumbers that we wouldn't normally see until late July. Our farmers' market, like all farmers' markets, is an ongoing experiment, a lively one in which customers and farmers both take part.

AN EARLY MARKET MENU

Spring Risotto with Sorrel (page 69)

Chicken Breasts and Leeks Poached in an
Herb Broth (page 78)

Shredded Salad of Many Greens (page 20)

Apple-Rhubarb Pandowdy (page 307)

Mustard Greens Braised with Ginger, Cilantro, and Rice | SERVES 4 TO 6

By the time the greens have cooked for 45 minutes, their sting is gone and they're tender and silky. If you prefer slightly milder greens, use one bunch each of mustard greens and chard, or all chard.

2 big bunches mustard greens, coarse
    stems removed

3 tablespoons vegetable oil

1 onion, diced

¼ cup white rice

2 tablespoons finely chopped ginger

1 teaspoon ground cumin

1 teaspoon paprika

1 cup chopped cilantro stems and
    leaves

sea salt

plain yogurt, Goat's Milk Yogurt with
    Cilantro and Mint, page 240, or
    lemon wedges

1. Wash the mustard greens well, then chop, but don't dry them.

2. Heat the oil in a wide, heavy pot over medium heat. Add the onion, rice, ginger, cumin, and paprika. Stir to coat with the oil. Cook for 2 minutes, then add the cilantro and the mustard (and/or chard) greens. Sprinkle with 1 teaspoon salt, cover the pan, and cook until the volume has reduced, 10 to 15 minutes. Give everything a stir, then reduce the heat to low, re-cover, and cook slowly for 40 minutes. There should be ample moisture in the pot, but check once or twice to make sure that nothing is sticking on the bottom. If the pan seems dry, add a few tablespoons of water.

3. Cook until the greens are really tender, 10 to 15 minutes more. Serve warm or at room temperature, with yogurt spooned over the top or a squeeze of fresh lemon.

Sautéed Spinach Leaves with Hedgehog Mushrooms | SERVES 4 TO 6

My notes for the Hollywood farmers' market read simply, "Everything plus." The "plus" part consists of things that are *not* common to all markets, such as quince, pineapple guavas (feijoas), strawberries (yes, in October), fresh dates, green pistachio nuts, miniature lawns for apartment-bound felines, and an unusual selection of mushrooms. The "everything" part includes all the standard vegetables from A to Z, except that in this market almost nothing is ordinary. The cauliflower is salmon colored, and the green beans are extreme—the largest of the large (Blue Lakes) and tiniest of the small *(haricots verts)* I've ever seen. The shallots are breathtaking in their papery russet skins, and French-style goat cheeses are especially tempting in their rustic baskets.

Arriving an hour early to meet my friend food writer Amelia Saltsman, I also have time to discover that this is a great market for people watching and for eating. Come hungry and you can calm the pangs with a warm slice of focaccia covered with mascarpone, mozzarella, and sage, with a steamed tamale, or with a cappuccino and a pastry. Then pick a spot and watch the parade pass by. Some people enter the market looking as if they just finished a 5K run on the beach. Others look as if they haven't even been to bed yet. And I've never seen such a great assortment of hats!

When Amelia arrives, we head off to the mushroom table. She is particularly enthusiastic about these mushrooms and their seller, David West, who is very knowledgeable about his exotic flora—and not reluctant to share. I have watched him in action before on other visits, and it's clear that he's a natural teacher.

Wild mushrooms and the more exotic cultivars are not uncommon finds at farmers' markets. Chanterelles, porcini, morels, lobster mushrooms, utterly perfect fawn-colored oyster mushrooms, portobellos, and shiitake are just some of what you might find. Today David has shiitake, matsutake, pink and yellow oyster mushrooms, hedgehogs, black trumpets, and golden chanterelles. I watch a Japanese woman carefully consider some expensive matsutake mushrooms, highly prized in Japan. While she's thinking about them, David is busy explaining about his mushrooms to other customers and telling them how to cook them. He is passionate. We spend a good half hour watching him give out advice along with his bags of fungi. "Black trumpets—the Merlot of the mushroom world, smoky, strong. Chicken-of-the-woods? It tastes like grilled lemon chicken!" "Grill the portobello gill side up, and don't tip it! You'll want those juices!" The patter is still going strong when we finally pull ourselves away. Some of David's advice goes home with Amelia, along with a pound of hedgehog mushrooms and a big bag of baby spinach. The dish she made that night definitely got the thumbs-up.

1 pound hedgehog mushrooms,
    brushed clean
1 pound baby spinach leaves
3 to 4 tablespoons olive oil
1 sweet onion such as Maui or Vidalia,
    or 1 red onion, cut into ¼-inch
    dice
sea salt and freshly ground pepper

1. Leave the mushrooms whole, but snip off the ends of the stems if they feel tough. Wash the spinach well.
2. Heat 2 tablespoons of the olive oil in a large skillet over medium heat. Add the onion and sauté until softened, about 3 minutes. Turn the heat to high, add the mushrooms, and sauté until they're tender and most of the liquid, if any, has evaporated, about 5 minutes. Season to taste with salt and plenty of pepper. Transfer to a serving bowl or platter.
3. Return the skillet to medium-high heat. Add another tablespoon of olive oil, swirl the pan, and in batches quickly sauté the spinach just until wilted and a deep vibrant green. Season with salt and pepper, then toss with the mushrooms and onion.

Oyster Mushrooms with Cumin | SERVES 4 AS AN APPETIZER

Here's something good to do with those velvety oyster mushrooms that show up in so many markets. The mushrooms cook gently with onions or shallots and are seasoned in the end with cumin and cilantro. I serve these often as a first course, with grilled bread that's been lightly brushed with olive oil, sprinkled with sea salt, and cut into fingers, or on a bed of greens, such as mâche or deer tongue lettuce..

½ pound oyster mushrooms
2 tablespoons olive oil
1 small onion or 2 large shallots,
    thinly sliced
sea salt and freshly ground pepper
¼ to ½ teaspoon ground cumin
few drops sherry vinegar or
    lemon juice
2 tablespoons chopped cilantro,
    to taste

1. Separate the mushrooms and slice them lengthwise into pieces between ½ and 1 inch wide.
2. Heat the oil in a medium skillet. Add the onion and sauté for about 2 minutes over high heat, then add the mushrooms and sauté 1 minute more. Reduce the heat to medium-low, season with ½ teaspoon salt and some pepper along with the cumin. Cook gently, turning the mushrooms in the pan every so often, until they are tender, about 20 minutes, and browned a bit around the edges. Season with a few drops of vinegar, taste for salt, toss with the cilantro, and serve.

A big bank of steel-gray clouds is moving swiftly toward town. Pulses of lightning illuminate them, like *luminarias.* There is a low and continuous rumble of thunder, a wind is rising, and it looks as if all hell will break loose about the time the market is in full swing. But in the end the whole mass just blows over, dragging a blue sky behind it. Later that day, though, a storm does materialize, and it arrives with a volley of cracks that sound like gunshot. Outside hailstones as large as pullet eggs are bouncing off the roof. I run outdoors and gather a bowlful. They're oval shaped, having been spun through the clouds before slamming to earth. I have never seen hail so large or so perfectly formed. It stays in the freezer until we move from this house.

While this was a terrific storm to watch, hail can destroy a crop in a matter of minutes. One August a farmer and I stood in his field and watched the sky turn black and then unleash its sharp blast of ice. It lasted two, maybe three minutes. When it passed, what had been salad greens were now shredded leaves beaten into the mud. A good portion of his year's income was gone. When it hit a neighboring farmer's field of kale and chard, the leaves were punctured rather than shredded. She brought them to market and explained that the holes in the leaves weren't from bugs, but few would buy. A farmer in Virginia tells me that they have "hail sales" when this happens, so that they'll get at least something for the greens before they begin to spoil where they've been punctured. Even though potatoes form safely underground, if their foliage is destroyed before the tubers have developed, there will be no crop. Light hail can leave apples and melons—even tomatoes—pockmarked. They're not so pretty, but they're not exactly ruined either. However, hail can absolutely destroy a crop of stone fruits, such as peaches.

I recently witnessed a performance of a hailstorm, given by Mas Masumoto, the Fresno farmer who wrote the beautiful *Epitaph for a Peach,* and his fifteen-year-old daughter Nikiko. Reading against the dramatic punctuation of their *taiko* drums, Mas described the massive hailstorm that passed over his orchard and destroyed his family's crop of Sun Crest peaches one summer. The drums spelled out the fury of thunder, the sharpness of hail, the delicacy of the rain that followed, and the wash of dismay, anger, and acceptance Mas experienced as he stood, mute witness to destruction. This performance was given in San Francisco, but it took his urban audience right up to his front step and his view of the orchard, the storm, and the considerable risks that farmers take.

Later Mas told me something I hadn't considered: After a storm, there's also the matter of the shredded leaves and hail-sliced peaches, which soon begin to rot. Cleanup can take weeks, and it takes a farmer right into the loss, day after day. This, I imagine, is when one's commitment to farming must be strong enough to include destruction along with the hope and promise that is renewed each spring.

Of course hail isn't the only bad news for farmers. One March morning I called market manager Lynn Weddach in St. Augustine, Florida. I got her on her cell phone. "Are you at the market right now?" I asked. I needed to ask her a question about citrus fruit.

"Actually, I'm just closing the market because of the tornado warnings," she said, then added that in spite of all the big weather warnings the previous night, the day had turned out to be sunny and calm.

"So you could have had a market anyway?" I asked her.

"We could have, but the fields were actually too wet to allow picking, so it all worked out."

Farmers always need rain, but too much of it can be a problem if they can't get into their fields. Drought, of course, can also spell disaster. Hot, drying winds are death to flower growers; the blossoms wilt before they're even picked. Freak winds swooping down from the Arctic in mid-summer can slow down the summer crops for a week or more, during which customers give up on the market because "there aren't any tomatoes." Early freezes put a sudden end to peppers, tomatoes, and eggplants, only to be followed by six weeks of warm, unflawed weather: Indian summer. As if the weather itself weren't problematic enough, the extreme conditions produced by it often leave crops vulnerable to disease and insect infestation later in the season or the following year. No place is exempt from weather. No wonder farmers talk about it.

On the nightly news the forecast is always oriented to those who want nice weather for their weekend, even when rain is desperately needed. But if we experience our food as truly local, then we know that we're all in the same boat when it comes to weather. In a way we become a community through our shared concern. Farms feed us, so weather affects us all. Farmers shouldn't need a special farm report. What's good for the farmer is good for everyone else.

Spaghetti with Overgrown Arugula and Sheep's Milk Ricotta | SERVES 2 TO 4

Once it gets hot out, those farmers who've been providing you with tender, small arugula may suddenly start bringing big, overgrown bunches to market. The leaves are too spicy to enjoy in a salad, and the stems are way too stringy to eat, but the leafy material can be plucked from the stems and cooked. Sheep's milk—as well as cow's milk—ricotta is a good match with the peppery arugula.

sea salt and freshly ground pepper

½ pound whole wheat spaghetti

1 large bunch or bag (about ½ pound) mature arugula

3 tablespoons olive oil, plus extra virgin to finish

1 plump garlic clove, chopped

several pinches red pepper flakes

½ cup walnuts, toasted and chopped

½ cup sheep's milk ricotta

freshly grated pecorino cheese

1. Heat plenty of water for the pasta. When it comes to a boil, add salt to taste and the spaghetti. Cook until al dente and drain. While the spaghetti is cooking, stem the arugula, chop coarsely, and wash. Do not dry.

2. Warm the oil in a large skillet with the garlic and pepper flakes. Cook over medium heat until the garlic turns light gold, a minute or so, then add the arugula with the water clinging to its leaves. Season with a few pinches of salt and cook until wilted and tender, about 3 minutes. Add the cooked spaghetti directly to the pan, then toss with the walnuts, ricotta, and grated cheese. Season with pepper and serve with extra virgin olive oil drizzled over the top.

Shredded Salad of Many Greens | SERVES 4

I've always liked the way a chiffonade of greens looks with all the different lengths and shades of color wrapped around each other, but the taste is even better. Here is where you can use those greens that might be a little overwhelming on their own, such as dandelion, radish leaves, and sorrel. I often see people step back in surprise when they taste tart sorrel for the first time at the farmers' market, but when it's part of a collection of greens it becomes a highly desirable addition. As for the mix, there's no one way, but here's one—more or less—that I like.

2 cups finely sliced napa cabbage

2 cups finely sliced romaine, red leaf, or butter lettuce

1 cup slivered dandelion greens

2 cups finely slivered spinach, amaranth, or *quelites*

1. Wash and dry all the greens, then toss them together in a bowl.

2. Mix the shallot and lemon juice and zest with ¼ teaspoon salt, then whisk in oil to taste.

3. Toss the greens with a few pinches of salt, then with the dressing. Mound on plates and serve.

1 Belgian endive, slivered

½ cup slivered parsley or half as
    much lovage

a few sorrel leaves, stems removed
    and leaves thinly sliced

1 shallot, finely diced

2 teaspoons fresh lemon juice plus 1 teaspoon grated zest

sea salt

4 to 5 tablespoons extra virgin
    olive oil

CHICORIES: THE BITTER GREENS

When I ordered the roasted radicchio with fresh mozzarella in a Los Angeles restaurant, the waiter told me flat out that I wouldn't like it. I guessed it was because of the bitterness of the radicchio—lessened when cooked, but often a challenge for the sweet American palate. I can imagine that by this Sunday evening the waiter was tired of having had customers send back the special all week. He remained skeptical of my promise not to do that and was sullen until I had cleaned my plate.

Mild to strong bitterness is a characteristic shared by all of the chicories, which include radicchio, Belgian endive, escarole, curly endive or frisée, the speckled Castelfranco, *pain de sucre* or sugar loaf. All members of this group of leafy greens respond well to the heat of searing, grilling, and roasting. Heat seems to temper their bitter edge so that the underlying notes of nuttiness, which make chicories such an interesting group of plants, come forward. Even so, some bitterness will remain, which many people find pleasing. It's not meant to go away.

On the other hand, the bitterness shouldn't be so strong that you can't stand it. I've noticed that the long Treviso type of radicchio can be very strong indeed. With practice you can determine whether a brief blanching or an hour-long soaking in cold salty water is needed to soften the punch. If you discover your chicory is too bitter only after cooking it, don't throw it out, but consider chopping the leaves and adding them to white beans, where they add pungency to blandness, or to a risotto based on winter squash, where they balance sweetness.

Because it's popular and commands a good price, it's no longer uncommon to see radicchio at farmers' markets, the red, cabbage-shaped Chioggia variety being the most common. The heads are often looser and softer than those you'll find in a supermarket. You might also find the Treviso type with its long scarlet leaves. When the root of the Treviso is harvested and then sprouted, it turns into a long-leafed sea-like plant called *tardivo,* something we may see more than just occasionally someday.

All the chicories are extraordinarily handsome plants, with strong, beautifully formed leaves. They seem to glow in the slanting fall light or the young spring light, the two seasons when they taste best, for a cold snap, as with so many vegetables, benefits their flavor. Once I was sent a box of four large heads of Castelfranco from a grower in Salinas, California. The cream-colored leaves were speckled and spotted with streaks of dark red, and they were every bit as beautiful as old-fashioned cabbage roses. In fact, it was hard to decide whether to cook them or arrange them. Fortunately there were enough to do both.

Freckles Meets Merlot in Vermont | SERVES 6 OR MORE

"This weather is unusually cold and windy for July," Ellen Ogden, co-founder of the *Cook's Garden Catalogue*, apologized to me as she offered me a jacket. I've noticed that we all do this, claim that the weather of the moment isn't what it should be. But chilly or not, I was delighted to be visiting Londonderry's little farmers' market with Ellen. The previous night we had eaten well from her garden; today we would see what others were growing.

This little market, which was set in a grassy field bordered by a creek on one side, had a familiar assemblage of midsummer vegetables, with a few stellar standouts, such as three kinds of big plump raspberries and enticing preserves made from all the different berries that grow in the Northeast. But it was the lettuces that were most striking, and I ended up using them in a class I was giving later that day.

Among the salad greens was a deep red loose-leaf lettuce named Merlot, which easily suggested the hue of that wine. There was also a selection of green and red-tipped oak leaf lettuces, a bronze-tinged iceberg, and the charming red-flecked romaine named Freckles. The leaves of these lettuces grouped themselves effortlessly into a luscious salad of red, purples, and greens, and although I might have stopped here, I couldn't help adding some of the market's plum-colored opal basil, flowering red oregano, and red scallions. The resulting salad was utterly alive and vivid for both the eye and the tongue.

There's always something like this happening at the market. Often it's not reproducible, for the following week that stunning speckled lettuce is gone, spotted by a shopper who arrived earlier, or perhaps the farmer has just run out. But if this combination is not to be had, quite assuredly another just as wonderful is waiting to be discovered.

---

1 head red romaine

1 head Freckles

1 head Merlot or other bronze lettuce

10 small opal basil leaves, torn

1 bunch red scallions

sea salt and freshly ground pepper

⅓ cup extra virgin olive oil

1½ tablespoons aged red wine
    vinegar

a few red oregano tips

1. Remove the outer leaves of the lettuces, then separate the rest by slicing them off at their bases. If small, leave the leaves whole; otherwise tear them gently. Wash and dry them well. Put them in a spacious bowl with the basil leaves and scallions. Toss with a few pinches of salt.

2. Whisk the olive oil, vinegar, and ¼ teaspoon salt in a bowl, then pour it over the salad. Toss well, add pepper to taste and the herbs. Toss again, then mound on a large platter. Scatter the scallions, if they've fallen to the bottom, over the top and serve.

Radicchio Seared in the Skillet with Mozzarella | SERVES 2 TO 4

For this dish I like to use a cast-iron skillet. Once it's hot, I sear the radicchio, turn down the heat, then let it cook slowly. It comes out with just enough bitterness to be enjoyable. Serve it as a side dish or as a vegetarian entree with a mound of soft polenta. The bitter, sweet, and nutty flavors of the radicchio and the corn make a good match.

1 large head radicchio
3 tablespoons olive oil
sea salt and freshly ground pepper
1 garlic clove, minced
2 tablespoons balsamic vinegar
1 (4-ounce) ball fresh mozzarella, cut
    into thin rounds

1. Rinse the radicchio, then cut it into wedges about 1½ inches across, keeping the root ends intact. Brush generously with olive oil and season well with salt and pepper.
2. Heat a cast-iron skillet over medium-high heat. When it's good and hot, add the radicchio. Press down on the wedges to ensure contact, reduce the heat to medium-low, and cook until browned, about 5 minutes. Turn and cook on the second side. The red will turn brownish, and the leaves should get crisp in places.
3. Scatter the garlic over the radicchio, add the vinegar, and cover with the cheese. Cover the pan and cook just until the cheese is soft, 2 or 3 minutes. Season with pepper, arrange on a platter, and serve.

Oven-Roasted Treviso Chicory | SERVES 4

You can cook most chicories this way—radicchio, sugar loaf, or Castelfranco. However, Treviso, the one shaped like romaine, lends itself especially well to this method. Taste it before cooking. If it's extremely bitter, either blanch it briefly in boiling salted water first or soak it in a bowl of salted water for an hour.

2 plump heads Treviso chicory
3 tablespoons olive oil
sea salt and freshly ground pepper

1. Preheat the oven to 400°F. Split the chicories lengthwise in half or, if large, into quarters. Rinse them well, but don't dry. The moisture will help them cook.
2. Lay them cut side up in a baking dish. Brush most of the olive oil over the leaves and season well with salt and pepper. Bake for 12 to 15 minutes, then turn and bake for 5 to 8 minutes longer. Turn them one last time so that the cut side is again facing up. When done the edges of the leaves should be nicely browned. Brush with the remaining oil and serve.

Pasta with Radicchio, White Beans, and Rosemary | SERVES 4 TO 6

The deep flavors of the rosemary, beans, their broth, and the radicchio make an all-vegetable dish that's remarkably robust. Gnocchi-shaped pasta or shells are perfect for the beans, which end up cradled in the folds of the dough. This isn't a particularly pretty dish—the radicchio turns brown—but if this bothers you, add a little chopped parsley before serving.

1 cup dried large white beans,
    such as cannellini, *gigante,* or
    runner beans
sea salt and freshly ground pepper
⅓ cup olive oil
1 red onion, finely diced
3 plump garlic cloves, chopped
2 tablespoons minced rosemary
1 to 1½ pounds radicchio, sliced into
    ½-inch ribbons
1 pound dried pasta, such as
    gnocchi or shells
freshly grated Parmesan

1. Sort through the beans, rinse them, then put them in a pressure cooker with 2 quarts water, 1½ teaspoons salt, and 1 tablespoon olive oil. Bring to pressure and cook on high for 30 minutes. Turn off the heat and allow the pressure to fall naturally, then open the pot. Take a taste. If the beans aren't fully tender, simmer them until they are. If you're not using a pressure cooker, soak the beans for 4 hours (or cover with boiling water and let stand for an hour), then drain. Rinse and re-cover with 2 quarts cold water. Add the salt and oil; bring to a boil and simmer, partially covered, until tender, about 1½ hours. Drain and reserve the cooking water.

2. Put on a pot of water for the pasta.

3. Heat 2 tablespoons of the remaining oil in a wide skillet. Add the onion and sauté over high heat until lightly browned around the edges, about 5 minutes. Add the garlic, half the rosemary, and the radicchio and season with 1 teaspoon salt. Sauté until the radicchio is limp, a few minutes longer, then add the beans and 1 cup of their cooking liquid. Bring to a boil, then lower the heat to a simmer. It's nice if there's a little broth at the end, so add liquid as needed.

4. Salt the pasta water, add the pasta, and cook until al dente. When done, drain and add it immediately to the pan. Add the remaining rosemary and season well with pepper. Toss everything together, then divide among heated pasta bowls. Drizzle the remaining olive oil over each serving, add another twist of pepper, and lightly grate the cheese over all.

White Pizza with Radicchio, Mushrooms, and Gorgonzola Cheese | MAKES ONE 12-INCH PIZZA

1 (4-ounce) ball fresh mozzarella

1 large head radicchio

olive oil

sea salt and freshly ground pepper

1 large portobello mushroom

½ recipe Pizza Dough, page 386

3 ounces Gorgonzola cheese

1. Preheat the oven to 500°F. Thinly slice the mozzarella and set on paper towels to drain.

2. Cut the radicchio into wedges about 2 inches thick. Brush with olive oil and season with salt and pepper. Heat a cast-iron pan and, when hot, add the radicchio. Reduce the heat to medium and cook for 5 minutes, pressing lightly to open the leaves. Turn and cook the other side until the leaves are brownish but seared in places, another 5 to 7 minutes. Remove and chop coarsely.

3. Remove the stem and scrape the gills from the mushroom. Slice into ½-inch strips. Add 1 tablespoon oil to the skillet, then sauté the mushroom over high heat until browned. Remove and season with salt and pepper.

4. Roll or press the dough into a 12-inch circle, leaving the edge slightly raised. Transfer to a pizza pan, or, if using a stone, a peel dusted with cornmeal. Lay the mozzarella over the dough, add the radicchio and mushrooms, and bake for 10 minutes.

5. Add the Gorgonzola and continue baking until the cheese is melted and the crust is browned, 10 minutes longer. Season with salt and pepper, then cut into wedges and serve.

Grilled Sugar Loaf Chicories | SERVES 2

This marvelous-looking plant, when trimmed of its outer leaves, forms an elegantly scrolled cone about the size of a loaf of bread. You can serve them whole or chop them up and dress them with vinegar and olive oil. Endive and escarole are also delicious grilled.

1 sugar loaf chicory (pain de sucre), halved lengthwise

olive oil as needed

sea salt and freshly ground pepper

best-quality balsamic vinegar or aged red wine vinegar

1. Rinse the chicory, then pat dry. Brush liberally with oil and season with salt and pepper.

2. Prepare a fire or heat a grill. Grill the halves, turning them every few minutes until they're browned, wilted, and singed in places. This should take at least 15 minutes. Remove them to a large platter, season again with salt and pepper, and drizzle with extra virgin olive oil and a few drops of vinegar.

Lucky shoppers at some of northern California's farmers' markets can buy packages of smooth white and red endive, raised by Richard Collins, the only commercial endive producer in the United States. Endive is not a common market vegetable, but it does appear now and then in markets around the country, whenever some adventurous gardener decides to give it a try. It's something of a challenge for, unlike other crops, it takes a two-part growing process to produce the plump chicons: Seed is planted, and a leafy head of chicory is formed. But instead of being eaten, it's lopped off in the field and the roots are harvested. The roots are then planted in complete darkness, where they eventually sprout a cone-shaped bud, which is detached and sold as endive. A raggedy open-leafed plant has become a smooth, silken cone of leaves that sit nicely in your hand. It's juicy, pleasantly crisp, and only slightly bitter.

Don't overlook this delectable vegetable if you're lucky enough to find endive at your market. Buy generously! It's easy to use in a salad, and it's even better baked or sautéed, and that's when a bag of endives can be a very attractive resource indeed. (In case you think this pale vegetable has no nutritive value, ounce for ounce it rivals the banana as a source of potassium; it's a decent source of vitamin B and fiber as well as microelements, which it metabolizes from the roots.) Endives keep well, but it's important to store them in the cold and the dark of your refrigerator so that the leaves don't turn green. They have intentionally been blanched to whiteness by being kept from the light, and that's the way you should keep them, too.

Endive and Celeriac Chowder | SERVES 4

Ladling this delicate, vegetable-laden chowder over toasted bread raises it to main-course status. If you don't want such a hearty dish, use a little less liquid and a few croutons to finish. Use only white endives for this soup. Red ones will make it look very dingy indeed.

3 (about ¾ pound) plump Belgian
    endives
2 leeks, white parts only, chopped and
    rinsed well
2 shallots, chopped
2 celery ribs, with leaves, diced
½ pound yellow-fleshed potatoes,
    peeled and diced into small cubes
½ pound celery root, peeled and cut
    into small dice
2 large carrots, diced
2 tablespoons unsalted butter
2 teaspoons thyme leaves, chopped
1 bay leaf
5 to 6 cups Vegetable Stock, page 385,
    chicken stock, or water
sea salt and freshly ground pepper
½ cup cream

TO FINISH

2 tablespoons finely chopped parsley
1 tablespoon snipped chives
1 teaspoon chopped tarragon
4 slices country bread
2 ounces Gruyère cheese, thinly sliced

1. Set aside 8 outer leaves of the endive, then quarter the remainder lengthwise and chop coarsely. Prepare the rest of the vegetables as suggested.

2. Melt the butter in a wide soup pot over medium-high heat. Add the vegetables, thyme, and bay leaf. Cook over medium-high heat, stirring frequently, until the vegetables smell good and there's a little glaze on the bottom of the pot, about 7 minutes.

3. Add stock or water to cover along with 2 teaspoons salt. Bring to a boil, then lower the heat and simmer, covered, until the potatoes are soft to the point of falling apart, about 25 minutes. Press a few against the side of the pot to break them up or puree 1 or 2 cups of the vegetables to give the soup body. Pour in the cream, taste for salt, and season with pepper. Stir in half the herbs.

4. Finely sliver the reserved endive leaves. Toast the bread and cut each piece into halves or quarters. Divide the pieces among 4 bowls and cover with the cheese. Ladle the soup over the toast and serve garnished with the remaining herbs and slivered endive.

Endive on Toast with Gruyère Cheese |

Slivered sautéed endives can be made from start to finish in less than 15 minutes. This is one of my favorite appetizers or, made larger, last-minute suppers. The appearance of cooked endive is generally a bit dingy, but the flavor is nutty and the texture silky. Lemon juice helps keep the color lively, but don't overdo it.

3 or 4 fat Belgian endives, about 5 ounces each

2 tablespoons unsalted butter

½ lemon

8 baguette slices or 2 large slices country bread

½ cup grated Gruyère cheese

sea salt and freshly ground pepper

1. Quarter the endives lengthwise, then cut them into long slivers or chop them into ½-inch pieces.
2. Melt the butter in a nonstick skillet. When foamy, add the endive and cook over high heat, stirring frequently, until browned in places, about 12 minutes in all. Squeeze a little lemon over the endive.
3. Meanwhile, preheat the broiler and toast the bread. Cover the toasted bread with as much of the cheese as it will easily hold. Stir the rest into the endive when it's finished cooking.
4. When the endive is done, broil the toasts until the cheese is soft, then remove. Season the endive with salt and pepper, then spoon it over the toast and serve.

VARIATION WITH FONTINA AND PROSCIUTTO: The flavor of thin slices of prosciutto is very good with endive—and so is a glass of Belgian beer. Make the Endive on Toast, using Italian Fontina in place of Gruyère cheese. Serve with the prosciutto draped over the endive.

Frisée and Endive Salad with Mint and Pomegranate Seeds | SERVES 6

Frisée is the frizzy-leafed member of the chicory group. When blanched in the garden, the leaves are pale green—almost white—the flavor is mild, and the texture tender enough to use as a winter salad green.

Blanching is accomplished either by planting the frisée plants very close together or by tying the outer leaves around the inner ones. Grower Ric Gaudet said that one year the oats and other grasses, which went unweeded, grew up around the chicories and provided the shade and crowding they needed to remain tender and pale inside.

⅓ cup pine nuts

sea salt

1 head frisée

2 Belgian endives, red or green

1 bunch watercress

1 small pomegranate

⅓ cup fresh mint leaves, torn into
    small pieces

3 scallions, including the firm greens,
    thinly sliced

5 tablespoons extra virgin olive oil

1 tablespoon red wine vinegar or
    lemon juice, or more to taste

1. Toast the pine nuts in a small skillet over medium heat, shuffling the pan back and forth until they're golden. Immediately dump them into a bowl and toss with a pinch of salt.

2. Separate the frisée leaves at the base, discarding the tough outer leaves. Sliver the endives. Remove the large, coarse stems from the watercress. Wash and dry the greens. You should have between 8 and 10 cups in all. Refrigerate until needed.

3. Quarter the pomegranate and gently pry the pieces apart so that they don't spurt. Pick out the seeds from the membranes.

4. Toss the greens with the mint and scallions. Sprinkle with salt and toss again. Pour the oil over them and toss until the greens are lightly coated. Add the vinegar, toss well, and taste for tartness and for salt. Divide among salad plates and garnish with the pine nuts and pomegranate seeds.

June 1, and we're one month into our market season. There are not a lot of vegetables. The few beets and carrots sold out while I was making a tour to see what was there. But there are salad greens, some herbs, asparagus—a real treat—and some delectable green garlic.

Everyone's green garlic is slightly larger than it was last week. The heads are now beginning to reveal their separate cloves, whereas last week there weren't any membranes dividing them, at least not noticeable ones. The garlic probably won't last more than a few weeks longer, but then it will begin to show up in its mature form, the heads hard, the cloves clearly distinct.

The same thing is happening with the spinach. Instead of the baby spinach leaves of the week before, there are large bouncy heads of some gorgeous crinkly variety grown by Stanley and RoseMary Crawford, two farmers who are actually best known for their garlic and for Stanley's writings about garlic. Today all of their garlic is secure in the field, but their spinach is not, and it's irresistible. I've never seen such vigorous-looking greens. They seem to stand upright in their crates, ready to jump out. I have the impression after cooking this spinach that there is definitely more volume than I'm accustomed to seeing from this water-filled green.

There are cartons of beautiful big brown eggs, rounds of fresh goat cheese, and rhubarb. There is also bread, for, like other markets, we have good bakers as well as farmers. Today there is a new bread, called Nativo, made with organic wheat, which has been grown and milled in northern New Mexico as wheat used to be. These loaves are the result of years of effort on the part of the baker and many others in the farming community, who wanted to see wheat return to our area. The bread is delicious.

I have invited a new friend to lunch tomorrow, Sunday, so I am shopping this small market with that in mind. In spite of the meager offerings, a menu isn't difficult to compose. And everything was from New Mexico, even the champagne!

A SUNDAY LUNCH FROM NEW MEXICO

Gruet Champagne

Nativo Bread with Radish Butter (page 51)

Asparagus Braised with Peas and Spring Onions (page 38)

Spinach and Green Garlic Soufflé (page 242)

Rhubarb with Berries and Candied Ginger (page 53)

A Cool-Weather Miscellany 2

"When you go to the grocery store, everything is in season all the time." It's Richard McCarthy talking, and we're standing in the Crescent City farmers' market in New Orleans, which he manages. He's making a point that crosses my mind every time I venture into the supermarket and see plums from Chile in February, feijoas from New Zealand in March, clementines from Spain at the same moment they're plentiful in California. True, these are all in season somewhere, but what's truly in season has to do with where *you* live. It's not some abstraction expressed in a magazine or the timeless season of the supermarket.

Spring, bringing apple blossoms, moves ever northward. Asparagus tips puncture sandy soil in succession from southern California to Washington; migrant workers follow the harvest from south to north. Altitude plays a part, too, for the higher you climb, the cooler the weather, which means peas will be flourishing from July to September if you live at eight thousand feet and apricots will ripen, if they ripen at all, sometime after mid-August. Artichokes appear in New Orleans for Mardi Gras, along with the potherbs used to make the Lenten dish of *gumbo z'herbes* immediately afterward. In the same week it might well be snowing in upstate New York, while the mercury has finally climbed to nearly fifty degrees in Albuquerque. Such disparity means that it's impossible to talk about season without, in the same breath, talking about place.

What we do share, albeit at different dates, are moments when cool weather means warm but not hot days, nights that bring a chill but no killing frost. In my market visits I've seen the same cool-weather vegetable miscellany from Mesa, Arizona, to San Francisco; Atlanta to Washington to Missoula—but at wildly disparate months. The date-anchored equinoxes and solstices apprise us of day lengths, but season is something we know more viscerally by the feel of the air, the foods we crave, and the foods that mature together. Curiously, foods that are in season together always taste good together, which is why you can feel confident when cooking intuitively from the farmers' market. Ratatouille, succotash, grapefruit and avocado salads, and rhubarb-strawberry pie offer proof of this maxim's validity.

Cool-weather crops are more or less the same wherever one goes. They include asparagus and artichokes, fennel, leeks, green garlic, greens of all kinds, spring onions, fava beans, peas, as well as chives and soft, minty sage. Rhubarb makes its appearance when it's still cool, too.

Some of these spring vegetables will return in the fall, the other cool season, the one that's cooling down instead of warming up. There's the fall season of artichokes and fennel. Spring-planted leeks will have matured, and shallots are plentiful, though not so chives. The sage has a stronger flavor than it did a few months earlier. Asparagus does not return in the fall, but chicories and greens do. This means that we'll see some of the same vegetables, but in a slightly different alignment—artichokes with potatoes, shallots, and rosemary, say, instead of artichokes with asparagus, spring onions, and chervil. All share a liking for cool, steady temperatures rather than the hot ones that are so appealing to the nightshades and summer squashes.

A LIGHT COOL-WEATHER LUNCH FOR SPRING	A HEARTY COOL-WEATHER SUPPER FOR FALL
Radish Salad with Vella's Dry Jack Cheese (page 51)	Radicchio Seared in the Skillet with Mozzarella (page 24)
Fennel Soup with Saffron Dumplings (page 48)	Artichokes and Jerusalem Artichokes Braised with Black Lentils (page 40) with artisan pasta
A Cherry-Almond Loaf Cake (page 283)	Pear-Hazelnut Torte (page 326)

ASPARAGUS AND ARTICHOKES

Wilfred Guttierrez, our lone farmer who grows asparagus, told me that for years he had been intending to diversify his garden with an asparagus planting but just hadn't gotten around to it. When a neighbor offered him crowns to plant, he protested that he didn't know how, but he planted them anyway. Three years later he was in the market with a large blue ice chest, a piece of cardboard with the word *asparagus* scrawled across it, and a long line of customers. Big and little stalks were mixed together; their uniformity lay in their extraordinary taste, not their shape or size. Some were violet tipped; others inadvertently blanched to whiteness due to a heavy covering of mulch. It was good to see asparagus that wasn't choked with rubber bands, and even nicer to be able to rove through the pile and choose the spears you wanted. I think the fat ones are much tastier and more fun to eat because there's something there. But fat or thin, if you've waited until June to eat asparagus, you are happy to eat it every night until it's gone.

Although Castroville is known as "The Artichoke Capital of the World," artichokes do grow in other places. I've met many southerners who grow them on a regular basis and those from colder climes who take them on as a challenge. They may have to be treated as annuals, planted yearly, and harvested only once, unlike the California artichokes, which have a spring and fall season. But you can find them. I found them in the Crescent City market in New Orleans, in Montpelier, Vermont, in Maine, and even in New Mexico. Without a doubt they're elsewhere, too.

Roasted Asparagus with Citrus Butter | SERVES 4

The first asparagus of the season and the last citrus fruits have a great affinity for each other. Try tart Eureka or sweet Meyer lemons, blood oranges or calamansi limes, or other citrus juice and zest.

1½ pounds asparagus

1 teaspoon olive oil

sea salt and freshly ground pepper

¼ cup fresh citrus juice

3 tablespoons cold unsalted butter, chopped into chunks

1 teaspoon grated citrus zest

1. If the asparagus is thin, snap off the tough parts of the stalks where they break naturally. If thick, slice off the tough ends with a knife—you can usually see a change in color where the stalks turn tender—then peel them up to the tips.

2. Soak the asparagus in cold water while you preheat the oven to 425°F, then drain and put them in a gratin dish. (They needn't be dry.) Toss with the oil and season with salt. Bake until the stalks are tender when pierced with the tip of a paring knife, 20 to 40 minutes, depending on their thickness.

3. Boil the juice in a small skillet until it has reduced to about 1½ tablespoons. Remove from the heat, whisk in the butter, then add the zest, a pinch of salt, and some pepper. When the asparagus is done, remove it to a platter and spoon the sauce over it.

Asparagus and Wild Mushroom Bread Pudding | SERVES 6 GENEROUSLY

After a damp spring day spent visiting the organic biodynamic gardens on the UCSC campus in Santa Cruz, a town that is unusually committed to using its local produce, it was time for dinner. There is always a moment during asparagus season when you want something hearty, and this was the day. Fortunately, the chef had the dish for it—a golden bread pudding studded with asparagus.

I like to simmer the milk with green garlic (immature garlic whose leaves are still green) for flavor. If you live where fresh chanterelles or morels are in season as well as asparagus, here's a good opportunity to use them, too. But dried chanterelles or morels from the previous year are also delicious.

1 head green garlic

3 cups milk

1 (1-pound) loaf good firm white
    bread, cut into thick slices

1 to 2 pounds asparagus, preferably
    thick, peeled

sea salt and freshly ground pepper

3 tablespoons unsalted butter

1 large shallot, finely diced

½ to 1 pound chanterelles or
    morels, cleaned and coarsely
    chopped

4 large market eggs

⅓ cup chopped parsley

3 tablespoons chopped tarragon or
    marjoram

2 cups grated Fontina or Gruyère
    cheese

1. Preheat the oven to 350°F. Lightly butter or oil an 8 x 12-inch gratin dish. Coarsely chop the garlic, add it to the milk, and bring to a boil. Turn it off and set it aside to steep.

2. If the bread isn't stale, lay it on a sheet pan and bake until golden and crisp (but not hard); otherwise your pudding will be mushy. Break it into chunks, put it in a large dish, and strain the milk over it. Let it sit while you prepare the vegetables. Occasionally turn the bread so that it soaks up as much of the milk as possible.

3. Slice the asparagus on the diagonal about ⅓ inch thick, then soak in cold water for a few minutes. Fill a skillet with water and, when it boils, add salt to taste and the asparagus. Simmer until bright green and partially tender, about 3 minutes. Drain, then rinse with cold water to stop the cooking.

4. Melt half the butter in a medium nonstick skillet. Add the shallot, cook for 1 minute, then add the mushrooms. Cook over high heat until they brown in places, exude their liquid, and are tender, after several minutes. Season with salt and pepper and set aside.

5. Break the eggs into a large bowl and beat them until smooth. Add the herbs, 1 teaspoon salt, and plenty of pepper. By now the bread should have soaked up most of the milk. Add the bread and any milk that is left to the bowl, along with the asparagus and mushrooms plus any juices, and two thirds of the cheese. Toss well.

6. Pour the mixture into the prepared dish, even it out some, and dot with the remaining butter. Scatter the remaining cheese over the top and bake until puffy and golden, about 45 minutes. Let cool for a few minutes, then serve.

Asparagus and Artichoke Sauté with Toasted Bread Crumbs | SERVES 4 TO 6

3 large or 4 medium artichokes,
    trimmed and quartered,
    page 389
sea salt and freshly ground pepper
1 pound asparagus, peeled if thick,
    then thinly sliced on the
    diagonal
½ pound mushrooms, thinly sliced
1 bunch scallions, including an inch
    of the greens, chopped
2 medium zucchini, sliced
    ¼ inch thick
½ cup parsley leaves
2 garlic cloves
1 teaspoon grated lemon zest
½ cup fresh bread crumbs
¼ cup olive oil
¼ cup white wine
1 cup chicken stock or water
freshly grated Parmesan cheese

1. Simmer the artichoke quarters in 1 quart water with 2 teaspoons salt until tender-firm, 5 to 7 minutes. Remove and slice them thinly. Cut the rest of the vegetables as described.

2. Chop the parsley, garlic, and lemon zest together. Brown the bread crumbs in 1 tablespoon of the oil in a small skillet, then set aside.

3. Heat the remaining oil in a wide nonstick skillet. When hot, add the artichokes, asparagus, and zucchini. Sauté over high heat until they take on some color, then add the scallions and mushrooms and sauté for 5 minutes more. Season with 1 teaspoon salt.

4. Add the wine. Let it sizzle and reduce, then add the stock and simmer for a few more minutes or until the vegetables are cooked to your liking. Toss them with the chopped parsley, slide them onto a platter, and garnish with a light dusting of freshly grated cheese. Or, pass the cheese separately at the table.

Asparagus Braised with Peas and Spring Onions | SERVES 4 GENEROUSLY OR 6 MODESTLY

This delicate braise can become a vegetable main course if you spoon it over soft polenta or mix in some tender cheese ravioli. If morels or chanterelles are in season, cook them right along with the onions and garlic.

1 pound asparagus

2 pounds shelling peas

3 tablespoons unsalted butter

5 spring onions or other small, fresh
   onions, thinly sliced

1 head green garlic, thinly sliced

½ cup white wine

sea salt and freshly ground pepper

a few basil leaves or a small handful
   chervil

1. Peel the asparagus stalks. If they're thick, trim the bases. If they're thin, snap them at the breaking point. Slice them diagonally into several pieces, then put them in a bowl of cold water to soak while you shuck the peas.

2. Melt 2 tablespoons of the butter in a skillet. Add the onions and garlic and cook over medium heat until they look as though they're starting to fry, then add the wine. Once the wine cooks down, add 1 cup water and the asparagus. Simmer until the asparagus is nearly tender, about 7 minutes. Add the peas and cook until they're done, about 2 minutes. Sprinkle with salt and add a twist of pepper and the last bit of butter. Tear the basil leaves right into the dish or add the chervil, then turn off the heat and serve.

Sautéed Artichokes and Potatoes with Garlic Chives | SERVES 2 TO 4

Garlic chives are often found in farmers' markets. They always seem to come in big bunches. Flat, rather than round like the more familiar garden chives, they can go wherever garlic goes but are far milder. Garlic scapes (see page 76), the curlicue tops of hardneck garlic, are another spring find. They can also be chopped and sautéed with the artichokes and potatoes.

4 medium artichokes, trimmed and
   quartered, page 389

3 tablespoons olive oil

6 fingerling potatoes, such as Ratte,
   Ruby Crescents, or Rose Fir Apple

sea salt and freshly ground pepper

½ cup chopped garlic chives, or
   more to taste

2 tablespoons chopped parsley

a few drops truffle oil, optional

1. Thinly slice the artichoke quarters lengthwise and toss them with a little of the olive oil. Peel the potatoes and slice lengthwise about ¼ inch thick. Drop them into a pot of boiling salted water for 3 minutes, then drain.

2. Heat the oil in a nonstick skillet. Add the potatoes and artichokes and cook over medium-high heat, tossing every few minutes, until golden brown and tender when pierced with a knife, about 20 minutes. If they look done but aren't quite tender, add ½ cup water, lower the heat, and cook gently, covered, until tender. Season well with salt and pepper and toss with the chives and parsley.

3. Slide onto a platter and drizzle a few drops of truffle oil, if you like, over all.

Artichokes and Jerusalem Artichokes Braised with Black Lentils | SERVES 4

A recipe for the fall crop of artichokes, this has all the warm earthy colors and flavors that go with the season. Use black "caviar" lentils or dark green Le Puy lentils for flavor and drama. This makes a robust vegetarian main dish served with small, dried pasta, such as orecchiette, or an accompaniment to roasted chicken or duck.

⅓ cup dried green or black lentils, sorted and rinsed

sea salt and freshly ground pepper

2 large artichokes trimmed and quartered, page 389

juice of 1 lemon

8 Jerusalem artichokes, scrubbed

4 shallots, peeled and sliced about ⅓ inch thick

1½ tablespoons olive oil

1 garlic clove, minced

2 teaspoons chopped tarragon or marjoram

2 tablespoons unsalted butter

1 tablespoon chopped parsley

1. Cover the lentils with 2½ cups water. Bring to a boil, add ½ teaspoon salt, and simmer until tender, 25 to 30 minutes. Drain but reserve the broth.

2. Dice the artichoke hearts into pieces about 3 times the size of the lentils. Thickly peel and dice the stem as well. As you work, put the finished pieces in a bowl with the lemon juice and just enough water to cover. Slice the Jerusalem artichokes about the same thickness as the shallots. If the pieces are large, chop them coarsely.

3. Heat the oil in a medium skillet. Add the artichokes, Jerusalem artichokes, and shallots and sauté over medium heat for 4 to 5 minutes. Season with ½ teaspoon salt and some pepper, then add the garlic and ¾ cup of the reserved lentil broth. Simmer, covered, for 20 minutes. If the pan becomes dry, add more lentil broth or water.

4. Add the lentils to the pan with some of their cooking liquid and the tarragon to make a little sauce. Cook for 5 minutes more or until the vegetables are tender. Just before serving, stir in the butter, then taste once more for salt and season with pepper. Garnish with the parsley and serve.

Elixir of
Fresh Peas | SERVES 4 TO 6 AS A FIRST COURSE

This pale green froth of a soup is the essence of fresh peas. Peas can travel in every flavor direction imaginable, but this soup needs nothing, although a few drops of truffle oil are intriguing. Plan to make it just before you serve it unless you want to serve it chilled. The light, fragrant stock is made while you shuck the peas, and cooking time for the soup is about 4 minutes.

1 bunch scallions or 2 small leeks, including 2 inches of the greens, thinly sliced

5 large parsley stems with leaves

sea salt and freshly ground white pepper

1½ pounds pod peas, bright green and moist looking

1 teaspoon unsalted butter

½ cup thinly sliced fresh onion or young leek

½ teaspoon sugar

truffle oil

1. Bring 1 quart water to a boil. As it's heating, add the scallions, parsley, and ½ teaspoon salt. Add about 3 cups of pea pods as you shell them. Once the water comes to a boil, lower the heat. Simmer for 20 minutes, then strain.

2. Melt the butter in a soup pot and add the sliced onion. Cook over medium heat for about a minute, then add ½ cup of the stock so that the onion stews without browning. After 4 to 5 minutes, add the peas, ½ teaspoon salt, and the sugar. Pour in 2½ cups of the stock, bring to a boil, and simmer for 3 minutes.

3. Transfer the soup to a blender. Drape a towel over the lid and give a few short pulses to make sure it won't splatter. Then puree at high speed for 1 minute. Pour into small soup bowls and serve immediately, adding a few drops of the truffle oil to each bowl.

Everyone is rich with peas. Sugar snaps, snow peas, and pod peas are abundant. Some farmers have heaped their peas into bushel baskets; others arrange them neatly in plastic berry containers. Their skins are smooth and unmarred. Occasionally there's a tendril, a stem, or a flower, but what we don't have are the pea greens, which are so often available at other markets, particularly where Laotian, Chinese, and other Asians shop—like the Civic Center market in San Francisco. At our "Shop with the Chef" demonstration, Lynn Walters simmers sugar snap peas for about 2 minutes in a little water, drains them, and tosses with butter and chopped mint. They're unbelievably good, and the children love them.

If you measure the season by what's available, then it's still spring for us—in mid-July!—for in addition to peas, there's also asparagus, sorrel, sweet onions, springy greens, and cherries, the first of the stone fruits. Elsewhere, peas have been gone for weeks if not months.

But there are beets. Among the golden beets and scarlet Chioggia beets, there's a large albino that seems frankly naked without its color. All the beets come with a luxurious crown of greens attached, which give you an entire second vegetable. So when Marion Carter says that a huge Mangel beet with its endless stems and great ruffles of greens is "a dollar a pop," it seems like the right price. Rainbow chard has made its first appearance, the stems glowing yellow, orange, red, and pink. The cilantro has an almost buttery texture. Bugs have found the Asian greens attractive, and they're partially laced with holes, but they'll be fine to eat. Icicle, Easter Egg, and French Breakfast radishes are still crisp and sweet. They make wonderful sandwiches and are good cooked, I've found. Arugula, dill, parsley, marjoram, lemon thyme, and thyme fill out the herb department, while the lettuces are coming to an end. It *is* July, after all.

There are also those vegetables that shoppers walk by without noticing—kohlrabi, broccoli, and cauliflower. But these are sweet and pure tasting, with a delicacy I've seldom experienced. There's no bitterness, no sulfurous taste, no wash of chemicals doing battle with the innate but oft-concealed sweetness of these robust vegetables. Although I try to build enthusiasm for them in my chef demonstration, I detect a slightly sullen response. What people really want is tomatoes. Rather, what people really want is for it to be summer, and when the tomatoes are here, summer will be, too.

MENU FOR A COOL JULY

Freckles Meets Merlot (page 23)

Market Ragout of Turnips, Kohlrabi, and Peas (page 94)

Polenta

Mixed Cherry Pie with a Double Crust (page 285)

Pea and Spinach Soup with Coconut Milk | SERVES 6

Peas are as good with cilantro and coconut milk as they are with the more predictable mint and basil. If you haven't explored this direction, do! Serve this soup unblended, completely blended, or just blend a cup or so and stir it back into the pot to provide some background texture and color.

2 tablespoons unsalted butter

2 tablespoons white basmati rice

2 cups thinly sliced sweet white onions

sea salt and freshly ground pepper

2 teaspoons curry powder

4 cilantro sprigs, plus extra for garnish

1½ to 2 pounds pod peas

4 cups spinach leaves

1 quart Vegetable Stock, page 285, or water

¾ cup coconut milk

1. Melt the butter in a soup pot over medium heat and add the rice, onions, 1½ teaspoons salt, the curry powder, 4 cilantro sprigs, and 1 cup water. Simmer over medium-low heat for 12 minutes.

2. Meanwhile, shuck the peas and wash and coarsely chop the spinach. Add both vegetables to the pot, along with the stock. Bring to a boil and cook for 3 minutes. Turn off the heat and add the coconut milk.

3. Puree about a cup of the soup in a blender and return it to the pot. Taste for salt, season with white pepper, and serve, garnished with fresh cilantro leaves. Or puree all of the soup until smooth, about 1 minute, then pass it through a strainer and serve.

Stir-Fried Snow Peas with Pea Greens | SERVES 4

Tangles of vining pea greens aren't the same as sprouted peas, or pea shoots, which you can sometimes find in the supermarket, but are bits of the vine itself, complete with curling tendrils and sometimes a small pea or pea blossom. You can dip pea greens briefly into salted boiling water to bring out their color and flavor, then use them to garnish a dish of peas or a pea soup. Or you can stir-fry them as is done here. Lacking the greens, you can use pea shoots in their place.

½ pound snow peas

¼ pound or more pea greens

1½ tablespoons roasted or plain peanut oil

1 garlic clove, chopped

sea salt

1. Trim and string the snow peas. Wash the pea greens in a bowl of cold water, then remove and shake off the excess water.

2. Heat a large skillet or a wok. Add the oil, swirl it around, then add the garlic and snow peas. Stir-fry the peas for 1 minute, then add the pea greens and a pinch of salt and stir-fry until the leaves are tender and bright green. Serve right away.

Pasta with Peas, Fresh Sage, and Bread Crumbs | SERVES 2 TO 4

The shape of pasta makes a difference. Radiatore, lumache, shells, and other curved pastas keep the peas and pasta together, which otherwise tend to go off in separate directions. Fresh sage may sound like a surprising choice of herb, but early in the season its undertones are minty, making it a natural with peas. Make the sauce while the pasta is cooking.

sea salt and freshly ground pepper
½ pound small pasta shapes, such as
    radiatore or lumache
4 tablespoons unsalted butter, olive
    oil, or a mixture
¼ cup finely diced shallot or scallion
1 pound pod peas, shucked
3 tablespoons chopped sage
1 teaspoon grated lemon zest
½ cup fresh bread crumbs
⅓ cup chopped parsley
sage blossoms, if available

1. Bring a large pot of water to a boil and add salt and the pasta.

2. While the pasta is cooking, heat 2 tablespoons of the butter in a large skillet, add the shallot, and cook gently for a few minutes, until softened. Add the peas, sage, and 1 cup of the pasta water and stew until the peas are bright green and tender, 1 or 2 minutes. Add the lemon zest.

3. Crisp the bread crumbs in the remaining butter or oil in a small skillet. When the pasta is done, drain it, add it directly to the peas, and toss. Taste for salt, season with pepper, and toss with the parsley and bread crumbs. Garnish with the purple sage blossoms, if available.

Fennel and Winter Greens Salad with Mushrooms and Truffle Oil | SERVES 4 TO 6

If I had to choose just one, this would be my favorite winter salad. The bitter edge of the greens, the clean flavor of the fennel, the dank mushrooms, and the haunting fragrance of the truffle oil—what could be better? Serve this salad as a first or last course so that it can stand alone.

1 head butter lettuce

1 medium head radicchio

1 plump Belgian endive

1 fennel bulb, trimmed

6 large mushrooms, thinly sliced

1 large shallot, finely diced

1½ tablespoons aged red wine vinegar
　　or fresh lemon juice

sea salt and freshly ground pepper

5 tablespoons extra virgin olive oil

truffle oil

a chunk of Parmigiano-Reggiano at
　　room temperature

1. Gently tear the butter lettuce into bite-sized or larger pieces, leaving the smaller heart leaves whole. Tear the radicchio into smaller pieces. Quarter the endive lengthwise, then sliver lengthwise. Wash and dry the greens and put them in a salad bowl. Slice the fennel paper-thin on a mandoline and add it to the greens along with the sliced mushrooms. Cover with a damp towel and refrigerate until needed.

2. Combine the shallot, vinegar, and ½ teaspoon salt. Let stand for at least 5 minutes, then whisk in the olive oil. Taste on a lettuce leaf— it can be a little on the tart side. Toss the salad with enough vinaigrette to coat well, then drizzle on a teaspoon or so of truffle oil and toss again. Pile lightly onto plates. Shave some thin curls of cheese over each serving, add pepper to taste, and serve.

FENNEL

Fennel, or anise as it's also called, has become a regular feature of farmers' markets everywhere, a welcome sight to my eyes, for this is a delicious and versatile vegetable.

In the supermarket fennel bulbs tend to be compact and roundish, hefty for their size—they can weigh up to 10 or 12 ounces. Fennel bulbs at the farmers' market are so frequently small and more elongated than round that I suspect it's not an easy vegetable to grow. But it is an easy vegetable to use. Slice the bulbs for the pasta dish and soup recipe that follow, or thinly slice them on a mandoline or benriner cutter when you want them for a salad. Raw, fresh fennel, sliced into long pieces and set out with a little sea salt, makes a crisp and cooling appetizer, and the greens can be used as a garnish or seasoning wherever the bulbs are called for.

Pasta with Golden Fennel | SERVES 4 TO 6

Caramelized fennel is the only vegetable in this pasta, but it's enormously flavorful. You can also serve the fennel as a vegetable. Cut it into thicker, heftier pieces, but still cook until golden and caramelized.

2 or 3 large fennel bulbs, including the greens
2 tablespoons unsalted butter
1 tablespoon olive oil
sea salt and freshly ground pepper
grated zest and juice of 1 lemon
1 garlic clove, minced
¾ to 1 pound fettuccine
Parmigiano-Reggiano or Dry Monterey Jack cheese

1. Peel or discard, if badly bruised, the tough outer layers of the fennel, then quarter the bulbs, setting aside the greens, and slice thinly. (The core will cook to tenderness.) Heat a large pot of water for the pasta.

2. Melt 1 tablespoon of the butter with the olive oil in a wide skillet. Add the fennel and sauté over high heat, stirring occasionally, until browned in places, 7 to 10 minutes. Season with 1 teaspoon salt. Toss with the lemon juice, then add 1 cup water. Reduce the heat and cook, covered, until the liquid has evaporated. Add another ½ cup water and continue cooking in this fashion until the fennel is very soft and deep gold in color, about 25 minutes in all. Season with pepper. Chop a handful of fennel greens—enough to make about ⅓ cup—with the garlic and lemon zest and set aside.

3. Add salt and the pasta to the boiling water and cook until the pasta is al dente. Scoop it out and add it to the pan with the fennel and the chopped greens. Taste for salt and season with pepper. Serve with the cheese, finely grated or thinly shaved over the top.

VARIATION WITH RICOTTA CHEESE: When my friend Michele Anna Jordan came to visit one winter, she brought 3 pounds of fresh ricotta from Bellwether farms in Sonoma country. It's an exquisite cheese—light, delicate, and very pure tasting—and we used it in everything all week, including this pasta.

Toss a cup or so of fresh whole-milk ricotta with a little grated lemon zest, a few pinches of salt and pepper, and a teaspoon or so of olive oil. Add it to the dish at the very end. A good fresh ricotta will practically melt into the pasta. You can also simply season the ricotta like this, then spread it over little toasts for an appetizer.

Fennel Soup with Saffron Dumplings | SERVES 4

Saffron is not commonly seen at farmers' markets, but I know some farmers who have given it a try, my brother, Mike Madison, and his wife, Dianne, being two. They grow mostly flowers on their small farm in northern California, but one year they decided to venture into saffron, which involved plucking the stamens from large lavender crocus blooms. When they sent me home with a bag of fennel and a packet of saffron, this soup with these dumplings immediately came to mind.

THE SAFFRON DUMPLINGS | MAKES 20 SMALL DUMPLINGS

½ cup milk

2 tablespoons unsalted butter

2 pinches saffron threads

sea salt and freshly ground pepper

¼ cup minced fennel greens

½ cup all-purpose flour

2 eggs

1. Heat the milk with the butter, saffron, ½ teaspoon salt, and a little pepper. When the butter has melted, stir in the fennel greens, then add the flour all at once. Remove the pan from the heat and beat vigorously with a wooden spoon to make a smooth paste, then return the pan to low heat and work the paste until it leaves a film on the bottom of the pan. Turn off the heat and beat in the eggs one at a time, until completely smooth.

2. Bring a large skillet of water to a simmer and add 1 teaspoon salt. Drop loosely heaped teaspoons of batter into the pan. Cook gently until they're firm, turning once, about 5 minutes. When done, transfer the dumplings to a plate and set them aside until needed.

THE SOUP

1 hefty or 2 smaller fennel bulbs, about 6 ounces

1 bunch scallions, including a few inches of the greens

1 large artichoke

1 quart Vegetable Stock, page 285, light chicken stock, or water

¼ cup finely chopped parsley

2 tablespoons chopped cilantro

1 tablespoon finely snipped chives

sea salt and freshly ground pepper

extra virgin olive oil to finish

1. Quarter the fennel bulb(s) and slice very thinly crosswise. Chop enough of the greens to make ¼ cup. Trim the scallions and slice them crosswise about ¼ inch thick. Pare and quarter the artichoke, removing the leaves and the choke, and slice thinly (see page 389).

2. Put the stock into a saucepan. Add all of the vegetables, half of the herbs, and 1 teaspoon salt. Bring to a boil, then simmer gently until the vegetables are tender, about 20 minutes. Turn off the heat and add the remaining herbs and the dumplings. Let steep for 10 minutes, then pepper lightly. Serve with a thin drizzle of olive oil in each bowl.

RADISHES

Radishes abound at farmers' markets year-round, but they always taste best when it's cool out, whether spring or fall. When the weather turns hot, their flavor gets hot and spicy, too. It's easy to take these cheerful little vegetables for granted, but I've seen a few farmers stop selling them because of the time it takes to tie them into neat little bunches, their greens intact.

Radishes can be like tofu—we buy them with every intention of eating them, but in the end they linger until the greens are wilted and the roots are puffy and soft. It's partly that we don't know what to do with them. One of the easiest and best things to do is just to put them on the table while they're impeccably fresh, with their greens. Add a dish of sea salt for those who like to dip them, butter, and a fresh baguette. As simple as it sounds, this is absolutely delicious.

As with carrot tops, there's a use for the greens. Finely slivered, they make a lively addition to a salad, and they can go into a green vegetable soup. Radishes can also be cooked. Their bright colors fade to delicate pastels, and their flavor mellows. You might, for example, braise them in stock or water, combine them with other spring vegetables such as little carrots and turnips, and finish with mustard butter and sprinkle with chives.

Easter Egg radishes are round and come in bunches of pinks, purples, reds, and whites. French Breakfast radishes are long, with white tips on the end. Daikon are the giant white radishes that can vary anywhere from six inches to a few feet in length! In a Sacramento market I saw forty-pound bags of enormous daikons. They can be grated and used as a condiment—popular in Japanese restaurants and households, cut into chunks and simmered in a miso-based vegetable stew, or sliced into ribbons and then stewed with leeks and a touch of cream—an effective base for crispy pieces of roasted chicken. They are also delicious shredded and sautéed, as in the recipe on page 52.

Less frequently seen but certainly the most exotic varieties are those large Chinese and Korean radishes that resemble small turnips on the outside, but on the inside anything goes. Red Meat and Beauty Heart are two with pale green skins and the most gorgeous deep rose-red interiors. Misato is another rose-fleshed type that's varied with paler-colored concentric rings, and there's also a green-fleshed Misato as well as long, tapering pink- and green-fleshed varieties.

These pretty, big radishes tend to be sweeter and less peppery than other kinds. If you slice them paper-thin on a mandoline, soak them briefly in cold water, then drain and refrigerate them for an hour or so, the nearly transparent rose-colored slices curl gracefully so that they resemble a ruffle you might want to sew on a dress. In fact you can just put them out in a bowl, a big, cheerful tangle, with some good salt, such as Malden sea salt, for dipping or sprinkling. And, of course, these can also go into or on top of a radish sandwich.

Radish Butter for Radish Sandwiches | MAKES ½ CUP

A good radish sandwich can be nothing more than sweet butter spread on bread and topped with sliced radishes and sea salt. But you might find that this is an easier way for getting the radishes and butter on quickly (and getting them to stay on), especially if you're making radish sandwiches for a crowd.

6 radishes—French Breakfast radishes or a mixture of red, purple, and pink radishes

4 tablespoons unsalted butter

1 teaspoon finely grated lemon zest

sea salt

1. Wash and trim the radishes. If the leaves are tender and fresh, set a dozen or so aside, stems removed. Slice the radishes into thin rounds, then crosswise into narrow strips. Each should be tipped with color. Chop the leaves. You should have about ½ cup.

2. Mix the butter with the lemon zest until it's soft, then stir in the chopped radishes, radish leaves, and a pinch of salt. Spread on slices of crusty baguette and serve.

Radish Salad with Vella's Dry Jack Cheese | SERVES 6

The Vella family's Dry Jack cheese from Sonoma County in California is one of our national food treasures. It's increasingly possible to find nationwide, but if you can't get your hands on some, use Parmigiano-Reggiano. This is a very pretty, bright, and lively little salad. You can stray successfully from its utter simplicity by adding some freshly blanched and peeled fava beans, radish sprouts, or very small arugula leaves.

2 bunches French Breakfast radishes or mixed varieties, including small daikon and Chinese Red Meat

2 tablespoons thinly sliced chives

olive oil

2 to 4 ounces Dry Jack cheese or Parmigiano-Reggiano

sea salt and freshly ground pepper

radish sprouts, leaves, or arugula greens, optional

1. Set aside a handful of the most tender radish greens. Trim the radish roots, leaving just a bit of the stem, and wash them well. Wick up the excess moisture with a towel, then slice thinly, either lengthwise or crosswise. Put them in a bowl and toss with the chives, radish greens, and enough oil to coat lightly.

2. Put the radishes on a platter, shave the cheese over them, and add salt and pepper and the greens, if using.

Shredded Daikon with Scallions and Sesame Seeds | SERVES 2 TO 4 AS A SIDE DISH

Although plentiful in the market, daikon is often too peppery to enjoy raw in quantity. However, it cooks down into a deliciously mellow dish. Choose firm, glowing roots and use them within a few days since moisture is lost quickly through their thin skins. Tender tops can be simmered or steamed, then chopped and added to the cooked daikon.

1½ pounds firm daikon, peeled
1 bunch scallions, including the firm
    greens
1 tablespoon sesame seeds
1 tablespoon light sesame or
    vegetable oil
1 teaspoon dark sesame oil
sea salt
soy sauce

1. Coarsely grate the daikon or cut into matchsticks. Slice the scallions on the diagonal into large pieces.

2. Heat a nonstick skillet and toast the sesame seeds, shaking often, until they smell good, about 3 minutes. Pour them into a dish, return the pan to the heat, and add the oils. Add the scallions, cook for 1 minute, then add the daikon. (If it feels wet—it will exude water as it sits—squeeze it before adding it to the pan.) Season with ½ teaspoon salt, sprinkle lightly with soy sauce, and sauté over high heat, stirring occasionally, for 5 minutes. Taste for salt, add more soy if needed, toss with the sesame seeds, and serve.

Rhubarb with Berries and Candied Ginger | SERVES 4

Rhubarb, the earliest spring fruit, arrives in—or at least persists into—strawberry and mulberry season and is notoriously excellent with berries. This is a much simpler dessert to produce than a pie, and you'll end up with rosy pieces of fruit that dissolve into a puree—that is, if your stalks were red. There's also an heirloom variety that has green stalks—every bit as delicious, but a bit dingier in color.

Serve this compote garnished with strips of candied ginger (it turns slightly medicinal when baked), cream, and a ginger cookie. Or spoon it over ice cream. Plan to spread any leftovers on your morning toast.

1½ pounds rhubarb
½ cup light brown sugar, packed, or
    maple syrup
1 teaspoon minute tapioca
juice and long strands of zest of
    1 small orange
⅛ to ¼ teaspoon ground cloves
a handful to a few pints strawberries,
    mulberries, or blackberries
cream and crème fraîche
4 slices candied ginger, cut into thin
    strips, for garnish

1. Wash the rhubarb, trim off the ends of the stalks, then slice them crosswise into ½-inch chunks. If the stalks are very thick, halve them lengthwise first. Toss with the sugar, tapioca, orange juice, zest, and cloves. Arrange in an 8 x 10-inch gratin dish and let stand while you preheat the oven to 400°F. Cover with foil and bake until the fruit is tender when pierced with a knife, 35 to 45 minutes.

2. Meanwhile, if you're using strawberries, rinse them quickly, then slice thickly. Plunge mulberries briefly into water and remove any stems. When the rhubarb is done, remove it from the oven, scatter the berries over the top, and let stand with a piece of foil placed loosely over the top. The heat of the rhubarb will open the flavor of the berries, cooking them slightly. Serve chilled or at room temperature, garnished with cream and crème fraîche whipped together until billowy, and the candied ginger.

At a farm stand in a Kansas City farmers' market, a thicket of signs growing out of the produce practically obscures the vegetables. It's not usually this way, though. Many farmers don't bother with signage—then they complain about how tired they get of telling everyone how much something costs or what it is. That couldn't possibly occur here, I thought, but no doubt it does. People often don't bother to read. I overheard a teenage girl helping her mother at another market complain, "Why do we have to put out the signs? People never read them." "Some do," her mother said. But perhaps some people just prefer to talk.

I love market signs, especially the pictures people draw of their farms and their animals. Sometimes they express the spell of the place and you can see how the land speaks to the farmer. "Harmony Valley Farms" depicts three red hearts in a circle, wreathed with fruiting grapevines. The sign for Monte Vista farm shows a big tree, its roots spreading through the earth and emerging out of the field to spell the name. Rio Loco's farm depicts a Churro sheep drinking from the river, a New Mexican landscape in the background, recognizable to anyone who's been to New Mexico. Another shows, in a rustic fashion, a map of Earthheart Farm—the horse, the cottonwood trees, the gardens, and the house. Those who have taken a farm tour will see that sign in a different way, having walked through the fields and petted the horse. But the most poignant aspect of this sign was a big radish shaped like a heart.

Signs are, of course, for advertising. "Eat Me! Mmm Good!" is scrawled on a piece of cardboard stuck in a display of apples, grapes, and walnuts in Torrance, California. And what a good idea to serve all those together for dessert.

"The last of the season!" declares a sign on a bin of nectarines. That's useful to know if you want to stock up on crisp nectarines, which some people love.

"Organically grown," "Pesticide Free," "Grass Fed," "No Hormones or Antibiotics" is the kind of information that's important for many customers to know, while simply naming foods is essential to others. It's only through naming that you can find out what it is you like, return to it, and build a relationship to it and to its grower. A sticker with a number pasted to a plum is useless. We need to know that it was a Santa Rosa, a Friar, or a Damson we enjoyed if we want to eat it again next year.

Sometimes varieties aren't identified because they've been around for so long that farmers no longer know what they are exactly. They may have been foods that were planted generations ago. "Oh, we just call those yellow cherries," says one farmer who grows twelve kinds of named cherries. "That's Spanish basil," says another, pointing to her basil. Wild plums, Indian plums, Spanish plums are just three names of the same small fruits that grow around northern New Mexico.

Humor has its place in the market, too. Consider this string of signs over a corn booth in the Dane County (Wisconsin) Market:

"We are only trying to market our corn, not corner the

market. But we would like everybody to try our corn and melons. We would all be better off!"

"Eugsters corn is grown in real dirt. You can taste the difference!"

"Eugsters corn was picked by Norwegians. Uffda! What could be better than that?"

"When you care enough to eat the best, take some home and have a good meal."

While meat is displayed in cleverly constructed glass-topped boxes, the meat resting on ice packs below, signs are frequently used to draw attention to chicken and other meats. The Rullos in Cleveland had a chicken tea cozy with a sign saying, "Ask about our free range chicken!" In Minneapolis one family had big white plastic chickens standing in for their meat. I've seen lots of wonderful paintings of turkeys, chickens, goats, and buffalo. In fact many signs are as good as what they're advertising. The Ithaca farmers' market in particular seemed to have an abundance of beautiful signs. Two, one for potatoes and the other for garlic, were so handsome that a customer had bought one, along with the garlic and potatoes. I wanted to buy the other, but the farmers pleaded that they didn't have time to make a replacement.

The sign that symbolized for me what it is every farmer wants to see at the close of the market was one with lines drawn through each of its long list of offerings: Snake Hill Farm had enjoyed a successful day. With many days like this, perhaps, eventually, their great-great-grandchildren would be able to have a sign like one I saw in Wisconsin. Beside a picture of a round red barn and a tree full of red apples were the words:

> "Our Family Farm for 160 Years.
> Enjoy the Fruits of Our Labor."

The last digit, I noticed, could easily be replaced.

Herbs and Alliums 3

"I can't seem to get people interested in herbs!"

Khasia Hartwell, who sells her soft bundles of fragrance at our market, is just plain frustrated. Customers will gladly eat her lemon thyme shortbread or basil-scented cookies, but will they buy a bunch of herbs? Apparently not. Traffic in culinary herbs isn't as swift as it might be, except of course when it comes to Genovese basil, parsley, and chives, the Big Three. But the exotics—a spicy Lesbos basil, all the lemon-scented herbs, pungent epazote that's so deliciously authentic with black beans, anise hyssop with its lavender blooms—are left over at the end of the day.

This is a shame, for herbs are one of the most magical—and practical—components of our cooking. They're the lively border collies of the plant world, whose task is to urge fruits and vegetables in this or that direction. Herbs can take a vegetable on the most amazing journeys, changing a food from savory to sweet and back again, and they can make one vegetable seem like five. Corn with Italian basil is completely different from corn with Thai basil and is different yet again from corn with sage, cilantro, or dill. You can cook corn every night of the week and never have it taste the same. Herbs provide one of the easiest ways to bring variety to the foods you already know how to make and may be a little bored with.

Herbs take little effort to prepare, there's no waste, and they're pure pleasure to handle. Our reluctance to try a new herb probably has to do with not being able to imagine its effect. There are excellent cookbooks devoted to the culinary possibilities of herbs, but you don't need a book to start learning about the herb you're holding in your hand at the market. Start by crushing a leaf between your fingers, then deeply inhaling its scent several times. Next take a little bite, close your eyes, and let its flavor travel over your tongue so you can pick out the hints of sweetness, tartness, bitterness. Saturate your senses, and a pairing might just come to mind. You could suddenly find yourself thinking, I wonder if rosemary would be good with those sweet potatoes I bought? (It is.) Or you might decide that anise hyssop would go with beets—or with figs—(and it does, with both). If you give them a chance to enter your senses, herbs can often reveal the directions they best travel in.

Members of the onion family, the alliums are not usually thought of as herbs with the exception of chives. But although onions, scallions, shallots, and garlic are occasionally treated as vegetables most often they are used as seasonings, just as herbs are. Even the Sweet and Sour Onions with Dried Pluots and Rosemary on page 74 are treated more as an accent than a vegetable. As with herbs, a small amount of garlic, chives, scallions, and shallots goes far to influence a dish.

Chicken, lamb, beef, as well as far more exotic meats are a regular feature of many farmers' markets now. The quality is often very high. Personally, I'm always more interested in what meat goes with than in the meat itself, and herbs and alliums enhance and harmonize with these foods beautifully, just as they do with vegetables. Included here are some recipes that draw especially on these small but very full-flavored members of the plant world.

Fresh herbs are used plentifully throughout this book, but this chapter features some of the herbs we might not find at the supermarket, or dishes that amass a concentration of herbs. And if your market is limited to parsley, dill, and basil, then try mixing them together to make a kind of superherb that goes far beyond the impact of any single one.

Herb Teas
or Tisanes

A tisane is an herb tea, but it's not a musty little package of dried herbs. Far better, a tisane is a handful of fresh green herbs that are steeped in boiling water. The essence that ensues is then poured into glasses or cups or cooled and poured over ice.

Many herbs—virtually all of them, really—can be used in this way. But some that are especially suited for tisanes are mints of all kinds, lemon thyme, lemon verbena, and lemon balm; chamomile, anise hyssop, marigold, pineapple sage, and culinary sage, if the leaves are fresh and new. You can be even more adventurous with herbs like dill, lovage, rose geranium, and other edible scented plants. Wild herbs, such as cota and apple mint, traditionally used here for their very mild medicinal qualities, can be found in our market and, no doubt, others. And you can mix different herbs together. If you steep your herbs in a glass teapot, you'll have the added pleasure of seeing the deepening color of the herbs emerge.

For about 6 cups, take a good handful of fresh herbs. Give them a good rinse and pluck any unattractive leaves off the stems. Place them in the teapot and cover with boiling water. Let steep for 5 minutes, or longer if needed, then pour into glasses or teacups.

For 1 person, place several clean sprigs in a glass, such as a Moroccan mint-tea glass, and pour in the boiling water.

For iced tea, make the tisane, then chill well. Pour over ice and add a sprig of fresh herb to the glass.

Herb
Sugars | MAKES ABOUT 2 CUPS

If you like to sweeten tea with a whisper of lavender, sprinkle rose-scented sugar over a fresh cream cheese, or sweeten a fruit compote with a potpourri of lemon verbena and lime zest, then you'll want to have some herbed sugar on hand. You can use any number of the sweet herbs, such as lemon verbena, rose geranium, lavender, mints, or lemon thyme, and you can also add a few strips of orange, lime, bergamot, or Meyer lemon zest as well.

Here's a general formula:

¼ cup leaves and flowers of sweet
    herbs
2 cups sugar
zest of 1 citrus fruit, optional, in strips
    rather than finely grated

Gently bruise the herbs with a mortar to bring out their aromatic oils, then mix them with the sugar and citrus zest. Put the herbs and sugar in a jar and cover tightly. For the next two weeks, give the sugar a shake or a stir every few days to spread the aromatic oils around and to break up any clumps. After 2 weeks, the sugar will be infused with the herbs' flavor. Strain the sugar, discard the herbs and zest, and store, tightly covered.

Herb Vinegars

With all the herbs you're likely to find at the farmers' market, it's very tempting to make your own herb vinegars, for your own use or to give as gifts. The results, which are both tasty and pretty, are easily accomplished.

The method for making herb-flavored vinegars is simply to pour simmering vinegar over a handful of clean herbs (about 3 cups vinegar to 1 handful of herbs), cap, and let steep for about 2 weeks. The herbs needn't be chopped or removed from their stems. Turn the jar occasionally to distribute the flavor.

It's easiest to steep the vinegar in a wide-mouthed jar, then, once the flavor has developed, decant it into bottles and add just a fresh sprig of the herb you've used as a pretty reminder of the chosen flavor.

Herbs should always be clean and dry and your jars and lids sterilized. Wash the herbs in a bowl of cold water, then spin them dry or let them dry on a clean towel. As for the jars and lids, wash them well in hot, soapy water, then plunge into a pot of boiling water to cover and boil for 15 minutes (20 at higher altitudes). Lift them out of the water with tongs and let them dry on a clean towel. Now you can add the clean, dry herbs and simmering vinegar. If you like, include a clove of peeled garlic or shallot as well.

WHICH VINEGARS AND HERBS TO USE:

There isn't any rule, but in general the robust flavor of red wine vinegars favors more robust herbs, such as rosemary, hyssop, oregano, thyme, bay, and nonherbal additions such as garlic and shallot.

White wine or rice wine vinegars are more delicate, so they favor the softer herbs, like chervil, mint, tarragon, chives (including garlic chives and scapes), lemon verbena, the different basils, spring sage, dill, lovage, and marjoram. Dill and lovage can be used in lesser amounts than the others—½ cup to 3 cups of vinegar. Although arugula and sorrel are considered herbs, they're too volatile to be useful in herbal vinegars. You can mix herbs, and you can include other seasonings such as peppercorns, dried coriander, allspice, and bay leaves.

Lovage Oil

| MAKES ½ CUP

An emerald-green oil that makes a delicious herbal seasoning for steamed new potatoes, cucumber salads, and salmon—or all 3 together on a single plate.

1 cup lovage leaves, more or less
sea salt
½ cup olive oil

Pick lovage leaves that are young and flavorful. Rinse them, then blanch in boiling salted water for about 30 seconds. Drain and squeeze out the excess moisture. Puree the leaves with the olive oil for 1 minutes, then set aside to steep for 30 minutes. Pour through a strainer and discard the solids.

Sage Oil

| MAKES ½ CUP

Sage is such a natural accompaniment to fall and winter foods that I make this often. Use it as a sauce for the Herb Dumplings on page 66 or with roasted winter squash, sweet potatoes, roasted potatoes, white beans, and so forth. I start by browning butter for its good, nutty flavor, then finish it with oil. If you prefer, you can use all olive oil. When you're done, you'll end up with a lot of crispy sage leaves to use for a garnish.

4 tablespoons unsalted butter
24 sage leaves
⅓ cup olive oil

Melt the butter in a small skillet over medium heat until it turns pale gold and smells pleasantly nutty. Skim off any foam, add the sage leaves, and let them sizzle for a minute or so. Pour in the oil, reduce the heat to low, and cook for 10 minutes. Pour through a strainer and re-serve the sage leaves.

Not all markets are large and thriving; some are just starting out, and like seedlings, they can look small and fragile, barely there at all. The market in Socorro, New Mexico, was such a market when I visited it one late July several years ago. It is now a thriving market, but then it was only two years old, and no signs announced its presence. But many New Mexican towns still have their old plazas, and that was the place to look. There, in the green shade of the elms, a half dozen farmers sat with their wares displayed on card tables. Another few vendors were parked on the street, selling, among other things, pecan pies from their cars. Thunder was rumbling, and the gusts of cool wind that precede a storm urged measured haste.

I didn't have high expectations, but it's always nice to be surprised. The first farmer I stopped before had something very surprising—black shell beans in their pods. Not that they'd taste that much different from dried, but I was intrigued. The long pods cradling their cargo of shiny black seeds were tender shades of rose and cream. The ride home would offer plenty of time for shelling them. She also had plump fennel bulbs, and behind a bushel of pickling cucumbers was a bucket of flowers, among them a spray of Joseph's Coat, a rose whose buds are yellow but fringed with pink and orange. They open, like the bean pods, to a mass of pink and cream petals with the fragrance of raspberries. This exquisite little flower was surrounded with the feathery fronds of asparagus she had thought to include in her bouquet. I was starting to get very excited.

But I soon had to shift gears. A tall, thin farmer was sitting in at the next table, his face darkly tanned from the sun. His son stood by him. Their offerings consisted of just a few carrots and a bowl of Red Dale potatoes. The carrots were beautifully formed and the potatoes freshly dug, but the display looked forlorn. To make matters worse, while they chatted with their neighbors, both men kept breaking off the carrots and munching on them, further diminishing their supply. They seemed so unconcerned about making any sales that I had to cajole them into selling me some potatoes. When I leaned over to pay, I saw that this small showing was bogus, for hidden behind their table was a huge crate of carrots and a big bucket of potatoes!

These two weren't the only farmers committed to such a nonaggressive sales approach. There was the young man who had twenty Sun Gold tomatoes and three zucchini. He sat behind *his* table reading a book. I bought the tomatoes, then he asked me if I couldn't please buy the squash too so that he could go home. Apparently he always shows up with two or three squash, a cup of tomatoes, a single head of lettuce, and a book.

Farmers around the world have found that it's best for business if they flaunt their wares by piling them into heaps. That way shoppers can choose this beet or carrot over that one, always taking what they think is the best. People everywhere like to congratulate themselves on their ability to select well, and we tend to feel more confident about choosing food than we do other things. Plus, a mound, a pile, a heap, be it artichokes, turmeric, or lemons, always draws us to it. When there's just a handful of plums or a single bunch of whatever, it makes things harder, not easier, because it appears to be what's left over, the ones not chosen.

When farmers don't have much to offer, they can get around the paucity problem by displaying their five cucumbers, say, in a little box, as I saw done in a New York market. Some farmers at our market put their few bunches of basil in a toy wagon but keep more in the cooler. Five ordinary red tomatoes set on a red plastic plate looked stunning in another market. Little tricks like these frame what's there and make it special. Then everyone wants it.

The last farmer I spoke with in Socorro restores ancient carpets when she's not farming. Most farmers, it seems, have other jobs. She had boxes of freshly dug Bintje, Yukon Gold, German Butterball, and Peruvian Blue potatoes—beautiful, clean, and perfect. Bunches of tender arugula and chard stood next to the table, along with herbs, a single bowl of sky-blue borage blossoms, and lush bouquets of zinnias, cosmos, and sunflowers. There wasn't a lot of any one thing, but it was all fresh and fragrant. I packed the zinnias and greens in my cooler, then it was full and time to go.

It would have been easy to drive past such a little mar-ket, but I was thrilled with what I found there. And what I also appreciated about this and other small markets was that the experience wasn't overwhelming, the way large markets often are. Both have their advantages, but every time I find a little farmers' market I enjoy it immensely. There's always a treasure to be found, and limited choices are often a blessing.

Three years later Patrick and I were having lunch in Socorro. Salads came first, a very tasty mix of tender greens that were clearly locally grown. Patrick's pizza was strewn with fresh oregano; mine with basil. Everything tasted as if it had been brought into the kitchen while we were reading our menus. When we told the young waiter how good everything was, he proudly said that the lettuce and herbs were locally grown. A few months later I ran into Cecilia Mc-Cord, a farmer and the manager of the Socorro farmers' market, and mentioned this lunch to her. "Oh," she said, "that was my lettuce!"

AN ALL-VEGETABLE SUPPER FROM SOCORRO

Sun Gold tomatoes

Carrot Top Soup (page 204)
garnished with borage blossoms

Salt Potatoes with Butter and Herbs (page 214)

Chard, as cooked for The Simplest Tender Greens (page 3)

Shaved fennel and arugula with
Shallot Vinaigrette (page 392)

Apricot Custard Tart (page 288)

White Pizza with Sage | MAKES ONE 12-INCH PIZZA

You can adapt this easily for bruschetta if you don't have the time or inclination to make pizza dough.

2 (4-ounce) balls fresh mozzarella
½ recipe Pizza Dough, page 386
olive oil
15 to 20 sage leaves
a chunk of Parmigiano-Reggiano
red pepper flakes
sea salt

1. Preheat the oven to 500°F. Thinly slice the mozzarella and set it on paper towels to dry.
2. Roll or pat the dough into a circle 12 or 13 inches across, keeping it a little thicker at the edge. If using a baking stone, generously dust a peel with cornmeal and lay the dough over it. Otherwise, put the dough on a sheet pan or pizza pan. Lay the mozzarella over it, drizzle with a little oil, and bake for 7 minutes. Remove, add the sage leaves, and bake until the crust is golden, another 8 to 10 minutes.
3. Remove from the oven, grate a little Parmigiano-Reggiano over the pizza, season with pepper flakes and a pinch of salt, and paint the edge with olive oil. Cut into wedges and serve immediately.

Salsa Verde with Basil, Cilantro, and Mint | MAKES ABOUT ⅔ CUP

A dip, a spread, a garnish, it's also a terrific seasoning for scrambled eggs, tacos, and corn dishes. If you use a food processor, everything will be very fine and smooth; chopped by hand, the chiles and herbs will be suspended in the oil.

1 jalapeño chile, seeded

1 large bunch cilantro, stems removed

½ cup basil leaves

¼ cup mint leaves

2 small garlic cloves

½ cup plus 2 tablespoons olive oil

grated zest and juice of 1 lime

sea salt

1. Chop the first five ingredients very finely, then stir in ¼ cup water, the oil, and the lime zest and juice.
2. Taste for salt and adjust the balance of the lime juice to oil, if needed. Or, pulse the chile, herbs, and garlic in a food processor, then gradually add the water, oil, and lime zest and juice to taste.

Marjoram Pesto with Capers and Olives | MAKES ABOUT ⅔ CUP

When you find marjoram at your market, skip the basil and reach for it instead. It may be a while before you go back to basil. I usually serve this with cold beets, fresh egg noodles, or spread on toast, then covered with tomatoes. In fact, if it's in the house, it gets eaten with everything.

1 small slice country bread

2 tablespoons aged red wine vinegar

1 garlic clove, coarsely chopped

sea salt and freshly ground pepper

¼ cup marjoram leaves

3 tablespoons drained capers

½ cup pine nuts

1 cup finely chopped parsley

2 tablespoons pitted green olives

½ cup extra virgin olive oil

1. Remove the crusts from the bread, then soak it in the vinegar on a plate.
2. Pound the garlic with ½ teaspoon salt in a mortar until smooth, then work in the marjoram, capers, pine nuts, parsley, and olives until you have a coarse puree. Add the bread and the olive oil and work until the pesto is well amalgamated. Season with pepper, taste for vinegar, and add a little more if you think it needs it. The pesto will be very thick.

Herb Dumplings for Soups and Ragouts |

These dumplings are easy to make. The only secret to their success is to be gentle every step of the way. The base is potato, and all kinds of herbs go well with potatoes—from a big baroque mixture to a single herb. I usually start with a base of parsley, then add others. You might start the market season using chervil mixed with some chives and tarragon leaves. Come midsummer, marjoram, dill, basil, and lemon thyme will prevail. As soon as the weather cools, turn to rosemary and sage. These are delicious drizzled with the Sage Oil on page 61.

1 russet potato, about ½ pound,
    peeled and cut into chunks
sea salt and freshly ground pepper
2 medium or large eggs, beaten
½ to ¾ cup finely chopped parsley
¼ cup chopped tarragon, marjoram, or
    rosemary
1 cup all-purpose flour, plus extra as
    needed

1. Cover the potato with cold water, add 1 teaspoon salt, and bring to a boil. Cook until tender, then drain. Gently mash or pass through a potato ricer.

2. Stir in the eggs, then add the herbs, 1 teaspoon salt, and a few grinds of pepper. Gently stir in the flour, taking care not to overwork the dough, which should end up fairly stiff but still somewhat tacky. (Once it becomes too stiff to work, you can turn it out on a counter and gently knead in the rest.) Dust with flour, cover loosely in plastic wrap, and let it rest for 30 minutes.

3. Dust a counter lightly with flour and gently roll or pat the dough into a rectangle, approximately 10 x 4 inches. Cut the rectangle lengthwise into thirds, and then cut each third into 10 to 12 pieces. Gently roll them between your palms or leave them in little squares.

4. Bring a wide skillet of water to a boil. Lower the heat to a simmer and add a third of the dumplings. Simmer gently until they float to the top, 7 or 8 minutes. Transfer them to a buttered dish and continue cooking the rest. Add them to your soup or ragout a few minutes before serving so that they'll warm up.

VARIATION: Roll or pat the dough into a much larger piece, one that ends up with a thickness of ¼ inch, then cut out shapes with a knife or cookie cutters—squares, diamonds, or rounds, or other simple shapes.

Herb Salad | MAKES 4 TO 6 SMALL SALADS

Herb salads are astonishing. A vivid parade of flavor marches across your tongue with each bite, leaving it surprised and fully awake. Such salads don't need additions like croutons or cheese, but good bread tempers the salad and prolongs its enjoyment.

Although largely an extemporaneous affair, composing an herb salad does ask for a moment of thought before starting. This is not, perhaps, the best place for those aggressive herbs such as rosemary, mature sage, savory, hyssop, and culinary thyme. More suitable are the more volatile, soft-leaf herbs—chervil, marjoram, the basils, anise hyssop, chives and garlic chives, lovage, to name a few. Lemon thyme is good in small quantities; the other lemon-scented herbs in larger ones. I always include some lettuce, preferably a soft butterhead type, as background, along with a few handfuls of odd greens, such as orach, amaranth, miner's lettuce, and *quelites* (see page 8). Baby spinach leaves can be used in place of such greens.

Herb blossoms are always welcome in these salads. Although tiny and fragile-looking, they convey more than you might expect of the personality of the herbs they come from. Besides, what could be prettier than violet chive flowers, purple sage blossoms, sky-blue borage, periwinkle rosemary, or the bright and fragrant yellow-orange blossoms of Mexican tarragon (mint marigold)?

Here's a sample salad and some other ideas for combinations to work from.

2 cups butter lettuce leaves

2 cups mixed greens (see headnote)

2 tablespoons marjoram or
    basil leaves

½ cup celery leaves

several lovage leaves

½ cup parsley leaves

½ cup purslane sprigs

sea salt

sunflower seed oil or extra virgin
    olive oil

fresh lemon juice or apple cider
    vinegar

purple sage, chive, or thyme
    blossoms

1. Tear the greens into bite-sized pieces. Keep the marjoram leaves whole and tear the basil leaves, unless they're the tiny *piccolo fino* variety. Tear the celery, lovage, and parsley leaves, keeping them in fairly large pieces. Snap the purslane into clumps and wash well since it tends to be sandy.

2. Toss everything with a pinch of salt, then again with just enough oil to coat. Season with lemon juice or vinegar to taste, then toss again with the blossoms.

OTHER POSSIBLE HERB COMBINATIONS:

Parsley, dill, cilantro, watercress, mint

Thai basil, spearmint or perilla, lemon verbena, chives, cilantro

Cilantro, parsley, spearmint, garlic chives, lemon thyme

Chervil, chives, parsley, marjoram, salad burnet

Dill, salad burnet, tarragon, sorrel

Red and Golden Beets with Anise Hyssop | SERVES 6

The Chioggia beets no larger than an inch across and some similarly sized shiny red onions that I found at a late-summer market were irresistible. They fell right into place with a cooked red beet waiting at home, and some purple-tufted anise hyssop. Of course it needn't be this combination exactly. What's enjoyable is to be led by what you find at the market.

2 large red beets

20 small golden or Chioggia beets

2 small red onions

3 tablespoons champagne vinegar

sea salt and freshly ground pepper

10 leafy flat-leaf parsley sprigs

6 large and 12 small anise hyssop
　　leaves, plus the blossoms if
　　possible, or 1 tablespoon
　　chopped dill

a handful small arugula leaves or
　　pea shoots

extra virgin olive oil

1. Steam the large beets until tender-firm when pierced with a knife, about 35 minutes. Steam the little beets until tender-firm, about 20 minutes. Chill both. Using 5 or 6 neat strokes of the knife, peel and trim the red beets. Slip off the skins of the smaller beets with your hands. Leave the smallest ones whole. Quarter and halve the rest.

2. Peel, then thinly slice the onions into rounds, toss with the vinegar, and sprinkle with salt. Refrigerate for at least 20 minutes.

3. To compose the salad, slice the large beets on a mandoline or very thinly by hand, then overlap them on a large platter. Scatter the small beets on top, then add the onions. Drizzle some of the vinegar over all, salt lightly, and season with pepper. Finely mince the parsley and the large hyssop leaves and sprinkle them over the salad. Add the arugula and the small whole hyssop leaves, along with their violet flowers. Drizzle olive oil over all and serve.

Spring Risotto with Sorrel | SERVES 4

One of the many good things about the farmers' market is being able to buy sorrel by the bagful, and that's what's needed to make a statement here. If the leaves are soft and tender, with tiny little stems, just lop off the stems and slice the leaves. But if the sorrel is a little more weather worn—the leaves thicker, the stems larger— fold the leaves, then pull the stem all the way up to the tip and discard. The chopped leaves will melt into a dark, olive green puree.

2 tablespoons unsalted butter

1 large new red onion, finely diced

6 ounces sorrel (3 to 4 cups trimmed leaves)

sea salt and freshly ground pepper

1½ cups Arborio rice

6 cups simmering Vegetable Stock, page 385, or chicken stock

¼ cup crème fraîche or cream

½ cup chopped chervil or ¼ cup chopped parsley plus 2 tablespoons chopped tarragon

freshly grated Parmigiano-Reggiano, optional

1. Melt the butter in a sauté pan, add the onion, and cook over medium heat, stirring often, for about 5 minutes. Add the sorrel and cook until it has collapsed into the onion after several minutes. Season with ½ teaspoon salt.

2. Add the rice, stir it about, and cook for 1 minute.

3. Pour in 2 cups of the stock. Simmer until it has been absorbed, then raise the heat to high and begin adding the rest, ½ cup at a time. Stir energetically and continue adding liquid after each addition is absorbed. When the rice is tender, stir in the crème fraîche and chervil. Taste for salt, season with pepper, and serve, with a light grating of cheese, if you wish.

Crostini with Chive-Scented Ricotta | MAKES 2 CUPS, ENOUGH FOR 20 CROSTINI

This is amazingly simple and good—especially if you start with delicate, fresh ricotta. You can also use this ricotta as a sauce for pasta, and any leftovers will find a good home folded into an omelet or scrambled eggs.

2 cups fresh cow's or sheep's milk
    ricotta
2 tablespoons olive oil
sea salt and freshly ground pepper
¼ cup very finely snipped chives
chive blossoms, cut at the base
20 slices baguette, ciabatta, or a nutty,
    dense whole wheat bread

Mix the ricotta, oil, salt and pepper to taste, and chives together. Toast the bread until golden, then spread the cheese on top. Add a tiny bit of additional pepper and a few chive blossoms to each slice.

Scallion Crêpes with Stir-Fried Greens | MAKES 12 CRÊPES

A scribble in an old notebook said, "Make scallion crêpes with flowering Chinese greens." These beauties, which actually had succulent red stems beneath their yellow flowers, appeared just one year in our market, but they left a lasting impression. Baby bok choy is a good choice too, and is easy to find, but you can use any tender Chinese green.

THE SCALLION CRÊPES

3 large eggs
1 tablespoon dark sesame or roasted
    peanut oil
1 tablespoon vegetable oil, plus extra
    for the pan
1 cup water
¾ cup milk or soy milk
½ teaspoon salt
1 cup all-purpose flour
1 bunch scallions
¼ cup black or white sesame seeds

1. To make the crêpes, combine the first 6 ingredients in a blender on high speed. Add the flour; blend again for 10 seconds, then stop. Scrape down the sides and blend briefly once more. Pour the batter into a bowl and set aside to rest.

2. Trim and wash the scallions, including an inch or more of the greens. Slice them very, very thinly on the diagonal. Toast the sesame seeds and set them aside. Preheat the oven to 250°F.

3. Heat a 9-inch nonstick pan (about 7½ inches at the base) with a little vegetable oil. Spread it around with a paper towel. When the pan

6 baby bok choy

1 cup snow peas

a few handfuls pea greens, optional

sea salt

1 tablespoon roasted peanut oil

is hot, add ⅓ cup batter and swirl it around the pan. Scatter some scallions and sesame seeds over the top and cook until golden on the bottom, about one minute. Loosen the crêpe, flip it over, and cook the other side until it's dry, then slide it onto a plate. Continue making crêpes until all the batter is used, stacking them on top of one another. If a crêpe sticks, wipe out the pan before going on to the next. Wrap the crêpes in foil and put them in the preheated oven when you start the vegetables.

4. Cut the bok choy lengthwise into quarters, or sixths, if they're on the plump side. Sliver the peas on the diagonal and wash the pea greens.

5. Bring a wide nonstick skillet of water to a simmer; add salt and the bok choy. Simmer for 2 minutes, then drain. (This can be done ahead of time, but if so, rinse the bok choy to keep it from cooking as it cools.)

6. Return the skillet to the stove and turn the heat to high. Add the peanut oil, swirl it around the pan, and add the vegetables. Stir-fry until tender-crisp and bright green. Season with salt and turn into a serving dish. Present the crêpes in a stack, the greens in a dish, and let each person assemble his or her own. Or place an open crêpe (sesame side facing up) on a plate, with some of the vegetables in the middle. This is a very pretty presentation.

VARIATIONS: Stir-fry cleaned and butterflied shrimp with the greens. Or, going in a different direction altogether, fill the crêpes with sautéed or steamed amaranth greens or wild spinach, flavored with chopped cilantro.

Scallion, Potato, and Herb Puree | SERVES 4

Scallions come in many shapes and sizes, from tiny and red to thick and green and very, very long. A stack at the St. Paul market labeled "table onions" were nearly as long as King Alfred leeks and just as sweet. Potatoes are, of course, delicious with leeks, so you can expect they'd be good with scallions, and they're a perfect vehicle for herbs, whether bracing parsley, a handful of chervil, tarragon, or whatever herb you love.

It's completely optional, but I often add a little cheese—goat cheese or sheep's milk feta for a bit of tang, Gruyère for a richer version. Leftovers are delicious browned in clarified butter or olive oil. Measurements are flexible.

2 large (1 pound or a little more) russet potatoes

sea salt and freshly ground pepper

4 tablespoons unsalted butter

2 to 3 cups chopped scallions, including an inch of the greens

⅓ cup chopped parsley, chervil, or other favorite herb

½ cup crumbled goat cheese, optional

1. Peel the potatoes and cut them into chunks. Put them in a saucepan, cover with cold water, and add 1 teaspoon salt. Bring to a boil and cook until soft, about 25 minutes. Set aside a cup of the cooking water, then drain.

2. Melt 1 tablespoon of the butter in a skillet, add the scallions, and toss to coat. Season with ½ teaspoon salt, add ½ cup water, and cook gently until softened, about 15 minutes.

3. Combine the scallions and potatoes in a bowl and mash with the remaining butter, parsley, and enough of the reserved cooking water to make a smooth, light puree. (Use warm milk or cream if you prefer a richer dish.) Stir in the cheese if using. Season to taste with salt and pepper.

Leek, Scallion, and Fennel Gratin | SERVES 4

Serve this delicate gratin for early spring or fall as an accompaniment to fish or roasted chicken or as a vegetable main course.

3 large leeks, white parts only

2 fennel bulbs, about 6 ounces each

sea salt and freshly ground pepper

1½ tablespoons unsalted butter

1. Preheat the oven to 375°F. Lightly butter a 2-quart gratin dish. Chop the leeks into ½-inch pieces and wash them well in plenty of water, separating the rings. Let them soak while you trim and quarter the fennel. Slice it very thinly, including the core. Bring a skillet of water

1 bunch scallions, including an inch
of the greens, sliced

¼ cup chopped fennel greens or
2 tablespoons each chopped
parsley and tarragon

1 teaspoon grated lemon zest

2 large eggs

1½ cups milk or half-and-half

½ cup freshly grated Parmesan or
Gruyère cheese

to a boil; add the fennel and a pinch of salt. Simmer until the fennel is translucent, about 2 minutes, then drain.

2. Melt the butter in a wide skillet. Lift the leeks out of their soaking water and add them to the pan along with the fennel. Season with 1 teaspoon salt and cook over medium heat, stirring frequently, until the leeks are tender, about 10 minutes, adding the scallions after 5 minutes. Add the fennel greens and lemon zest, taste for salt, and season with pepper. Scrape the vegetables into the prepared dish.

3. Beat the eggs and milk together and add ½ teaspoon salt plus the cheese. Pour it over the vegetables, then bake until the top is browned here and there in places, about 40 minutes. Let rest for a few minutes, then serve.

VARIATION WITH ENDIVE: Slice or chop 1 or 2 white Belgian endives and cook them with the leeks and fennel.

Whole Wheat Spaghetti with Late-Summer Onions | SERVES 4 TO 6

This is a minimal dish with maximal flavors. It is best made with those cured onions that come on in late summer and the fall, rather than summer's fresh onions, which are a bit too sweet and watery.

4 tablespoons unsalted butter

5 large yellow onions, 2½ to 3 pounds,
sliced or chopped

sea salt and freshly ground pepper

½ cup white wine

2 tablespoons chopped parsley

1 tablespoon chopped rosemary

1 pound whole wheat spaghetti

freshly grated Parmesan or pecorino
Romano cheese

1. Melt the butter in a wide nonstick skillet. Add the onions, stir to coat them with the butter, then cover and cook over low heat for 1 hour, occasionally checking on them and giving them a stir. Season with 1½ teaspoons salt and a few grinds of pepper, and cook for 30 minutes more or until they're thoroughly soft and starting to color.

2. Raise the heat to reduce any juices that remain, then add the wine and cook until the onions are glazed and the wine has reduced to a syrup, 12 to 15 minutes. Stir in the herbs. Because they're so sweet, the onions may need more salt and pepper than you're used to using. Season to taste.

3. Cook the spaghetti in plenty of salted boiling water until al dente, then drain and toss with the onions. Serve with freshly grated cheese.

Sweet and Sour Onions with Dried Pluots and Rosemary | SERVES 4 TO 6

Onions, vinegar, dried fruit—this ever-enticing combination can be realized with all kinds of onions, different types of vinegar, and an assortment of dried fruits, from the plump Red Flame raisins to apricots and pluots, a plum-apricot cross. The smallish, disk-shaped cipolline onions are most attractive here.

If carefully tended in their final stages, these onions should come out burnished with gold, with the pluots adding succulent sweet-tart bites. Serve warm or at room temperature, with simple grilled chicken.

16 (about 2 pounds) cipolline onions
(or boiling onions, parboiled for
1 minute, then peeled)
2 tablespoons olive oil
1 tablespoon unsalted butter
6 dried pluots, cut into quarters
2 tablespoons red wine vinegar
2 teaspoons honey
2 teaspoons finely chopped rosemary
sea salt and freshly ground pepper

1. Trim the onions of any tough skins or root ends, but leave them whole, removing as little as possible so that they'll keep their shape.

2. Heat the oil and butter in a nonstick skillet large enough to hold the onions in a single layer. Add the onions; give them a stir to coat them with the oil and butter, then cook over medium heat, shuffling the pan back and forth frequently, until they have browned in places, about 6 minutes. Add water to cover, bring to a boil, then simmer until the onions have begun to soften, 15 to 20 minutes. Add the pluots, vinegar, honey, rosemary, and a few pinches of salt.

3. Once all the liquid has boiled away, the onions will start to color nicely. Cook them gently, over the lowest heat, adding more water—a tablespoon or two at a time—until they are perfectly tender and golden. Season with pepper.

HARDNECKS, SOFTNECKS, AND OTHER FORMS OF GARLIC

There's a buzz around garlic that's usually reserved for tomatoes and peppers. Shoppers can be heard using words they'd never heard a few years ago, such as *rocamboles, hardnecks, softnecks, green garlic, scapes,* and names like Music, Persian Star, and Chinese Purple. Nearly every market, it seems, has at least one farmer who is passionate about garlic.

A type of garlic that's new to many shoppers is the stiffneck or hardneck garlic. Its neck grows upright early in the season, then it takes off at a right angle, circles back on itself, and zooms off, ending in a blossom. When these curlicues are still green and soft, they're clipped and sold as "scapes," which can be stir-fried or sautéed. Eventually the necks harden. The mature bulbs have only five to ten cloves per head, which are large and very easy to peel. Some hardneck garlics such as the rocamboles are favored for their hot, spicy flavor. Spanish Roja is the standard for this group, one you may see at the market. Some of the most stunning varieties are those stiffnecks in the "Porcelain group," whose white papery wrappers give pink heads (such as Music) and red ones (such as Georgian Crystal) a gorgeous blush.

Unlike stiffneck garlic, the heads of softneck garlic have from sixteen to forty cloves. Those at the very center of the head are often very small, but those on the outside are large and peel easily. Their soft necks make it possible to weave these garlic heads into braids. California Early and California Late, the main commercial varieties, are favored because they keep well and because their taste is soft and mild rather than fiery. Some, such as lumpy-looking Dushambe, are practically mahogany colored, while Spanish Morodo is intensely purple. One could go on endlessly with depictions of variations on this theme—white papery heads tinted, splashed, or overcome with reds, pinks, and purples. Inchellium Red, an heirloom variety found in Washington State, is one of the new favorites of the softnecks.

Green garlic is simply garlic that's picked while the leaves are still green and the heads are immature. The plants, which may be thinnings from the farmer's field—slender shoots the size of a scallion or small leeks—are one of the first vegetables, besides greens, to appear in the early season of the market. You'll find them as early as January in Austin, February in Phoenix, March in Santa Monica and New Orleans, May in Albuquerque, and June in Des Moines and Montpelier. They provide a little early income to the farmer while exciting shoppers with their elusive flavor, which deepens with every passing day.

Leek and Green Garlic Risotto | SERVES 4

This allium special is loaded with sweet green garlic and the first leeks of the season. If there are any fresh, green garlic shoots, set them aside to add, minced, at the end.

Leek roots and greens, trimmings from the garlic (the stalks and roots), parsley stems, plus some bay leaf and thyme can be used to make a vegetable stock.

THE GREEN GARLIC AND LEEKS

4 medium leeks, white parts only

3 large heads green garlic

2 tablespoons unsalted butter

½ cup white wine

sea salt and freshly ground
    pepper

1. Quarter the leeks lengthwise, cut them crosswise into ¼-inch slices, and wash them well. Remove any tough papery husks from the garlic, then finely chop the bulbs.
2. Melt the butter in a sauté pan. Add the leeks and garlic, stir to coat, then add the wine and cook over medium-low heat until the leeks are tender, about 10 minutes. Season with salt and pepper and set aside while you cook the rice.

THE RICE

6 cups Vegetable Stock, page 385 (see
    headnote), or chicken stock

2 tablespoons unsalted butter

1½ cups Arborio rice

½ cup white wine

½ cup cream or crème fraîche

1 cup freshly grated Parmigiano-
    Reggiano cheese

½ cup chopped chervil or ¼ cup
    chopped parsley and
    1 tablespoon chopped tarragon

sea salt and freshly ground pepper

1. Have the stock simmering on the stove. Melt the butter in a wide soup pot over medium heat. Add the rice and cook, stirring, for 1 minute.
2. Pour in the wine and simmer until it is absorbed, then add 2 cups of the stock. Simmer until it has been absorbed, then raise the heat to high and begin adding the stock ½ cup at a time. Stir energetically and continue adding liquid after each addition is absorbed. When the rice is done, stir in the leeks, cream, cheese, chervil, and any minced garlic shoots. Taste for salt, season with pepper, and serve.

Chicken Breasts and Leeks Poached in an Herb Broth | SERVES 4

These chicken breasts are tender, flavorful, and pretty with their topping of herb-flecked leeks. Serve plain or with any of the green herb sauces. The leftover poaching liquid can go into a soup or risotto.

6 parsley branches

6 tarragon or cilantro sprigs

4 lemon thyme or lemon basil sprigs

1 garlic clove, slivered

1 large piece lemon zest

1 bay leaf

10 peppercorns

sea salt and freshly ground pepper

4 slender leeks, white parts only

Salsa Verde with Basil, Cilantro, and Mint, page 65, or Marjoram Pesto with Capers and Olives, page 65, optional

4 chicken breast halves, skinned, boned, and neatly trimmed

1. Bring 2 to 3 quarts water to a boil in a skillet large enough to accommodate the chicken breasts. Tie the herbs together and add them to the water with the garlic, lemon zest, bay leaf, peppercorns, and 1 teaspoon salt. Simmer while you wash the leeks and make a green herb sauce, if using.

2. Slice the leeks into rounds ⅓ inch thick. Separate the rings, wash them well in a bowl of water, then scoop them out, add them to the pan, and simmer for 5 minutes. The water should barely be moving. Slide the chicken breasts into the pan and cook until the meat is cooked but still very tender, 8 to 10 minutes per side, depending on the size of the breast. The leeks should be done after 25 minutes.

3. Discard the bundle of herbs and transfer the chicken to a cutting board. Lift out the leeks, shake off the excess water, and toss them with enough sauce to coat lightly, if using. Taste for salt and season with pepper. Slice each breast on the diagonal into 4 or 5 pieces. Lay them on each plate and spoon 2 teaspoons sauce over each. Spoon the leeks over each breast and serve.

Roast Chicken with Herbs Under the Skin | SERVES 4 TO 6

Whether you use a small chicken or a great big roaster, this makes a succulent bird that's as good cold as it is hot. The juices, which are flavored with the garlic, wine, and herbs, make delicious pan gravy.

1 roasting chicken, 3 to 5 pounds

½ teaspoon black peppercorns

1 large garlic clove

¼ cup rosemary needles

¼ cup chopped parsley

2 tablespoons marjoram leaves

1 teaspoon sea salt

2 tablespoons aged red wine vinegar

2 tablespoons olive oil

½ cup red or white wine

1 tablespoon all-purpose flour, optional

sea salt and freshly ground pepper, optional

1. Preheat the oven to 400°F. Rinse the chicken and pat it dry.

2. Pound the peppercorns in a mortar. Coarsely chop the garlic with the herbs, then add them to the peppercorns and pound into a paste. Stir in the sea salt, vinegar, and oil.

3. Carefully slide your hand between the skin and the flesh of the chicken, loosening it over the breasts and the legs as far as possible. Rub about half the herb mixture into the flesh. Spread the remainder over the chicken and into the cavity. Truss, then place the chicken in a roasting pan.

4. Bake the chicken for ½ hour, then add the wine and lower the heat to 350°F. Roast until the juices run clear from the thigh, about 1½ hours for a 3-pound bird. While the chicken is roasting, baste it several times with the juices. If it appears to be getting too dark on top, cover it loosely with foil. Serve hot or cold.

5. To make a sauce for hot chicken, remove the bird from the pan and put the pan over a burner on low heat. Whisk in the flour and stir, scraping up the bits from the bottom of the pan. Simmer for 10 minutes. If the sauce is too thick, add stock to thin it out. It should be well seasoned already, but taste and season, if needed, with additional salt and pepper.

Grilled Lamb Chops with Fresh Oregano and Lemon | SERVES 4

The lamb chops at our market are little, offering only a few succulent bites each.

½ cup olive oil

1 large handful chopped
    oregano

½ teaspoon sea salt

½ teaspoon red pepper flakes

8 lamb chops

1 lemon, sliced

1. Combine the oil, oregano, salt, and pepper flakes. Pour it over the lamb, turn to coat it well, then add the lemon. Marinate at room temperature for 1 hour or cover and refrigerate for several hours. Bring it to room temperature before grilling.

2. Preheat a gas grill to hot or build a wood fire. Grill 4 inches or so from the heat, allowing 3 to 5 minutes per side, depending on the thickness.

Lamb Shanks Braised with Onions and Rosemary | SERVES 4

Onions that are too small to bother chopping are very attractive in this braise. Serve with a root vegetable puree—such as potatoes mixed with rutabagas or parsley root (pages 216 and 217), followed by a green salad dressed with a tart lemon vinaigrette.

4 lamb shanks

3 garlic cloves: 1 crushed, 2 slivered

sea salt and freshly ground pepper

¼ cup all-purpose flour

3 tablespoons olive oil

16 small onions, about an inch across,
    peeled and left whole

2 tablespoons finely chopped rosemary

3 thyme sprigs or ½ teaspoon dried

1 cup Merlot or Pinot Noir

⅓ cup parsley chopped with 1 large
    garlic clove

1. Rinse the shanks and pat them dry. Rub the crushed garlic over them and insert the slivers into the folds of the meat. Season with salt and pepper, then roll the shanks in the flour, patting it on with your hands so that they're well coated.

2. Heat the oil in a Dutch oven. Add the shanks and cook over medium-high heat, browning them all over. Transfer them to a platter and add the onions, rosemary, thyme, and any remaining garlic to the pot. Cook until the onions are browned lightly, about 7 minutes.

3. Return the shanks to the pan, add the wine, and simmer until it has reduced by about half. Pour in 3 cups water, bring to a boil, then lower the heat to a simmer. Cover and cook over low heat until completely tender, with the meat falling off the bone, about 2 hours. Serve with chopped parsley and garlic over all.

Bruce Aidells's Roast Beef with Herb and Garlic Paste | SERVES 8, PLUS LEFTOVERS

"Roast beef!" Bruce Aidells blurted out without a moment's hesitation when I asked him what single beef dish he would include in this book. As the author of many fine books on meat, which he faithfully sends me, I knew I should look to Bruce for guidance when it came to beef. He has kindly shared his thoughts on the subject and this recipe, which he adapted from *The Complete Meat Cookbook*.

Most shoppers seem to buy steaks for summer grilling, but Bruce had his reasons for considering a roast. "You can make a roast beef for a simple family dinner, a Sunday lunch, known in England as the Sunday 'joint,' or holiday and other special occasion meals." And whatever you find in season should determine the side dishes. "In spring," Bruce says, "I might serve roast beef with roasted asparagus, sautéed spring greens, and nettle-potato cakes." Even the customary potatoes become something else when you're using tiny summer potatoes, gorgeous All Reds, or long fingerlings. And any of the seasonal vegetable recipes in this book could, conceivably, do as well, from the Roasted Asparagus on page 36 to the Slow-Roasted Roasted Tomatoes on page 175 and the Parsley Root and Potato Puree on page 217. Sautéed mushrooms are always a good choice, and of course, the herb paste itself can also follow the seasons.

1 4- to 6-pound whole beef top loin,
   the fat trimmed to ¼ inch

2 tablespoons minced garlic

3 tablespoons chopped fresh
   thyme, fennel, marjoram,
   sage, rosemary, or savory or
   2 teaspoons dried

1 tablespoon chopped fresh rosemary
   or 1 teaspoon dried

1 teaspoon freshly ground pepper

1 tablespoon olive oil

1. About 2 hours before cooking, remove the meat from the refrigerator. Combine the rest of the ingredients in a small bowl and set aside.

2. Preheat the oven to 450°F. Lay the roast beef flat side up on a rack in a shallow roasting pan. Coat the top, ends, and sides of the roast with the herb paste.

3. Place the meat in the middle of the oven and roast for 15 minutes. Turn the heat down to 350°F and continue to roast for 35 to 45 minutes. After about 25 minutes, begin to check the internal temperature in the thickest part with an instant-read thermometer. Remove the roast from the oven when it reaches 115–120°F for rare meat, 125–130°F for medium-rare, 130–140°F for medium. Cover the meat loosely with foil and let rest for 15 to 20 minutes so that the meat juices and internal temperatures can equilibrate. The final temperature should be about 10 degrees higher than when it was removed from the oven.

4. Carve the meat into slices ⅜ to ½ inch thick and serve with your choice of vegetables.

It was a pleasure to finally visit the St. Paul farmers' market one August weekend. Although my friend Kathleen Craig and I arrived early, the market was so densely packed that it was difficult to wend our way down the aisles. But everyone was good-natured and relaxed about the crowding. This seems to be generally true at farmers' markets. There isn't much rage. I think people enjoy getting along with each other.

We met up with Patty Brand, who used to sell at the market, then became its manager for thirteen years, and now heads the Friends of the Market, which supports market education and development. "There are," Patty told us, "160 farmers under the covered aisles and more waiting to get in." This is a large farmers' market.

Mandated in 1853, the St. Paul market is also one of the oldest farmers' markets. "It's actually been in existence longer than Minnesota has been a state. Some families have had a continuous presence there since the late 1800s," Patty explained between greetings to farmers as we bumped along. "At present," she shouted back to us when we got caught in a jam, "there's a nine-year waiting list to get a permanent spot in this market!" Nine years? This was the longest wait I had ever heard of. But it's easy to see why—*everyone* was doing a good business.

"The farmers' market has traditionally served as a jumping-off point for new immigrants," Patty explained. "First the Swedish immigrants, then the Italian and German, and so on. Today the new immigrants are the Hmong from Southeast Asia, and there is a strong belief that they will be followed by the Somalian and Hispanic nationalities." If you take many cab rides, you get the impression that there are a lot of Somalians in the Twin Cities, and there are Somalian restaurants where you can find traditional foods. Some of the seasonings they use are provided by the Hmong.

The Hmong vendors, who make up about a third of the market, grow beautiful lettuces and tomatoes, but they diversify the market by selling bitter melons, huge bunches of lemongrass, very hot chiles, culinary and medicinal herbs, and the most interesting eggplants. *Kitelee,* which look like bracts of dark green currant tomatoes, are, a Hmong farmer told me, used in Somalian curries and stews. Other stunning tomato-sized eggplants were yellow and violet to deep purple to green and white striped. They were exotic looking, but they were being bought by the sackful by typical-looking midwesterners. "For pickling," they explained when I asked how they used them.

Minnesota's regional foods also stood out at this market: crab apples, wild rice, ground-cherries (Cape gooseberries), maple syrup, local meats and cheeses, pickled beets. Sweet corn was displayed handsomely, the greens carefully trimmed to reveal the kernels, and a luscious melon called Passport was practically tropical tasting. There were huge bunches of dill for pickling, an array of peppers from stuffers to habaneros, and even biscuits for the pooch.

Kathleen and I shopped heavily for a cooking class the following day. While we drove around visiting other markets, everything that was shy of being perfectly ripe finished ripening in the car. Never has a car smelled so good! While this happened to be fine for our purposes, it *is* a good idea to take a cooler to the market filled with ice packs to keep things fresh so that you don't have to eat all of your purchases as soon as you get home.

After our tour Patty mentioned, "This market, for all its diversity, has been the gathering place for the community, and while crowded, it is a safe, happy, and exciting place to wander about, bring your family, meet your friends, or even make new friends."

There were lots of children helping their parents sell or shop. I watched one small boy push his plastic shopping cart down an aisle, taking a single potato from one farmer, a tomato from another. He was quite serious about his task and was making his way in a very deliberate fashion. When his mother finally caught up with him, she explained that this wasn't the supermarket, where you go to a checkout stand; that here a particular farmer grew each vegetable and that was the person to pay. They retraced his steps and bought each item directly from the farmer.

Everything at this impressive market is produced or grown within a fifty-mile radius of the Twin Cities. As long as there's farmland close to urban centers, farmers can, it appears, make a living. Certainly they are giving urban dwellers something they want, for customers here were described as not only being loyal but also tending to develop relationships with the growers. "They get to know them and their families through their weekly contact at the market and through visits to their farms," Patty commented. Which means that when they sit down to eat, they are sitting down to high-quality food grown by people they know—a rare experience in our world today.

A MENU FROM THE ST. PAUL MARKET

Crostini with Roasted Eggplant and
Pine Nut Puree (page 168)

Squares of Zucchini Frittata with Ricotta and
Marjoram (page 236)

Extravagant Platter Salad, showered with herbs
(page 124)

Warm Corn Custard with Berries (page 121)

Hazelnut Crisps (page 366)

Cabbages, Kale, and Other Crucifers 4

All of the members of this robust family of plants, the crucifers, produce flowers whose four single petals form the shape of a cross. Hence the name. With wild radishes the innocent-looking blooms are white, yellow, and pink. Arugula blossoms are cream colored with tiny blood-red veins. Broccoli, when allowed to blossom, puts out clusters of tiny yellow cross-shaped flowers. They're all edible if you wish to scatter them in a salad.

For many shoppers it may seem odd to find kohlrabi, cauliflower, turnips, and broccoli at the summer market next to tomatoes and melons. We're accustomed to thinking of these as winter vegetables, with Brussels sprouts being confined mainly to Thanksgiving. But summer-into-fall is when some of these so-called winter crops are peaking. In areas that are moderate and cool, they may be at their sweet best now.

Kohlrabi, for example, is definitely not what we think of as summer food. In fact we scarcely consider it at all. But when small, kohlrabi is thin skinned, sweet, and juicy. You would need only to slice one and sprinkle it with sea salt to have a crisp and original crudité or combine it with turnips and peas to make a delicate vegetable ragout (see page 94).

Summer cabbages, with some of their vast number of outer leaves left intact, look magnificent. In the ground they're huge, as big as turkeys. Those extra leaves may go to the compost, but in the meantime they shade the plant and keep it cool. One delightful farmer I saw was cooling herself at a midday market with a "hat" made of cabbage leaves that fit neatly over her head.

You may see some interesting heirlooms at your farmers' market, such as Early Jersey Wakefields, which are cone shaped, as are Winningstadt, only even more so. A farmer might bring cabbages weighing only half a pound or less—an easy fit in the fridge and fine for a single meal. Or you may see an enormous flat Dutch cabbage, like the one we found in Cortez, Colorado, weighing as much as fifteen pounds. Savoy cabbages, whose leaves resemble faience pottery when they haven't been stripped down to tight little balls, are always prized for their delicate flavor, plus you can use the crinkled outer leaves as serving ware for your coleslaws.

Other finds in this department are cauliflowers with pristine white curds or those that are picked when they're only a few inches across. They may be thinnings for the farmer, but for you and me they are perfect for a single serving and just the size to delight a child. Similarly, De Cicco broccoli produces a small (four-inch) head instead of the mammoth ones we're used to seeing at the supermarket. And smaller varieties are often sweeter. Sprouting side shoots with their delicious tender leaves might also be found here too, as well as the spiraled whorls of the green Romanesco cauliflower (or broccoli). The tender leaves of all these vegetables are edible and delicious. And, of course, they are among the most healthful of vegetables.

Braised Broccoli with Olives | SERVES 4

Broccoli needn't only be cooked fast until bright green and al dente. In fact the flavor is amplified when it's braised slowly until as tender as can be. You can enjoy this as a vegetable side dish, spoon it over garlic-rubbed bruschetta, or toss it with pasta and freshly grated pecorino or Parmesan cheese.

4 small heads broccoli or 1½ or more
    pounds broccoli sprouts
sea salt and freshly ground pepper
¼ cup olive oil
1 onion
1 tablespoon chopped marjoram or
    oregano
3 garlic cloves, coarsely chopped
2 tablespoons olive paste or finely
    chopped Gaeta olives
grated zest of ½ lemon

1. Separate the stalks from the broccoli crowns. Thickly peel and trim the stalks and chop them into ½-inch pieces. Peel the base of the broccoli crowns, then separate them into florets.

2. Bring 2 quarts water to a boil; add salt, then the broccoli. Cook for 5 minutes (even if the water barely returns to the boil), then scoop into a colander to drain, reserving a cup of the water. Chop into small pieces just smaller than bite-sized.

3. Warm the olive oil in a wide skillet, then add the onion, marjoram, and garlic. Cook over medium-low heat, stirring now and then, until the onion is softened, 5 to 7 minutes. Stir in the olive paste; add the broccoli and stir to coat well. Taste for salt, season with pepper, and add the lemon zest. Add the reserved broccoli water and simmer gently until the broccoli is very tender, 15 to 20 minutes.

Broccoli and Broccoli Rabe on Bruschetta | SERVES 4

There never seems to be enough of those succulent broccoli rabe nubbins, so I sometimes mix in the shoots of sprouting broccoli that are sold at the market.

1 pound broccoli florets

1 large bunch (1 pound or more) broccoli rabe

sea salt

2 tablespoons olive oil

2 large garlic cloves: 1 minced, 1 cut in half crosswise

several pinches red pepper flakes

2 tablespoons chopped oregano

aged red wine vinegar

4 large slices hearty country bread

¼ to ½ pound fresh mozzarella, thinly sliced

1. Thickly peel the broccoli stems. If longer than a few inches, coarsely chop them. Peel the larger of the broccoli rabe stalks, then chop them along with the thinner stems. Coarsely chop the greens.

2. Bring a large pot of water to a boil. Add salt, then the vegetables. Cook until tender, about 5 minutes, then scoop them into a colander to drain. Reserve 2 cups of the cooking water.

3. Warm the 2 tablespoons oil in a nonstick skillet. Add the vegetables along with a cup of the reserved cooking water, the minced garlic, pepper flakes, and oregano. Turn with tongs to mix in the garlic, then lower the heat. Make sure there's ample liquid in the pan. The greens shouldn't fry, plus you'll want the extra liquid to spoon over them. Taste for salt, then season with a few drops of good, strong vinegar.

4. Preheat the broiler. Toast the bread, then rub it with the halved garlic clove. Immediately lay the cheese over the top, then broil just until it begins to droop or bubble a little. Transfer the toasts to plates, then cover them with greens and their juices. Add a few drops of olive oil to each, as well as any remaining pan juices.

Harriet's Hot Roasted Cauliflower | SERVES 4

Few recipes are as simple as this one, but if Harriet Bell hadn't told me about it, I might never have known what a great little dish this is. If you should be fortunate to find some undersized cauliflower at your farmers' market, bake them whole and serve one per person.

1 larger or 4 small cauliflowers, about 1 pound

olive oil

sea salt

Preheat the oven to 400°F. Leave small cauliflowers whole, but slice a larger vegetable into wedges about 1½ inches wide at the widest point. Brush with olive oil, season with salt, and place in a baking dish in a single layer. Bake until browned on top, about 25 minutes, then turn to brown the second side (if cut into wedges).

Green Cauliflower with Parsley and Green Olives | SERVES 4 TO 6

Of course the color doesn't really matter, but one of those lime-green cauliflowers or a whorl of broccoli Romanesco makes a stunning-looking dish, as does a mixture of green and white cauliflowers.

1 large head cauliflower, broccoflower, or broccoli Romanesco

1 bunch flat-leaf parsley, stems removed, leaves finely chopped

2 tablespoons finely chopped tarragon

½ cup chopped Spanish green olives

2 tablespoons drained capers, rinsed

⅓ cup olive oil

sea salt and freshly ground pepper

Manchego cheese

1. Cut the cauliflower into small florets; peel and dice the stems. Put the parsley, tarragon, and olives in a bowl with the capers, oil, ½ teaspoon salt, and plenty of pepper.

2. Steam the cauliflower over salted boiling water until tender, about 5 minutes. Dump it into the bowl and toss well. Taste for salt and season with pepper. Serve with a little Manchego cheese grated or shaved over the top.

Whole Little Cauliflowers with Crispy Bread Crumbs | SERVES 4

Here's a way to showcase those tiny cauliflowers that you sometimes find at the farmers' market—cooked whole and still wrapped in their pale green leaves. If you're using a large one, cut it into florets and steam until tender, then toss with the rest of the ingredients.

4 small cauliflowers, about 5 inches across

½ cup fresh bread crumbs

½ cup finely chopped parsley

2 to 4 tablespoons unsalted butter

1 teaspoon Dijon or coarse mustard

sea salt

¼ teaspoon red pepper flakes

freshly grated Parmesan or pecorino cheese

1. Wash the cauliflowers well. Toast the bread crumbs in the oven or in a skillet until crisp and golden. Melt the butter.

2. Steam the cauliflower, the curds facing down in the pot, until tender, 6 to 8 minutes. Set them on individual plates or a platter. Mix the melted butter with the parsley, mustard, ½ teaspoon salt, and the pepper flakes. Pour it over the cauliflower, then add the bread crumbs and grate a little cheese over all.

Brussels Sprouts with Cauliflower and Mustard-Caper Butter | SERVES 8 OR MORE

One should never feel merely obligated to eat Brussels sprouts. They're good, especially when they're tossed with nubbins of pale green broccoli Romanesco and white cauliflower. Besides, who can resist them when farmers bring them to markets on their stalk, complete with a "hat" of cabbage leaves? Here is the most Dr. Seuss–like vegetable one could hope for. People walking through the market cradling a stalk that bristles with tiny cabbage seem to smile proudly as if they have just captured something rare. And they have.

THE MUSTARD-CAPER BUTTER

2 garlic cloves

sea salt and freshly ground pepper

6 tablespoons unsalted butter, at
    room temperature

2 teaspoons Dijon-style mustard,
    more or less

¼ cup drained small capers, rinsed

grated zest of 1 lemon

3 tablespoons chopped marjoram

Pound the garlic with ½ teaspoon salt in a mortar until smooth, then stir it into the butter with the mustard, capers, lemon zest, and marjoram. Season with pepper. The butter can be made a day ahead and refrigerated. Bring back to room temperature before serving.

THE VEGETABLES

1 pound Brussels sprouts or 1 whole
    stalk, stripped of its sprouts

1 small head white cauliflower

1 small head broccoli Romanesco

sea salt and freshly ground pepper

1. Trim the base off the sprouts, then slice them in half or, if large, into quarters. Cut the cauliflower and broccoli into bite-sized pieces.
2. Bring a large pot of water to a boil and add salt. Add the Brussels sprouts and cook for 3 minutes. Then add the other vegetables and continue to cook until tender, about 5 minutes. Drain, shake off any excess water, then toss with the Mustard-Caper Butter. Taste for salt, season with pepper, and toss again.

Setting aside for a moment such virtues as quality, variety, flavor, and freshness, one of the other things I love most about farmers' markets are the unexpected treasures one finds. For example, one August a farmer handed me a shoebox. Inside were about two hundred extremely infant fennel bulbs, thinnings, to be precise. They were sweet and delicate and a lot of fun to use over the next few days.

Later in the season, another farmer had a lot of Chioggia beets. They were too small to bother bunching, so he had just clipped off their greens and tossed them in a basket. Their small size made them perfect to use whole in a salad, where they looked like jewels. On more than one occasion I've found tiny cauliflower, broccoli heads, and Delicata squash that are just the right size for a single serving and perfect for a child-size portion. It may be that gigantic fifteen-pound flat-head cabbage that's got your name written all over it, or an enormously long, curled summer squash called Tromboncino.

There are lots of odd and funny vegetables that would never meet supermarket standards: eggplants with noses on them, three-legged carrots, winter squashes covered with warts, heart-shaped potatoes, the occasional five-pound onion or turnip. In the category of sheer beauty I once saw an eggplant so marvelously ruffled that it looked like a satin evening purse.

It's always wonderful to come across a fruit or vegetable that you've only heard of and never seen, like those green peanuts and muscadine grapes in Alabama or hickory nuts in Wisconsin. Or there might be the pleasure of finding foods from a home you no longer live in. For me figs, quince, and muscat grapes fill that role. And there's the fun of seeing something completely new—the fresh lychees in a Hawaiian market, the unusual Hmong eggplants at St. Paul's, or the Swedish peanut potatoes in Mesa, Arizona.

The farmers' market is often where new varieties of vegetables and fruits are first encountered by chefs and the public at large. The market provides a place where an experimental botanist can bring the exotic fruits he's been cultivating, such as the dramatic cerise pitahaya fruits I saw in a Los Angeles farmers' market. It's also a place where a shopper can encounter unusual varieties of fruits, sometimes referred to as "backyard" fruits, such as unusual varieties of persimmons grown by Japanese-American families who brought them from Japan many years ago.

The market is also a place where a traveler with a keen interest in food can introduce a new crop. Laura Avery, manager of the Santa Monica farmers' markets, told me about a restaurant forager who brought back Fagiola d'Espagna beans from Italy. He gave them to a farmer at the market who specialized in beans and peas, who grew them out. They are now used in Los Angeles's Campanile restaurant. At our market, Elizabeth Berry spent years growing heirloom beans, until there were enough for local chefs to taste and determine which ones were best eating. (They aren't all alike.) Once they were grown in real quantity, customers lined up for these beans, which were unlike any others seen or tasted before.

Experimentation and collaboration among farmers, customers, and chefs are characteristic of farmers' markets. They are marketplaces of ideas, translated into foods, which become those unexpected treasures customers might find.

LUNCH OF UNEXPECTED TREASURES

Crudités: Three-legged carrots and tiny whole fennel

Salad of little Chioggia beets and
heart-shaped potatoes

Whole Little Cauliflowers with Crispy Bread Crumbs (page 89)

Scarlet prickly pears with Rangpur limes

A Rough and Ready Turnip Potage | SERVES 3 TO 4

On one equinoctial day everything imaginable was in the market, but sudden rain, wind, and cold meanly undermined what should have been the fulfillment of the season's promise. Like others, I scurried home as soon as I could. While putting away my produce, I decided what I needed was a big pot of soup. I quickly chopped some leeks, a half dozen turnips, and a potato, then stewed them all in a little butter with a few sprigs of thyme. Salt and water were added, and I went out into the garden. The cold had chilled me, but it had also made me energetic, so I got to work cleaning up my beds and forgot about the soup. When I finally came inside, it had simmered down to a thick and chunky potage.

I rather liked the uneven shapes and varied textures that came from hurried cutting. It had a pleasing rough and ready look. A smidgen of cream went into the pot, some freshly ground pepper, and I served myself a bowl. I had another bowl, then started dipping into the pot. This soup was no less compelling to me than chocolate cake might have been to another. Of course, nothing tastes better than what we eat when we're really hungry. That's when the tongue can detect anything that's not of the first quality, any little slip, flaw, or falsity that might be present. There was none with these vegetables.

6 slender leeks, about ¾ inch across

3 small Yukon Gold potatoes

6 small turnips

1½ tablespoons unsalted butter

a few thyme sprigs

sea salt and freshly ground pepper

cream

chopped parsley or thyme

1. Slice the white parts of the leeks crosswise and wash them well. Scrub the potatoes, quarter them lengthwise, and chop. If the turnip skins are tender looking, quarter and chop the turnips without peeling.

2. Melt the butter in a soup pot. Add the vegetables, give them a toss, then add ½ cup water and the thyme. Simmer for 5 minutes, then add 5 cups water and 1½ teaspoons salt. Bring to a boil, then simmer until the vegetables are tender, 25 to 30 minutes. Taste for salt, season with pepper, and stir in a few spoonfuls of cream. Garnish with chopped parsley or thyme.

VARIATION: A more refined bisque can be made with the same ingredients and a few minor changes: Use a good vegetable stock or chicken stock to enrich the flavor; don't let it cook down so much, puree it, and add a cup of light cream. If you have the greens, simmer them until they are completely tender, then chop them up and add them to the soup. Garnish with fresh thyme and its blossoms.

Market Ragout of Turnips, Kohlrabi, and Peas | SERVES 2 TO 4

This pretty vegetable ragout should prove, if any doubt lingers, that members of the cabbage family can be delicate and pretty—especially in early summer. I've made this with vegetables from the Mesa, Arizona, farmers' market in January, from Santa Fe in June, from California in March, and again from Santa Fe in October, when a new crop of vegetables is ready. Improvise with what your market offers—small onions or red scallions, spring leeks or green garlic, shallots in the fall, bunched spinach or loose leaves.

1 tablespoon unsalted butter

6 spring onions or shallots, halved

6 or more small turnips, scrubbed and quartered

2 or 3 small kohlrabi, about golf ball size, peeled and quartered

1 thyme or lemon thyme sprig

sea salt and freshly ground pepper

1 pound pod peas, shelled

a few handfuls baby spinach

dollop crème fraîche

4 large basil leaves, slivered

1. Melt the butter in a skillet and add the onions, turnips, kohlrabi, and thyme. Add water to cover halfway and a teaspoon of salt. Simmer while you shuck the peas.

2. As soon as the vegetables are tender, after 12 to 15 minutes, add the peas and spinach and cook until the spinach has wilted down, a few minutes more. Stir in the crème fraîche and add the basil. Taste for salt and season with pepper. Serve this as a side dish or a course by itself. With a starch (puff pastry, ravioli, even buttered toast), it can be offered as a vegetarian main dish.

The village of Angel Fire, New Mexico, puts on a fund-raiser each September to raise money for library books or a kitchen for the community center. It does this by celebrating local food. During the day there's a farmers' market and at night a dinner is cooked entirely from food grown in New Mexico, much of it near Angel Fire. It is a night of good food and drink, and there is always a strong appreciation for what is grown locally and how good it is.

A lot of things are auctioned off during the dinner. One year the most amusing item was a basket of vegetables grown by Ed May, a local farmer and the main organizer of the event. Hardly the basket of exquisite delicacies you might be imagining, this was a laundry basket crammed with examples of verdant gigantism. Among these were huge daikon, enormous potatoes, rutabagas, and turnips of astounding heft, a five-pound onion, eggplants with "noses," Siamese twin carrots, and other vegetable oddities that farmers see but shoppers seldom do. Laughter grew as each vegetable was held up. The mayor's husband purchased the entire collection and the next morning it fell to me to turn these vegetable beasts into breakfast for a crowd of volunteers.

I woke up sobered by the task of facing these big fellows and got to work. After an hour or so the giant roots were transformed into a delicious mess of home fries, seasoned with the fresh thyme and garlic I found hidden in the basket. Were the five-pound rutabagas and turnips woody, bitter, or bad in any way? Not in the least! They were sweet, firm, and full of flavor. Plus they were easy to work with;

cubes of vegetables grew quickly into a large heap with just a few strokes of the knife. Huge was terrific.

Had these vegetables been raised in the heat of the Rio Grande valley below, they probably would have been bitter, woody, and tough. The cool weather at Angel Fire's eight-thousand-foot elevation, the mountain rains, plummeting night temperatures, and soft volcanic soil all worked in concert to produce turnips and rutabagas that were as good as they were large. They were a far cry from those sad thickly waxed specimens languishing miles away in supermarket bins. With vegetables like these, people would happily tuck into those good-for-you brassicas—and come back for seconds.

Prior to World War II, this area supplied the greater Southwest with lettuce, cabbage, kohlrabi, turnips, and potatoes. Underground potato bunkers from that time can still be seen in the valleys that were once potato fields. Today virtually all the productive land, following the ruinous path of so much fertile ground in America, has been converted to golf courses or ranchettes or is simply neglected while waiting to be developed. However, a few people, like Ed, have begun to farm the area again, growing heirloom potatoes, root vegetables, cooking greens, and other crops that thrive in cool weather. They are even building new bunkers so that potatoes can be stored properly over the winter. This means that we can open our chilly May market with potatoes, so good with the green garlic and sorrel, instead of waiting until July, when the new crop comes in.

Cabbage and Potato Gratin with Sage | SERVES 4 TO 6

Cabbage really is one of the nicest vegetables, and it's always very friendly with potatoes. I like German Butterball potatoes here, which are not as sweet as Yukon Golds, although you can certainly use them, too. Fingerlings, French Nosebags, the exotic purple-blushed Huckleberry, new to many markets, or any other waxy potato can be used here as well.

1 pound potatoes (see headnote)
1½ pounds Savoy or other green
    cabbage
sea salt and freshly ground pepper
4 tablespoons unsalted butter
3 tablespoons chopped sage
1 garlic clove, chopped
1⅓ cups milk
3 eggs
½ cup freshly grated Parmesan
⅓ cup all-purpose flour

1. Preheat the oven to 350°F. Lightly butter an 8 x 12-inch gratin dish. Bring a gallon of water to a boil while you prepare the vegetables: Peel and slice the potatoes ¼ inch thick; slice the cabbage into 1-inch ribbons.

2. Add 1 tablespoon salt to the water, add the potatoes, and boil until nearly tender, about 6 minutes. Scoop them into a colander, then add the cabbage to the pot and cook for 5 minutes. The water may not return to a boil. Drain, rinse under cool water, then twist in a kitchen towel to remove the excess moisture. Get it as dry as you can. Combine the cabbage and potatoes in a bowl.

3. Melt the butter in a small skillet with the sage and garlic. Cook for about 1 minute without letting the garlic brown. Pour it over the cabbage and potatoes. Toss well, taste for salt, and season with pepper. Transfer to the baking dish.

4. Whisk the remaining ingredients together, pour them over the vegetables, and bake until firm and lightly browned, about 50 minutes. Let cool for at least 10 minutes, then cut into pieces and serve.

Savoy Cabbage and Fennel with Parsley-Lemon Butter | SERVES 4

This tender mess of pale green ribbons flecked with yellow lemon zest is the kind of dish I'd make a meal of with some egg noodles thrown in. But it also makes a delicious bed for monkfish, cod, or wild salmon.

½ small Savoy or other green
    cabbage
1 large fennel bulb, quartered
1 large leek, white part only
4 tablespoons unsalted butter
sea salt and freshly ground pepper
juice and zest of 1 Meyer lemon
3 tablespoons chervil or parsley
    leaves

1. Cut the cabbage, fennel, and leek into very thin slices and wash. Don't dry, though.

2. Melt 1 tablespoon of the butter in a large, wide skillet. Add the vegetables and sprinkle with ½ teaspoon salt. Cover the pan and cook gently for 10 minutes. Check after 5 minutes and make sure there's a little moisture so that the vegetables steam and don't brown. Meanwhile, simmer the lemon juice in a small skillet until only 1 tablespoon remains. Remove from the heat and whisk in the remaining butter.

3. Finely chop the lemon zest with the chervil. Stir half into the butter and add the other half to the vegetables. Toss well, taste for salt, and season with pepper.

The North Pole Farmers' Market? The notion of farmers' markets in Alaska sounded unlikely to me, but they're there—eight of them, which is two more than Wyoming has and close to the number in Arizona. I didn't make it to Alaska, but it didn't seem right to leave our big northern state out, so I spoke with Doug Warner, the farmers' market representative from the Alaska Department of Agriculture, and Bill Webb, manager of the Anchorage Downtown Farmers' Market, who filled me in over the phone one day.

"Maybe I should tell you what we don't have," Doug said, when I asked him what a shopper might find at an Alaskan farmers' market in mid-July. This seemed a bit of a stretch. Surely they didn't have corn, did they?

"Yes, we do."

"Tomatoes?" I asked skeptically.

"Oh yes." His reply was laconic.

"Okra?"

"Well, there's not much market for it, but we *could* do it."

Summer and winter squash are in the market too, but in the prolonged daylight the zucchini grow even quicker than they normally do. "Big enough to make a canoe out of," joked Bill.

Doug did admit that they didn't grow watermelons, al-though there is a Siberian heirloom variety. And they don't grow peaches. But they do grow strawberries, blueberries, bush cranberries, lingonberries, marionberries, and apples. Rose hips, along with blueberries and lingonberries, are natives. The big crops are cabbages and many, many kinds of potatoes. "Then there are radishes, green onions, zucchini, turnips, lettuce, beets, winter squash, and quite a few Asian vegetables as there's a large Asian population in Anchorage," Bill adds. "People bring in wild mushrooms, and we also have leeks, chard, and kale, but no spinach for some reason. Cucumbers are very much in demand, especially picklers, and I love those yellow tomatoes!"

Even though corn and tomatoes come to market, corn is in its experimental stage—it's transplanted from the green-house—and tomatoes remain in the greenhouse through-out the season. Cabbages are what northern climes are famous for. "The long light makes them pretty large," Doug said. "Last year one weighed in at 107 pounds. It won first prize at the Alaska State Fair." And because of the cool soil temperature, the conversion of sugar to starch in plants is slowed down so that foods end up with higher sugar contents. "Even the potatoes are sweet," Doug explained, and Bill remarked that he had never eaten turnips that were as sweet and delicious as those grown in Alaska.

Twice the government has made an effort to lure farmers to Alaska, once in the 1950s and again in the 1980s. In spite of subsidies and massive loan offers, however, the farming community has remained small. "There are maybe only thirty active farmers in the biggest section of arable land near Anchorage," Bill explained. "Some farmers have enough volume to sell wholesale, but the others come to market."

The main obstacle that Alaskan farmers face is not climate as much as getting help during the harvest. There is no migrant worker population, and everyone in this underpopulated state seems to be pretty busy. "At one time they used to run buses filled with teenagers out to help with the harvest," Bill said, "but they don't now." The high cost of locally grown food reflects the high cost of labor among other things, but it all sells. The markets are very successful. "We haven't lost any," Doug reports. "In fact we've just started a few more. People want something fresher than what they can normally buy, and they want organic. Attendance has been increasing."

The Alaskan markets have from five to twenty-five farmers. The Anchorage market is actually a huge crafts fair. There are about twenty-five farmers to three hundred other kinds of vendors. "Hundreds of customers come hours early to buy the produce," says Bill. Some reselling is allowed to bring diversity to the markets—those peaches, for example. The markets begin in May, largely with crafts and resale, and continue to mid-September, although a market manager can keep the market open as long as the local farmers have food to sell.

A SUMMER SUPPER IN ANCHORAGE

Carrot Salad with Parsley, Lovage, and Mint (page 203)

Grilled or poached salmon

Savoy Cabbage and Fennel with Parsley-Lemon Butter
(page 97)

Warm Berry Compote (page 265) with ice cream

Napa Cabbage Salad with Peanuts and Cilantro | SERVES 4 TO 6

Although this salad can be made at the last minute, it doesn't suffer from being dressed hours earlier, which makes it a good picnic salad. Add the peanuts just before serving so they'll be nice and crunchy.

THE SALAD

½ cup skinned raw peanuts

1 teaspoon peanut oil

1 large carrot

4 cups thinly sliced Napa cabbage

2 cups slivered lettuce leaves

3 thin scallions, including some of the greens, finely sliced diagonally

¼ cup chopped cilantro

2 tablespoons chopped mint leaves

2 tablespoons torn basil leaves, preferably Thai basil

THE DRESSING

½ jalapeño chile, finely diced

¼ cup rice vinegar

1 teaspoon sugar

¼ teaspoon sea salt

¼ cup roasted peanut oil

1. Heat the peanuts in the oil over medium-low heat, shaking the pan occasionally, until lightly browned after a few minutes. Blot with paper towels and set aside.

2. Peel the carrot with a vegetable peeler and discard the skins. Then, with the vegetable peeler, continue removing long strips of the carrot until you've reached the core.

3. Combine the cabbage, lettuce, and carrot with everything except the nuts. Whisk the dressing ingredients together and toss with the greens. Add the peanuts just before serving.

Priest Stranglers (Strozzapreti) with Black Kale, Sage, and Potatoes | SERVES 4

A variant on *pizzoccheri,* this dish unites pasta, potatoes, and kale with Fontina cheese but uses wheat pasta in place of buckwheat. The name *priest stranglers* refers to the pasta shape, which resembles folded and twisted ribbons of fettuccine or tagliatelle. Gemelli and other similarly twisted pastas work well here, and spaghetti does too.

4 tablespoons unsalted butter

3 large garlic cloves, peeled and
    smashed with the side of a knife

10 sage leaves

2 bunches cavolo nero (black kale),
    stems discarded

sea salt and freshly ground pepper

2 cups finely diced yellow potatoes,
    about ¾ pound

¾ pound pasta (see headnote)

5 ounces Italian Fontina cheese,
    coarsely grated or cubed

freshly grated Parmigiano-Reggiano

1. Bring a large pot of water to a boil for the pasta. While it's heating, heat the butter, garlic, and sage in a small skillet over medium heat until the butter is lightly browned and nutty smelling. Turn off the heat and discard the garlic.

2. Chop the kale coarsely. When the pasta water boils, add salt and the kale. Boil for 4 minutes, then add the potatoes and cook for 6 minutes more or until both are tender. Scoop them out, shake off excess water, and dump them into a bowl. Cook the pasta until al dente, then drain and add it to the kale and potatoes.

3. Pour the butter and sage over all, then, using a pair of tongs, pick up some of the pasta and use it to wipe out the pan. Add the Fontina, a generous grating of Parmigiano-Reggiano, and toss. Season with pepper, and serve.

KALE AND CAVOLO NERO

What people tend to fear, or so they tell me, about cabbages and kale is that they'll be strong tasting. This is never true when cabbages are fresh and properly cooked, and it's certainly not true of kale, although it always looks as if it might be tough, overly hearty, and hard to tame. In fact its flavor is mild, and it cooks to tenderness in a very short time.

Here's cause for celebration, a new kale! I have seen it in so many markets the past few years that I no longer think of it as a newcomer. Still, *cavolo nero* is a fairly recent addition to our national vegetable repertoire. *Black kale, black cabbage, dinosaur kale, dragon tongue, Tuscan kale,* and *lacinato* are just some of the names for this extraordinary-looking leaf vegetable. Slate green–black in color, the leaves do have the shape of a tongue, with a pronounced waffled texture. It cooks in 5 to 7 minutes and retains half its volume (unlike spinach) as well as its lustrous hue. Its color makes it hard to resist dramatic pairings with any food of contrasting values, such as white beans, cauliflower, yellow-fleshed potatoes, or paler Savoy cabbage. The flavors in such partnerships hold up as well as the visuals.

In Italy, grower Lucio Gomiero told me, cavalo nero is treated seasonally and enjoyed only after the first frost. As with most hearty greens, cold conditions favor its flavor. In fact, kale is so cold-hardy that it may persist in your market until the very end of the season. Other kales you'll find are more familiar: the ruffled gray-green variety, Red Russian kale, which has a purplish cast to the leaves and red veins, and Redbor, which is plum-purple-red.

All kales have ropy stems that run down the center of each leaf. They're too tough to eat, so just strip the leaves from the stems by sliding a sharp knife along the stem and letting the leaves fall away. (Some prefer to use their hands.) Bring a skillet or pot of water to a boil—you don't need a lot—and add salt, then the kale. Simmer until tender, 5 to 10 minutes, then drain in a colander and press out the excess water. You can season cooked kale with garlic and olive oil, sauté it with the same, add it to soups, toss it with cauliflower or boiled potatoes, and so forth. Lucio says that he makes a kind of pesto from it, which he spreads on crostini or tosses with pasta. Two bunches of kale, about 2 pounds, will serve 4 to 6, assuming you want more than one or two bites—and you will.

Redbor Kale with Red Beans, Cilantro, and Feta Cheese | SERVES 4

A limited cupboard can sometimes prove an asset. I had dark red kidney beans from a California market, feta cheese, cilantro, and what seemed like an armload of Redbor kale. They worked well together, much to my surprise. In truth, any variety of kale is fine here, and so is chard and other greens, such as collards.

1½ cups dried red kidney beans,
    soaked for 4 hours or overnight

2 bay leaves

½ teaspoon thyme leaves

sea salt

1 white onion, finely diced

1 large bunch kale (see headnote)

2 tablespoons olive oil, plus extra
    to finish

¾ cup chopped cilantro

3 ounces feta cheese, crumbled

1. Drain the beans, cover them with plenty of cold water, and bring to a boil. Remove any scum that rises to the surface, then add the herbs, 1½ teaspoons salt, and all but ½ cup of the onion. Lower the heat and simmer until tender, about 1½ hours.

2. Slice the kale leaves from their stems with a knife. Chop coarsely into 1- or 2-inch pieces and rinse well. Bring a few quarts water to a boil; add salt and the kale. Simmer until tender, 5 to 7 minutes, then pour into a colander to drain.

3. Heat the oil in a wide skillet. Add the remaining ½ cup onion and ½ cup of the cilantro. Cook over medium heat until the onion has softened, about 10 minutes, then add the kale and the beans with enough of the cooking liquid so that there's plenty of sauce. Simmer together for at least 10 minutes, then serve garnished with crumbled feta cheese and the remaining cilantro.

White Beans with Black Kale and Savoy Cabbage | SERVES 6 TO 8

If you add water or stock, you can make this into a hearty minestrone to serve with garlic-rubbed toast. One day I decided to stop before adding the liquid and just enjoyed the two greens entwined with the beans. You can still serve it over toast, making a hearty bruschetta, over pasta, or as a side to a roast chicken.

1 cup dried cannellini, navy beans, or *gigantes*, soaked for 4 hours or overnight

sea salt and freshly ground pepper

1 large onion, finely diced

2 leeks, white parts only, diced

1 bunch cavolo nero (black kale), the leaves stripped from the stems and slivered

1 small Savoy cabbage, quartered, cored, and chopped

2 plump garlic cloves, minced or pounded with a pinch salt

½ cup chopped parsley

2 tablespoons olive oil, plus extra to finish

1. Drain the soaked beans, then put them in a pot and cover with cold water. Bring to a boil, add ½ teaspoon salt, then lower the heat and simmer, partially covered, until the beans are tender, about 1½ hours.

2. While the beans are cooking, chop all the vegetables. Rinse the leeks, kale, and cabbage, but don't dry them.

3. Warm 2 tablespoons of the oil in a heavy wide skillet. Add the onion and leeks and cook over medium-low heat until the onion is soft but not browned, about 12 minutes. Add the kale, cabbage, garlic, parsley, and 2 teaspoons salt. Cook with the heat on low and the pan covered until the vegetables are soft and the volume greatly reduced, about 30 minutes.

4. When the beans are done, add them, along with a cup or two of their cooking liquid, to the pot. Simmer until the greens are completely tender. Taste for salt and season with pepper. Serve with, or over, garlic-rubbed toast, drizzled with olive oil.

Cortez lies about an hour's drive from the Four Corners, a point where one can walk in a tiny circle across the corners of Colorado, New Mexico, Arizona, and Utah. Durango is located about an hour east of Cortez. Both small towns hold their farmers' markets on Saturday, but the Cortez market is in full swing by 7:00 A.M., while Durango gets its start around 10:00. An ambitious shopper can attend both markets, which my husband, Patrick, and I did one August morning.

Plain and flat, Cortez is a town shaped by farming and ranching, and a lot of the businesses there have to do with farm equipment and trucking. The absence of chain restaurants and malls is refreshing. The mannequins in the clothing store on Main Street still wear their hair in a bubble, but there is an espresso bar in the lobby of the supermarket, which supports the convivial atmosphere there in a more contemporary way. Durango, on the other hand, is set in a valley edged with mountains and filled with the Victorian bric-a-brac of its mining past. It is filled with tourists who gawk in that unhurried tourist way at the gingerbread architecture, then move on, more energetically, to the Ralph Lauren outlet store.

But it was the farmers' markets we came for, and we started in Cortez, where, we discovered, there are actually two markets. Cortez has had some form of farmers' market since 1911, and until a few years ago the farmers gathered on an empty city lot on the main street to sell their vegetables. When they had the chance to move to a new market site in a tiny city park a few years ago, some of the older farmers chose to stay on at the old site.

We headed for the new site. It was a relaxed market. Some farmers parked in the street and sold from their trucks, some were set up on the sidewalk, while others were selling in the park itself. Dogs wandered about free of their leashes, and there were plenty of babies and children. For such a small market, there was a surprising amount of good food: Ivory bell peppers, heirloom tomatoes, eggplants, including the delicious Rosa Bianca, Costata Romanesco zucchini, tiny filet beans, sweet corn, white Babcock and Red Haven peaches, and the muskmelons for which this area is known. Although small—there were no more than a dozen vendors—it resembled our Santa Fe market with its mix of goods. And it was not only a place to buy the best produce imaginable, but also a place where neighbors—some of whom might live many miles apart—could meet and catch up on news and the weather, the most important topic in any farming community.

One farmer had enormous Dutch flat-head cabbages, weighing twelve or more pounds apiece, a very hefty armful. His potatoes and garlic were also unusually large, as was he. When I asked him why everything he grew was so big, he shrugged his shoulders and said, "Well, we're completely organic. Don't use any chemicals." But even I know that doesn't say it all. Organic farmers can grow puny food, too. One has to know *something*. Our rancher friend with whom we were shopping suggested that being organic to this farmer probably meant digging a lot of composted manure into his garden because he couldn't afford the chemical inputs. Well, good for him, I thought. It looked as though he was doing fine. We bought a cabbage along with some garlic and potatoes. Later that day we hollowed out the cabbage and filled it with a mixture of lamb (Colorado is also lamb country), rice scented with herbs and spices, tomatoes, and the cabbage center that had been sautéed with some onions. We nestled the whole thing into a large Mexican casserole, covered it with a blanket of spare cabbage leaves, and left it to bake for several hours. It was served that evening in succulent glory, the cabbage saturated with juices and the rich flavor of the lamb, garlic, and spice.

At the renegade market around the corner, the farmers, who were much older, seemed more interested in chatting with one another than selling to the few customers who happened to pass by. One farmer had bagged his vegetables and scrawled the price on each bag, leaving him free to talk with his neighbors without pesky customers asking "How much?" We found some tart wild cherries and bran milled from local wheat. But most curious of all was a table of homemade jams packed in every conceivable size and shape of jar, the old labels left on and only partially covered with a scrawl announcing their new identities. With a stroke of the pen, Mary Ellen's grape jelly had become apricot jam, the contents of a jar of kosher dills had been replaced with applesauce, and so forth. It had a kind of "buyer beware" attitude that I liked: You'd better pay attention when you dip into that jar of jam. It could be something else entirely.

Over in Durango, no signs were posted announcing the whereabouts of the market, but people walking by with sacks of corn and armloads of sunflowers led us to it. This little market was tucked behind a large brick schoolhouse, which stood on a pleasant grassy plot. Some of the twenty or so vendors were the spouses of the farmers we had just seen in Cortez, selling the same mix of produce. But there was also grass-fed beef, lamb, fresh trout, smoked trout, and pastured chickens, making the farmers' market more of a farmers'-*ranchers'* market. Actually, meat and fowl at farmers' markets is a growing trend. Often this is the only place where wholesome meats, raised without hormones or antibiotics, can be bought in a community and at prices that seem fair to farmers and affordable to customers.

We shopped and chatted with the growers, and then it was time for lunch. We found a Greek restaurant and sat on the patio, our patient dog now joining us. The special that day was an Ivory bell pepper filled with eggplant, peppers, and tomatoes, braised with North African spices. The menu also featured the lamb and grass-fed beef from the market. While we were eating, a farmer we had spoken with only an hour before walked in with coffee cans stuffed with fragrant fresh basil. Lunch was delicious. It was a rare joy to be able to eat so directly from garden, farm, and ranch.

By dessert, our dog was asleep at our feet. Our waiter gently laid a few scraps of beef by her nose. She simply sighed and without as much as opening her lazy eyes, extended her tongue, wrapped it around the morsel, and took it into her disbelieving mouth. She was as happy and astonished as we were.

A LATE-SUMMER MENU

Crostini with Slow Roasted Tomatoes (page 179)

Lamb Kebabs Marinated in Yogurt (page 240)

Roasted Eggplant and Chickpea Stew (page 173)

Steamed Potatoes (page 213)
with Green Chile Paste (page 188)

Ripe melons with limes

Corn and Beans

It's late August, and there's corn and beans in markets everywhere. When it comes to corn, everyone wants the super-sweet varieties with names like Kandy Korn, which leave no doubt where corn syrup comes from. Old-fashioned corn is now too starchy for the general public's taste, but occasionally you'll find someone in a market growing Golden Bantam, an heirloom variety, for customers who claim they like that old-fashioned flavor. But, the farmers' complain, in the end they don't buy it because it's too starchy! So virtually all of the corn is sweet corn. Sometimes it's just loose in a trailer that the farmer has hauled from the field. But in St. Paul and other midwestern markets, displays are generally set out with care, one ear of each variety set apart, the greens neatly cut and pulled away to reveal the kernels.

Some farmers grow dent corns, popcorn, and the variously colored Indian corns, which, in our case, really are grown by native Americans. Each year a family from the Santa Domingo Pueblo brings large fantastically colored ears to market tied into corn ladders. Other farmers just have their ears out for you to go through, while still others have woven their blue, yellow, red, and piebald ears into ristras to hang on a wall or a front door. Not all dried corns are for decoration, though. South-western markets are likely to have *posole* (corn cured in lime, then dried), *chicos* (corn dried in the sun or *horno*), *atole* (a fine cornmeal for drinking), and cornmeal.

Corn growers everywhere dislike it when you paw through the ears and then pull back the husks. The husks are there to protect the kernels and keep them moist. As soon as they're loosened, the corn begins to dry out, especially in the arid climates of the western mountain states. One of our farmers growls, "You peel it, you buy it." A farmer's sign at the Dane County Farmers' Market states, "Corn'ography is when you strip the ears too far back. Let your 'corn'science be your guide." Tacked to a barn in the Ohio countryside is a sign with serious warnings about corn stripping, and a sign at a New York market begs shoppers, "Please, do not husk the corn!" They point out that if you husk it and don't buy it, neither will anyone else, even if it's a perfectly good ear.

If you need to know more about the corn you're buying than what you can see, try feeling the kernels through the husks. Press your fingers along the ears, letting them search for the plumpness that tells you the kernels are well filled out. Of course what most people are really checking for are worms. There's a great fear and loathing of worms in food, but far better worms than the pesticides, and commercial corn is *very* heavily sprayed just so you don't have to encounter that little worm. If you find a worm when you get home—and it's almost always on the tip of the ear—just knock it off, then slice off the end where it's been nibbling and proceed. You'll forget about it, and no one else will ever know.

Fresh beans appear about the same time corn does, but over the course of a market season, we see beans go from dried to fresh to dried again. In between are shell beans, beans that are too large to be eaten in their pods but not yet fully dried either. Any bean, left to mature, can become a shelling, or shell, bean. Over the course of my market visits, I've seen many kinds of shell beans— Black Valentine, borlotti, cranberry, white runner beans, even pintos. Fava beans are not usually thought of this way, but they too are shell beans, as are *edamame,* or green soybeans, and black-eyed peas.

For varieties, we tend to favor what we grew up with. Some gravitate to the old-fashioned Blue Lake, Kentucky Wonder, Venture, and Derby. Others prefer yellow wax beans, Slankettes, or Royal Burgundies. Those of Italian inclination will reach for the broad Romano beans and shelling beans. Midwesterners have their fresh limas, while markets in Arkansas, Alabama, Georgia, and Oklahoma feature field peas, a world that encompasses a host of small peas with eyes—cowpeas or black-eyed peas, crowders, Purple Hull, Lady Peas, Mississippi Whites, and others. New-crop pinto and bolita beans, however, are a cause for excitement in New Mexico.

Pretty much everyone now has access to the skinny French filet beans. These are the most expensive beans. Michael Abelman of Fairview Gardens in Goleta, California, told me he probably loses money on filets because they take so long to pick—and this is at $6 a pound. But everyone wants them, so they keep on planting them. Crouching in the sun and searching for thin green beans among the green leaves and green shadows is not that easy!

A good fresh bean that's not overgrown, whether a French, an American, or an Italian bean, is one that a child will eat, provided it's not overcooked. Beans want just a bit of crunch at the heart of their tenderness. Modern varieties are free of strings. They simply need to be tipped and tailed—if that—dropped into plenty of boiling salted water, and cooked uncovered until tender but not mushy. It seems quite normal to pick them up with your fingers, like asparagus, and they are every bit as good as this favored vegetable.

Corn and Chanterelle Chowder | SERVES 4 TO 6

Chanterelles and corn, if it's a mushroom year, come into season at the same time, at least in the mountain states, and they fit seamlessly together. All mushrooms are good with corn, but chanterelles are my favorite.

There are two parts to this recipe, the stock and the vegetables. The stock is made with the trimmings from the vegetables, aromatics, and milk, including chanterelle trimmings. You'll want to use every bit of these glorious fungi.

THE VEGETABLES

4 large ears sweet corn, shucked

2 long leeks or 2 cups chopped

2 German Butterball or other yellow waxy potatoes, scrubbed

2 tablespoons unsalted butter

2 teaspoons chopped thyme

sea salt and freshly ground pepper

2 or more cups chanterelles, cleaned and sliced about ¼ inch thick

½ cup cream

2 tablespoons each chopped parsley and snipped chives

THE STOCK

1 tablespoon unsalted butter

1 large onion, chopped

1 celery rib, chopped

2 bushy thyme sprigs

handful parsley stems

1 bay leaf

1 quart milk, whole or 2 percent

1. Slice off the corn kernels, cutting no more than two thirds of the way into the kernels. Reverse the knife and press out the scrapings. Snap the cobs into 2 or 3 pieces. Put them in a bowl for the stock.

2. Slice off the root ends of the leeks, rinse them, and add them to the corncobs. Cut off the leaves, coarsely chop a cup or so of the firmest parts, wash them well, and add them to the corncobs, too. Quarter the remaining white parts lengthwise and chop.

3. Peel the potatoes and dice them into small cubes. Put the skins with the stock ingredients.

4. Make the stock: Melt the butter in a wide pot, add the vegetable trimmings, the onion, celery, herbs, and 1 teaspoon of salt. Stirring them frequently so that they don't brown, cook over medium heat for 10 minutes, then add the milk. Slowly bring to a boil, then reduce the heat to as low as possible, cover the pan, and simmer for 30 minutes. Check occasionally to make sure nothing is sticking. When done, carefully strain the stock, watching for any grit in the bottom.

5. Melt half the butter in a wide soup pot and add the leeks, potatoes, and half the thyme. Add 1 cup water, sprinkle with ½ teaspoon salt, and cook over medium heat for 5 minutes. Add the corn.

6. Heat the remaining butter in a wide skillet. When foaming, add the chanterelles and sauté over high heat, turning them frequently, for about 5 minutes. Add them, with their juices, to the soup pot, then pour in the stock. Bring slowly to a simmer and cook until the potatoes are fully tender. Stir in the cream and add the remaining thyme, the parsley, and the chives, and season with pepper.

A LOOK AT THE MARKET IN TRENTON, NEW JERSEY
AUGUST 25

Food writer Joe Colanero sent me a market report from Trenton, New Jersey, one August. There were none of the justly famed Jersey tomatoes at this market. But there were those luscious Sun Gold tomatoes, lots of Jersey sweet corn, and in between a wide range of vegetables from Chippewa potatoes to Scotch Bonnet peppers, seven kinds of eggplant, Blue Gem cabbage, squash, green beans, garlic, herbs, and more. Fruit included plums, Yellow Doll and Crimson Sweet watermelons, Bartlett and Seckel pears, peaches, nectarines, and McIntosh apples. While more modest than August markets elsewhere, there was ample variety to make a meal of many tastes and textures.

AN ABUNDANT AUGUST SUPPER

Corn Fritters with Aged Cheddar and Arugula (page 115)

A Platter Salad (page 124) featuring Slankette beans and lemon cucumbers

Steamed Potatoes (page 213), Sun Gold tomatoes, and tuna

Peach Shortcake on Ginger Biscuits (page 299)

Lemon thyme tisane (page 59), iced

Creamy Corn and Shallots | SERVES 4

This couldn't be simpler or faster to make. Savor it by itself or serve it as a side dish.

6 ears freshly picked sweet corn

2 tablespoons unsalted butter

2 shallots, finely diced

sea salt and freshly ground pepper

¼ cup cream

1 tablespoon chopped parsley, torn
     basil leaves, or chopped dill

1. Shuck the corn and remove the kernels with a sharp knife, cutting no more than two thirds of the way into the kernels. Reverse your knife and force out the scrapings, keeping them separate from the kernels.

2. Melt the butter in a wide nonstick skillet. Add the shallots and cook over medium heat for 2 minutes. Add the corn kernels, sprinkle with ½ teaspoon salt, and raise the heat. Cook for 2 minutes, then add the scrapings and cream and cook for 1 minute more. Turn off the heat, season with pepper, and stir in the herb.

Corn Pudding | SERVES 4 TO 6

This pudding is the essence of corn—sunny yellow and filled with sweet kernels that burst in your mouth. Add a cheese from your market, whether it's a soft goat, pungent sheep, smoked Gouda, or aged Cheddar—all will be good with corn—but don't forget the dash of paprika.

1½ tablespoons unsalted butter

1 cup finely diced yellow onion

6 large ears sweet corn, enough to
     yield approximately 3 cups
     kernels

2 eggs, lightly beaten

1 cup cream, evaporated milk, or fresh
     milk

1 cup grated or crumbled cheese

2 tablespoons chopped parsley

1 tablespoon chopped marjoram

sea salt and freshly ground pepper

paprika

1. Preheat the oven to 350°F. Lightly butter a 6-cup gratin dish. Melt the butter in a skillet over low heat. Add the onion and cook, stirring occasionally, just until it's soft and lightly colored, about 10 minutes.

2. While the onion is cooking, shuck the corn and rub off the silk. Using a sharp knife, slice off the top halves of the kernels, then turn your knife over and, using the dull side, press it down the length of the cob, squeezing out the rest of the corn and the milk. Set these aside. Bring a quart of water to a boil, add the corn kernels, and cook for 1 minute, whether or not the water returns to a boil. Drain.

3. Beat the eggs and add the cream, corn kernels, corn milk, cooked onion, cheese, herbs, and 1 teaspoon salt. Season with pepper and pour into the baking dish. Shake a few dashes of paprika over the top. Bake on the center rack of the oven until puffed and golden, about 45 minutes. Serve warm.

Corn Fritters with Aged Cheddar and Arugula | SERVES 6 AS AN APPETIZER OR A LIGHT SUPPER

These crunchy fritters are all corn, not just a few corn kernels suspended in batter. I like the sharp, aged Cheddar I found at the Minneapolis market against the sugary sweetness of today's corn, but corn is versatile and good with every kind of cheese—fresh goat, sheep's feta, Swiss, Gouda, Jack.

6 ears sweet corn, enough to yield
    3 cups kernels

2 eggs, beaten

4 scallions, including an inch of the
    greens, finely sliced

½ cup chopped parsley

2 tablespoons shredded basil or dill

1 cup grated or crumbled cheese (see
    headnote)

⅓ cup all-purpose flour

sea salt and freshly ground pepper

unsalted butter or oil for frying

3 handfuls arugula, stems trimmed

1. Slice the tops of the kernels off the corn, then reverse your knife and press out the milk. Mix the kernels and scrapings with the eggs, scallions, herbs, cheese, and as much flour as can easily be absorbed. Season with ½ teaspoon salt and some pepper.

2. Melt enough butter or heat enough oil to cover a wide skillet generously. Divide the batter roughly into sixths and drop into the skillet. Fry over medium heat until golden, about 2 minutes, then turn and brown the second side.

3. Place a fritter on each of 6 plates and top with the arugula leaves. Serve right away.

We have no trouble finding the farmers' market at all. Signs on the freeway announce the exit, which raises our expectations enormously. But where we end up is at the wholesale produce market, a part of which is given over to farmers. It feels wrong, and we hesitate at the gate. But a guard assures us that we're in the right place. "Come on in!" he shouts, and he ushers us in with a grand sweep of his arm.

The area is so vast that we drive, rather than walk, to each of the three farmers. Presumably there is more activity on other days. Restaurants we have eaten at in Birmingham indicate that there is an appreciation of local produce, and you'd think this would be the source. It is in part, I learn later, but today it's dispiriting with these few farmers waiting in their pickups for customers to come and buy their gunnysacks of field peas. A few young men are lounging by a truck full of watermelons. They see us and begin holding up their forefingers and motioning toward us, signaling that the price of their melons is a dollar. We drive over and spend a half hour with them—they are a pleasant chatty bunch—then we buy a huge, heavy striped Rattlesnake melon, hardly a convenient purchase for out-of-town travelers. Fortunately we are invited out to dinner, and it proves to be an excellent melon.

There is little else to see. We gather that it's too late in the morning, so we come back earlier the next day, when there are two or three more farmers. What's going on here? I wonder. Then someone explains what should be obvious: The season is about over. This is hard to comprehend, because at home our market is probably enjoying its peak day of the year. But this is the South. Chris Hastings, chef-owner of the popular Hot and Hot Fish Club, says that when the market *is* running, he buys a lot of his produce from the farmers. "It varies," he says, "from bring-a-tear-to-your-eye-gorgeous to root average," but on the whole the farmers are really good at growing southern produce, "which is what we like to cook with." On a return visit a year and a half later,

Chris gives me an in-depth tour of the market but also tells me about a new farmers' market in another neighborhood that's wildly successful, selling out every week—the Pepper Place Saturday Market.

For now, though, we wander into a produce store at one end of the market, and that's where I find the foods I have only, until this moment, read about, starting with sacks of Jumbo Red and Spanish White "green" peanuts, fresh from the field. They are moist, like shell beans, which they are, in effect. An elderly gentleman, who is buying a great deal of them, tells me to get some, boil them in salted water, then just "peel 'em and eat 'em." I take his advice, and when I get home, I boil them in salted water, but I don't think I've got it right because they're not very good. When I next return to Alabama, I discover that I didn't have it right at all. Real boiled peanuts are delicious and nothing like the ones I attempted. "It's a fairly standard formula," Damon Lee Fowler, author of *Beans, Greens, and Sweet Georgia Peaches,* told me when I asked him about how to get a good boiled peanut. "You use a very mild brine—a tablespoon of salt for every quart of water—and cover the peanuts by at least an inch—more if you can. The only way to get them gooshy and tender is loooong, slow simmering. You just have to be patient and let them cook for hours." An innkeeper I met in Louisiana confirmed this when she told me that she always has a pot of peanuts simmering on the back of the stove. I'm immediately hooked and can now understand why southerners love their peanuts, which show up reliably at farmers' markets there.

A lot of the produce here bears local names: Mississippi Bogards (probably Beauregards) and Alabama Cullmam Reds are sweet potatoes. Chandler Mountain green tomatoes are piled into wooden trugs, and small Gates apples are bagged for canning, I'm told. Some spectacular yellow-skinned "yams" that must weigh a good three pounds apiece are designated as pie potatoes, as are the big beige

Cow Pumpkins. There are heaps of field peas: purple hull, pink eyes, black eyes, and white zipper or Mississippi crowder peas. One can buy them already shucked, but the twisted pods are irresistible with their shades of purple, pink, and green. The pole beans are big, green, and cool-looking. And you can tell that this is where serious okra eaters live: The okra is carefully laid out in baskets—long pods for pickling, medium pods for stewing, and short pods for frying. In New Mexico, the farmers just throw all the different pods together, making no distinctions for size or use, and they're nearly always picked too large to be acceptable to anyone from the South. We are not okra eaters.

For the first time in my life I get a taste of muscadines, the native grape of the South. They are as large as wild plums, their skins russeted and tough, but the flavor is roundly sweet and full. The women buying them say they are planning to use them for juice and jelly. (Muscadine jelly is for sale in places everywhere we visit.) Collards and turnip greens are piled into enormous heaps, taller than a man. Never have I seen such abundance or greens so fresh and dark that they practically shout out their vitamin content.

Could anyone possibly doubt that these are good for you? Another regional difference is that shoppers are buying them by the armload, not just one bunch at a time.

After our market visit, we go to a nearby restaurant, where we join a very long line of chattering customers who are shuffling steadily forward. Every ten feet or so there's a post telling how much longer before it's your turn to order. Surprisingly quickly, we arrive at the head of the line, where customers order their "meat and three, four, or five." We go for an "eight" and no meat, which allows us to sample the produce we've been looking at. Our plates are heaped with the collard greens, long stewed and delicious with their dousing of pepper sauce; stewed okra and fried okra; sweet potatoes; stewed summer squash; stewed tomatoes; black-eyed peas; and fresh lima beans. Everything is stewy, soft, and sweet, but it's also delicious and very fresh. Later that night we experience more local foods, this time from the Pepper Place farmers' market and at two uptown restaurants where they are turned into bright, contemporary dishes by chefs Chris Hastings at the Hot and Hot and Frank Stitt at the Highland Bar and Grill. Both ways, we win handsomely.

NONE AND SIX:
A PRODUCE-INSPIRED MENU FROM BIRMINGHAM

Corn and Squash Simmered in Coconut Milk with Thai Basil | SERVES 4

The minute I added Thai basil to the corn instead of Italian basil, the direction I had in mind for this dish changed radically. All at once I was using roasted peanut oil, coconut milk, and tofu to make a fragrant vegetable stew.

1 tablespoon roasted peanut oil

1 package fresh, firm tofu, drained and diced into ½-inch cubes

2 medium zucchini, diced into ½-inch cubes

sea salt and freshly ground pepper

4 large ears sweet corn

1 serrano chile

1 heaping tablespoon cilantro

1 heaping tablespoon Thai basil leaves

1 bunch red or green scallions, including half of the firm greens, sliced into ½-inch pieces

1 (15-ounce) can coconut milk

1 teaspoon mushroom soy sauce

3 cups cooked basmati rice

cilantro sprigs and slivered basil leaves for garnish

1. Heat the oil in a wide nonstick skillet over medium-high heat. When hot, add the tofu and zucchini and sprinkle with ¼ teaspoon salt. Cook for 8 to 10 minutes, shaking the pan occasionally to brown all the sides of the tofu.

2. While the tofu is cooking, slice the corn off the cob, then, reversing your knife, press out the milk. Set aside on the cutting board. Finely chop the chile with the cilantro and basil.

3. Add the scallions, chile-herb mixture, and corn to the pan. Add the coconut milk to the pan, then rinse out the can with a little water and add that as well. Stir in the soy sauce, an additional ½ teaspoon salt, and a few twists of black pepper. Simmer until the corn is heated through, 3 to 5 minutes. Taste for salt. Serve over rice garnished with the additional herbs.

Lazy Corn Stew with Taxi and Sun Gold Tomatoes |

Made with yellow and orange tomatoes, this ends up a sunny-looking dish. Of course, if your corn is white, your zucchini green, your tomatoes red, that's fine, too. Use what's available. This little stew is as pleasant to eat at room temperature as it is warm, so it could travel on a picnic.

1 bunch red or green scallions

½ pound yellow summer squash:
Gold Bar, Sunburst, Zephyr, etc.

4 ears sweet corn

3 (about ¾ pound) yellow tomatoes such as Taxi

1½ tablespoons unsalted butter or olive oil

sea salt and freshly ground pepper

½ jalapeño chile, seeded and finely diced

several sprigs green or purple basil

10 Sun Gold tomatoes

1. Cut the scallions, including the firm greens, into ½-inch lengths. Cut the squash lengthwise into quarters or sixths, then into ⅓-inch dice. Shuck the corn, then slice off the top two thirds of the kernels with a sharp knife. Reversing your blade, press out the corn milk.

2. Peel and seed the yellow tomatoes, squeezing the seeds and juice into a strainer placed over a bowl. Cut the flesh into ½-inch pieces and set aside.

3. Melt the butter in a wide skillet over medium heat. When bubbling, add the scallions and cook for about 30 seconds. Add the squash, season with ½ teaspoon salt, and stir. Cook for about 2 minutes, then add ¼ cup water.

4. Lay the tomato pieces over the squash, add the strained juice, and cover with the corn and half the chile. Bury 2 large sprigs of the basil into the vegetables, then cover the skillet. Reduce the heat to low and cook for 15 minutes.

5. Meanwhile, slice the Sun Gold tomatoes in half and set them in a bowl. Add 2 tablespoons torn basil leaves and the remaining chile. When the vegetables are finished cooking, taste for salt and season with pepper. Strew the Sun Gold tomatoes over the top and serve.

CORN AS A CONSTANT

To a great degree, we tend to see vegetables as constants when we shop in the supermarket. The extraordinary buying power of supermarket chains means that they can reach far and wide to keep corn looking more or less the same throughout most of the year. Ears don't vary much in size, the kernels are perfectly filled, the husks, if there are any, may not be green and glistening, but you'll never find a worm. If you shop at a farm stand or a farmers' market, however, you will get a view of how quickly produce runs through its cycle from tenderness to maturity to being gone. Carol Ann Sayle, of Boggy Creek Farm in Austin, Texas, describes it like this:

"The first Saturday, the corn is sublime. Eating it is a euphoric, transfiguring experience, one not often enjoyed by modern folk. By Wednesday's market, it is still magnificent, but the quality has slipped just a tad. By the next Saturday, the slip is more noticeable: The resident worms have eaten more of the kernels, then moved on. This Wednesday will be Gleaners Day. Those who can tolerate ears bereft of half their kernels and possessing more starch than sugar will get a free pass to enter the corn patch. There they can wade through the scratchy leaves and emerge, if not with great corn, then with a profound appreciation for what it takes to harvest corn for market."

And after that? The corn is gone until the next season, or until the next crop of a later, staggered planting is ready for harvest. In all, there were just two short weeks during which its quality arched quickly upward to the sublime moment, then curved steadily downward to the half-eaten, starchy end of the corn cycle.

Warm Corn Custard with Berries | SERVES 6

The sweet corn taste is most detectable when the custard is still a little warm from the oven. These custards are delicious plain, but the corn flavor is perfectly pitched with sweetened blackberries. Other fruit contenders are huckleberries, raspberries, blueberries, sliced peaches, and the plum compote on page 293. Serve the custards in their dishes with a spoonful of the fruit and a little softly whipped cream.

1¾ cups whole milk or light cream

⅓ cup sugar

⅓ vanilla bean, split lengthwise

3 ears sweet corn, shucked

1 tablespoon all-purpose flour

3 eggs

1 egg yolk

1 cup berries (see headnote)

1 tablespoon or more light
    brown sugar

whipped cream, optional

1. Preheat the oven to 350°F. Heat a kettle of water. Slowly heat the milk with the sugar and vanilla bean until it comes to a boil. Turn off the heat and let steep for at least 10 minutes. Scrape the seeds from the vanilla bean into the milk and set the pod aside to dry. You can embed it in sugar to make vanilla sugar.

2. Slice the top two thirds of the corn kernels off the cobs and then reverse your knife and press out the milk. Scrape up the kernels and milk and put them in a blender with the flour. Add the warm milk and puree at the highest speed for at least 2 minutes. Pour the corn-milk into a fine strainer set over a 1-quart measure. Work a rubber scraper back and forth over the strainer, pressing the milk through. You should end up with about 3½ cups liquid. Rinse out the strainer and set it aside.

3. Beat the eggs and yolk in a bowl, then whisk in the corn-milk. Pour it once again through the strainer to get rid of any bits of egg white, then pour the milk into 6 custard cups and set them in a baking dish. Put the dish in the oven and remove one of the cups, to make it easy to pour in enough hot water to come about halfway up the sides. Return the single cup to the pan. Reduce the heat to 325°F and bake until the custard is set except for a wobbly dime-sized circle in the center, about 50 minutes. Remove and let cool in the water bath to finish cooking.

4. An hour before serving, toss the berries with the sugar and set aside. (If the berries are tart, you might want to use a little more sugar.) Serve the custards with the berries on top, and whipped cream, if you like.

Summer Posole
with Cilantro Salsa | SERVES 4 GENEROUSLY

Posole is corn that's been slaked with lime to remove the outer skin. This process gives the corn a rich, nutty flavor. After sampling New Mexican cooking, visitors to our farmers' markets often buy dried *posole* to take home. This recipe, however, is lighter and greener than the *posole* served in New Mexican restaurants. The cilantro salsa and garnishes are added at the end, Mexican style, so that their colors and flavors remain bright and fresh.

THE *POSOLE*

1 pound dried *posole*

1 large white onion, finely diced

3 plump garlic cloves, minced

1½ teaspoons dried oregano, Mexican if possible

6 large green New Mexican chiles

sea salt

SALSA AND GARNISHES

1 bunch scallions, including a few inches of the greens, finely chopped

1 cup finely chopped cilantro

1 jalapeño chile, seeded and minced

1 teaspoon cumin seeds, toasted in a skillet, then ground

pinch sea salt

¼ cup light olive or vegetable oil

1 avocado, diced into chunks

4 corn tortillas, slivered

1 cup thinly sliced green cabbage

1 lime, quartered

warm tortillas for serving

1. Put the *posole* in a large soup pot with the onion, garlic, oregano, and a gallon of water. Bring to a boil, then cover and simmer until tender. This can take as long as 3 hours, so check the pot occasionally and add water as it boils away. The *posole* will swell considerably, and the kernels will split open.

2. While the *posole* is cooking, roast the chiles (see page 390), then place them in a bowl and cover with a plate to steam for 15 minutes. Slip off the skins, pull out the seeds, and chop. Add the chopped chiles to the simmering *posole* along with 4 teaspoons salt. Continue cooking until the *posole* is completely tender. Taste for salt.

3. Preheat the oven to 350°F. To make the salsa, combine the scallions, cilantro, chile, cumin, and salt in a bowl. Stir in the oil, add water as needed to thin, and add the avocado. Toast the tortilla strips in the oven until crisp, or fry them in vegetable oil.

4. To serve, stir the salsa into the *posole* and garnish with a nest of cabbage and tortilla strips and a wedge of lime. Accompany with warm tortillas.

Yellow Wax Beans with Lemon Thyme and Yellow Tomatoes | SERVES 4

This is a pretty dish of beans, and pretty good to eat, too.

1 pound yellow wax beans or other
    fresh beans, as you prefer

sea salt

1 tablespoon unsalted butter

1 tablespoon olive oil

2 shallots, minced

1 yellow tomato, peeled, seeded, and
    diced

2 teaspoons finely chopped lemon
    thyme

champagne vinegar

1. Tip, tail, then cut the beans into 3-inch lengths. Boil them in plenty of salted water, uncovered, until tender-firm, about 5 minutes. Taste to make sure, though. Beans can take a while, depending on their size.

2. While they're cooking, melt the butter with the olive oil, add the shallots, and cook over medium heat for 2 minutes, then add the tomato and thyme.

3. Drain the beans as soon as they're done, add them to the pan, and cook briefly, coating them with the sauce. Season with a few drops of vinegar and serve.

Platter
Salads

A large Italian platter has long provided the answer. The question is: How can I use everything I see at the market?

Platter salads are a blessing for those of us who can't make up our minds about what to focus on when faced with abundance. Following the maxims that foods in season together taste good together, and that botanical families offer a unique coherence of flavor, platter salads are bound to turn chaos into success. These salads are simply collections of compatible vegetables, cooked when appropriate, left raw when not, arranged on a large platter, showered with herbs, and bathed with a fine olive oil. The herbs can be as common as parsley, dill, and chives, but the effect of combining them produces such a layering of flavor that you may hear yourself say, as one guest did, "Every bite tastes different!" Of course you can stray toward more exotic herbs as well.

No matter what combination you come up with, platter salads always make a painterly tableau for the eye. My preference is for the big, bright, baroque arrangements, but sometimes I yield to more minimalist leanings. A salad for mid-August might include several varieties of potatoes, green and yellow Romano beans, filet beans, Sun Gold and Green Grape tomatoes, lemon basil, capers, and fresh red onions bathed in olive oil and spiked with aged red wine vinegar. One of my favorite salads was finished with thin rounds of purple peppers and sprays of tiny currant tomatoes from a children's farmers' market in St. Paul. A different version, inspired by the market in Ithaca, might include grilled small eggplants and zucchini with fresh sheep's milk cheese. In late August shelling beans and roasted peppers could go on the platter, while by late October you might turn to shredded kohlrabi and turnips, slivered sweet Jersey Wakefield cabbage, and steamed cauliflower, all drizzled with a mustardy vinaigrette and garnished with leafy accents of arugula or tatsoi.

Sometimes I select a color as the guiding principle. Gold Rush zucchini or rich yellow Sunburst, orange peppers, yellow wax beans, golden beets, and yellow and orange tomatoes of various kinds together make a dazzling sea of yellow, orange, and gold. Opal basil leaves or amaranth greens make irresistibly gorgeous accents.

Bright flavor elements to include on platter salads are capers, olives, anchovies, and pickled vegetables. Cold roasted meats, grilled chicken, tuna packed in oil, smoked albacore, hard-cooked eggs, or wedges of frittata turn a platter salad into a complete meal.

The process of making these salads is very fluid and far more difficult to describe than actually to do. First of all, let the market guide the composition. Washing, tipping beans, and that sort of thing can be done ahead of time. The most important consideration for me is to dress cooked vegetables while they're warm, which is the most flavorful way, and to try to cook them as close as I can to serving so that they keep their colors and aromas. Other than that, you're on your own, improvising madly and always assured of success.

June Platter Salad of Green Beans, Potatoes, and Tuna | SERVES 4 AS A MAIN DISH

It's pre—tomato season in June, at least in Santa Fe, but the first green beans, tender little carrots, and French Breakfast radishes fit quite nicely with a few handfuls of lettuce, herbs, and fleshy purslane leaves. Tuna packed in oil or smoked fish—salmon, tuna, albacore, which can often be found at farmers' markets—makes the salad into a meal.

1 sweet onion, thinly sliced into
    rounds

¼ cup aged red wine vinegar

1 pound small potatoes, any waxy-
    fleshed variety (fingerlings are
    always choice)

sea salt and freshly ground pepper

1½ pounds green beans, one variety or
    several

1 bunch little carrots

several handfuls salad greens or small
    head lettuces

a handful purslane sprigs or
    big sunflower sprouts

several herb sprigs, such as chervil,
    marjoram, lovage,
    chives

2 garlic cloves

1 can anchovies, packed in olive oil

1 teaspoon Dijon mustard

⅓ cup extra virgin olive oil

2 (6-ounce) cans tuna packed in oil,
    drained, or an 8-ounce chunk
    smoked albacore, thinly sliced

3 tablespoons smallest capers,
    rinsed

1 bunch radishes

1. Heat a large pot of water for the vegetables. Toss the onion with 2 tablespoons of the vinegar and set in the refrigerator.

2. Wash the potatoes, then put them in a small saucepan, cover with cold water, add 1 teaspoon salt, and bring to a boil. Simmer until tender when pierced with a knife, about 25 minutes, then drain. Cut the stem ends off the beans, along with the tails if they're tough. If the carrots are small and tender, you don't need to peel them. Leave them whole or halve lengthwise with about an inch of the stems. Wash and dry the lettuces and herbs.

3. Mash the garlic with ½ teaspoon salt and 2 anchovies in a mortar. Whisk in the mustard, the remaining 2 tablespoons vinegar, and the oil, making a thick, emulsified dressing.

4. When the water boils, season well with salt, then add the beans and cook until tender but still a little firm, 4 to 8 minutes, depending on the varieties. Scoop them out and put them on a towel to dry briefly, then toss them, while still hot, with half of the dressing. Season with salt and pepper and heap them in the center of the platter. Boil the carrots until tender-firm, 4 to 6 minutes or so, then drain and dress lightly.

5. Arrange the lettuces on the platter. Place the tuna at either end, breaking it up slightly. Halve the potatoes and arrange them on the platter. Spoon the remaining dressing over the lettuce and potatoes and scatter capers over all, along with the onions, drained of their vinegar. Lay the remaining anchovies over the potatoes. Tuck in the radishes and carrots; add the purslane and herb sprigs. Season everything with pepper. Present the salad arranged. Toss it before serving.

Fava Bean, Herb, and Wax Bean Soup with Fried Pita Bread | SERVES 2 TO 4

You can make this Lebanese soup with a light chicken stock, but the leek trimmings, an onion, a few extra wax beans, and cilantro stems will make a fine vegetable stock. In either case, the stock should be delicate enough that it doesn't overwhelm the vegetables.

Very small fava beans needn't be peeled, but larger ones (thumbnail size) should be. Peeling is time consuming, but silky orbs of shimmering green are the payoff.

3 cups Vegetable Stock, page 385,
    or light chicken stock

1 cup shelled fava beans, about 1¼
    pounds pods

5 very slender leeks, white parts
    plus an inch of the greens,
    thinly sliced

1 small red onion, finely diced

1 garlic clove, crushed

12 yellow wax or other fresh beans,
    cut into 2-inch lengths

1 small zucchini, thinly sliced

¼ cup chopped parsley

¼ cup chopped cilantro

2 tablespoons slivered mint leaves

sea salt and freshly ground pepper

1 pita bread

2 tablespoons olive oil

1. Heat the stock. Add the fava beans if they're small, along with the leeks, onion, garlic, and wax beans. (If the favas are large, blanch them separately for 1 minute, then peel and add them to the soup with the zucchini.)

2. Bring to a boil, then lower the heat and simmer, covered, for 12 minutes. Add the zucchini, simmer for 10 minutes more, then stir in the herbs. Taste for salt and season with pepper. Turn off the heat and allow the soup to rest so that the herbs can infuse the broth.

3. Meanwhile, cut or tear the pita bread into small pieces and fry in the olive oil over medium-high heat until crisp and golden. Serve the soup with several pieces of bread floating in each bowl.

Shelly Beans with Pasta and Sage | SERVES 4

Shelly, shell, or shelling beans are the tender stage of what will become dried beans. At this point their pods are tough, twisted, and dry, far past the stage for eating. But the beans within are still moist. Any bean can be a shelling bean if grown to the right stage. For this dish, cranberry beans would be my preference.

Shelling beans do cook more quickly than dried beans, but they still require some time on the stove.

2 tablespoons olive oil

1 onion, diced

2 bay leaves, 1 parsley sprig, and a few
    thyme sprigs, tied together

2 tablespoons chopped sage

3 garlic cloves, minced

3 cups shelled fresh cranberry beans,
    about 3 pounds in their pods

5 to 6 cups Vegetable Stock, page 385,
    chicken stock, or water

sea salt and freshly ground pepper

¾ pound lumache shells

¼ cup chopped parsley

Sage Oil, page 61, or extra virgin
    olive oil to finish

freshly grated Parmesan

1. Heat the oil in a wide sauté pan or casserole with the onion, herb bundle, and sage and cook over medium heat for 8 minutes, stirring frequently. Add the garlic, beans, enough stock to cover by 2 inches, and 1 teaspoon salt. Simmer, covered, until the beans are soft, about 40 minutes. Check occasionally to make sure they're covered with liquid. Remove the herb bundle from the beans. Mash or puree about half the beans, then return them to the pan and thin with the extra stock or water. Taste again for salt and season with pepper.

2. Bring plenty of water to a boil, add salt, and cook the pasta until just tender. Drain and add it to the beans. Add the parsley, taste for salt and pepper, and toss well. Serve in pasta plates, spoon Sage Oil over each serving, and dust with a grating of cheese.

On this Labor Day weekend there are heaps of sweet corn, tomatoes, and green beans at the Ohio farm stand I'm visiting. And there, next to the fat Blue Lake beans, is something I've never seen before: flattish, succulent green pods about four inches long. The green is so dark and lustrous, the shape so full and promising, I am drawn in. Each pod is edged with what looks like a seam. Little tips at either end suggest pulling. I pull, and a string the length of the pod comes off, but I'm no closer to opening it than I was before. I twist the pod in the middle, and it pops open. Inside are four perfect beans, my first fresh limas. They *smell* green, and they seem to be lit from within. Their luminous yellow-green skins are tipped with the tiniest lines of a green just slightly darker than the whole. Unlike frozen limas, they are utterly alive.

Lots of good things can be done with lima beans. You can make a delicate green puree seasoned with rosemary and chives or a Lebanese soup of limas, fava beans, and fresh coriander (cilantro). You can always just cook them and toss them with butter, sea salt, and pepper. And, of course, there's succotash.

I fly back to Albuquerque with my big bag of lima beans, take a detour to a farm that I know still has sweet corn, then drive home to Santa Fe. There I make my first real succotash, and it is easily the best part of our Labor Day supper. I had no idea until now, having known only the frozen version, how completely seductive succotash can be and how truly wonderful lima beans are.

Succotash | SERVES 4

6 ears super-fresh sweet corn,
   preferably yellow
1 pound or more fresh lima beans,
   shucked
2 tablespoons or more unsalted
   butter
sea salt and freshly ground pepper

1. Shuck the corn, pull off the silk, and slice off the tops of the kernels. Turn your knife over and press it down the length of the cobs, squeezing out the rest of the corn and the milk. Keep the scrapings separate from the kernels.

2. Cook the beans in a saucepan with water to cover until tender, 25 to 40 minutes. When done, transfer them to a 10-inch skillet along with the corn kernels, butter, and enough of the cooking water just to cover. Bring to a boil, then reduce the heat and simmer for 5 minutes. Stir in the corn scrapings and continue to cook gently, without stirring, for 10 minutes. Most of the water will have cooked off, leaving the sweet corn and beans bound with the corn milk. Season with salt, a few grindings of pepper, and more butter if you wish.

Fresh Green Lima Beans with Scallions and Yogurt | SERVES 4 TO 6

Lovage always seems like the right bean herb to me because it's so lively. But dill, cilantro, basil in summer, or about half as much rosemary in the fall can be used to equally good, but quite different, effect. Serve these warm with fresh pita bread or garlic-rubbed toast to put them on or scoop up the sauce.

2 pounds fresh lima beans, enough to yield about 2 cups shelled

1 bunch thick scallions with nice, firm greens

2 tablespoons olive oil

¼ cup chopped parsley

2 tablespoons chopped lovage

sea salt and freshly ground pepper

water or stock

¼ cup whole-milk yogurt

1. Shell the lima beans. Finely slice the white parts of the scallions and an inch of the greens. Chop the rest of the greens into ½-inch pieces, keeping them separate from the bottoms.

2. Warm the oil in an 8-inch nonstick skillet. Add the scallion bottoms and cook over medium heat for 1 minute. Add the beans, two thirds of the parsley and the lovage, 1 teaspoon salt, and water to cover. Simmer until the beans are soft, about 10 minutes. Add the scallion greens and cook until the beans are completely tender, another 10 minutes or so. Taste for salt and season with pepper.

3. Turn off the heat, stir the yogurt into the hot beans, and add the remaining parsley and lovage. Serve warm.

Edamame (Green Soybeans) | SERVES 4

Edamame are soybeans at the shell-bean stage, the same beans that are served in Japanese restaurants. Recently, *edamame* have been appearing at farmers' markets here and there across the country. They're sometimes referred to as "edible" soybeans, as opposed to those that are grown for livestock feed or manufacturing.

You can tell that sometimes it takes a few seasons to figure out how to grow a new vegetable to its best advantage. Those in our market have been a little too dry and too small, but each season they get better. I've no doubt that soon they'll be perfect. Here's how to cook them.

1 pound green soybeans in their pods

2 tablespoons sea salt

1. Pluck the pods off the stems if that hasn't been done already and rinse them well.

2. Bring 2 quarts water to a boil; add the salt and beans. Boil for 3 minutes, then drain. Wick up extra moisture with a towel, then pile the pods into a bowl and sprinkle with more salt. Chill if the day is a hot one or serve warm. Be sure to put out a big bowl for the pods.

White Bean and Sage Fritters | SERVES 6 TO 10

I love these soft, chewy fritters. They were inspired by those I ate in Badalucco, Liguria, where they were served as one of many little appetizers.

The beans, which are special to this area and designated as one of Slow Food International's Ark Foods, appear to be a cross between cannellini and borlotti beans. Large and white with mottled golden eyes, they have a creamy texture and delicate taste. I use cannellini beans in their place since the beans are not available here. Fred Plotkin, whose method this is (and who describes them in his book *Recipes from Paradise*), says that black-eyed peas come much closer to the flavor of the Ligurian beans. Whichever way you go, I think these fritters are very good. You'll just need one or two per person.

1 cup dried cannellini or 2 cups fresh
    black-eyed peas

1 garlic clove

¼ cup chopped sage, plus extra
    leaves for garnish

olive oil

sea salt

1½ cups all-purpose flour

1 to 1½ cups sparkling mineral
    water

1 white onion, very finely diced

1. Cover the beans with water and set aside until plump and smooth, about 6 hours. Drain and cover with plenty of fresh water. Bring to a boil, then lower the heat to a simmer. Add the garlic, a few sage leaves, a tablespoon of oil, and 1½ teaspoons salt. Cook until the beans are tender, 1½ hours or so. Store in their cooking liquid until ready to use.

2. Place the flour in a bowl and gradually add enough mineral water to make a thick paste, gently working the mixture with a wooden spoon. Add the beans, drained of the liquid, the onion, and the chopped sage. Mix together as well as you can. Cover and let stand for at least 30 minutes. The batter should be pliable but not runny. (It may not look very promising at this point.)

3. Preheat the oven to 250°F. Have ready an ovenproof platter and a plate lined with paper towels. Heat ½ inch olive oil in a cast-iron or other heavy pot. When hot, drop in the batter by spoonfuls. Fry over medium-high heat until golden on the bottom, then turn and fry the second side, about 1½ minutes on each side. When golden, drain briefly on the towels, then transfer to the oven to keep warm.

4. When you've finished frying as many fritters as you wish to serve, fry a few large sage leaves for about 1 minute, then drain. Arrange the fritters on a platter, grind a little sea salt over each, top with a sage leaf, and serve.

Shell Beans and Summer Vegetables Stewed in Their Own Juices | SERVES 4 GENEROUSLY

This humble braise more or less cooks itself. The vegetables are cut into large pieces (quick to prepare) and are meltingly tender when finished. Some might say they're overcooked, and they *are* soft, but this only brings out their flavors. Once, when I added some pesto at the end, the familiar flavors told me that I had made a *soupe au pistou,* only a heartier version.

3 tablespoons olive oil

2 bay leaves

2 onions, chopped into large pieces

7 plump garlic cloves, peeled and halved

3 thyme sprigs

6 sage leaves

12 small (3- to 5-inch) carrots

sea salt and freshly ground pepper

¾ pound small new potatoes

½ pound yellow wax or green beans, ends trimmed

5 medium tomatoes, peeled, seeded, and chopped into large pieces, juice reserved

1 bell pepper, yellow or orange if possible, cut into 1-inch strips

1 pound summer squash, cut into large pieces

1 to 2 pounds shelling beans, shelled

THE BASIL PUREE

packed ½ cup basil leaves

1 garlic clove

3 tablespoons olive oil

½ cup freshly grated Parmesan cheese, optional

1. Warm the 3 tablespoons oil with the bay leaves in a large casserole or Dutch oven over low heat. When fragrant, add the onions, 6 of the garlic cloves, 2 of the thyme sprigs, and the sage. Cover and cook while you prepare the vegetables.

2. Leave small carrots whole or cut fat ones into 4-inch lengths. Add them to the pot right away since they take the longest to cook. Season with a little salt and pepper. If the potatoes are like large marbles, leave them whole. But quarter larger ones and cut fingerlings in half lengthwise. Lay the potatoes on top of the onions and carrots. Add salt and pepper. Cut the beans into 3-inch pieces and add them, along with all the rest of the vegetables except the shelling beans, to the pot, seasoning each layer with salt and pepper.

3. Strain the tomato juice over all, then cover and cook until the vegetables are tender, about 40 minutes to an hour. If tightly covered, the vegetables will produce plenty of flavorful juices. If the pot seems dry, add a few tablespoons water or white wine.

4. While the vegetables are cooking, simmer the shell beans in water to cover with the remaining garlic and thyme and a little olive oil. When tender, after 30 to 45 minutes, season with salt and pepper. Add the beans, with any liquid, to the pot.

5. Make the Basil Puree shortly before serving: Chop the basil and garlic in a food processor with the oil and enough water to make a puree. Stir in the cheese, then taste and season with salt.

6. Serve the vegetables in soup plates and spoon the Basil Puree over them.

Chickpea Salad with Coriander and Cumin | SERVES 4 TO 6

Dried chickpeas are among the first and last offerings of our market season. At the end of summer, you can use them, along with tomatoes, to make this salad.

THE CHICKPEAS

1⅔ cups dried chickpeas, soaked,
    or 4 cups, cooked

sea salt

⅓ cup vegetable oil

3 medium onions, finely diced

6 thin slices ginger

1 tablespoon ground coriander

2 teaspoons ground cumin

½ teaspoon ground turmeric

2 teaspoons garam masala

2½ tablespoons fresh lime juice

THE GARNISH

5 San Marzano, or other
    paste tomatoes, seeded
    and diced

1 cucumber, peeled, seeded, and diced

1 jalapeño chile, seeded and finely
    diced

3 tablespoons chopped cilantro

1 tablespoon Dijon mustard

lime wedges

1. Pour the soaking water off the chickpeas, cover them with 3 quarts fresh water, add 1 tablespoon salt, then bring to a boil. Simmer, partially covered, until tender. The time for cooking chickpeas can vary from 1¼ hours to 3 hours, so check while they're cooking. When done, drain, setting the broth aside.

2. Heat the oil in a wide skillet, then add the onions and ginger. Cook over medium-high heat until golden, stirring occasionally, 12 to 15 minutes. Add the dried spices and cook for 1 minute more.

3. Add the chickpeas, 1 cup of the broth, and 1 tablespoon of the lime juice. Cook for about 5 minutes or until most of the liquid has evaporated, then taste for salt. Let cool to room temperature, then mound on a platter.

4. To make the garnish: Combine the tomatoes, cucumber, chile, cilantro, and mustard in a bowl with the remaining lime juice, then spoon this over the chickpeas. Garnish with lime wedges and serve.

Soupy Pinto or Bolita Beans | SERVES 4 TO 6

Some of our farmers grow bolita beans, a small pinkish tan bean that's even smaller than a pinto. Elsewhere I've seen yellow Peruvian beans, Italian *soranos,* scarlet, black, and white runner, Speckled Cranberry, Black Valentines, white *gigantes*—in all, a great mix of form and color. Beans are one of the most beautiful and diverse foods.

Because they're delicate (some would say bland), you can do a lot with beans if you want to. But for the same reason, you can enjoy them very simply cooked. I usually just throw beans into the pressure cooker, add water and salt, and cook on high for 20 minutes. If that's not enough time, I finish them on the stove. The beans should come out soft and creamy and full of flavor. Add a spoonful of crème fraîche and a little chopped scallion, and they're even better.

If you don't have a pressure cooker, you can start with beans that have been soaked, or not. Unsoaked beans require more water for cooking and take somewhat longer, but not a lot. Either way, cover the beans amply with fresh water and bring to a boil. Boil hard for 10 minutes and skim off any foam that rises to the surface, then reduce the heat to a simmer. Cook until tender.

Most beans take roughly 1½ hours to cook. But the actual time depends on the type of bean, how old they are, the hardness of your water, and the altitude you're cooking at.

2 cups dried pinto or bolita beans

4 teaspoons sea salt

¼ to ½ cup crème fraîche

4 scallions, chopped

⅓ cup chopped cilantro

1. Sort through, then rinse the beans. Put them in a pressure cooker with 2 quarts water and the salt and bring to pressure. Keep on high (15 pounds) for 20 minutes, then quickly release the pressure. Remove the lid, then taste to see if they're done. If not, simmer until completely tender.

2. Stir in the crème fraîche. Taste for salt. Serve with chopped scallions and cilantro.

I had heard so much about Atlanta's Morningside farmers' market that in my mind it was huge. When I finally got there, I was surprised by how small it was. Shoehorned into a tiny parking lot were maybe twenty vendors in all. But this market was overflowing with beautiful food, including some of the most perfect, pristine lettuces I've ever seen. Shoppers and growers were friendly, informed, and enthusiastic. By the time I left, Morningside's stature was firmly restored.

Few markets are all organic. Most are a mixture of organic and conventional producers. However, this market was started by a group of organic farmers who were adamant about not sharing the platform with conventional farmers. Cynthia Hizer, a farmer and one of the market founders, explains, "It's hard to have a conventionally grown tomato selling for a dollar a pound next to a beautiful organically grown heirloom tomato that took a lot more effort and should sell—and does sell—for much more. People still go for what's cheap, not what's of value. Plus it's darn hard growing organically in Georgia. Bugs love humidity. What's amazing is that we can actually do it! We succeed, but there are drawbacks."

The quality of food in this market is outstanding, but its small size coupled with the challenge of farming organically in humid Georgia means that there's a limited range of offerings. "It's pretty bold of us not to have peaches in May. Georgia is peach country, but they're practically impossible to grow here organically," Cynthia says. "We'd like to have a regular cheese maker, a pasta maker, and be able to afford a band every week *and* do lots of advertising. But a small group of farmers simply doesn't have the money for ad blitzes."

Nonetheless, the market is well attended, and the fact that it's small makes it very much a neighborhood market. "Most of our customers walk to market. They bring their dogs, their strollers, they meet neighbors, so it's very social," Cynthia says. "We tried putting the market on a major thoroughfare to attract more customers, but the traffic moved so fast that no one stopped. In fact it didn't even get noticed, so we were pretty happy to come back to this spot. We have such loyal customers here that they come out in sleet storms—even when we don't."

In addition to the interesting mix of vegetables similar to those grown elsewhere in the country, the Morningside market has a lot of local foods that make it very much a regional market. "Southern greens are a big hit, of course," Cynthia says. "But instead of growing mustard greens that are two feet long, our farmers bring them in when they're only six to eight inches long, when they're really tender. Turnips are grown for the greens, not the roots. And there's one plant called Tender Green that cooks like spinach but tastes like collards. And if it tastes like collards, it'll sell here."

This market also has some very unusual and interesting

figs, unusual backyard varieties, whose season was just ending when I visited. And there was a special honey—sourwood. But there were more vegetables, too.

"We have our Georgia sweet onions, of course, and eggplant is very popular. It's kind of an old-timey vegetable in Georgia. There's a man who brings in his kettle and boils peanuts—southerners love their peanuts. And this is definitely bean country. We have dozens of beans: zippers, black eye, pink eye, baby butter beans, crowders, half runners, shelly beans, and the queen, White Acre Pea, also called Cream Pea, the size of a BB, which turns to cream when cooked. We even have fresh soybeans, even though they aren't a classic southern offering. It's great fun here in the summer! Beans and peas are one of the things we do best, and folks love them like they love the collards—the more the better."

When I visited the market, Cynthia was selling something people were lined up for that didn't taste like either beans or collards. It was goat's milk mixed with jojoba oil, and it was for bathing in. She gave me a bottle. I admit that I had my doubts about bathing in milk. I always thought that a "milk bath" was just a metaphor for luxury. But that night in my hotel tub I understood why there was the line at Hazelbrand farm's stand—a milk bath does make your skin feel luxuriously soft, and it has a most calming effect.

Many people talk about how the farmers' market draws people together and makes "a village out of a city." But Cynthia sees it another way, too. "Organic farmers are such a minority here that this market gives *us farmers* a place to come together. Before we had the market, we saw each other once a year at our organic farming conference. Now we have a weekly venue, and it has really been good for us. Our farmers are still helping each other out, not falling over each other in competition. They share equipment, seeds, advice, and even customers."

AN ATLANTA-INSPIRED MENU FOR FALL

Crudités: thinly sliced Chinese red radishes with sea salt,
slivered red bell peppers, olives

A Rough and Ready Turnip Potage (page 93)

A salad of flawless lettuces

Goat's Milk Panna Cotta with Sourwood Honey
(page 248)

Vining Fruits and Vegetables

This group of curvaceous fruits and curling vines includes sweet, savory, and utilitarian plants such as cucumbers, squashes, melons, and gourds. In the fall you'll undoubtedly discover Cinderella pumpkins and other magnificent old varieties of winter squash. Or you might come across a pretty orange Pocket melon that you carry around just because it smells good. There's the charming heirloom watermelon called Moon and Stars for the big golden moon and countless little "stars" peppering its dark green skin, and wart-covered or three-lobed winter squash. Certainly this group captures the imagination as easily as the glamorous nightshades do.

Perhaps because people have long enjoyed complaining about the reproductive powers of zucchini, our farmers weren't growing much of it for a while. For a few years they were even hard to find, but the squash gap has been closed, and they're back in greater number and variety, along with big baskets of the golden squash blossoms to enjoy on your counter during the day before cooking them in the evening.

A new variety of summer squash has caught my eye. Called Zephyr, it's light yellow except for two inches of the tip, which is pale green and very faintly striped—delicious and lovely. Another fine zucchini is Costata Romanesco, an Italian gray-green squash with prominent raised ribs than run down the length of its body. Its flesh is dense and exceptionally flavorful, especially if you cook it for more than a brief moment. Round zucchini, called *calabacitas* in the Southwest, look exactly like the French Ronde de Nice. When allowed to grow to immensity, their name becomes *calabasas Mexicanas*. These, along with Black Ravens, dark green Embassy, bright yellow Gold Rush, and pale green Lebanese zucchini, show that summer squash embodies a world of colorful diversity.

While you'll undoubtedly find so-called baby summer squash, which are as cute as can be, you may come to conclude that they don't have the lush flavor that squash that has been given a chance to grow has. In fact, they can be on the bitter side. Look for squash roughly between six and eight inches long if you want the most flavor. Mammoth ones, as everyone knows, become seedy and dull. I don't always buy just one kind of summer squash. Invariably my hands rove through a variety of squashes and I am equally attracted to all of them, be they pattypans, pale green or black zucchini, round calabacitas, or yellow crooknecks. But when I go to cook them, there's always the question of how to cut these different-shaped squashes.

Since I don't like them to lose their distinct characteristics, I cut each type in the way that best preserves its form: lengthwise for the zucchini, crosswise for pattypans and round squash, lengthwise again for crooknecks, capturing the curve at the stem end. You'll end up with an assortment of different shapes, each revealing the identity of the squash you used. Cut them all the same thickness, and they'll cook in the same amount of time. It's a small and simple technique, but the results definitely catch the eye.

Zephyr Zucchini with Opal Basil, Pine Nuts, and Parmigiano-Reggiano | SERVES 4

Slender, pale yellow, and tipped in pale green, Zephyr zucchini are far too pretty to chop. Instead, halve them lengthwise to retain their pretty markings, cook, then shower them with purple basil, freshly grated Parmesan, and pine nuts—the elements of pesto but brought together in the mouth rather than the mortar. The plum-colored opal basil is especially gorgeous here. Of course you can use other basils—or summer squashes for that matter—to make this dish. Regardless of varieties used, this is easy, attractive, and very good.

1 pound or more Zephyr or other
    zucchini, 6 to 8 inches long
sea salt and freshly ground pepper
¼ cup pine nuts
extra virgin olive oil
freshly grated Parmigiano-Reggiano
10 large opal basil leaves, torn

1. Slice the squash in half lengthwise, then steam or simmer in salted water until tender. Meanwhile, toast the pine nuts in a dry skillet over medium heat until golden.
2. When the squash is done, arrange it on a platter, cut side up. Drizzle olive oil over it and season with salt and pepper. Grate a veil of cheese over the squash, add the pine nuts and basil, and serve.

Slow-Cooked Thin-Sliced Summer Squash Showered with Herbs | SERVES 4 TO 6

I could eat summer squash every day, especially when it's cooked like this. Savor these fragrant vegetables by themselves or turn them into supper by heaping them on garlic-rubbed toasted levain bread with thinly sliced fresh mozzarella. Regardless of its color, shape, or size, all summer squash cook in about the same amount of time, so you can use all and any varieties you find.

2 pounds mixed summer squash
3 tablespoons olive oil
½ cup simmering water
sea salt and freshly ground pepper
⅓ cup chopped flat-leaf parsley
2 tablespoons chopped marjoram or
    oregano or torn basil leaves

1. Slice the squash ¼ inch thick.
2. Heat the oil in a wide skillet. Add the squash and cook over medium-low heat, flipping the squash in the pan every 3 or 4 minutes until it's tender and golden, about 20 minutes. Add the water and continue cooking until none remains. Season with salt and pepper and shower the herbs over all. Slide onto a platter and serve.

Penne with Green and Gold Zucchini and Ricotta | SERVES 4 TO 6

Having approximately the same shapes, the pasta and zucchini mimic each other in this dish. Or if you have really small zucchini, you might cut them crosswise and pair them with orecchiette. Use the freshest ricotta you can get, preferably whole milk, so that it melts nicely into the pasta. You can also use a fresh goat cheese or a mixture of the two.

1 cup fresh ricotta, cow's milk or sheep's milk

2 pounds zucchini, mixed green and yellow

2 tablespoons olive oil

3 plump garlic cloves, chopped

3 tablespoons chopped marjoram or opal basil

sea salt and freshly ground pepper

1 pound penne

freshly grated Parmesan or Dry Monterey Jack cheese

1. Put water on for the pasta. Remove the ricotta from the refrigerator and spoon it onto a plate so that it will warm to room temperature. Slice the zucchini on the diagonal a scant ½ inch thick, then slice into strips so that each piece resembles the quill-shaped pasta.

2. Heat the oil in a wide skillet. Add the zucchini and sauté over medium-high heat until golden, about 5 minutes. Add the garlic and the marjoram, toss with the squash, and turn off the heat. Season well with salt and pepper.

3. When the water boils, add salt and the penne. Cook until al dente, then drain and add it to the zucchini. Toss, season with salt and pepper, then add the ricotta cheese in spoonfuls. Grate the cheese over the dish and serve.

Summer Squash and
Squash Blossom Risotto | SERVES 4

This risotto is a sunny, golden dish that uses masses of squash blossoms, golden squash, and yellow tomatoes. A number of different yellow tomatoes come to market, from the deep orange Sun Gold cherry tomatoes and the yellow-orange Italian paste tomatoes to Italian Golds and lemon-colored fruits. My choice would be the yellow-gold paste types or any thick-walled tomatoes, but try whatever is available to you.

THE TOMATOES

1 pound or more ripe yellow tomatoes
1 garlic clove, minced
2 tablespoons chopped marjoram
2 tablespoons chopped parsley
1 tablespoon olive oil
sea salt

THE RICE

1 pound bright yellow zucchini
5 to 6 cups Vegetable Stock, page 385
2 tablespoons unsalted butter
⅓ cup finely diced shallots
1½ cups Arborio rice
½ cup white wine
1 cup freshly grated Parmigiano-
 Reggiano
20 to 30 squash blossoms, slivered
sea salt and freshly ground pepper

1. Cut the tomato walls (sides) into small neat pieces and finely mince the cores. Put them in a bowl with the garlic, herbs, oil, and a few pinches of salt and set aside. Cut the zucchini into small dice, about twice as large as the grains of rice. Have the stock simmering on the stove.

2. Melt the butter in a wide pot. Add the shallots and squash and cook over medium-low heat, stirring occasionally, until the squash has begun to color, about 15 minutes.

3. Add the rice and stir to coat it with the butter. Pour in the wine and simmer until it's absorbed, then add ½ cup stock and simmer until it's absorbed. Keep adding stock in ½-cup increments until the rice is cooked, using 5 to 6 cups in all. Turn off the heat and stir in the tomatoes and cheese. Stir in the squash blossoms, taste for salt, and season with pepper.

VARIETY AT THE MARKET: A SELECT MARKET LIST
AUGUST IN SANTA FE

CUCUMBERS: Yamato cucumbers, Armenian, Lemon, pickling, cornichons, Painted Serpent

EGGPLANTS: Purple Rain, Rosita, Neon, Farmers Long, Purple Blush, Ichiban, Black Knight, Machiaw, Asian Bride, Rosa Bianca

HERBS: basil (Green Gem, Genovese, Thai, cinnamon, lemon, Osmonds Purple), lovage, marjoram, thyme, sage, lemon thyme

MELONS: native melon from Santa Domingo Pueblo, Charentais, Ogen, Canary, Jakes, Baby Dolls watermelons, Moon and Stars watermelons, Cavaillon

ONIONS: Red scallions, cipolline, giant sweet onions, leeks, shallots, eight kinds of garlic

POTATOES: Yukon Gold, Rose Fir Apple, German Buterballs, Red Rose, Red Dale, Russian Banana, fingerling, French Nosebags, Peruvian Blues, Caribe

SUMMER SQUASH: Embassy, Costata, white bush Lebanese zucchini, Sunburst pattypans, Cocozelle, Gold Bar, crooknecks, Tromboncino, *calabacitas,* Ronde de Nice

TOMATOES: Mercado Sweets (little reds), Lemon Boy, big beefsteaks, peach and persimmon tomatoes, Sun Golds, red and yellow-orange paste tomatoes, Black Krim, Carmello, Costoluto Genovese, and more

A BIRTHDAY LUNCH FOR A LEO

White Bean and Sage Fritters (page 131)

Chilled Sun Gold Soup with shallots and avocados
(page 179)

Chicken Braised in Red Wine Vinegar (page 377)

Slow-Cooked Thin-Sliced Summer Squash
Showered with Herbs (page 141)

Cornmeal Crêpes with Plums and Honey Ice Cream (page 294)

Strawberry–Passion Fruit Cream Cake (page 256)
(if you live in Los Angeles!)

Zucchini and Cilantro Soup with Chile and Mint | SERVES 6

July's sweet onions, shiny green zucchini, and big bunches of buttery-leafed cilantro, or fresh coriander, inspired this aromatic soup. A corn tortilla thickens it and gives it a briny, limed-corn taste. Serve chilled or warm.

1 poblano or 2 Anaheim chiles

3 zucchini, 10 to 12 ounces

1 bunch cilantro, about 2 cups in all

1 large fresh white or red onion

3 tablespoons sunflower seed or
    olive oil

3 tablespoons chopped parsley

2 tablespoons chopped mint

2 corn tortillas

sea salt

5 cups water or chicken stock

juice of 1 or 2 limes

sour cream, optional

1. Roast the chiles (see page 390), peel, and remove the seeds, then chop them coarsely. Quarter the zucchini lengthwise, then chop into ½-inch pieces. Wash the cilantro very thoroughly, including the stems. Finely slice the stems and chop the leaves, setting aside a few pretty branches for garnish. Thinly slice the onion.

2. Heat half the oil in a soup pot over medium-high heat, then add the onion, zucchini, cilantro stems, parsley, and mint. Cook, stirring occasionally, until the onion is limp and the zucchini is fairly soft, about 10 minutes. Tear one of the tortillas into pieces and add it to the vegetables.

3. Add 2 teaspoons salt and the water or stock and bring to a boil. Simmer, covered, until the zucchini is completely soft, about 15 minutes, then add the remaining cilantro. Let cool to room temperature, then puree until smooth. Season with salt and lime juice to taste.

4. Cut the remaining tortilla into skinny strips and heat the remaining oil in a skillet. When hot, add the tortillas and cook until crisp. Set them on paper towels to drain. Serve the soup garnished with a dollop of sour cream, a little mound of tortilla strips, and a sprig of the cilantro in each bowl.

CUCUMBERS

No matter where you live, market cucumbers are bound to be crunchy and sweet, their skins thin and free of wax. This means that you can eat the skins. But it also means that you shouldn't wait too long after buying cucumbers to fully enjoy their cool, watery nature. Without the wax they won't last as long, but then the season moves quickly and there will be more to buy at the next market.

At the farmers' market you'll undoubtedly find varieties you won't encounter elsewhere. There are the striped Painted Serpent cucumbers, for example, which twist and curve and are only an inch or so across. It's great fun to heap them in a tangle on a platter and put out a knife—a thoroughly edible arrangement. In contrast, there are the small round Lemon cucumbers, an heirloom variety with bright yellow skins that resemble lemons in size and shape as well. You can just cut them into wedges and add them to a salad plate. The pale green, grooved Armenian cucumbers are as pretty as flowers, for when sliced into rounds their scalloped edges are revealed. Smaller pickling cucumbers, including gherkins, invite home pickling.

Cucumbers can be prepared in many ways, but one of the nice things about cucumbers is that you don't really need to do much to enjoy them. A memorable lunch on a farm consisted, in part, of a plate of cucumbers from the garden, sliced and sprinkled with sea salt. They were so sweet and crisp I can still taste them. If that seems too plain, go ahead and add a fresh herb, maybe a spoonful of yogurt or sour cream. You can always include them on a platter salad or make them into a relish to flatter other foods.

Cucumber and Pepper Relish | MAKES ABOUT 3 CUPS

Like cucumbers, market peppers are free of wax. If you like the bite, include a teaspoon of minced hot chile. Spoon this relish over pulled string cheese, fresh cheese curds, or grilled fish.

1 or 2 (about ¾ pound) dark green
    cucumbers
1 small sweet pepper, any variety, very
    finely diced
3 scallions, including an inch of the greens,
    thinly sliced
2 tablespoons chopped dill
1 tablespoon chopped lovage or cilantro
1½ tablespoons rice wine vinegar
sea salt and freshly ground white pepper

Score the cucumbers with the tines of a fork or a citrus zester. Cut them lengthwise into quarters, slice off the seeds, then chop the flesh into small pieces. Toss with the remaining ingredients. Taste for salt and adjust the level of acidity if needed. Let stand for 30 minutes if time allows. Use within a day or two.

Cucumber Salad with Chile and Roasted Peanuts | SERVES 4 TO 6 AS AN APPETIZER

This could be the place to use those searing habanero chiles that you find in markets everywhere. I'll stick with serranos and jalapeños, but those who are inclined can go ahead and try the superhots.

1 long cucumber, English or Armenian
1 bunch scallions, including ½ inch of the
    greens
½ serrano chile, finely diced
grated zest and juice of 2 limes
1 tablespoon light soy sauce
1 tablespoon light brown sugar
4 teaspoons roasted peanut oil
⅓ cup roasted peanuts, chopped
6 mint leaves, slivered
6 Thai basil leaves

1. Peel the cucumber, halve it lengthwise, and cut it into long strips. Or remove long thin slices with a vegetable peeler. Thinly slice the scallions on the diagonal, making them long and thin. Combine the cucumbers, scallions, and chile in a bowl.
2. Combine the lime zest, juice, soy, sugar, and oil.
3. Toss the vegetables with the dressing, then add the peanuts and herbs and toss again.

Short-Term Cucumber-Onion Pickles | MAKES ABOUT 3 CUPS

Here's a great use for all the different cucumbers and onions that find their way into the farmers' market. And what a nice dish to have at the ready, for these sweet pickles keep for about 5 days in the refrigerator.

For vinegar, scout around your market and try what's locally made. Perhaps there's some lovely apple cider vinegar infused with herbs. Usually a lighter-style vinegar is desirable with cucumbers so that their delicate flavors aren't overwhelmed. Since vinegar dulls the herbs, you might refresh the pickles with a new sprig just before serving.

⅔ cup white wine or apple cider
   vinegar
⅓ cup sugar
pinch salt
2 shiny fresh red or white onions
2 cups thinly sliced cucumbers, peeled
   only if the skins are tough
a few lovage leaves, fennel greens, or
   dill sprigs
1 teaspoon mixed whole peppercorns
3 tablespoons olive oil

1. Mix the vinegar, sugar, and salt and set aside, stirring occasionally, until the sugar is dissolved.
2. Thinly slice the onions into rounds, then toss them with the cucumbers, herb, and peppercorns in a noncorrosive bowl.
3. Add the oil to the vinegar, stir well, then pour over the vegetables. Toss well, then cover and refrigerate. It's best if the pickles can sit for a day before being used.

Winter Squash Risotto with Seared Radicchio | SERVES 4

Blue Hubbard squash is rich and meaty. It's one you'll do well with here, but also consider Buttercup, Hokkaido, Queensland Blue, and any other smallish squat green-skinned varieties. Many of these heirloom varieties have dense, dark yellow flesh with deep flavor and creamy texture. Butternut, as always, works well, too. In any case, you need only a cup of cooked squash to season this risotto. (To bake winter squash, see page 151.)

Pumpkin seed oil—certainly optional if you can't find it—is dark green and redolent of pumpkin, an appropriate and beautiful garnish that picks up the flavor of the squash.

6 cups Vegetable Stock, page 385, or
    chicken stock

1 cup cooked winter squash

1 head radicchio, cut into wedges 1 to
    2 inches wide

olive oil

sea salt and freshly ground pepper

balsamic vinegar

3 tablespoons unsalted butter

1 yellow onion, finely diced

1½ cups Arborio rice

1 cup freshly grated Parmigiano-
    Reggiano

2 teaspoons pumpkin seed oil,
    if available

1. If you're making a vegetable stock, begin it first. Be sure to use any seeds from the winter squash.

2. Mash the cooked squash with a fork to smooth the flesh. Brush the radicchio generously with olive oil and season with salt and pepper. Heat a skillet, add the radicchio, and cook on both sides until wilted and brown, about 5 minutes per side. Douse lightly with the vinegar, then transfer to a cutting board and chop coarsely.

3. When you're ready to begin cooking the risotto, have the stock simmering on a burner. Melt the butter in a wide soup pot. Add the onion and cook over medium heat until wilted and lightly colored but not browned, about 5 minutes. Add the rice, stir to coat, and cook for 1 minute. Turn the heat to high, add 2 cups of the simmering stock, and cook at a lively boil, stirring just a few times. When the first batch is fully absorbed, begin adding stock ½ cup at a time, stirring constantly. Once you've used 4 cups in all, stir the squash into the rice. Continue cooking, stirring, and adding liquid until the rice is tender, but still a little resistant, and the sauce is creamy.

4. When the rice is done, add the radicchio. Cook for a minute more to heat the radicchio, then turn off the heat and stir in the cheese. Taste for salt, season with pepper, and divide among heated plates. Season with pepper and drizzle a little of the dark-green pumpkin oil into each dish.

These vegetables are real characters with big and in some cases unforgettable personalities. They're a fascinating brotherhood, especially some of the heirloom varieties, such as three-lobed blue-gray Triamble or the heavily warted Hubbards. Deep-orange *Rouge Vif d'Etampes* is the classic Cinderella pumpkin, with deeply ridged sections and a flattened coachlike shape. Although described as decorative, and it certainly is that, it's also fine eating, far better than most pumpkins in fact.

Variations among winter squashes have to do with color, texture (from superfine to stringy), and degree of sweetness. Golden Hubbard has dryish, pale flesh, not entirely dissimilar to pale-skinned sweet potatoes, while other winter squashes have deeper orange, moister, and sweeter flesh, such as Perfection. Other differences have to do with kitchen issues, such as how tough the skins are (Hubbards are notoriously hard), the possibility of peeling them (few), and so forth.

Despite the fact that this group is highly varied and interesting, we often turn to the trusty butternut, perhaps the most serviceable winter squash of all. Its smooth skin makes it easy to peel, the flesh is always creamy, and its flavor is rich. But even with the butternut, there's more than one kind. Some have long curved necks and a small, bulbous base. Others are almost straight from top to bottom. One farmer at Atlanta's Morningside market had grown a gorgeous butternut type with seeds he had collected in Africa. It had an ex-

ceedingly long neck (a very practical feature) and skin that was richly hued with golds and browns. The flesh was a brilliant deep-orange color. My brother cultivated the seeds I sent him but reported that no one would buy the squash at market. They were just a little too unfamiliar. We're not always easily persuaded to be adventurous, it turns out. It's easier, it seems, to try something unfamiliar in a restaurant, where someone else has figured out for us exactly what to do with it.

another or more or less stringy than thought. All of a sudden people are trying new varieties that may well become new favorites. If your market hosts demonstrations, try to arrange for a tasting. If you're curious about winter squashes, probably others are, too.

Except for the smooth-skinned butternut and Delicatas, winter squashes are hard to peel. Sometimes the easiest way to get to the flesh under those convoluted exteriors is to bake the squash first.

Preheat the oven to 375°F or whatever temperature is convenient if you're using the oven for something else. Cut the squash in half, scoop out the seeds and strings, brush the cut surface with oil, and place cut side down on a sheet pan. Bake until very soft when pressed with a finger, about 40 minutes, though the time depends on the size. Now you'll be able to scoop out the tender cooked centers.

Of course cutting the squash in half can be quite a challenge in itself. There have been moments when I wished someone made a kitchen chainsaw for this very purpose. I once had a giant Blue Hubbard that was so hard that I had to bake it whole until the skin softened, then cut it in half. But mostly, a cleaver and a mallet, or a big chef's knife, will do the job.

Early in the season, when the squash is still a little green, it may exude a lot of liquid when baked. It's quite sweet, and if you leave the squash on the pan for 15 minutes or so, it will probably reabsorb it. If not, you can add it to whatever dish you're making.

Accountably, one of the most popular demonstrations at our market came about when a few of us cooked up every variety of winter squash available and offered tastes. Shoppers were glad to have a chance to taste them side by side without having to go through the baking exercise themselves. A taste, it turns out, is worth any amount of words. A spoonful goes into the mouth and someone says, "Oh! *That's* what that is! I always wondered how that tasted." Or a shopper might discover that one squash is sweeter than

Winter Squash Braised in Pear or Apple Cider | SERVES 6

Winter squash, apples, and pears arrive earlier than you might guess. Summer apples, or Transparents, begin in July, and the first winter squash are often here by August. However, we scarcely notice them until the fall weather has cooled everything down enough to make them seem appealing. It's then that we might remember that squash and apples make a comfortable pairing, especially with a robust herb like rosemary, which unifies the sweet and savory notes of both parties.

Apple and pear ciders from the market are likely to be excellent, for fruit growers take great pride in making their own cider blends. Butternut and Delicata squash will be the easiest varieties to use for this dish because they're so easy to peel. You can also make this dish using sweet potatoes, the starchy Japanese varieties, or the sweeter, moister Jewel and Garnet types.

2 pounds Delicata or butternut
    squash
2 tablespoons unsalted butter
2 tablespoons finely chopped
    rosemary
2 cups fresh unfiltered apple or pear
    cider
sea salt and freshly ground pepper
apple-balsamic or organic apple
    cider vinegar, to taste

1. Peel the squash, then dice it into ½-inch cubes or even smaller pieces. If using Delicata, remove the seeds with a long spoon, then slice it into rounds.
2. Melt the butter in a wide skillet and add the rosemary. Cook over medium heat to flavor the butter. After 3 minutes, add the squash and cider plus water to cover. Bring to a boil, add ½ teaspoon salt, and simmer until the squash is tender, 20 to 25 minutes, by which time the juice will have reduced enough to provide a glaze for the squash. If not, raise the heat to reduce it quickly. Sprinkle on a teaspoon of vinegar and taste for salt. Add additional vinegar if you need to balance the sweetness, then season with pepper.

Kent Whealy, with his wife Dianne, founded the Seed Savers Exchange in 1975. Kent does a lot of public speaking on behalf of genetic diversity, and his talks fill his audiences with awe, inspiration, and an appreciation for what biological diversity in the plant world looks like.

There are a lot of slides in Kent's presentation, breathtaking portraits of the heirloom members of botanical families. Kent has seen his slides hundreds of times, but he still responds to them with enthusiasm. "Isn't this just gorgeous!" he'll say more than once during a presentation, as if he's seeing an image for the first time. The audience agrees with collective gasps of astonishment, but there's a reason for the beauty. "Most people fail to see genetic erosion as a threat," Kent says, "so you have to show people the beauty of diversity." *Gorgeous* is one word you walk away with. *Diversity* is the other. Perhaps this is nature's trick to get us to take care of our world, or our environment.

As the slides come up on the screen, Kent gives some numbers. You see 10 beautiful beans, and he mentions that there are 3,600 known varieties. He shows a slide of an unusual golden snow pea. "There are 950 varieties of peas," he says. A stunning salad that comprises 20 more types of tomatoes becomes a tease when he mentions that there are at least 4,000 known varieties. Watermelons? There are 125 kinds. Six hundred squash, 175 sunflowers, 650 potatoes, and 220 garlics. And these are not modern hybrids, but varieties that, when their seeds are planted, come true to form. They don't revert to something else. These are the foundations of the vegetable world. "These are the sparks of life that feed us all" is how Kent puts it.

One slide that seems to be everyone's favorite is of an old wooden wagon that tilts forward. From its bed flows an immense river of winter squash that spills to the ground and flows over the grass. In this river is every color, size, shape, and marking that can be imagined—and many that can't. It is a picture of sheer exuberance, of the great diversity of life. *Wows* pass through the audience, and you can feel the excitement in the room. Then, with perfect timing, Kent says, "*This* is your true heritage." And there is silence. It is very humbling to see the vastness of life's

gifts and to realize how very little we know about them, how little we've actually experienced them. We think we know variety when we see five kinds of apples in the supermarket, but there are eight hundred known varieties of apples (all growing at the Seed Savers Exchange Heritage Farm)—and that number is a fraction of what has already been lost.

A shopper in the Portland, Oregon, farmers' market says, "This is where you go to get an heirloom variety that's special." Indeed heirloom varieties seem to be of special interest to many of the farmers who grow for farmers' markets because they can grow for reasons that agribusiness farmers can't. These wonderful-looking and -tasting fruits and vegetables don't necessarily ship well, produce in a uniform way, or keep for months on end in cold storage. But they have other virtues, taste being but one, and their seeming fragility is overcome when they are enjoyed locally.

Each heirloom vegetable, fruit, and flower has a story: where it was found, who brought it to America, how long it's been grown, who carried it in his or her catalog, which seed bank it was found in. Many of these plants are descended from seeds that were brought by immigrants, starting with the first settlers and continuing up to the present as new Asian and Latin immigrants arrive, bringing with them seeds from their homelands. Other heirlooms come from seeds that have been grown traditionally by Native Americans and the Mennonite and Amish communities. These plants are part of our heritage as Americans. Quite literally the ingredients for our big national stew, they feed our imaginations, describe our histories, and tell the stories of our changing geographic and climatic circumstances. But for heirlooms (species of turkeys, cattle, and other animals are also considered heirlooms, incidentally) to be a viable part of our culture, they must be grown, eaten, and known as food as well as protected and saved. At the farmers' market, we are very likely to have a chance to participate in keeping diversity alive. Try the heirlooms you find there and become a living part of genetic diversity.

(The Seed Savers' Heritage Farm is open to the public during the summer. See www.seedsavers.org.)

Spaghetti Squash Gratin with Chanterelles | SERVES 6

The chanterelles were at the Bellingham, Washington, farmers' market on Columbus Day. My farmer friends had spaghetti squash in their garden, so we put them together for dinner. I wouldn't have thought so, but they made a wonderful dish and one that's incredibly easy to prepare. As always, foods in season together taste good together.

1 large spaghetti squash, about
    3 pounds
1 pound chanterelles
5 tablespoons unsalted butter
sea salt and freshly ground pepper
2 garlic cloves, chopped
1 cup half-and-half or cream
freshly grated Parmesan cheese

1. Lightly butter a shallow baking dish and preheat the oven to 375°F. Poke a few holes in the squash and bake until it's browned and soft, about 1½ hours.

2. While the squash is baking, clean the chanterelles with a brush. (Avoid washing them if possible—they drink up water like a sponge.) Slice or dice them into small pieces. Melt half the butter in a skillet. When foamy, add the chanterelles and cook over medium heat until tender, 10 to 15 minutes. Season with salt and pepper, add the garlic and half-and-half, and simmer gently until the half-and-half and mushroom juices are reduced by about a third, about 10 minutes.

3. When the squash is done, cut it in two and scoop out the seeds. Now pull away the flesh with a fork, heaping it into spaghettilike strands. Toss with the remaining butter and season with salt and pepper. Spread the squash in the baking dish, spoon the chanterelles and half-and-half over it, and cover lightly with cheese. Return to the oven until heated through and the top is crisped and browned in places, 15 to 20 minutes.

Winter Squash "Pancake" with Mozzarella and Sage | MAKES APPROXIMATELY 3 CUPS, SERVING 3 TO 6

With a bowl of leftover roasted butternut squash, a ball of fresh mozzarella, and half a bunch of sage leaves, this dish was inevitable. Sage is a natural with winter squash. If you have any Sage Oil, you can use it to cook the "pancake." Adding the sage leaves is optional in this case.

1 butternut, Buttercup, or Blue
    Hubbard squash, 2 to 3 pounds
sea salt and freshly ground pepper
3 tablespoons unsalted butter or
    Sage Oil, page 61
10 large sage leaves
1 (4-ounce) ball fresh or smoked
    mozzarella
3 tablespoons parsley leaves
1 garlic clove

1. Bake the squash as described on page 151. Scoop out the flesh and beat it with a fork to smooth it out. Season it with a little salt to taste.

2. Melt the butter or heat the oil in a medium nonstick skillet. Add the sage leaves and cook over medium heat for a minute or two to flavor the butter. Leaving the leaves in the pan, add the squash and smooth it out. Cook for 15 minutes, then give it a stir, scraping up the browned undersides and pressing a new layer to the bottom of the pan. Continue in this manner as long as you have time for. The more it browns, the better it will be.

3. While the squash is browning, thinly slice the cheese and chop the parsley and garlic together. Just before serving, pat the squash evenly in the pan once more, lay the cheese over the top, then cover and cook for a few minutes longer for the cheese to soften. Remove the lid, add the parsley-garlic mixture, drizzle on a little more Sage Oil, if using, and serve right from the pan.

The sun is shining, kites are flying, the bay is blue, there are boats on it, and I can't imagine why on earth I ever left San Francisco. California has it all.

At the Ferry Plaza Market the seasons are mixed as befits October markets most everywhere. Thanks to the erratic Bay Area weather, today is a good day to shop for heirloom tomatoes and Italian zucchini. But as tomorrow could be foggy, you're completely justified in thinking of pasta with shell beans, braised leeks, and a baroque platter of fall fruits and nuts.

This is a splendid market in every way, but best of all, I see farmers I've known for years. A farmer from my hometown is there. There's Al Courchesne of Frog Hollow Farm, whose peaches are so exceptionally good that I can recognize them before I recognize him. And there are farmers from my former residence, Green Gulch Farm, with their pretty fingerling potatoes and fog-happy lettuces. I see other familiar faces as well, so I can anticipate the special joy of preparing a meal where everything in it has been grown by someone I know.

Some standouts at this market are the spectacular Dutch leeks called Pancho with shanks about 1½ feet long. The most efficient leek I've ever seen, it could have been bred for the airlines—if they used rounds of leeks—they're so long and so even. There is the primitive-looking Chinese pear, a Yali, and Chinese dates, or jujubes. Bunches of herbs are so large that they beg to be crushed and inhaled. An industrious shopper might come home with Black Angelina plums, cape gooseberries, French butter pears; fresh Bahri dates on their stems as well as dried Medjools, muscat grapes and white nectarines, pomegranates, persimmons, figs, quince, raspberries, and new-crop almonds and walnuts. This is a market that truly inspires the cook!

And there are lots of big French pumpkins, *Rouge Vif d'Etampes*. At Greens I used to fill these with cream, bread, and Gruyère cheese, bake them, and then serve a whole pumpkin to each table. It was quite a challenge to time everything right so that none would split in the oven and spill. It's much easier to do this at home, where you're cooking just one at a time. Give this a try when you need a culinary adventure some weekend. The beauty of winter squash and pumpkins is that you can enjoy keeping them around the house until the perfect moment presents itself.

SOME MARKET-INSPIRED DISHES

Leek, Scallion, and Fennel Gratin (page 72)

Sautéed Artichokes and Potatoes with Garlic Chives (page 39)

Shelly Beans with Pasta and Sage (page 128)

Quince and Goat Cheese Tart (page 322)

Raspberry Cream Tart (page 259)

A baroque fruit platter of Chinese pears, Fuyu persimmons, Medjool dates, fresh dates, Muscat grapes, white peaches, raspberries, and black plums

Butternut Squash Rounds with Dates and Pistachios | SERVES 4 TO 6 AS A SIDE DISH

This Persian-inspired dish was further inspired by the offerings of a southern California market. Choose a butternut squash with a long straight neck (or several Delicatas peeled and sliced crosswise) and you'll have the perfect rounds in no time. They're fried slowly in olive oil until caramelized, then baked with a sweet-and-sour mixture of dates, almonds, pistachios, citrus, and mint.

1 large butternut squash, about 3 pounds

3 tablespoons olive oil

sea salt and freshly ground pepper

2 tablespoons unsalted butter

2 shallots, finely diced, about ⅓ cup

2 garlic cloves, minced

⅓ cup slivered almonds

⅓ cup peeled pistachios, preferably unsalted, slivered or chopped

1 tablespoon grated zest from 1 Meyer lemon or orange

6 Medjool or Deglet Noor dates, pitted and chopped

2 tablespoons finely chopped parsley

1 tablespoon chopped mint

¼ teaspoon ground cinnamon

juice of 1 Meyer lemon or 1 Persian lemon

1. Preheat the oven to 400°F. Lightly butter a large baking dish. Peel the neck of the squash and slice into rounds about ⅓ inch thick. Heat the oil in a wide nonstick skillet. Add the squash in a single layer and cook over medium heat until golden, then turn and brown the second side, 8 to 10 minutes per side. When the pan becomes dry, add ⅓ cup water. Cover the pan and steam the squash until tender when pierced with a knife, about 10 minutes. Check while it's cooking and add more water as needed. Season with salt and pepper.

2. Melt the butter in a medium skillet over medium-low heat. Add the shallots and garlic and cook without browning, stirring occasionally, for 5 to 7 minutes.

3. Add the nuts, zest, dates, herbs, and cinnamon and raise the heat. Season with ½ teaspoon salt and some pepper. Cook, stirring frequently, for 2 minutes, then add the lemon juice, cook for 1 minute more, and turn off the heat.

4. Arrange the squash rounds in the baking dish and scatter the dates and nuts over them. Add ¼ cup water and bake until heated through and the topping is barely crisped, about 15 minutes.

Cinderella Pumpkin Soup Baked in the Pumpkin | SERVES A CROWD FOR THANKSGIVING

I don't know why this should be the case, but this soup just tastes more like pumpkin than you ever thought imaginable. My friend Krista put it this way: "It's as if you went out into the field, opened a pumpkin, and just bit into it!" It's more civilized than that, of course, but you get the idea—this is the essence of pumpkin realized in your kitchen.

Start with one of those French Cinderella pumpkins, *Rouge Vif d'Etampes.* They're big and orange and sort of flat, with nice bulging sides. Cut a lid off the top, scoop out the seeds and fibers, then rub the inside with sea salt. Set the pumpkin in a big ovenproof dish, such as a large Mexican *cazuela,* or a roasting pan. You don't want to take any chances with it collapsing over your oven.

For a 5-pound pumpkin you'll need approximately 2 quarts whole milk, half-and-half, cream, or a mixture. Heat it with 15 large fresh sage leaves, 2 teaspoons sea salt, some freshly milled pepper, and 3 plump garlic cloves, slivered. Pour the hot liquid into the pumpkin, lay a piece of foil over the top, and set the lid on that. (Otherwise it's likely to fall into the pumpkin.)

Put the whole thing in the oven, the temperature set at 375°F. Cook for about 2 hours or until the pumpkin feels soft when you press your finger against its side. Remove it from the oven, set the lid aside, and carefully begin drawing the cooked flesh into the hot liquid. If all goes well, meaning the flesh is smooth and creamy and the sides don't fall in, you can bring the whole thing to the table just like this. If the flesh is stringy (my latest pumpkin was this way) or the sides have caved in, just scoop everything—the liquid and flesh—into a bowl or blender, then puree. Taste for salt. Stir in a handful or two of Gruyère cheese and garnish with a little chopped Italian parsley.

If you want to play it very safe, use 2 pumpkins. Use one pumpkin to make the soup—in a pot, not the pumpkin itself. Hollow the other to use as a container. You can bake it a bit first, if you like, or just use it as a tureen, uncooked.

MELONS

Melons reside at the sweet end of the cucurbit spectrum. As with the tender-skinned summer squash and harder-skinned winter varieties, there are lots of melons besides cantaloupes and honeydews to choose from. Not that there's anything wrong with these! Like most fruits, even the most common melon can be exquisite when grown well and picked ripe. And certain areas in the country are known for their good cantaloupes. Rocky Fords from Colorado are one example; melons from Pecos, Texas, another.

However, French melons, such as the Charentais, at last are starting to be grown in this country. An extremely delicious melon that's highly prized in France, it has a pale, almost bluish gray skin, dark green stripes (or *sutures,* as they're called), and luscious orange flesh that rivals the best of peaches. Small, they're ideal for one or two people to enjoy.

There are several green-fleshed melons with tropical flavors that rival the mango. An Israeli melon called Galia is perhaps the best known, but the most fragrant may be one called Passport. Both have pale green flesh and an intense, tropical perfume. When I walked past a bin of Passports at a Minnesota market, I was stopped in my path. I couldn't imagine what tropical fruit was growing here! There are other green-fleshed melons that are not among the tropical-scented types but are good to eat, such as the heirloom Jenny Lind.

You're also likely to find Spanish melons at the market, such as Canary, and even crisp but sweet-fleshed Asian melons. I've occasionally encountered Native American melons that taste like a cross between a cucumber and a melon, as if they can't make up their mind what they are. They're ideal for making *agua frescas,* because they aren't at all cloying.

Watermelons can now be found in a great profusion of colors and sizes, partially as a result of heirloom seeds being grown out. The classic Rattlesnake type, so called because of its pattern of stripes, is mostly a southern type of melon, but there are quite a few that come from northern climes, too. Some seeds come from as far north as Russia, such as the yellow-fleshed Sweet Siberian or, closer to home, Cream of Saskatchewan, a small (for a watermelon) pale green variety. Certainly, smaller melons are much easier for customers to carry to their cars and store once they're home. But it always seems that at least once during the summer you're going to want a great big old-fashioned red-fleshed watermelon for a party. There's just nothing like it.

Melon Salad with Thai Basil | SERVES 6 TO 8

Santa Fe chef Peter Zimmer demonstrated a rather complex fall salad at the market one Saturday, at the heart of which was a variety of melons—Charentais, honeydew, Persians, cantaloupes—all finely diced and dressed with a salsa of Thai basil, cilantro, and mint. There were several more parts to his dish, but I loved the melon by itself. Here it's featured, cut larger, and set on pungent greens. Keep this in mind especially when you have several melons open at once.

1 large shallot, finely diced

juice and zest of 2 limes

sea salt and freshly ground pepper

1 cup cilantro leaves

⅓ cup Thai basil leaves

¼ cup mint leaves

1 jalapeño chile, finely diced

1 teaspoon minced ginger

1 small garlic clove, minced

1 tablespoon nut oil or olive oil

1½ to 2 pounds melon, chilled

1 bunch arugula or watercress

1. Put the shallot in a bowl with the lime juice, zest, and ¼ teaspoon salt. Finely chop the herbs and add them to the bowl along with the chile, ginger, garlic, and oil. Stir and taste for salt.

2. Halve the melon, remove the seeds, and cut into wedges. Slice off the skins, then cut the melon diagonally into bite-sized pieces or into very small cubes, as you prefer.

3. Pour the dressing over the melon and toss well. Season with pepper. Arrange the greens on small plates and spoon the melon into the center. If the melons are extra-sweet, add an extra lime wedge to each plate. Garnish with the purple-tipped Thai basil leaves.

Melon in
Moscato d'Asti

Although you can do things with and to melons—make them into drinks or sherbets, float them in syrups—
I'm generally happy doing nothing to them. They're so intensely sweet that lime, black pepper, chile, salty
cheeses, and prosciutto are more to my liking for accompaniments. However, covering sliced melons with a
froth of sparkling *moscato d'Asti* easily transforms melons into a light and festive dessert. While port is traditional with certain muskmelons, such as the Charentais or Cavaillon, it has always seemed a bit heavy to me,
especially since melon weather is usually hot weather. The Muscat is much more flowery, like melons themselves, plus the bubbles aerate all that flavor too, making it more effervescent. But a nonsparkling Muscat wine,
a chilled Beaumes de Venise, is also delicious with melon, especially Charentais.

Choose a single melon, one that's ripe and full of
fragrance, or several kinds. Remove the seeds and
cut the flesh into attractive bite-sized pieces. Put
them in a compote dish and chill. When it's time
for dessert, uncork a bottle of *moscato d'Asti* and
pour it over the melon. Serve in fruit bowls. Alternatively, you can serve the diced melon in wineglasses, then add the *moscato* and serve.

Melon and Cucumber Agua Fresca | SERVES 6 TO 8

Dual purposes are served here: The first is to make a drink that is greenly cool and refreshing; the other is to use up that extra melon you just couldn't get to. Adding the cucumber diminishes the sweetness of the melons. A few times I've run across native melons from the Santa Domingo Pueblo that are already a nice balance of melon and cucumber. Given their close botanical relationship, it's not surprising that this blending of flavors should occur.

Agua frescas are always best drunk the day they're made.

4 cups honeydew or other melon,
    cut into chunks
1 medium cucumber, peeled and
    chopped
Simple Syrup, page 388
zest and juice of 1 or 2 limes
handful mint leaves, lemon
    verbena, or pineapple sage
2 cups spring or mineral water
for garnish: sprigs of mint, lemon
    verbena, salad burnet, or borage
    flowers

Puree the melon and cucumber in a blender or food processor just enough to break them up without letting them get too foamy. Pour the juice into a large pitcher; add the syrup to taste, lime zest and juice, and herbs. Chill well. Stir in the spring water and serve over ice. Garnish with any of the herbs or borage flowers. Both salad burnet and borage have overtones of cucumber.

Tropical Melon Soup
with Coconut Milk | MAKES 1 QUART, SERVING 4 TO 6

Here's the recipe especially for Passport, Galia, or Ogen melons, those scented varieties that Johnny's seed catalog describes as having "A taste of the tropics." These melons go especially well with the coconut milk, lime, and Thai basil, but you can certainly try other types, such as cantaloupes or a really ripe, sweet honeydew type.

3 pounds Galia melon (see headnote)

1 (15-ounce) can coconut milk

grated zest and juice of 1 large lime

1 serrano chile, minced, or 1 jalapeño, seeded and diced

1 teaspoon grated ginger

1 tablespoon chopped Thai basil

1 tablespoon chopped mint

¼ teaspoon sea salt

small basil or mint leaves for garnish

1. Halve the melon, scoop out the seeds, and cut into 3-inch sections. Set 1 section aside. Slice the skin away from the flesh and puree the flesh.

2. Add the rest of the ingredients to the melon puree. Dice the reserved section into small pieces and add them to the soup. Chill well. Serve garnished with little sprigs of the basil or mint leaves.

Watermelon
Agua Fresca | MAKES ABOUT 1 QUART

Watermelon makes a delicious pink, green, or yellow drink, depending on the type of melon used, that attracts a number of appealing additions, such as blackberries or wild strawberries, lime juice, and orange flower water. A splash of tequila is another option.

3 pounds watermelon, with rind

½ cup Simple Syrup, page 388, if needed

2 large limes

pinch salt

1 tablespoon orange flower water

1. Remove the skin, scrape away the seeds, chop the melon into chunks, and puree in a blender or food processor. Taste and sweeten with the syrup if needed.

2. Remove 4 lime slices for garnish and squeeze the rest into the puree. Add the salt and orange flower water to taste and stir. Pour the juice over ice and garnish each glass with a slice of lime.

One of the surest signs that the Santa Fe farmers' market is in full gear is the presence of Jake West and his trailer of melons. Jake is one of the last farmers to arrive at the market after a four-hour drive. Until he pulls into his spot, the most commonly asked question for the market manager is "Is Jake coming today?"

People can't wait to eat his melons. His corn is great too, but it's the melons that have everyone buzzing around his truck. He has watermelons, casabas, Canaries, Persians, honeydews, and one he claims comes from a seed he found washed downriver. "Jakes," as these are called, are the collective favorite. I never think I care much for watermelon until Jake thrusts a piece into my hands. I slurp it up, and it's so good that I take one home too. As the crowd collects around him, a lot of women get not only melons but also one of Jake's big, warm hugs. A farmer who's visiting from Texas assures me that those wonderful hugs are merely good salesmanship. I'm guessing that he knows from his own experience, and his wife confirms that this is so. But we don't care.

Jake, his wife, some of his sons and grandsons stand in the trailer, choosing melons to fit their customers' needs. They pass a small Ogen melon to a small lady who will eat it over the next few days. A hefty watermelon is tossed to one of the security guards who's squeezing in a moment of shopping. Here's a melon that will be ready in two days for one customer and a riper one for someone who needs one for a dinner party this evening. The whole family is knowledgeable and accommodating.

Jake doesn't need signs or labels or enticing displays to sell his melons. Everyone knows they're great. Even visitors from out of town go to the market especially for them. I recently found an old photograph of the market taken from above. What stood out most was a huge mass of people swarming six or more deep around Jake's truck.

"These melons put us five boys through college," one of his sons brags to me. He says it a bit defensively, as if he's responding to some insult directed toward farmers at large. But Jake and his boys are proud of their farming, as well they should be. Not only do they succeed at it; they grow something so good that a portion of our diverse community is briefly united each year in its enthusiasm for melons. Even though the sons all have careers of their own now, they often show up at market with their own kids to help their dad and their mother sell. Recently, Mrs. West has added ostrich meat and eggs to their wares. When you see the giant eggs, it doesn't seem so surprising. They just look like more melons.

A SUMMER PICNIC

Radishes with their greens

Tomato Juice Sipped Through a Lovage Straw (page 175)

Cold Roast Chicken with Herbs Under the Skin (page 79)

or

Savory Goat Cheese Tart with Leeks (page 245)

Short-Term Cucumber-Onion Pickles (page 148)

Melon in Moscato d'Asti (page 162)

The Vegetable Fruits of Summer: Eggplants, Tomatoes, and Peppers

Shoppers at markets everywhere spend a good part of their time wondering when the eggplants, tomatoes, and peppers will be here and hoping it will be soon. These shiny, sexy nightshades are synonymous with summer itself, proof that it exists. And the window for them is so small that we don't want to miss even a week of their presence.

Over the years I've gradually ceased buying eggplants out of season; cold storage seems to make them bitter. I don't want wax on my peppers, nor do I want to pay $5 a pound—or more—for peppers that have traveled thousands of miles from Holland. This just isn't necessary. And when it comes to tomatoes—well, everyone knows that a good tomato requires the kind of care and conditions that supermarkets can't manage. So I wait. Eventually there will be an overwhelming selection of truly great tomatoes, peppers of all sorts, all without wax, and sweet eggplants that never need salting.

I suspect that the diversity at any farmers' market expresses itself most with the nightshades. There is just so much variety, and they're all so pretty. I can't imagine a shopper—or a farmer—who isn't seduced by this alluring group.

Crostini with Roasted Eggplant and Pine Nut Puree | MAKES 1 CUP PUREE

If you have a chance, make this puree using the pale green or white eggplants or the violet Rosa Bianca—all of which are delicate and sweet. You can make it all in a large mortar or a food processor.

1 pound eggplant or a little more
olive oil
⅓ cup pine nuts or walnuts
1 garlic clove
sea salt and freshly ground pepper
fresh lemon juice
1 tablespoon chopped mint
2 tablespoons chopped parsley
2 tablespoons chopped opal basil,
    plus basil leaves for garnish
12 slices toasted baguette or crackers

1. Preheat the broiler. Peel the eggplant and slice it into rounds about ½ inch thick. Brush both sides of each slice lightly with oil, set on a sheet pan, and broil about 6 inches from the heat until golden, 12 to 15 minutes. Turn and brown on the other side. When done, stack the eggplant slices so that they'll steam and finishing cooking. Toast the pine nuts in a dry skillet over low heat until golden. (If using walnuts, toast them in a 350°F oven for 7 to 10 minutes, until fragrant.)

2. Pound the garlic and pine nuts with ½ teaspoon salt until smooth. Coarsely chop the eggplant, then work it into a somewhat rough puree with the pestle or in a food processor. Add a little lemon juice to sharpen the flavors, taste for salt, season with pepper, and stir in the herbs. Spread the puree on the toasted bread or crackers, garnish with a basil leaf, and pass around as an appetizer.

Savory Eggplant "Jam" with Cumin and Coriander | MAKES ABOUT 1½ CUPS

Unlike the preceding dish, this one is dark and robust, flecked with purple from strips of skin. Although summer eggplant is seldom bitter, I salt it anyway and let it sweat for an hour or more so that it won't absorb as much oil as it might otherwise. Serve with crackers or pita bread.

1 pound eggplant, purple or white, slender or round

sea salt and freshly ground pepper

2 tablespoons olive oil

1 large garlic clove, pressed

½ teaspoon ground cumin

½ teaspoon ground coriander

2 tablespoons finely chopped cilantro

juice of ½ small lemon

lemon wedges, tomato wedges, and olives, to finish

1. Remove wide ribbons of the eggplant skin, leaving vertical bands of skin. Slice the eggplant into ½-inch rounds, salt generously, and set on a plate for an hour, or longer if time allows. Rinse, then squeeze the eggplant dry in a towel. (If you're using white eggplant, peel all of it, because the skins tend to be tough.)

2. Heat the oil in a large nonstick skillet. Add the eggplant and cook over medium-high heat, turning occasionally, until well browned on both sides, about 15 minutes. Add the garlic, about ½ cup water, the cumin, and coriander, reduce the heat, and mash the eggplant with a fork until it's broken into a jamlike consistency. This can take 15 to 30 minutes, depending on the eggplant. Add more water as it cooks, to help it break down. You can let the excess cook off when the eggplant is finally soft. Add the cilantro and lemon juice. Taste for salt and season with pepper. Mound in a shallow bowl and serve warm or at room temperature, plain or garnished with lemon wedges, tomato wedges, and olives.

SHORTS AND EGGPLANTS:
A COOK'S GUIDE

It's usually not until August that eggplants appear at our market. When they finally do arrive, there's a stunning number of varieties to choose from, as if to make up for the shortness of the season. We see, for example, scarlet Rosita and dark pink Neon, orange Thai eggplants, pure white Casper, the skinny lavender Farmers' Longs, pretty Rosa Biancas that look like evening purses, Purple Rain (royal purple splashed with white), short finger-size Japanese and Italian varieties, and a new pale green Thai eggplant called Thai Green. Some are hybrids; others are heirloom varieties. All of them are beautiful enough that I end up buying some to put on the table just to look at and some more to cook. The most truly unusual eggplants I saw at any market were those in St. Paul. Grown by Hmong farmers, these were small, round vegetable fruits with purple and yellow colorations, a bit like a bruise or an evening sky after a rainstorm. The Hmong farmers also had tiny little green eggplants that looked a lot like a bract of unripe currant tomatoes, each fruit no larger than my pinky fingernail, called *kitelee*. They are, apparently, popular with the many Somalians who live in the Twin Cities area.

At most markets you will probably find a shiny Black Beauty, the heirloom parent of the supermarket eggplant, only it will be inconceivably better than any eggplant you have bought at the supermarket. The best thing about truly fresh eggplants that haven't been subjected to cold temperatures and long-term storage is that they aren't bitter. Therefore, they don't need salting, although you can salt if you want to. Salting does keep them from absorbing so much oil when fried.

I often teach dishes based on eggplant in classes during the summer, and three things always happen. The first is that people say that they never liked eggplant before but that this is different—they love it! The second thing is they ask if they can freeze it. And third, they ask what kind of eggplant they should use in December if they want to make this for Christmas. They understand with their tongues that *now* they like something they never liked before, but it's harder to grasp *why* it's now and not later that this dish is so good. Gradually they figure out that it's eating food in its true season that indeed makes the difference. Freshly picked summer eggplant is the only eggplant to eat. Make it as seasonal as shorts and you'll find every eggplant dish you make is delectable.

PICNIC MENU
FOR A DRIVE TO THE MOUNTAINS

Good bread from the market and market cheeses

An Eggplant Gratin (page 171)

Roasted Peppers and Tomatoes Baked with
Herbs and Capers (page 194)

Plum Kuchen (page 297)

An Eggplant Gratin | SERVES 6

This dish is adaptable. Like a frittata, this pudding-gratin is good warm from the oven or at room temperature. It can be set up in advance, and it can be reheated. When it comes to its place in the meal, you can serve it as a side dish or as a meatless main course. Leftovers, should there be any, can be cut into pieces and served garnished with Sun Gold tomatoes tossed with balsamic vinegar. *And* this recipe can be made with other vegetables as well, such as summer squash, artichokes, and asparagus.

As for the eggplant, you can use any variety. Since I often buy several types just because I love to look at them in my kitchen, I end up using them all in this dish. Otherwise larger varieties are the easiest to work with.

2½ pounds eggplant, peeled if white

sea salt and freshly ground pepper

¼ cup olive oil

1 large or 2 medium onions, sliced

4 large eggs

1 cup milk or light cream

1 cup freshly grated Parmesan cheese

1 tablespoon balsamic vinegar

10 large basil leaves, torn into small
    pieces

1. Preheat the oven to 350°F. Lightly oil a 2-quart gratin dish. Cut the eggplants into rounds or slabs a scant ½ inch thick. Salt if you wish and set aside while you prepare the rest of the ingredients.

2. Heat 1 tablespoon of the oil in a large nonstick skillet, add the onions, and cook over medium heat, turning frequently, until soft and light gold, about 12 minutes. Scrape into a bowl. While the onions are cooking, beat the eggs with the milk; stir in the cheese, vinegar, ¾ teaspoon salt, and some freshly ground pepper.

3. If you salted it, rinse the eggplant, then wick up the water with a towel. Heat the remaining oil in the skillet. When hot, add the eggplant and immediately turn it in the pan so that all the pieces are coated lightly with the oil. Cook over medium heat, turning occasionally, until the eggplant is golden. This will take about 25 minutes in all, but you don't need to stand over the pan. This is a good window of time to make a quick tomato sauce for the dish or another part of the meal.

4. Season the eggplant with salt and pepper to taste, then toss with the onions and basil. Put it in the prepared dish and pour the custard over the top. Bake until golden, firm, and puffed, 30 to 40 minutes. Let cool for at least 10 minutes before serving.

Braised Farmers' Long Eggplant Stuffed with Garlic | SERVES 4

One day Eremita Campos had some exceptionally pretty eggplants, a variety that is normally picked when dramatically long. But an inexperienced helper had picked them when they were only about 8 inches in length. Because they were scarcely an inch across, I cooked them whole, studded with garlic. They ended up golden, tender, and sweet. You can treat any slender eggplant this way; fatter types, such as Little Fingers, will need a little more time to cook.

8 to 12 long, skinny eggplants,
    such as Farmers' Long
2 plump garlic cloves, thinly sliced
2 tablespoons olive oil
sea salt and freshly ground pepper
chopped flat-leaf parsley
vinegar for serving

1. Cut several slits in each eggplant and insert a sliver of garlic into each.

2. Heat the olive oil in a wide skillet and add the eggplant. Cook until the eggplant starts to sizzle and color a bit, about 5 minutes. Add 1 cup water and ½ teaspoon salt and bring to a boil. Reduce the heat to medium-low, cover the pan, and cook until the eggplants are completely tender, 20 to 30 minutes. You may have to add more liquid as they cook. When tender, remove the lid and cook until the water has evaporated and the eggplants are golden, about 10 minutes. Arrange them on a platter, season with pepper, and shower with parsley. Serve with vinegar for those who like a bit of sharpness with the eggplant.

Roasted Eggplant and Chickpea Stew | SERVES 6

All the nightshades are braised together in a sauce of basil and cilantro, two herbs that are quite possibly even better in combination than they are separately. Serve warm or at room temperature with a spoonful of garlic-infused yogurt or a wedge of lemon.

sea salt and freshly ground pepper

1½ pounds Yellow Finn, Russian Banana, or other waxy potatoes

2 large peppers, red and/or yellow bells or cubanelles

vegetable oil

1 cup packed basil leaves

1 cup packed cilantro leaves

3 large garlic cloves

3 tablespoons olive oil

½ teaspoon roasted ground cumin

2 large onions, peeled and cut into eighths, or 16 very small onions

1 pound short oblong eggplants, such as Ichiban, quartered lengthwise

2 or 3 large meaty red tomatoes, peeled, seeded, and diced

1½ cups cooked chickpeas (1 15-ounce can, rinsed)

1. Preheat the broiler. Bring 6 cups water to a boil and add 1 teaspoon salt. Slice the potatoes lengthwise about ½ inch thick, boil them for 5 minutes, and drain. Halve the peppers lengthwise, press to flatten them, then brush with vegetable oil. Broil, cut side down, on a baking sheet until blistered but not charred. Stack them on top of one another and set aside to steam. When cool, remove the skins and cut the pieces in half. Set the oven temperature at 350°F.

2. Coarsely chop the basil, cilantro, and garlic, then puree in a small food processor with the olive oil, cumin, and ½ teaspoon salt.

3. Toss all the vegetables with 1 teaspoon salt, some freshly ground pepper, and the herb mixture. Using your hands, rub the herb mixture into the vegetables, especially the eggplant, then add the chickpeas and toss once more. Transfer everything to an earthenware gratin dish. Rinse out the herb container with ½ cup water and pour it over all. Cover the gratin dish tightly with foil and bake until tender, about 1½ hours. Remove the foil, brush the exposed vegetables with the juices, and bake for 20 minutes more. Let cool for at least 10 minutes before serving.

Regardless of the virtues that other vegetables enjoy, tomatoes are what people want most at the farmers' market. Even those who are very savvy about food will say, when our market is bursting with possibilities, "There wasn't much at the market. There weren't any tomatoes!" Tomatoes define summer. The fruit world is slightly more democratic, but peaches probably come closest to holding the tomato title. Proof of our passion for tomatoes lies in such gardening inventions as Walls-of-Water and the fact that farmers and gardeners everywhere figure out how to grow tomatoes, even in parts of the country—and the world—that aren't at all hospitable to them.

When it comes to taste and pleasure, the gap between a locally grown tomato in summer and a long-distance tomato the rest of the year is enormous. (This holds even for the heirloom tomatoes that are starting to appear in supermarkets.) The gap is there for every fruit and vegetable, of course, but with tomatoes it's more pronounced. Good tomatoes don't travel. And because getting them at the peak of their flavor depends on picking them at their peak of fragility, tomatoes are more wedded to their site than other foods. Good tomatoes fetch a consistently good price, as well they should.

Several years ago I watched a shopper pick up an enormous Brandywine and ask its grower, Eremita Campos, how much it cost. It

weighed nearly two pounds. It was easily salad for four. "Four dollars," Eremita said. The customer threw it down and said, "I work too hard to pay four dollars for a tomato!" Eremita crossed her arms and quietly said, "And I work too hard to sell it for less."

Prompted by this stalemate, I spent a day on the farm, finding out from Eremita and her daughter, Margaret, what it takes to grow a good, organic heirloom tomato. I concluded that $4 was a bargain. (Try picking off those big green horn worms in the hot sun for even fifteen minutes, and you'll most likely agree.)

Last year I happened to be standing once again with Eremita when the scene repeated itself. Only this time four or five customers jumped into the fray and explained to the probably frightened shopper why Eremita's price was fair.

Bit by bit, shoppers are learning what the true cost of growing good food is and what the right price should look like. It shouldn't be cheap. The effort is enormous, and the reward is discovered when you slice a tomato, then lift a bite to your mouth.

Alan Chadwick, the biodynamic gardener who inspired so much of the good gardening that has been done in this country, used to say, "Food is really cooked in the garden. It's merely finished in the kitchen." Tomatoes, perhaps more than any other vegetable, are proof of the truth of this statement.

Tomato Juice Sipped Through a Lovage Straw | MAKES A SCANT 2 CUPS

Imagine having your own fresh tomato juice. Strained but not cooked, the juice has a consistency far lighter than what comes out of a can. It's especially fine if you can sip it through the hollow stem of lovage, yet another good reason for having a lovage plant in the garden.

1 pound ripe, juicy tomatoes, any
    color, coarsely chopped
½ cup ice
sea salt and freshly ground pepper
fresh lemon juice, to taste
2 lovage stalks, fennel stalks, or lemon
    basil sprigs for garnish

Puree the tomatoes and ice in a blender, then pour through a strainer. Add a pinch of salt, some pepper, and lemon juice to taste. Let stand for a few minutes for the air bubbles to dissipate, then pour 2 glasses and serve with the lovage straws or herb sprigs.

Slow-Roasted Tomatoes | MAKES 16 TO 20 PIECES

Slow roasting requires rather little effort for the succulent results that are produced. It concentrates the flavor of tomatoes, leaving them intact but meltingly tender. I serve them perched on a little toast. (You can spread with ricotta cheese first.) But I've been advised that they freeze well for winter use, too. They can also be cooked with other vegetables or with meats. A combination of red Principe Borghese and yellow Italian paste tomatoes, such as Italian Gold, is especially striking. Oblong, dense paste tomatoes have scant amounts of juice and thick, meaty flesh.

1½ pounds paste tomatoes
2 to 3 tablespoons olive oil
sea salt and freshly ground pepper
1 teaspoon chopped oregano, thyme,
    or marjoram
1 garlic clove, minced

1. Preheat the oven to 300°F. Lightly oil a large shallow baking dish. Slice the tomatoes in half lengthwise. Set them cut side up in the dish, then brush the tops with the oil, using about a tablespoon in all. Sprinkle with salt and pepper and add the herb and garlic.
2. Bake, uncovered, for 2 hours. Check after an hour and drizzle a little more oil over the surfaces if they look dry. If you don't plan to use the tomatoes right away, store them in the refrigerator, or freeze and use in soups and stews come winter.

A Big Tomato Sandwich | SERVES 4 TO 6

Taking the feast-or-famine approach, we live on tomato sandwiches from the moment tomatoes appear in the market to the first killing frost. Then none until next year. Crusty, strong-textured ciabatta is the ideal bread. The holes drink in the juice, but the bread is strong enough that it won't fall apart. These big stuffed breads look great, taste great, and are invariably messy to eat. Tomatoes of choice are Brandywines, Striped Germans, Carmello, and Costoluto Genovese.

1 large (1-pound) loaf ciabatta

Herb Vinaigrette, below

2 or more big ripe, juicy tomatoes
    (see headnote)

1 large yellow or red bell pepper,
    roasted, peeled, and quartered,
    page 390

4 ounces fresh mozzarella, goat, or
    other favorite cheese, sliced

sea salt and freshly ground pepper

1. Slice the top third off the loaf of bread and set it aside. Pull out the inside. (You can use it to make bread crumbs.)

2. Paint the inside of the bread with some of the dressing, then make layers of sliced tomatoes, pepper, and cheese. Bathe each layer with the dressing and season with salt and pepper.

3. Add the top, press down, then cut into quarters or sixths. This packs well if wrapped tightly.

THE HERB VINAIGRETTE

¼ cup basil leaves

1 tablespoon chopped marjoram

1 tablespoon chopped parsley

1 small garlic clove, minced

⅓ cup extra virgin olive oil

4 teaspoons aged red wine vinegar

sea salt and freshly ground pepper

Finely chop the herbs with the garlic, then add the olive oil. Add the vinegar and ¼ teaspoon salt and season with pepper. Taste and adjust the seasonings if needed.

Chilled Sun Gold Soup |

I've been making Sun Gold tomato soups ever since sipping one that was astonishing at Casablanca restaurant in Cambridge, Massachusetts. The little yellow-orange tomatoes are so sweet that you really have to have the vinegar. (At the restaurant they used a full-bodied Spanish Chardonnay vinegar.) You needn't serve more than a taste of this sweet-tart soup. It makes a stimulating, eye-opening start to a summer meal on a hot day.

2 pints Sun Gold tomatoes

2 shallots, finely diced

sea salt and freshly ground pepper

3 tablespoons Spanish Chardonnay
    vinegar or champagne vinegar,
    plus a few drops sherry vinegar

2 teaspoons finely diced and seeded
    serrano chile, optional

2 tablespoons extra virgin olive oil

1 firm avocado, finely diced

1 tablespoon chopped basil or
    cilantro

1. Pluck the stems off the tomatoes and rinse them. Add them to a heavy saucepan with a tight-fitting lid with half the shallots, ½ teaspoon salt, and 1 cup water. Cook over medium-high heat, keeping one ear inclined to the pot. Soon you'll hear the tomatoes popping. Take a peek after a few minutes to make sure there's sufficient moisture in the pan—you don't want the tomatoes to scorch. If the skins are slow to pop, add a few tablespoons water. Once they release their juices, lower the heat and cook, covered, for 25 minutes.

2. Run the tomatoes through a food mill. You'll have about 2 cups. Chill well, then taste for salt.

3. Just before serving, combine the remaining shallots in a bowl with the vinegar, chile if using, oil, avocado, and herbs. Season with a pinch or two of salt and some pepper. Spoon the soup into small cups, divide the garnish among them, and serve.

Golden Pepper and Yellow Tomato Soup | SERVES 4

This September soup is flushed with the colors of early fall. In addition to their attractive appearance, the yellow-gold hues signify more sweetness in the peppers and less acidity in the tomatoes, making a soup with a softer flavor than if it were made with the green peppers and red tomatoes bought, perhaps, a few weeks earlier. If you have thick, meaty peppers and the time to grill them first, they'll make the soup slightly smoky and silky textured. Otherwise, just chop them with the skins on. Smoked Spanish paprika (*pimentón de la Vera*) will also give the soup a hint of smoke.

1 pound yellow or orange tomatoes
⅓ cup white rice
sea salt and freshly ground pepper
1 onion
2 garlic cloves
3 yellow or orange bell peppers
2 tablespoons olive oil
pinch saffron threads
1 bay leaf
2 thyme sprigs, leaves plucked from
    the stems
1 teaspoon sweet paprika or
    ½ teaspoon smoked Spanish
    paprika
1 tablespoon tomato paste
1 quart Vegetable Stock, page 385,
    chicken stock, or water
slivered opal basil or chopped
    marjoram and parsley
    for garnish

1. Bring 2 quarts water to a boil. Slice an X at the base of each tomato. Plunge them, 2 at a time, into the water for about 10 seconds, then remove and set aside. Add the rice and ½ teaspoon salt to the water, lower the heat to simmer, and cook until the rice is tender, about 12 minutes. Drain.

2. Chop the onion. Mince the garlic with a pinch of salt until mushy. Dice the peppers into small squares, removing the seeds and membranes first. You should have about 2 cups. Peel and seed the tomatoes, reserving the juice, then dice the walls and mince the cores.

3. Warm the oil in a soup pot and add the onions, peppers, saffron, bay leaf, thyme, and paprika. Cook over medium heat, stirring occasionally, until the onion has begun to soften and color, about 6 minutes. Add the garlic, then stir in the tomato paste and 1 teaspoon salt. Give it a stir and add ¼ cup water. Stew for 5 minutes, then add the tomatoes, their juice, and the stock. Bring to a boil, then reduce the heat to low and simmer, covered, for 25 minutes.

4. When ready to serve, reheat the soup with the rice, then ladle it into bowls. Or make a mound of rice in each bowl and spoon the soup around it. Season with pepper and garnish with fine slivers of opal basil leaves or marjoram chopped with a few parsley leaves.

Late-Season Tomato-Vegetable Soup | SERVES 4 TO 6

One October market yielded such diminutive leeks and carrots that they led me to keep all their shapes intact. If you don't have slender leeks and carrots, just cut whatever size you do have into small pieces.

For tomatoes, I like a mixture of big, meaty Brandywines and a few low-acid yellow tomatoes. I use them 4 ways: Their juice becomes the liquid for the soup, the walls are finely diced and stewed with the other vegetables, the cores are pureed for body, and the skins are fried to a crisp and used as a garnish.

If the soup is to be a main course, serve it with bread in the bowl, toasted first, rubbed with garlic, and covered with a soft cheese, such as Teleme. If you find yourself with leftovers, puree them and you'll have a perfect base for a cream of tomato soup to serve with the last of the basil.

2 tablespoons olive oil

6 very small leeks, including a little
    of the pale greens, finely sliced
    and washed

6 carrots, about 4 inches long, finely
    sliced into rounds, about 1 cup

1 small fennel bulb, finely diced

1 small red or orange, bell pepper, or
    2 pimientos, neatly diced

pinch saffron threads

1 garlic clove, minced

2 tablespoons chopped parsley

2 pounds ripe tomatoes

sea salt and freshly ground pepper

chopped tarragon, dill, basil,
    or lovage, optional

1. Warm half the oil in a soup pot over medium-low heat. Add the leeks, carrots, fennel, pepper, saffron, garlic, and parsley. Stir once, cook for 1 minute, add 1 cup water, and cover the pot. Stew over low heat.

2. Meanwhile, plunge the tomatoes into boiling water for 10 seconds to loosen their skins. Peel them, reserving the skins, then slice them in half crosswise and squeeze the seeds and juice into a strainer set over a bowl. Force the juice through the strainer by running a spoon through the contents. Cut the walls of the tomatoes away from the cores and neatly dice them. Puree or mince the cores.

3. By now the vegetables should be soft. Add the tomato juice, diced tomatoes, and puree and season with 1 teaspoon salt. If the mixture seems too thick, add water or stock to thin it to the right consistency. Bring to a boil, then lower the heat and simmer gently for 10 minutes or until the vegetables are tender. Turn off the heat.

4. When you're ready to serve, reheat the soup. Season with a little pepper and add some fresh chopped herb if you wish.

5. Heat the remaining tablespoon of olive oil in a small nonstick skillet. Add several large pieces of tomato skin in a single layer and fry until crisp. Remove and sprinkle them lightly with salt. Serve a few of these golden pieces piled onto the soup as a garnish.

Tomato and Avocado Salad with Lime-Herb Dressing | SERVES 3 TO 4

The farmers' market in Santa Barbara is filled with foods that most of us never even dream of seeing in our markets—Ice Cream bananas (their texture and flavor suggest ice cream), fresh shellfish from the ocean that's practically across the street, and different kinds of avocados. This salad brings the avocados together with crisp cucumbers, peppers, and tomatoes. Try cherry and currant types mixed with paste tomatoes, heirloom slicers, or whatever your market offers. To make this a main dish, I serve it with wedges of crisped corn tortillas spread with soft black beans and crumbled feta.

THE LIME-HERB DRESSING

1 tablespoon chopped mint

1 tablespoon chopped marjoram

½ cup chopped cilantro

4 to 5 tablespoons olive oil

1 jalapeño chile, finely diced

2 to 3 tablespoons fresh lime juice

¼ teaspoon sea salt

THE SALAD

1½ pounds tomatoes (see headnote)

1 large avocado, peeled

1 cucumber, peeled

1 sweet pepper—frying pepper, bell,
    or cubanelle

½ small sweet onion or several
    scallions, finely diced

2 cups chopped romaine hearts

sea salt

8 large pimiento-stuffed olives, sliced

2 ounces feta cheese, crumbled

1. Combine all the dressing ingredients in a bowl. Taste to make sure there's enough acid.

2. Cut the tomatoes, avocado, cucumber, and pepper into bite-sized pieces and put them in a roomy bowl with the onion. Add the lettuce and a few pinches of salt. Toss, add the dressing, salt lightly, and toss again with the olives and feta cheese. Pile on plates and serve.

A HARVEST DINNER
SEPTEMBER, SANTA FE

Surely today *must* be the high point of our season. On the other hand, I've made this note in my journal the past seven market visits. But today I'm sure that it really is so. This high moment is not necessarily sustained. It might last just this day, then fall to a hard frost, or it could last a while. In either case, like others, I shop until my last dollar is spent, according to eye and regardless of need. When I get home, there just isn't room for everything in the refrigerator. I make jam out of the figs that didn't get eaten last week and sauce from the leftover tomatoes. The eggplants stay out on the counter, where they're happier but won't last as long. The melons take up an enormous amount of space, so I leave them out, too, where their sweetness soon attracts a colony of fruit flies. We can't possibly eat so much food, but since it will never be as good as it is right now, we try.

Eventually the solution becomes obvious: It's time for a harvest dinner. What better way to celebrate our farmers and our market on a Labor Day weekend? Friends and neighbors are called, and they're pretty much in the same spot, so we make it a feast, a groaning board of market dishes.

Now I can relax, knowing there's a destiny for those five varieties of eggplant, the bowl of multicolored tomatoes, the corn, cucumbers, herbs, cabbages, all shapes, sizes, and colors of summer squash, beans, *and* the Concord grapes and Wolf River apples.

A HARVEST DINNER

Melon and Cucumber Agua Fresca (page 163)

TWO CROSTINI
Roasted Eggplant and Pine Nut Puree (page 168)
Ricotta with Roasted Chile and Mint (page 192)

VEGETABLE SIDES
Zephyr Zucchini with Opal Basil, Pine Nuts, and Parmigiano-Reggiano (page 141)
Braised Farmers' Long Eggplant Stuffed with Garlic (page 172)
Sliced cherry tomatoes tossed with minced garlic and olive oil
Succotash (page 129)

MAIN DISHES
Grilled Lamb Chops with Fresh Oregano and Lemon (page 80)
Shell Beans and Summer Vegetables Stewed in Their Own Juices (page 133)

DESSERTS
Concord Grape Mousse ("Grapette") (page 268)
Aged Cheddar and Gouda cheeses with heirloom apples
Fig Tart with Orange Flower Custard (page 272)

CHILES AND PEPPERS

Chiles and peppers must be fun to grow. At farmers' markets from San Francisco to Madison, from Atlanta to Missoula to New York, I've seen the most amazing collection of chiles. Often beautifully presented in small baskets, they include cayennes, Thai bird peppers, dragon peppers, Hungarian Hots, jalapeños, serranos, and so on up the Scoville heat scale to the red and orange habaneros. Slender, serpentine chilaca chiles are not nearly as hot, and they are delicious brushed with olive oil, grilled lightly, and seasoned with nothing more than sea salt. You can also just put them out to admire until they turn red and finally shrivel. Let them dry and you can crumble them into flakes or grind them into powder.

Peppers, which don't even rate on the Scoville scale, are just as varied in size, shape, and color. Some farmers lay them out in an ordered fashion, one variety to a basket. Others throw caution to the wind and just mix them all up. Either way, who can resist the curved Corno di Toros, or bulls' horns? Nardellos, Hungarian wax peppers, Ivory bells, chocolate bells, gypsy peppers, Italian sweet peppers—all good for slicing and frying because of their thin flesh, but for the same reason not so good for roasting: A hot fire would consume the flesh along with the skin if they were charred. Two bright red pimiento-type peppers, called Lipstick and Firecracker, surface predictably in markets. They're small enough that they're perfect for stuffing with goat cheese and fresh herbs. Red Cherries and Cherry Bombs are even tinier and sweeter, good for one bite. In contrast, if you were to stuff one of the huge, meaty cubanelles, you'd have a dinner for four! Well, two, maybe.

Bell peppers are always the last to arrive. Perhaps those big thick walls take longer to mature, but when they get here, they arrive in a profusion of color that is far from common. Shades range from the lightest pale ivory to the darkest purple-browns of the chocolate bells. In between, there are peppers of luminous dark green, blistering red, orange, and school-bus yellow. Imagine what beautiful salads or pepper sautés can be made with such vibrant colors. Such variety can transform the dishes we usually make into something breathtakingly gorgeous and delicious. And if you're not terribly fond of peppers, you can treat them as if they're flowers. The price of a bouquet will buy you a bag full of glossy color and sensual form simply to look at.

Sautéed Gypsy Peppers | MAKES 3 TO 4 CUPS

There's a whole class of peppers that are more thin-skinned than bells, just as sweet, and meant to be fried with their skins on. Frying peppers seem to be much better known in the East and Midwest than they are in the Southwest, although I've been seeing them more lately. Frying peppers can be found in many colors, but the green ones are what my Hungarian friend Esther Kovari uses for stuffing—these and never bell peppers, she says.

Serve this sauté hot or cold, as an appetizer or a side dish, on garlic-rubbed toast, in a sandwich, with pasta, or in a frittata.

1 pound frying peppers, such as
    Gypsy, Nardello, or Corno
    di Toros
2 tablespoons olive oil
1 small red onion, quartered and
    thinly sliced
2 garlic cloves, thinly sliced
1 tablespoon tomato paste
1½ tablespoons chopped marjoram,
    anise hyssop, or basil
sea salt and freshly ground pepper
1 tablespoon balsamic vinegar

1. Slice the peppers into strips ¼ inch wide or wider, removing the seeds and veins if you wish.
2. Heat the oil in a wide skillet, add the onion and garlic, and cook over medium heat until translucent, 4 to 5 minutes. Add the peppers, raise the heat, and sauté for 5 minutes, stirring every so often. Add the tomato paste, half the herbs, and ¼ cup water. Cover the pan, lower the heat to medium, and cook until the peppers are soft, another 10 minutes or so.
3. Season with salt and pepper to taste. Add the vinegar and raise the heat. Cook until the peppers are glazed, then stir in the rest of the herbs. Serve warm or cold.

Green Chile Paste (Zhough) | MAKES ABOUT ½ CUP

A chile paste from Yemen with a hint of sweet spice, *zhough* can be spread on pita bread or stirred into vegetable stews, soups, and sauces. Try it with grilled sweet potatoes or wherever you want extra heat and spice.

You can use jalapeños, serranos, Anaheims, poblanos, or perhaps another chile that grows in your area. I usually use jalapeños with 1 serrano thrown in for extra heat and flavor. Ripe red chiles, which you may come across at your farmers' market and in the grocery store on occasion, can also be used. Because they've ripened longer, their flavor is deeper and sweeter.

4 ounces fresh green or red chiles
  (see headnote)
1 teaspoon black peppercorns
1 teaspoon cumin seeds
1 teaspoon caraway seeds
½ teaspoon ground cardamom
½ cup coarsely chopped parsley
½ cup coarsely chopped cilantro
4 garlic cloves, peeled and chopped
olive oil to moisten
pinch sea salt

1. Remove the seeds and veins from the chiles, chop by hand or in a food processor, and set aside. (If using a food processor, stand back—the volatile oils can be irritating.)

2. Crush the peppercorns and spices in a mortar. Add the chopped chile, parsley, cilantro, and garlic and continue to work to make a smooth paste. Add oil to moisten—the *zhough* should have a paste-like consistency—and a pinch of salt. Keep refrigerated and use within a few days.

Small Roasted Chickens with Cumin-Chile Butter | SERVES 4

Not all the chickens at the market are the same size. Sometimes they can be very small indeed, Cornish hen size or a bit larger, which are perfect for 2 people, or they can be about twice that size. Either way, serve the chicken with couscous, tossed with the spicy juices that collect in the chicken.

1 (2½- to 3-pound) chicken or
   2 (1-pound) chickens

sea salt

2 garlic cloves

1½ teaspoons ground roasted cumin
   seeds

1½ teaspoons mild ground New
   Mexican chile or hot paprika

plenty of freshly ground pepper

4 tablespoons unsalted butter, at
   room temperature

12 fresh cilantro sprigs

1. Preheat the oven to 400°F. Lightly butter or oil a shallow baking dish that's large enough for the chicken(s).

2. Rinse and thoroughly dry the bird. Salt lightly, rubbing the salt into the skin. Gently slide your hand between the skin and the breast, loosening the skin as far as you can.

3. Pound the garlic to a very smooth paste with ½ teaspoon salt, then work in the cumin, chile, pepper, and butter. Use 1 tablespoon of the butter to rub inside the cavities of the bird. Use another to force underneath the breast skin. Melt the remaining butter over low heat with a teaspoon of water, then brush it generously over the chicken. Stuff the cavity with the cilantro, then truss the bird and place it, breast side up, in the pan. Bake until the liquid runs clear from the thighs, 45 to 55 minutes or about one and a half hours, depending on the size of the bird.

4. To serve, toss cooked couscous with the juices from the chicken. Then present the chicken whole and carve it at the table.

One of the great pleasures in New Mexico comes in August, when the farmers set up their roasters for the new green chile. Nothing smells better than the burning skins of these peppers. It's our equivalent of burning fall leaves, and there's always quite a buzz around this activity.

First you select a bushel of chile—mild, hot, or very hot. The farmer will tell you which is which—it all looks the same. Next you watch as it's dumped into a barrel-sized cage, which is turned slowly over a brace of fiery nozzles. As soon as the skins are charred—there are always bits of them flying through the air at this point—the chiles are dropped through a shoot into a waiting plastic bag. Although the bushel is now greatly diminished in size, it feels much heavier. By the time you get home, the skins, which have been steaming, are easy to slip off. You might pull some out for tonight's dinner, but the rest are skinned and packed for the freezer.

I know aficionados who have lugged sacks of wet roasted chiles home on airplanes. This isn't the easiest thing to do, and I'm sure they curse themselves while they grapple with twenty-five pounds of slippery wet chile in the overhead bin. But they'll be glad they went to the trouble when they bring a spoonful of green chile stew to their lips some dreary Saturday in January. For those who aren't up to storing a bushel's worth, it's usually possible to buy a 1-pound bag. Or you can buy a few fresh ones and roast them yourself.

A warm, roasted chile slipped into a fresh tortilla with a piece of local goat cheese is one of the best ways to satisfy that after-market hunger. Goat cheese isn't just a stylish conceit here; it was once the common cheese in New Mexico, for the goat thrived more cheaply and easily than the cow. At almost every farmers' market I've visited, someone is making goat cheese, a great addition regardless of whether it stems from some local tradition or not.

SATURDAY LUNCH AFTER MARKET

Soft Taco with Roasted Green Chile and Goat Cheese
(page 191)

Sliced cucumbers and tomatoes

Cold freshly pressed apple cider

Soft Taco with Roasted Green Chile and Goat Cheese | SERVES 1

2 long green chiles, such as New
    Mexican natives, Joe Parkers,
    Espanola Hots, or poblanos
1 large wheat tortilla
soft fresh goat cheese
chopped cilantro

Roast the chiles until charred (see page 390), then drop into a covered bowl to steam for 10 to 15 minutes. Slip off the skins and pull out the seeds, then pull into strips with your fingers. Place the tortilla in a dry skillet over medium heat. As soon as the bottom is warm, flip it over. Put the chile on top, crumble the cheese over it, and add the cilantro. (You can add salsa, too, if you like.) When the cheese starts to soften, slide the tortilla onto the counter, then fold it in half. Press down, wrap in a napkin, sit down, and enjoy.

Ricotta with Roasted Chile and Mint | SERVES 6 AS AN APPETIZER

This is one of my favorite appetizers to make when glossy poblanos are in season. Put out a bowlful to spread on warm corn tortillas or spread it on a slice of toasted nutty wheat bread. A spoonful can also perch on the base of an endive leaf.

2 poblano chiles

3 scallions, including an inch of the greens, halved lengthwise and thinly sliced, or 3 tablespoons finely snipped chives

2 tablespoons chopped cilantro, plus sprigs for garnish

1 tablespoon finely chopped mint

1½ cups ricotta

sea salt

6 small corn tortillas or 4 large slices nutty, dense wheat bread

4 large red radishes, thinly sliced lengthwise, then julienned

1. Roast the chiles until charred (see page 390), put them in a bowl, cover with a plate, and set aside to steam for 15 minutes. Meanwhile, stir the scallions, cilantro, and mint into the ricotta. Season with salt to taste.

2. Remove the chiles from the bag and slip off the skins. Wipe off any large flecks that remain, then remove the stems and seeds. Chop finely and stir into the ricotta. Taste for salt.

3. Wrap the tortillas in foil and steam or heat in the oven until warmed through. Serve tortillas and cheese separately. If you're using bread, spread the cheese over it, slice into fingers, then garnish with the radish slivers and a sprig of cilantro.

A Farmers' Stew | SERVES 3 TO 4

It's such an easy pleasure to make this dish, I always imagine it would be ideal for tired farmers at the end of the day—or tired anyone. While the onions sizzle in olive oil, you're cutting eggplant and squash into big bold pieces. Into the pan they go, a tight-fitting lid goes on top, down goes the heat, and the vegetables stew briefly in their own juices until tender.

You can be completely relaxed and improvisational with this stew, for it really reflects the generous spirit of the market with all its choice and variety. Any kind of squash, onion, or eggplant will be fine, in any proportion. I find that some of the skinnier eggplants are interesting here: Yellow squash definitely enlivens the appearance; pattypans can be cut into thick wedges; zucchini into 2-inch logs, then halved or quartered; etc.

Serve these vegetables with couscous or rice or mounded over a garlicky piece of toasted bread.

3 tablespoons olive oil

2 big onions, coarsely chopped

a few thyme sprigs

3 tablespoons chopped oregano

8 skinny eggplants, cut into 2-inch
    lengths

1½ pounds summer squash, cut into
    large wedges or lengths

2 tablespoons tomato paste

sea salt and freshly ground pepper

½ cup white wine or water

vinegar, optional

1. Heat the oil in a Dutch oven or other deep pot that has a tight-fitting lid. Add the onions, thyme, and oregano and cook over medium-high heat, shaking the pan occasionally while you prepare the rest of the vegetables. By the time they're all cut, the onions will have wilted and started to color in places.

2. Add the vegetables, give them a stir, and cook, keeping the heat high and shaking the pan occasionally, until they begin to give off an enticing smell. This should take 10 to 15 minutes. Stir in the tomato paste; add the salt and the wine or water. Cover the pan, turn the heat to low, and cook for about 10 minutes. The vegetables should have an invitingly tender appearance and be blushing with a faint glaze of red from the tomato. Season with pepper. Add a few drops of vinegar for sharpness if you like.

Roasted and Stuffed Firecracker Pimientos | SERVES 8

The prettiest little peppers you can imagine, they look more like ornaments than food, but they are real from the ground up. I found these at a fledgling farmers' market in Colorado Springs. They were grown by one of the few actual farmers (as opposed to resellers) who were selling there. He called them Firecracker pimientos, and like all pimientos, they were heart shaped, heavy for their size, perfect to roast and put aside to use during the winter. But as he had only 8, I decided to roast and then stuff them. They were the perfect size for an appetizer.

8 small pimientos, such as Firecracker
    or Cherry Bombs

½ cup fresh goat cheese

1 cup ricotta

1 tablespoon finely chopped thyme or
    rosemary

1 garlic clove, crushed or minced

sea salt and freshly ground pepper

olive oil

1. Roast the peppers until charred (see page 390), then put them in a covered bowl to steam for 15 minutes. Preheat the oven to 400°F. Remove the skins, cut a slit in the side, and gently pull out the seeds and core. Mix the 2 cheeses with the thyme and garlic. Season with salt and pepper. Add any of the pepper juice that might have accumulated.

2. Fill the peppers with the cheese mixture. Set them upright in a baking dish and brush with olive oil. Bake the peppers until thoroughly heated through, about 25 minutes.

Roasted Peppers and Tomatoes Baked with Herbs and Capers | SERVES 4 TO 6

With its silky texture and summery fragrance, this is one of the most pleasurable dishes to make. The short baking melds everything together, transforms the flavors, and yields juices so delicious they invite dunking. This is served cold as a little salad, but it also makes a great filling for a sandwich or frittata.

4 big bell peppers, red, orange, and
   yellow

1 large beefsteak-type tomato or 1¼
   pounds other ripe tomatoes

2 smaller yellow tomatoes

6 flat-leaf parsley sprigs

1 tablespoon marjoram or 12 large
   basil leaves

1 plump garlic clove

2 tablespoons capers, rinsed

12 Niçoise olives, pitted

3 tablespoons olive oil, plus extra for
   the dish

sea salt and freshly ground pepper

1. Roast the peppers until charred (see page 390). Drop them into a bowl, cover, and set them aside while you prepare everything else. Then wipe off the blackened skin, pull out the seeds, and core and cut into wide strips. Trim off any ragged ends and set them aside for another use.

2. Score the ends of the tomatoes, then drop them into boiling water for 10 seconds. Remove the skins, halve them crosswise, and gently squeeze out the seeds. Cut the walls into wide pieces. Reserve the cores for a soup or sauce.

3. Pluck the leaves off the parsley stems. You should have about ½ cup. Chop them finely with the marjoram and garlic, then put in a bowl with the capers, olives, and the olive oil. Season with ¾ teaspoon salt and some pepper.

4. Preheat the oven to 400°F. Lightly oil a small gratin dish. Add the tomatoes, peppers, and sauce and gently toss with your hands. Season with pepper.

5. Cover and bake for 20 minutes. Let cool before serving.

Robust End-of-the-Summer Spaghetti | SERVES 4 TO 6

Giving the last of the summer vegetables a lengthy time on the stove turns them into a robust and deep-flavored sauce, hearty enough for the beginning of fall.

1½ to 2 pounds eggplant, peeled and
    sliced a scant ½ inch thick
2 red or yellow bell peppers, or one of
    each, halved lengthwise
¼ cup olive oil, plus extra for the
    eggplant
1 onion, finely diced
1 garlic clove, minced
3 anchovies, chopped
⅓ cup chopped parsley, plus extra
    for garnish
2 pounds ripe tomatoes, peeled,
    seeded, and chopped
¼ cup Kalamata or Gaeta olives,
    pitted and chopped
¼ cup green Sicilian olives, pitted
    and chopped
3 tablespoons capers, rinsed
1 tablespoon dried oregano
sea salt and freshly ground pepper
1 pound spaghetti
1 cup grated pecorino Romano or
    Parmigiano-Reggiano

1. Preheat the broiler. Brush a sheet pan lightly with oil, arrange the eggplant on it, and brush the tops with more oil. Broil on both sides until browned, 12 to 20 minutes per side. Remove and cut into wide strips. Lightly oil the peppers, then broil, skin side up, until blistered. Stack them on top of one another to steam for 15 minutes, then peel and dice into small squares.

2. Heat the ¼ cup oil in a Dutch oven. Add the onion, peppers, garlic, anchovies, and the parsley. Sauté over medium-high heat until the onion and peppers are softened, about 5 minutes. Lower the heat and add the eggplant, tomatoes, olives, capers, oregano, and ½ cup water or juice from the tomatoes. Season with salt and pepper and simmer for 30 minutes.

3. Cook the pasta in a large pot of boiling salted water until done, then drain. Place in a large heated bowl. Present at the table with the vegetables spooned over the top and showered with the cheese and extra parsley. Then toss before serving.

ALL CAUGHT UP!
EARLY SEPTEMBER

I've just spent a morning visiting farmers all over the country via the Internet and the phone. Regardless of where we've started from—North or South, wet climates or dry, high altitudes or low—we are all the same right now. Every market report is remarkably like every other. There are a few variations—California and southern states are mentioning figs; high-altitude and coastal areas are reporting on peas and greens—but outside of these extremes every market manager mentions tomatoes, sweet corn, eggplants, peppers, and new potatoes. And for fruit we're looking at melons, peaches, plums, apples, and grapes. While every market has its constants—jams and jellies, honey, meats, eggs, and cheeses—the eggs will be starting to thin out with the shorter days while cider is coming in. A few markets mention the presence of winter squash, but they're on the early edge of their season, as are some other fruits and vegetables, such as Jerusalem artichokes and pears.

But right now, at this moment, every part of the country seems to be caught up with nightshades and corn. While what I appreciate perhaps most about farmers' markets are the regional differences across our land that show themselves so well, what I love about this moment is the opposite, that we can all eat the same foods at the same time. Like a national holiday that everyone takes, it's a moment of unity in a huge country with a diverse culture and geography.

A HEARTY LATE-SUMMER DINNER

Golden Pepper and Yellow Tomato Soup
(page 180)

Bruce Aidells's Roast Beef with Herb and
Garlic Paste (page 81)

Parsley Root and Potato Puree (page 217)

Caramelized Apple Tart
with Cinnamon Custard (page 312)

A VEGETARIAN SUPPER

Slow-Roasted Tomatoes (page 175)
on Croutons

Fava Bean, Herb, and Wax Bean Soup with
Fried Pita Bread (page 127)

Leek, Scallion, and Fennel Gratin (page 72)

Grapes with New Walnuts and
Crème Fraîche (page 266)

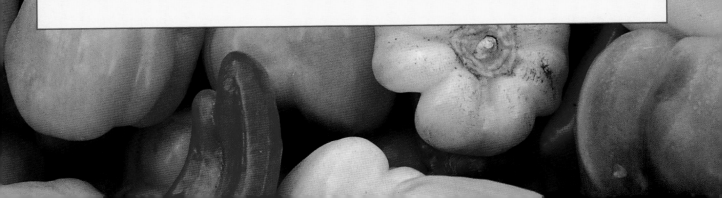

Roots and Tubers 8

Most of the vegetables we see at the farmers' market emerge above ground—leafy greens, squashes and melons, tomatoes and eggplants. But there are also the vegetables that grow underground. More dense and long lasting than their counterparts under the sky, roots and tubers are characterized by those satisfying textures that make them so good for hearty braises.

Most roots are naturally sweet, and that's a feature that can be intensified. Parsnips can be made into delicious breakfast fritters to eat with maple syrup. Sweet potatoes go into pies, of course, and they can be used to make the velvety custard on page 221.

But other roots are just plain rooty, in a good, sobering way. Gobo, or burdock, for example, a long skinny root that shows up quite frequently at farmers' markets, has a sharp earthy taste. Parsley root is clean and strong. Daikon is peppery.

Because so many roots keep well, we think of them as winter foods. However, roots also appear in the spring, and they can be as charming and welcome as asparagus. Sweet little carrots, turnips the size of two bites, the first spring radishes, early kohlrabi—these make the prettiest collection of root vegetables that taste as delicate as their spring colors.

The Ultimate Root Soup, Borscht | SERVES 8 TO 10

You can include parsley root, burdock, and celery root with perfect ease in this mélange of sweet root vegetables. Although we sometimes think of roots as dense and heavy, this soup is light, clear, and clean. The recipe makes a lot so that you can eat it over a number of days.

To keep the color of the beets glowing and red, don't add them until the rest of the vegetables have cooked for 15 or 20 minutes.

⅓ cup (1 ounce) dried porcini

2 large leeks

3 or 4 (¾ pound) small russet
    potatoes, peeled

1¼ pounds beets, peeled

3 celery ribs

1 carrot

finely chopped parsley or dill

3 bay leaves

7 garlic cloves, chopped

sea salt and freshly ground pepper

1 large onion

1 turnip, about ½ pound

2 tablespoons unsalted butter

3 cups shredded green cabbage

1 cup fresh or canned diced tomatoes
    (in puree or water)

1 tablespoon sugar

3 tablespoons white or red wine
    vinegar

½ cup sour cream mixed with
    1 tablespoon prepared
    horseradish

1. Cover the mushrooms with 2 cups warm water and set them aside while you make a vegetable stock. If you prefer to use water, skip to step 3.

2. Wash all the soup vegetables thoroughly since you'll be using the trimmings. These include 4 inches of leeks past the white part plus their roots, if available; potato peels; beet stems and peels; celery tips; carrot ends; and parsley stems. Put the trimmings in a pot with 2 bay leaves, 4 garlic cloves, and 2 teaspoons salt. Cover with 10 cups water and bring to a boil. Lower the heat and simmer while you chop the vegetables for the soup.

3. Finely chop the white parts of the leeks. Finely dice the onion. Chop the celery into ½-inch pieces. Dice the carrot into ¼-inch pieces. Peel the turnip and dice into ½-inch pieces. Dice the peeled potatoes. Cut the peeled beets into julienne strips.

4. Melt the butter in a large Dutch oven. Add the leeks, onion, celery, carrot, turnip, potatoes, cabbage, and remaining garlic. Toss with 1 tablespoon salt, cover, and cook over medium heat until the vegetables have wilted, about 20 minutes.

5. Add the beets, tomatoes, remaining bay leaf, and sugar. Chop the soaked mushrooms and add them, along with their soaking liquid, to the pot. Strain the stock, then add it (or 2 quarts water) and simmer until the beets are tender, about 25 minutes. Taste for salt and season with pepper. Stir in the vinegar. Serve hot or cold, with a spoonful of sour cream and horseradish in each bowl and a scattering of fresh green parsley or dill.

Three-Beet Caviar with Endive and Goat Cheese | SERVES 4

If your market offers the opportunity to make 3 different caviars using golden beets in one, red in another, and Chioggia in the third, go ahead and use all 3 kinds. They look like jewels. (Of course you can make this salad using just one kind of beet.) Serve the caviars in separate mounds, along with a mound of chopped endive and another of goat cheese, but encourage people to mix everything together at the table. If mixed beforehand, the red beets will stain the entire salad red.

I like to keep a supply of beet caviar in the refrigerator, especially during the summer. It's extremely refreshing and can be called into service as an appetizer, a relish, a salad, or an element on a salad plate. California's red endive makes a pretty edible holder for a bite-sized amount. Alternatively, spread mayonnaise on rye bread, then spoon the beets on top and add some pickled onions for an impromptu open-face sandwich.

6 beets: 2 golden, 2 Chioggia, 2 red

1 very small red onion, finely diced

3 tablespoons white wine vinegar

sea salt and freshly ground pepper

2 tablespoons chopped parsley or
   chervil

2 Belgian endives, red or white

4 ounces fresh goat cheese

olive oil

1. Leaving an inch of the stem and all of the roots, steam the beets un-til they're tender-firm when pierced with a knife, 25 to 45 minutes, depending on their size. Cool, then slip off the skins. Cut them into chunks, then pulse 6 to 8 times in a food processor until finely chopped, taking care not to turn the beets into mush. Alternatively, dice them by hand. Chop each color of beet separately.

2. While the beets are cooking, toss the onion in the vinegar with ¼ teaspoon salt and set aside. Toss each of the 3 types of beets with a third of the onion and vinegar. Taste for salt and season with pepper. Toss again with the parsley and chill.

3. Slice the endives crosswise into rounds and separate the pieces. Arrange mounds of the beets, a mound of endive, and a smaller one of goat cheese on each plate. Drizzle a little olive oil over the endive and cheese. Add pepper and serve. Toss everything together into a pile of confetti before eating.

Beets and Their Greens with Marjoram and Pine Nuts | SERVES 4

At the farmers' market beets usually come with their greens, which are uncommonly lush and fresh. Even though they may look tough, they cook quickly to tenderness. Their flavor is mild and sweet. Marjoram is an absolutely delicious herb with beets, every bit as companionable as dill.

2 small red onions, thinly sliced into
    rounds

white wine vinegar

8 to 12 small beets, golden and/or
    Chioggia, including the greens

olive oil

sea salt

Marjoram Pesto with Capers and
    Olives, page 65

1. Toss the onions with vinegar nearly to cover and refrigerate until needed. They will turn bright pink.

2. Discard the beet stems and any wilted leaves, wash the rest, and steam until tender, about 5 minutes. Set aside to drain, then chop coarsely. Toss with a little olive oil and season with salt.

3. Leaving an inch of the stems and the tails on the beets, steam until a knife pierces them easily, about 25 minutes. Slip off the skins. Trim the tops and tails, quarter them, and sprinkle with a little vinegar.

4. Make the pesto, setting aside half the toasted pine nuts as a garnish. Toss the beets with it, leaving ample streaks throughout. Place them over the greens. Remove the onions from the vinegar and strew them over the beets. Garnish with the reserved pine nuts and serve.

Carrot Salad with Parsley, Lovage, and Mint | SERVES 4 TO 6

It's the lovage and mint combined with sweet summer carrots that make this very simple salad sing. Lovage is a bit like celery—pungent and clean tasting. If you haven't any of this unusual, lively herb, add some chopped celery leaves in its place for now, then vow to plant your own.

1 pound carrots

2 tablespoons chopped parsley

2 tablespoons chopped lovage

2 tablespoons chopped mint

sea salt and freshly ground pepper

zest and juice of 1 lemon

1 to 2 tablespoons olive oil

Peel, then grate the carrots using the large hole of a box grater. Toss with the chopped herbs and ½ teaspoon salt. Add 1 tablespoon lemon juice, the zest, and just enough oil to coat the carrots lightly. Season with pepper and chill before serving if time allows.

Carrot Top Soup | SERVES 4

Don't just throw them away! The tender tops that come with your carrots are delicious in soups. Here's one that uses both the carrots and their tops.

1 bunch (6 small to medium) carrots,
 the tops and the roots
2 tablespoons unsalted butter
3 tablespoons white rice
2 large leeks, white parts only
2 thyme or lemon thyme sprigs
2 tablespoons chopped dill, parsley,
 celery leaves, or lovage
sea salt and freshly ground pepper
6 cups Vegetable Stock, page 385,
 light chicken stock, or water

1. Pull or pluck the lacy leaves of the carrot greens off their stems. You should have between 2 and 3 cups, loosely packed. Wash, then chop finely. Grate the carrots or, if you want a more refined-looking soup, finely chop them.

2. Melt the butter in a soup pot. Add the carrot tops and carrots, rice, leeks, thyme, and dill. Cook for several minutes, turning everything a few times, then season with 1½ teaspoons salt and add the stock. Bring to a boil and simmer until the rice is cooked, 16 to 18 minutes.

3. Taste for salt, season with pepper, and serve.

Stir-Fried Carrots and Burdock with Sesame Seeds | SERVES 4

Burdock, or gobo, is a long, dark-skinned root that has a clean, earthy flavor. I've seen it at quite a few farmers' markets. You may have wondered what to do with it, too.

This delicious condiment, *kinpira,* is often served in Japanese restaurants as an appetizer, and you can do the same, or serve it with nutty-tasting short-grain brown rice (and perhaps a dish of tofu braised with greens). However, there's no reason you can't add gobo to a Western dish, such as borscht or the root vegetable stew on page 223. It's tough but doesn't take long to cook if thinly sliced. It can also be parboiled to near tenderness before being added to a dish. Scrub the skin well; peeling is optional. Once cut, the flesh will darken if it sits around for long, so just keep it in water until you're ready to cook.

1 or 2 (8 to 10 ounces) burdock roots

3 carrots

2 tablespoons mirin

2 tablespoons soy sauce

3 teaspoons white sesame seeds

2 teaspoons vegetable or light
    sesame oil

2 teaspoons roasted sesame oil

1. Scrub the burdock roots with a stiff brush under running water to wash away the soil. Thinly slice them on the diagonal, then slice the pieces into matchsticks. Put them in a bowl of cold water. When all are sliced, parboil them for 1 minute, then drain.

2. Peel the carrots and slice into matchsticks. Combine the mirin and soy sauce. Toast the sesame seeds in a dry skillet until golden, then immediately pour them onto a plate to stop the cooking.

3. Heat a wok or a nonstick skillet, add the oils, and swirl it around the pan. Drain the burdock. When the pan is hot, add the burdock and stir-fry for 2 to 3 minutes. Add ¼ cup water, cover the pan, and steam for 5 minutes, then add the carrots and stir-fry for 2 to 3 minutes longer. Pour in the soy sauce mixture and continue to stir-fry until the vegetables are nicely glazed, after several more minutes. Toss with the sesame seeds and serve hot or at room temperature.

Taste of Spring: Young Root Vegetable Braise | SERVES 2 TO 4

I've found these charming spring vegetables—all of them small and sweet—at an Arizona market in January, a California market in March, and our farmers' market by May. And when the weather cools down again in the fall, most of the same cast returns for an encore.

To give this dish more heft, include a dozen or so of the Herb Dumplings on page 66, using tarragon and parsley for the herbs.

4 slender leeks, including a little of the
    pale green, or 1 bunch scallions
6 carrots, yellow and/or orange, 3 to
    4 inches long
12 little turnips with their greens
1 bunch radishes—pink, red, or
    purple—with ½ inch of their
    stems
sea salt and freshly ground pepper
1 pound fava beans, if available,
    shucked
2 tablespoons unsalted butter
2 tablespoons finely chopped parsley
1 tablespoon finely chopped
    tarragon
1 tablespoon fresh lemon juice

1. Slice the leeks crosswise about ¼ inch wide, then rinse them in a bowl of water and drain. Cut all but ½ inch of the carrot greens off, peel the carrots, and slice them in half lengthwise. Leave ½ inch of the turnip greens attached. Peel with a paring knife up to the shoulders. Leave smaller ones whole and cut larger ones into halves or quarters. Halve the radishes lengthwise, soak them briefly in a bowl of water, then rinse, especially the stems.

2. Bring 6 cups water to a boil and add 1½ teaspoons salt. Blanch the carrots, turnips, and radishes for 7 minutes, then scoop out and set aside. (There's no need to rinse them.) Drop the fava beans into the water for 1 minute, then scoop them out, saving the cooking water, and rinse to cool. Pop them out of their skins.

3. Melt half the butter in an 8- or 10-inch sauté pan. Add the leeks and cook over medium heat for about 2 minutes, stirring frequently. Add ½ cup of the vegetable cooking water, the blanched vegetables, half the herbs, and ½ teaspoon salt. Simmer until the vegetables are fully tender, 10 to 15 minutes, adding water in ⅓-cup increments so that the pan doesn't dry out. There should be a little sauce.

4. Add the fava beans, remaining butter, and lemon juice. Raise the heat and swirl the pan back and forth until the butter has melted into the juice. Remove from the heat, add the rest of the herbs, season with pepper, and serve. If you've made the dumplings, add them during the last 5 minutes so that they'll heat through.

I think that when we shop outdoors we are much truer to the moment. Without thinking much about it, we tend to ignore those foods that are at the far reaches of their season and gravitate toward those that are enjoying their prime. The weather itself, the air on our skin, tells us quite precisely what to eat. It's a rather animal-like impulse that overrides other considerations.

One October I was visiting New York's Union Square Greenmarket. It was a day that captured that shortest of market moments, that instant when all the glossy vegetable fruits of summer are there alongside the somber roots and tubers of fall. It's a moment that comes to nearly every market—exceptions being allowed for markets in southern California and Hawaii.

The day began with the tepid warmth and blue skies of autumn, but it quickly turned chilly, and suddenly it was coat weather. The sky took on dark, sooty tones and threatened rain. It even seemed that it might snow, and a few flakes floated to the sidewalk, but that was all. No one seemed to take much joy in lingering as people usually do at farmers' markets, even in fast-paced New York. Heads were down, shopping was quick and pragmatic. But the market was rich with possibilities.

Among the boxes of golden quince, Cortland and Golden Russet apples, and bins of hearty greens was an assortment of eggplants, Brandywine tomatoes, and golden bell peppers, the last of the season. They were handsome vegetables, but to me they were no longer appealing, whereas just weeks ago—days ago, in fact—weren't we all reaching over each other's arms and stuffing our bags with them? We were, after ten months of waiting for their arrival.

In spite of the warm and comforting foods one can cook from nightshades—a late-harvest ratatouille would have been quite apt for the moment—it simply wasn't summer anymore. The collective gaze was shifting. I watched as shoppers drifted away from the tomatoes to the Jerusalem artichokes, celery root, pumpkins, and leeks. I felt for those farmers who hadn't a single root or an onion, those who were standing in the drizzle with their peppers and tomatoes. When I picked up rosemary and sage instead of basil, I actually felt a twinge of guilt about turning my back on what I had desired so recently. But this act also made me feel like a human animal, and it felt good. Yes, I was fickle toward summer and all its offerings but true to the promise of winter, the time for rooty stews laced with robust herbs. That's just what happens in October.

A ROOT-WEATHER MENU FOR FALL

Three-Beet Caviar with Endive and Goat Cheese (page 201)

Celery Root and Wild Rice Chowder (page 209)

Green salad

Quince and Goat Cheese Tart (page 322)

Sunchoke Bisque
with Hazelnut Oil | SERVES 4 TO 6

Many customers draw a blank when it comes to these strange, nubbly tubers, but there are many good things to do with the humble sunchoke, also known as the Jerusalem artichoke. One is to make this soup. On a Saturday morning one November I served 12 gallons of it at the Union Square greenmarket, and the farmers selling Jerusalem artichokes couldn't believe what great sales they had once people could actually taste how sweet, nutty, and good these tubers are.

You don't have to peel sunchokes. Just scrub them well. Nut oils, especially pumpkin seed and roasted hazelnut oil, are very flattering to Jerusalem artichokes.

1 small onion

3 small red potatoes

1 pound Jerusalem artichokes

1 celery rib

2 tablespoons sunflower seed oil

2 garlic cloves, minced

6 cups Vegetable Stock, page 385,
    chicken stock, or water

sea salt and freshly ground pepper

2 bay leaves

milk or cream for thinning

½ cup croutons, crisped in the oven

roasted hazelnut or pumpkin seed oil

1. Wash all the vegetables, then chop them into ½-inch chunks. Don't bother to peel the sunchokes.

2. Heat the oil in a soup pot, add the vegetables, and sauté over high heat, stirring frequently, until lightly browned, about 10 minutes. Add the garlic during the last few minutes. Pour in the stock. Add 1½ teaspoons salt and the bay leaves. Bring to a boil, then simmer, covered, until the potatoes are tender, about 25 minutes.

3. Cool briefly, then puree until perfectly smooth. Return the soup to the stove and add enough milk or cream to thin it to the desired consistency. Taste for salt and season with pepper. Serve with a few croutons in each bowl and the oil drizzled in a thin stream over the top.

Celery Root and Wild Rice Chowder | SERVES 4 TO 6

Rich, fragrant, and chewy, this soup features wild rice you'll find at the St. Paul farmers' market and other markets in Minnesota and Michigan. The drop of truffle oil is optional, but just right with celery root.

If you want to make a vegetable stock, there are lots of good trimmings to work with—leek greens and roots, parsley stems, and the celery root peels (see page 385).

½ cup wild rice

1 celery root (about 1 pound)

2 large leeks, white parts only

2 tablespoons unsalted butter

1 celery rib, diced

1 cup thinly sliced russet potato

¼ cup chopped parsley, plus extra
    for garnish

1 bay leaf

1 large thyme sprig

sea salt and freshly ground pepper

2 cups Vegetable Stock, page 385,
    chicken stock, or water

2 cups half-and-half or milk

truffle oil, optional

1. Cover the wild rice with 5 cups water in a small saucepan. Bring to a boil, then lower the heat. Cover and simmer for about 45 minutes or until tender.

2. Thickly cut away the celery root skins, then quarter and chop the root into bite-sized pieces. You should have about 3 cups. Chop and wash the leeks.

3. Melt the butter in a soup pot. Add the vegetables, parsley, bay leaf, thyme, and 1½ teaspoons salt. Cook over medium-high heat for about 5 minutes, then add the stock. Bring to a boil, reduce the heat to low, and simmer for 20 minutes. Add the half-and-half and simmer until the vegetables are tender. Taste for salt and season with pepper. To give the soup a creamy background, puree a cup of the vegetables and return them to the pot. If the soup is too thick, thin it with some of the rice water or additional stock.

4. Divide the soup among 4 or 6 bowls and then add a mound of the wild rice to each. Garnish each bowl with parsley and a drop of truffle oil, if using, and serve.

Parsnip Galette with Greens | MAKES 1 LARGE GALETTE, SERVING 2, OR 6 SMALL ONES

This is a good dish for fall, when parsnips and greens are both at the market and in peak condition. It's an even better spring dish if you live where people wait until then to dig their parsnips out of the snow, as they do in places like Maine and Vermont. As a vegetable enthusiast, I like this for lunch or dinner as a main course. But you can also cut it into wedges and serve it alongside roasted chicken. Parsnips are naturally so sweet that they need some tempering effects, which they get here from the walnuts, sage, and blanched bitter greens. Look for parsnips that are firm and ivory colored.

½ pound (2 or 3) parsnips

sea salt and freshly ground pepper

4 cups mixed cooking greens: tatsoi,
    red mustard, green mustard, etc.

2 eggs

1 tablespoon all-purpose flour

¼ cup freshly grated pecorino
    Romano or Parmesan cheese

2 tablespoons unsalted butter

½ cup chopped sage

½ cup finely chopped walnuts

sunflower or olive oil for frying

1. Heat a large pot of water for the greens. While it's heating, peel the parsnips, then grate them lightly, stopping when you get to the core, which will be visible. You should have about 2 cups. Set aside.

2. When the water comes to a boil, add salt, plunge in the greens, and cook until tender, about 5 minutes. Taste to be sure. Drain, press out much of the moisture, then chop coarsely.

3. Beat the eggs, then whisk in the flour and 1 teaspoon salt. Stir in the parsnips, greens, and cheese. Season with pepper.

4. Melt the butter in an 8-inch nonstick skillet. Add the sage and walnuts and cook, stirring frequently, until they smell toasty and good, after just a few minutes. Add them to the parsnip mixture.

5. Wipe out the skillet and add enough oil to coat lightly. When hot, add the parsnip mixture and pat it evenly into the pan. Reduce the heat to medium-low and cook until golden, about 5 minutes. Slide the galette onto a plate, place the skillet over it, and, grasping both plate and skillet, flip them over. Cook the second side until golden and crisp, then slide the galette onto a counter, cut into pieces, and serve.

Parsnip Salad with Walnuts and Dates | SERVES 4

This autumn salad uses the new crops of dates and walnuts, the first Meyer lemons, and freshly dug parsnips. The combination may sound strange, but it's no stranger than one made of carrots and raisins. After all, parsnips are cousins to carrots, and dates, like raisins, are fruits with high concentrations of sugars.

1 or 2 (about 10 ounces) firm white parsnips

sea salt and freshly ground pepper

2 teaspoons Meyer lemon juice or more to taste

1 teaspoon grated Meyer lemon zest

2 teaspoons honey

8 large Medjool dates, pits removed

¼ cup yogurt, preferably whole-milk

6 walnuts, cracked and chopped

1. Peel the parsnips. Cut them in half crosswise and cut a slice off the very top so that you can see the ring of flesh surrounding the core. Grate them on a box grater without bearing down too hard so that the pieces will be thin. Keep your eye on the top of the parsnip and stop grating when you get to the core. Toss the grated parsnips with ½ teaspoon salt, some pepper, the lemon juice, zest, and honey.

2. Cut each date half into 4 pieces. Add these to the parsnips with the yogurt and toss well. Taste for salt and lemon, adding more if needed. Cover and refrigerate until ready to serve, then toss once more with the walnuts.

The Hmong people from northern Laos immigrated to the United States at the end of the Vietnam War and settled throughout the country. Cultural adjustment for the first generation of Hmong cannot have been easy, but they have survived, and their presence is particularly evident at farmers' markets. Unlikely to own land, at least at first, they have been willing to farm any land that can be leased, from the smallest backyard plot to marginal acreage at the edges of cities awaiting development. Since families and clan members work together, Hmong farmers have been able to grow more labor-intensive crops as well as take on more labor-intensive ways of presenting their vegetables at farmers' markets.

It is not difficult to recognize the Hmong displays, which are striking in their precision and very much the same from one market to the next. Haricots verts and yellow wax beans are bundled neatly with rubber bands, all the tip ends facing the same way. Narrow Asian eggplants are stacked vertically in green plastic baskets; long cayenne chiles are bound at the stems. Scallions and leeks are trimmed and stacked, the white ends whittled to a point and facing out—wasteful but alluring. Parsnips and carrots are bound by their stems, which are clipped so that the roots stand upright in little tepee-shaped piles. The same veg-

etables might also be stacked in plastic bags, the pointed ends out. At one market, the tiniest bok choy I have ever seen, probably twenty to a bunch, were tied neatly with string.

In Madison, Wisconsin, one morning I watched a Hmong woman, her head wrapped in a pretty traditional cloth, rapidly reduce a huge pile of beans to a mound of beautifully stacked bundles that were easy for her customers to pick up and tuck into a shopping bag. At the Missoula, Montana, farmers' market, quite a few young Hmong (who everywhere speak flawless English, I've noticed) were selling wild huckleberries, which they had packaged in open zip-close plastic bags, opened to make it easy to see the berries and for the berries to breathe. The Hmong way of presenting produce is so attractive that I've seen their techniques imitated by quite a number of farmers who can't remotely claim to be of Hmong descent. They obviously think it's an idea worth copying.

The only place I've seen Hmong produce rather casually, if not actually carelessly, displayed was at the Stockton market under the freeway. As far as I could tell, this was a completely ethnic market where no English was spoken and most of the shoppers were Asian and Middle Eastern. Perhaps there was no need for elaborate displays among friends and family. At least that's my guess.

Steamed
Potatoes

Potatoes are probably the most versatile vegetables of all. There are hundreds of things you can do with them. But when they first come into the market with their thin, papery skins, I keep turning to the steamer. I can never believe how amazingly good they are cooked this way and how different one variety tastes from another. Steaming lets you taste the essence of the potato. Their colors are surprisingly beautiful, too. There's also the surprise of opening a soft, hot potato, which you might have thought was a Red Dale, and discovering that it's pink inside (a Huckleberry), or yellow with swirls of rose (a French Nosebag).

Wash the potatoes, but don't worry about getting their skins off. Put them in a steaming basket over simmering water, cover the pan, and steam until tender. The time can vary enormously, depending on the size (very small ones can be done in 20 minutes; larger ones can take 45) and variety (boilers seem to take longer than wax-fleshed potatoes).

Salt Potatoes with Butter and Herbs | SERVES 6

When I've visited upstate New York in the summer, I've always seen sacks of salt potatoes for sale. Was there something about the potatoes that was salty, or was it the way they would be cooked? When I bought a plate of salt potatoes at a fair, I saw that they were new potatoes that had been boiled in brine and served floating in a pond of melted butter. This is an incredibly delicious way to cook the small new potatoes you find at your market, regardless of the variety, as long as they're not bakers. Traditionally the butter is plain, but it's good with herbs, too.

2 pounds small potatoes

2 cups sea salt

½ cup unsalted butter, melted

¼ cup finely chopped mixed herbs:
    marjoram, chives, lemon
    basil, etc.

freshly ground pepper

1. Scrub the potatoes, but don't peel them.
2. Bring 3 quarts water to a boil with the salt. Stir to dissolve the salt, then add the potatoes. Boil over medium heat until the potatoes are fork-tender, 15 to 30 minutes, depending on the size of the pota-toes. Drain the potatoes, then toss them in a bowl with the butter and herbs. Season with pepper and serve.

Potato and Onion Salad with Smoked Albacore | SERVES 4

Smoked albacore was an unusual find, discovered at farmers' markets in Washington and California. You can use any flaky-textured smoked fish in its place, however. For potatoes, use fingerlings or another waxy boiling type—Red Dale, Salad Red, Yellow Finn, or Yukon Gold.

1½ pounds potatoes (see headnote)

sea salt and freshly ground pepper

1 Walla Walla or other sweet onion, sliced into rounds, about 1 cup

3 tablespoons champagne vinegar

⅓ cup olive oil

16 black or green olives, pitted and halved

6 ounces smoked albacore, flaked

2 good handfuls coarsely chopped arugula or plucked purslane

2 hard-cooked eggs, page 230

1. Cover the potatoes with cold salted water and bring to a boil. While they're cooking, toss the onion with the vinegar, oil, olives, fish, and ½ teaspoon salt.

2. When the potatoes are fork-tender, drain them, then cut in half lengthwise. While still hot, add them to the bowl along with the arugula or purslane. Turn gently with a rubber scraper. Taste for salt and season with pepper. Serve garnished with the egg, cut into quarters or halves.

Rutabaga and Potato Puree | SERVES 6 TO 8

"When's the last time you ate a rutabaga?" Ed May's sign asked.

"They're sweet!"

Ed was frustrated that customers were buying his fingerling potatoes but overlooking his excellent though gnarly-looking rutabagas. People who pass these fall tubers by are missing out on a treat. They're delicious, they're mild, and they're a delicate buttery yellow color.

There's no need to worry about a specific blend here. You can use more rutabagas than potatoes, and you can include some turnips in the mix as well. Because rutabagas aren't as starchy as potatoes, you may not need to add milk, cream, or the cooking water. But if you do want to thin out the mixture, it's best if the liquid has been warmed first.

½ pound russet or other potatoes
1½ pounds rutabagas or mixed
    rutabagas and turnips
sea salt and freshly ground pepper
unsalted butter
freshly grated nutmeg
1 tablespoon chopped parsley and/or
    snipped chives

1. Peel the potatoes and rutabagas, then chop them into chunks, making the rutabagas about half the size of the potatoes (and turnips, if using) since they take longer to cook. Put them in a saucepan and cover with cold water. Add 1½ teaspoons salt and bring to a boil. Cook until soft enough to mash, about 25 minutes.

2. Drain, reserving a cup of the cooking water first, then return the vegetables to the pot and mash them with a potato masher, adding as much butter as you like. If the puree is too thick, add some of the reserved liquid or warm milk or cream to thin it. Scrape in a little nutmeg and taste for salt and season with pepper. Serve with the parsley or chives scattered over the top.

VARIATIONS:

Fold in toasted, chopped hazelnuts and serve the puree with a drizzle of hazelnut oil.

Add 1 cup grated aged Cheddar or freshly grated Parmesan cheese.

Brown any leftovers in butter and serve with an arugula salad.

Parsley Root and Potato Puree | SERVES 4 TO 6

Parsley roots are thin and unpromising in terms of volume but a huge treasure when it comes to flavor. Their taste is clean, bracing, and assertive enough to have a real presence in a potato puree or potato soup, which this can easily become with the addition of some extra liquid. In fact the vegetable-cooking water has so much flavor that any extra should be dedicated to soup.

1 bunch (½ dozen or so) parsley
    roots
handful of the parsley root greens or
    flat-leaf parsley
1 pound Yellow Finn or other waxy
    golden potatoes
sea salt and freshly ground pepper
butter
cream or half-and-half, optional

1. Peel the parsley roots. Wash the greens. Scrub and peel the potatoes. Coarsely chop the vegetables, then put them in a saucepan, cover with water, and add 1 teaspoon salt. Bring to a boil, then simmer until the vegetables are tender, 15 to 20 minutes. Drain, but reserve the liquid.

2. Return the vegetables to the pan and mash them, using the reserved cooking water to thin the mixture as needed. When smooth, stir in butter and cream, if using, to taste.

3. Finely chop the parsley, then stir them into the puree. Taste for salt, season with pepper, and serve.

This isn't its real name, but I had always heard friends refer to this market as the "XYZ" market. Actually, it's on W Street in Sacramento, and it's called the Sacramento Central CFM (Certified Farmers' Market).

I had heard that this Sunday market was where farmers went to get rid of what they didn't sell on Saturday. It was definitely not described in the glowing terms used for the more upscale market in nearby Davis, but there was plenty of good produce and some that was quite special. The displays were more haphazard than at the Davis market, but that's just another approach. And rather than being situated in a pretty park, this market was located under a freeway.

A number of markets across the country make use of the otherwise unutilized space under freeways. One I had visited the previous summer had offered cool and shady relief from the heat outside, as well as plenty of parking. But I'd wondered what it would be like to spend hours in the darkness of a concrete market during the winter. I found that it was bone chilling, especially for the farmers who were there for five or six hours, starting early in the morning. While it would have been much more pleasant to be out in the winter sun, there *was* plenty of room for everyone. Plus the freeway offered shelter from rains, which, if all goes well, are part of Sacramento winters.

I recognized some of the farmers I had seen the previous day in Davis with their apples, citrus, persimmons, and dried fruits. A chestnut farmer I had met in Auburn, Tim Broughton, was there, drawing customers to the warmth of his fragrant fire and samples of hot roasted chestnuts. Mr. Bariani was there with gallon jugs filled with his golden olive oil. Among some of the new faces I saw was a sweet potato farmer. But before getting to her interesting varieties of these tubers, let's try to clarify the sweet potato–yam confusion. Botanically, sweet potatoes and yams are two different vegetables. The yam is a tropical vegetable. It grows in West Africa and Asia. Sweet potatoes are what we grow here. However, the word *yam* has crept into the nomenclature, as in Garnet yams or Jewel yams, because growers and shippers decided years ago to use the word *yam* to distinguish these moist, sweeter, orange-fleshed sweet potatoes from the traditional pale-yellow, dry-fleshed ones. This probably shouldn't have happened, but it did, and it's not too confusing after all.

This sweet potato farmer, Tracee Canisso, who grows her fifty acres of tubers near Livingston, California, had varieties I had never seen before and some that I had. I bought some of each kind, took them home, and roasted them so that I could compare them. (To keep the varieties straight in situations like this, I simply write the names on the vegetables themselves. That way I don't lose track.) What I chose to taste and compare were the following:

KOTOBUKI: Long golden-skinned tubers with dry straw-colored, chestnut-flavored flesh

HANNA: Short and stubby tubers with pointy ends, slightly darker skin, and golden flesh; marvelous rich chestnut flavor

GARNET: Deep-purple skin, dark-orange flesh, moist, sweet, well balanced

DIANA: Purple skin, orange flesh, moist and extremely sweet but sharp

JEWEL: Another sweet, super-moist orange-fleshed sweet potato with a coppery rather than red-orange skin

BEAUREGARD: Quite similar to Jewel, with purple-rose skin and orange flesh

"Kotobuki and Hanna," Tracee explained, "are the sweet potatoes with the pale, dry flesh. They're the ones favored by Asians and East Indians." To me they tasted a lot like chestnuts, and I imagined that their cooked flesh could be used where chestnut purees are called for, whether savory or sweet. In fact, they both succeed as the ingredient in the subtle, velvety custard on page 221. Being nuttier and less sweet than the orange-fleshed varieties, they turned out to be more versatile, too—good in a salad with a garlicky dressing, compatible with curry spices, happy to be glazed with honey, ginger, and soy sauce (page 220). But they are also absolutely delicious simply roasted and eaten with butter and pepper.

In contrast, the Garnet and the Jewel yams were intensely sweet with very moist orange flesh. Although served as a vegetable, they are essentially ready-made desserts. (Try them sometime with a little molasses and cream.) Although you might be tempted to use them for a sweet potato pie, the sweet potatoes that I saw for sale at the Birmingham farmers' market that were specifically designed for pies were the paler variety—drier, not as sweet, but very tasty.

Garnet and Jewel "yams" are both very good eating and very popular, but a newcomer, Diana, was developed to replace the Garnet. Tracee explained that it has some shipping and storage problems due to its thin skin. When I bit into the cooked flesh of the purple-skinned Diana, I found it to be almost painfully sweet, with a somewhat sharp, even harsh, aftertaste. Of course, shipping shouldn't be a problem when food is grown and sold locally, as it is at farmers' markets, so perhaps local farmers can keep growing the Garnet.

Similarly, the Beauregard has been developed to replace the lovely Jewel. "But why?" I asked Tracee. "The Jewel is wonderful!"

"Because," she explained, "packers don't care for the way the eyes line up in a row, like a perforation."

For Pete's sake! I had never noticed this until I picked one up and looked. There it was, a tiny perforation, like a zipper, running up the length of the tuber. I can't believe this is a serious problem for anyone. Do you care if your sweet potato has a "zipper"? Perhaps this could be an asset. Fortunately, the Beauregard stays close to the original flavor of the Jewel.

You may be seeing fewer Garnets and Jewels in the future and more Dianas and Beauregards. "Strains of sweet potatoes don't last forever, so they can be expected to change every so many years," Tracee said. In fact, I noticed that Beauregards are being sold this year at my local market, which also carries what they call Japanese sweet potatoes. It's already happening.

A MENU FOR GINGER AND SESAME LOVERS

Stir-Fried Carrots and Burdock with Sesame Seeds
(page 204)

Soy-Glazed Sweet Potatoes (page 220)

Napa Cabbage Salad with Peanuts and Cilantro (page 100)

Roasted Chestnuts (page 381)

Vine-ripened kiwifruits and Satsuma mandarins

Sweet Potatoes Roasted in a Wood Fire

This is the best way of all to cook sweet potatoes. Rub clean tubers with sunflower seed oil or butter, wrap them individually in foil, and bake them in the hot coals until tender. An 8- to 10-ounce tuber should take about 30 minutes, but it's always tricky with wood fires. It's a good idea to choose one potato to be your tester, then test for tenderness with repeated pricks of a knife, leaving the rest securely wrapped. They'll emerge with a slightly smoky flavor mixed with the caramelized sugars. They are unbelievably delicious.

Soy-Glazed Sweet Potatoes | MAKES 12 PLUMP PIECES, SERVING 6

These take moments to ready for the oven and a little over an hour to bake. When done, they should be lacquered and even blackened in places. If you don't eat them all at the first sitting, reheat them in a nonstick skillet and they'll caramelize a bit. They're even more delicious the second time around.

3 large sweet potatoes, either the dry or the moist-fleshed types
1 tablespoon roasted sesame oil
2 tablespoons brown sugar
2 tablespoons mirin or sweet sherry
1 tablespoon minced garlic
3 tablespoons soy sauce
¼ cup water
1 tablespoon black or white sesame seeds, toasted

1. Preheat the oven to 400°F. Scrub the sweet potatoes and cut them lengthwise into quarters or halves. Place them in a baking dish roomy enough to hold them in a single layer.

2. Combine the rest of the ingredients except the sesame seeds. Brush all of the resulting sauce over the sweet potatoes, then cover the dish tightly with foil. Bake until nearly tender, 50 minutes to an hour. Remove the foil, baste the sweet potatoes with their juices, and return to the oven until the liquid has reduced to a glaze and the potatoes are fully tender, 15 to 20 minutes longer. Sprinkle with sesame seeds and serve.

Sweet Potato Flan with Warm Molasses and Sesame Tuiles | SERVES 6

Hanna and Kotobuki sweet potatoes make a luscious flan that could be mistaken for chestnut. In fact you could serve them with warm chestnut honey instead of molasses. A crisp sesame tuile offers a bit of crunch.

unsalted butter for the ramekins

2 cups whole milk

¾ cup sugar

½ vanilla bean, halved lengthwise

¾ pound Kotobuki or Hanna sweet potatoes, baked or steamed until tender

2 eggs

1 egg yolk

warm molasses

Sesame Tuiles, recipe follows

1. Preheat the oven to 325°F. Lightly butter 6 (½-cup) ramekins. Bring the milk, sugar, and vanilla bean to a boil in a saucepan, then turn off the heat. Stir to make sure the sugar is dissolved. Scrape the vanilla seeds into the milk and return the pods to the pan. Let stand for the flavor to infuse for 15 minutes.

2. Scoop the flesh from the sweet potatoes and measure ¾ cup. Puree with the eggs and the extra yolk. It will have a somewhat sticky texture. Add the milk and process just until well blended. You want a minimal amount of bubbles for a smooth custard.

3. Pour the liquid into the ramekins and set them in a large pan. Add boiling water to come halfway up the sides of the ramekins. Bake until set but just a bit wobbly at the very center, about 45 minutes. Leave the custards in the water bath until ready to serve. Run a knife along the edge of the cups, then turn them out onto serving plates. Drizzle with the warm molasses and serve with the tuiles.

SESAME TUILES | MAKES 2 DOZEN COOKIES

4 tablespoons unsalted butter

2 large egg whites

pinch sea salt

½ cup sugar

½ teaspoon roasted sesame oil

⅓ cup sifted all-purpose flour

½ cup white sesame seeds, toasted

You'll need a rolling pin for setting the warm cookies into their curved, tilelike shapes. Set on a cooling rack, they won't roll around.

1. Preheat the oven to 375°F. Cover 2 baking sheets with parchment paper or lightly butter and flour them. Melt the butter slowly over low heat, stirring occasionally. Set aside to cool.

2. Whisk the egg whites with the salt and sugar until foamy, then whisk in the sesame oil and flour. Stir in the melted butter and sesame seeds.

3. Drop heaping tablespoons of the batter onto the cookie sheets, leaving at least 3 inches between them. Spread the batter into a very thin circle. Bake for 6 to 8 minutes or until lightly browned around the edges. Turn the pans at least once while they're baking.

4. Slide a spatula under the tuiles, then lift them up and drape them over the rolling pin or bottles. As they cool, they'll harden. Then you can put them aside and continue baking until the batter is used up.

Braised Root Vegetables with Black Lentils and Red Wine Sauce | SERVES 6

This dish is for when you want to fuss a bit and make a celebration of root vegetables or for when you want an impressive vegetarian meal. It involves four elements: the sauce, the vegetables, the lentils, and some form of mashed potatoes or root vegetable puree. None of the parts are difficult or even terribly time consuming in and of themselves. However, you might choose to cook them over the course of 2 days. Only the potato-based puree is best made at the last minute, and even it can be held for an hour or so in a double boiler.

If making the dish from start to finish, start with the sauce, adding trimmings, such as carrot ends and parsnip cores, as you work. While it's simmering, prepare the vegetables and cook the lentils. You can have the potatoes scrubbed, cut, and waiting in a pot of cold water to cook close to serving.

THE RED WINE SAUCE

⅓ cup dried porcini

1 tablespoon olive oil

1 large onion, diced

1 large carrot, diced

2 celery ribs, diced

5 mushrooms and/or mushroom
    trimmings

parsnip tips and cores, from the
    vegetables, below

4 garlic cloves, smashed

aromatics: 2 thyme sprigs, 1 bay leaf,
    1 (2-inch) rosemary sprig

sea salt and freshly ground pepper

1 tablespoon tomato paste

2 tablespoons all-purpose flour

2 cups Merlot

1 tablespoon mushroom soy sauce,
    more or less

1 tablespoon unsalted butter

1. Cover the porcini with 1 quart warm water and set aside. Heat the oil in a wide soup pot. Add the vegetables, garlic, and aromatics. Cook over medium-high heat, stirring occasionally, until the vegetables are well browned, about 20 minutes. Season with 1 teaspoon salt and a little pepper.

2. Stir in the tomato paste and flour, then pour in the wine plus the dried mushrooms and their soaking liquid. Vigorously scrape the bottom of the pot to work in the juices, then bring to a boil, lower the heat, and simmer, covered, for 45 minutes. Strain into a 1-quart measure. You should have about 3 cups. Return it to the pan and simmer until reduced to 2½ cups, 15 to 20 minutes. Add the mushroom soy sauce, then taste for salt and season with pepper. Whisk in the butter. Set aside.

THE VEGETABLES

18 to 24 shallots or red pearl onions

3 large or 6 medium parsnips

6 medium carrots or 18 small
    carrots

5 large mushrooms

1½ tablespoons olive oil

2 tablespoons unsalted butter

sea salt and freshly ground pepper

aromatics: 1 bay leaf, 2 thyme
    sprigs, 1½ teaspoons minced
    rosemary

Parsley Root and Potato Puree or
    Rutabaga and Potato Puree (page
    217 or 216)

3 tablespoons chopped parsley,
    chopped with 1 garlic clove

1. Peel the shallots and separate them where their natural divisions occur. If using pearl onions, parboil for 1 minute, then drain and peel, keeping the root end intact.

2. Peel the parsnips and trim off the skinny tips. Cut the remaining vegetable into 3 segments of equal length. Quarter the thickest section and remove a portion of the core. Halve the middle section and keep the last section whole. (Use the tips and cores in the sauce as directed.)

3. Peel the carrots and cut them into 2- to 3-inch lengths. If they're tapered, cut the thick ends into quarters, cut the middles into halves, and keep the last skinny pieces whole. If they're the same diameter from tip to tail, simply halve them lengthwise. Thickly slice the mushrooms.

4. Heat the oil and butter in a wide skillet or Dutch oven. Add the carrots and shallots and cook over medium-high heat, turning occasionally, until well browned in places, about 10 minutes. Add the parsnips and mushrooms and cook for 10 minutes. Season with 1 teaspoon salt, then add the herbs. Pour in 1 cup of the sauce and 1 cup water, bring to a boil, then lower the heat and simmer until the vegetables are tender when pierced, 20 to 25 minutes. (Add more water if needed—there should be some moisture in the pan.) Season with pepper and set aside until needed.

THE LENTILS

½ cup black "Caviar" Beluga or French
    green lentils, sorted and rinsed

½ teaspoon sea salt

1 tablespoon unsalted butter

Cover the lentils with 3 cups water, add the salt, and simmer until tender, about 25 minutes. Drain, then stir in the butter and 1 cup of the sauce.

FINISHING THE DISH

Prepare the puree. Reheat the vegetables with the remaining sauce. Mound the puree in the center of 6 pasta plates. Place 2 or 3 spoonfuls of lentils around the potatoes, then fill in with the vegetables. Spoon the extra sauce around and over the vegetables and lentils, then garnish with the chopped parsley and serve.

Calgary is not a place where the image of the farm comes to mind, for this is a town that concerns itself with oil, banking, and beef. But in my several visits to Calgary I've found that Calgarians are enthusiastic about food. Cooking classes are filled, and there's always some new trendy restaurant. One of the best bakeries I've encountered is there, and there are excellent chocolate makers, for the cool, dry climate is ideal for chocolate work. There is also a farmers' market, which I visited late one September. The sky on this day looked like a big blue dome. Wind filled the air with leaves, and a sharp chill made it clear that Indian summer had run its course. Winter was only waiting for these few fall days to finish up before making its entrance. Its stay would be a long one.

It was the last day of the market. There weren't many customers, and they didn't come to linger. They got out of their jeeps, slammed the doors, zipped up their jackets, pulled down their hats, and did a cursory, purposeful shopping. With scarcely an exchange of words, they returned to their cars and were off. All but a few of the market's stalls were closed for the season. Wind kept slamming shut and then opening a loose door somewhere, only to slam it shut once more. It was a forlorn sound.

There were a few remnants of summer vegetables—actually quite a decent array of bell peppers, chiles, and eggplants from the Okanagan Valley, a province away. But mostly there were the sturdy foods of winter—six kinds of winter squash, including some huge warty Blue Hubbards; seven kinds of apples; pears and quince; parsley root (a rare find); celery root; parsnips; walnuts; and, surprisingly, poppy seeds. There was even thistle seed for the birds. This was the market to satisfy that deep urge for stocking root cellars and larders.

Like the first market of the year, there wasn't that much at the end of the season, but even the limited offerings of this market inspired all kinds of ideas for dishes to cook. That night I ate at the River Cafe, a handsome restaurant set in the woods on Prince's Island in the middle of the Bow River. There, chef Victoria Adams prepared a very refined root stew which made a celebration out of winter's earthly stores: a succulent root vegetable braise with a silken mushroom sauce, a few spoonfuls of black lentils, and luscious mashed potatoes. Since then, this is the dish I've chosen for my most special vegetarian winter meals. Roots, I've discovered, can both start and end the market season in proper style.

A MENU FOR A SPECIAL WINTER MEAL

Fennel and Winter Greens Salad with
Mushrooms and Truffle Oil (page 45)

Braised Root Vegetables with Black Lentils and
Red Wine Sauce (page 223)

Winter Mince Tart with a Lattice Crust (page 314)

Honey Ice Cream (page 379)

Eggs and Cheese at the Market

There are a dozen in each carton, but that's where the uniformity stops. Some of our farmers sell their eggs all mixed up—some tiny, some large, and many in between, but never all alike. Sometimes I overhear some customers complaining about this, but I rather like opening a box of mixed eggs. If I'm feeling ravenous, I reach for the giant ones. If I just need an egg to glaze a pastry, a tiny one is perfect, while a pullet egg is just the size for a small child. It's nice to have a choice, and in some ways it makes more sense than having every egg the same.

In the years I've been visiting farmers' markets, I've seen everything from duck eggs to yellow speckled turkey eggs, goose eggs packed in plastic bags, gigantic ostrich eggs, and the tiniest mottled quail eggs. Occasionally we have had guinea hen eggs at our market, sometimes duck eggs, but there are always chicken eggs, which may be blue, green, white, or varying shades of brown. Regardless of size or color, market eggs tend to have bright yellow yolks, firm, well-formed whites, and real flavor that even children appreciate.

"We've been going to Boggy Creek Farm for so long that our four-year-old daughter, Zibby, now knows the drill," Laurie Smith tells me. "Last week, when she saw Carol Ann, Boggy Creek's chicken lady, she tugged at her overalls. 'Can we collect some eggs, now?' she asked. She never liked eggs before, but when she could see where they came from and feel their warmth, that changed. Now she loves eggs. We cook an egg as soon as we get home."

I never really cared much for eggs either, until I started buying them at the farmers' market. Now I'm an egg eater, too. Because of these beautiful eggs, I frequently serve them for Sunday lunch or supper. Soft scrambled eggs with fresh herbs, a nettle frittata, and a spinach soufflé scented with green garlic are some of my favorites. But true farm eggs make delicacies out of familiar dishes such as custards and fried eggs, for they have a luster that ordinary eggs simply lack. Even an egg salad sandwich becomes something to anticipate.

Cheeses, like eggs, have long been part of farmers' markets, and they're getting better and better as our nation's new cheese makers become increasingly skilled. Goat cheese is now a common feature at many markets, and although most is made in the simplest fresh style, in California's San Rafael market I've seen goat's milk mascarpone and the markets I've visited in Vermont have some of the most impressive farmhouse goat *and* sheep cheeses I've encountered anywhere, including Europe. Quite a few of the artisan cheeses that have represented American cheese making at Slow Food's international cheese exposition in Italy can be found at farmers' markets.

Occasionally you'll find sheep's milk cheese. A sheep's milk feta is delicious with eggs, with cucumbers, and with apples, while a sheep's milk ricotta is likely to be delicate and creamy. While our local sheep's milk butter-cheese and feta are pleasantly tangy, a longer-aged sheep's milk cheese from the Ithaca farmers' market was quite strong. Local flavors vary.

In dairy states, such as Wisconsin, Minnesota, Vermont, and upstate New York, you can count on finding aged Cheddars, Goudas, and a host of other cow's milk cheeses. Some dairies will specify when their cheese or yogurt is made from Guernsey milk, the gold standard of cow's milks. Fresh ricotta of any kind is one of the very best market finds of all. It's pure and milky-sweet, with a light texture and no graininess. It makes any recipe that calls for ricotta absolutely stellar.

Cheese curds were present in every midwestern market I visited, and it seemed as if every other person I met in Minnesota told me about eating fried cheese curds at the state fair. Spongy and squeaky when you eat them, cheese curds are essentially day-old cheeses. At the Heart of the City

Market in Kansas City, a young man offered me a sample of his white and tangy goat cheese curd. "And what about your cheese?" I asked, assuming they'd have something more mature. "We don't even bother to make it anymore," the boy's father told me, "because we sell out of the curds every week." I took the curds home, drizzled them with olive oil, cracked pepper over them, and added chopped herbs—simple and obvious but good, especially with sliced pears. I'd no doubt buy them every week, too.

We have just one cheese maker at our market. Patrice Harrison-Inglis, who looks like the ur-dairy maid with her Dutch-cut blond hair, started out with goat's milk, goat yogurt, and a fresh goat cheese. Next she added herbs to her cheese, then she took off. She has been steadily developing her skills, and at this writing she offers a creamy Brie, a goat blue, a traditional New Mexican breakfast cheese, a stunning sheep's milk feta, sheep butter-cheese, salad goat cheeses in olive oil, and a sheep-goat Brie. She also makes *cajeta,* a thick goat's milk caramel that is delicious drizzled over ice cream. Her growing skill parallels what's happening all over the country.

The Boiled Egg

Everyone has a favorite method, but this is the one that always works for me. What makes a boiled egg perfect? The white is cooked, and the yolk retains moisture. It's not runny, but it's not dry, either. And, of course, there's no green ring encircling it.

Place the eggs in a pot of cold water, bring to a boil, and boil for 1 minute. Turn off the heat, cover the pan, and let stand for 6 minutes at sea level or a minute longer for every 1,000 feet over 3,000 feet elevation. (At 7,000 feet they need to stand for 10 minutes.) Pour off the water. If you're not planning to eat them hot, dump the eggs into a bowl of cold water (having some ice in it is fine) and run cold water over them to cool. Give them a few knocks against the side of the bowl to break the shells, which cools them down more quickly and makes the eggs easier to peel.

Egg Salad with Herbs Through the Seasons | SERVES 4 TO 6

When I brought this salad to market as part of a demonstration, people pounced on it. Perhaps because we don't make egg salad much anymore, we've forgotten how good it is. Of course made with real farm eggs, the simplest egg salad becomes remarkable. Put it on good bread with some arugula, and you will have one of the best sandwiches ever.

Following the progression of the seasons, in the spring, season this salad with liberal amounts of fresh chervil (and perhaps a clove or two of minced green garlic), then move on through the summer using dill, parsley, lovage, tarragon, fennel greens, lemon thyme, and marjoram. Chives (onion and garlic), scallions, and shallots always have a good place in an egg salad.

6 large market eggs

3 scallions, including an inch or so of the greens, thinly sliced

1 tablespoon chopped chervil or 2 teaspoons chopped tarragon or lovage

1 tablespoon minced parsley

1 tablespoon slivered chives

⅓ cup mayonnaise or more to taste

1½ teaspoons smooth mustard

sea salt and freshly ground pepper

vinegar or fresh lemon juice

Cook the eggs as described in the preceding recipe. After they've sat, dump them into a bowl of cold water and run cold water over them to cool. Peel them, place them in a bowl or pie plate, and coarsely mash them with a fork. Add the scallions and herbs, holding back a few of the chives, the mayonnaise, and the mustard. Season with salt and pepper and a few drops of vinegar or lemon juice to taste. Transfer to a serving bowl and garnish with the reserved chives.

Fried Eggs with Sizzling Vinegar | SERVES 1, BUT EASY TO MULTIPLY

This is so easy, yet it gives fried eggs an entirely new personality. Try these when you're having a fried egg for supper or a jazz breakfast. This vinegar sauce is also good with onion-based dishes, such as an onion frittata or Savory Custard with Caramelized Onions and Smoked Cheese on page 239.

3 to 4 teaspoons unsalted butter

1 or 2 fresh market eggs, any size

sea salt and freshly ground pepper

1 small shallot, finely diced

1 tablespoon or so sherry vinegar,
    aged red wine vinegar, or
    tarragon vinegar

1. Melt a teaspoon or so of butter in a nonstick frying pan and swirl it around. Once it's hot and the bubbles have subsided, break in the eggs. Season them with salt and pepper and cook them as you like—straight up, over easy, a bit firmer. (Be sure your bread is toasting at the same time.) When the eggs are done, slide them onto a plate.
2. Add the rest of the butter to the pan with the shallot, which will sizzle immediately. Add the vinegar, take the pan off the heat, and swirl it about to blend the vinegar and butter, allowing it to reduce some. Tip it right over your eggs.

Scrambled Eggs with Roasted Green Chiles and Corn | MAKES 4 BREAKFAST BURRITOS

From August on, you can count on buying a plastic bag full of roasted green chiles, still warm from roasting, beautiful eggs, a half dozen thick, homemade tortillas, and some fresh or aged goat cheese from our market. Having an ear of leftover roasted corn was how the corn got into the eggs, but you can start with raw corn, too.

6 long green chiles

1 ear sweet corn, cooked or raw

6 large market eggs

sea salt

2 tablespoons unsalted butter

½ cup goat or Cheddar cheese

4 large tortillas, whole wheat
    if possible

1. Roast the chiles (see page 390), then remove the skins and seeds from the chiles and chop them coarsely.
2. Slice the kernels off the corn. Break up the eggs in a bowl with a fork and season with ½ teaspoon salt.
3. Melt the butter in an 8-inch nonstick pan. When sizzling, add the corn and chile and stir long enough to warm them up. (If the corn was raw, cook it for at least a minute.) Add the eggs and the cheese, lower the heat, and cook, stirring gently, until the eggs are set.
4. Meanwhile, warm the tortillas in the oven or in a wide skillet. Serve them with the eggs.

A LUNCH ON THE PORCH
MID-APRIL

Boggy Creek Farm in downtown (practically) Austin has a farm stand that has become, in its decade-long life, an Austin institution. Fans drive down the tree-lined drive twice each week to buy whatever organically grown vegetables and fruits are in season, plus the farm's delicious eggs, local goat cheese, organic beef and chicken also raised nearby, and some exceptional value-added products, such as smoked dried tomatoes. On some occasions the owners, Carol Ann Sayle and Larry Butler, let customers into the fields to pick their own corn or strawberries, and some children have been known to collect their own eggs from the henhouse. It's tempting, after shopping, to linger in the shade of the old pecan trees or sit on the porch, and many customers do.

Farm stands are another way farmers can sell what they grow directly to the consumer. At some, money is just dropped into a jar in exchange for produce, on the honor system so that the farmer can keep working. But with others, like Boggy Creek, the public walks right into the heart of the farmers' life and livelihood. There they can really see exactly where their food comes from.

Shortly after turning in this book, I got a call from a friend in Austin with the bad news: Boggy Creek Farm had been hit by a tornado! The twister stayed in the tops of the sixty-year-old pecan and oak trees, snapping off limbs, which destroyed the chicken coop, the greenhouse, and a side of the farmhouse. Its force pulled some of these huge trees right out of the ground, unscrewing them like corks from a bottle. In addition, hundreds of smaller trees around the edge of the farm were snapped and broken, and crops were drowned in the deluge of rain that came with the storm.

The next day, various farm customers showed up, unasked, with chainsaws. They spent days cutting and hauling branches, making a pile in the street some 200 feet long. Out of gratitude, Larry in turn helped his neighbors with their clean-up efforts.

On another front, other friends were busy putting together a benefit so that the historic old farmhouse could be repaired. Patrick and I drove down to Austin to take part. We love the farm, too, and wouldn't have missed a chance to help out for anything. Hundreds of people—farm customers, chefs, musicians, other farmers, fans, and friends showed up for the auction event and did an amazing job raising money. It seems that we all donated what we could of our talents and goods, and bought as heavily as possible from one another. One of the most generous donors was Austin's Central Market, a grocery business that truly recognizes the importance of farms. There was a great sense of community that night, even though a lot of us didn't know each other. The words I kept hearing were, "It's a damn shame about that tornado, but isn't it great to be among so many people who care so much about Boggy Creek Farm!" It was, and the farm continues. And the farmhouse once again has walls and a roof.

A SPRING LUNCH MENU

Egg Salad (page 231) sandwiches
made with spring onions

Herb Salad (page 67)

Pure Luck goat cheese

Strawberries still warm from the sun

Thin Omelets with Saffron and Exotic Herbs | SERVES 3 TO 6

Founder of the FRESHFARM Markets in Washington, D.C., including the flourishing market at DuPont Circle, Ann Yonkers points out that by shopping at the farmers' market, you help your local farmers stay in business, which is undoubtedly the best way to preserve American farmland—staying in business. Chip Planck, who sells there, echoed this thought in a subsequent conversation when he said, "Without farmers' markets, I couldn't be in the vegetable-growing business today." With these words I believe that Chip speaks for a great many farmers.

On the opening day of the FRESHFARM Market one year, I was invited to do a chef's demonstration. Our market was opening on the same day, and although thousands of miles from New Mexico, and at sea level instead of 7,000 feet, both markets offered practically identical selections of produce—herbs, eggs, last fall's apples and potatoes, and a few spring greens.

I decided to make these thin omelets. The herbs are familiar. It's their commingling that makes them exotic and provides an interesting conversation of flavors. Serve these thin omelets with pita bread, a plate of sliced tomatoes and cucumbers, and some sheep's milk feta on the side.

pinch saffron threads

6 to 8 market eggs

4 scallions, including half the greens, finely chopped

1 tablespoon chopped dill

½ cup chopped cilantro

½ cup chopped parsley

1 tablespoon chopped basil

sea salt and freshly ground pepper

2 tablespoons olive oil, unsalted butter, or a mixture

sprigs of dill flowers for garnish

1. Cover the saffron with a tablespoon of boiling water to release the color and flavor.
2. Whisk the eggs, stir in the scallions, herbs, saffron, and a few pinches of salt and some pepper. Let stand for 15 minutes.
3. Preheat the broiler. Add 2 teaspoons of the oil and/or butter to an 8-inch, nonstick skillet over medium-high heat. When hot, pour in a third of the eggs. After a minute or so, lower the heat and cook until golden on the bottom and the eggs are mostly set, about 10 minutes. Slide the pan under the broiler to finish cooking the top. Slide onto a serving plate and repeat twice more. Cut the omelets into quarters and serve garnished with the dill.

Zucchini Frittata with Ricotta and Marjoram | SERVES 4 TO 6

Amenable zucchini is an obvious choice for summer frittatas, but what's not so obvious is the use of marjoram. If you haven't made its acquaintance, do, for it's every bit as good as basil, especially here. In fact this frittata can be served with Marjoram Pesto with Capers and Olives.

Grating and salting the squash draws out its moisture and keeps the eggs from becoming watery. Costata Romanesco, the ridged Italian zucchini, is the most dense and flavorful, the one to use if you can find it.

1½ pounds zucchini, preferably
    Costata Romanesco

sea salt and freshly ground pepper

2 tablespoons olive oil

6 large market eggs

1 large garlic clove, crushed or minced
    with a pinch sea salt

1 tablespoon chopped marjoram

⅓ cup grated Dry Monterey Jack or
    Parmesan cheese

½ cup ricotta, drained if very wet

1. Coarsely grate the zucchini, toss with 1 teaspoon salt, and set aside in a colander for 30 minutes. Rinse briefly, then squeeze dry.

2. Warm half the oil in a wide skillet over medium-high heat. Add the zucchini and cook, stirring frequently, until it's dry and flecked with gold, about 6 minutes. Transfer to a bowl and wipe out the pan.

3. Preheat the broiler. Beat the eggs with a few pinches of salt and some pepper, then stir in the garlic, zucchini, marjoram, Jack cheese, and ricotta. Allow the ricotta to remain streaky. Add the remaining oil to the pan and, when it's hot, add the eggs. Lower the heat, cook for a minute or so, then shuffle the pan a few times to make sure the eggs are loose on the bottom.

4. Cook over low to medium heat until the eggs are set and the top is nearly dry, about 10 minutes, then slide the frittata under the broiler to finish cooking the top. Invert the finished dish onto a serving plate.

VARIATIONS:

Stir ¼ cup Marjoram Pesto with Capers and Olives, on page 65, into the eggs before cooking.

Once the top of the frittata is nearly set, cover it lightly with toasted pine nuts.

Nettle Frittata with Green Garlic and Sheep's Milk Ricotta | SERVES 6

Admittedly nettles and sheep's milk ricotta will not be found at every farmers' market, but if not sheep's milk ricotta, another ricotta will be fine. Since nettles are an early-season green (those that are new and tender taste better than late-season nettles), you might be able to combine them with ramps (wild leeks) or green garlic.

½ pound (a plastic vegetable bag full) nettles

1 head green garlic or 2 mature garlic cloves, minced

1 small onion, finely chopped, or onion mixed with ramps to make 1 cup

2 tablespoons olive oil

sea salt and freshly ground pepper

6 to 8 market eggs

⅓ cup grated pecorino Romano cheese

½ cup sheep's or cow's milk ricotta

1½ tablespoons unsalted butter or olive oil

1. Preheat the broiler. Bring a large pot of water to a boil for the nettles. Wearing rubber gloves or using tongs, plunge them into the water long enough for them to turn bright green and limp, after a minute or 2, then drain. Press out the excess water, then chop finely. (Once cooked, they won't sting.)

2. Chop the green garlic or garlic cloves and the onion. If using ramps, chop, then rinse them well to get rid of any sand.

3. Warm 2 tablespoons olive oil in a 10-inch nonstick skillet. Add the garlic and onion and cook over medium-low heat, stirring occasionally, until softened. Add the nettles and cook until any water they exude has evaporated. Season with salt and pepper.

4. Beat the eggs lightly with ½ teaspoon salt, then stir in the nettles and pecorino cheese. Add the ricotta, leaving it streaky.

5. Wipe out the skillet and return it to the heat with the butter or oil. When the butter has foamed, then subsided (or the oil is hot), pour in the egg mixture. Slide the pan back and forth a few times, then turn the heat to medium-low and cook for several minutes until the eggs have set around the edges and are pale gold on the bottom. Slide the pan under the broiler and continue cooking until the top is set and lightly colored. Cool slightly or to room temperature before serving.

Leek and Sorrel Custards | MAKES FOUR ½-CUP CUSTARDS

Eat these warm savory custards right out of their ramekins for lunch or supper. You can make this leaving the texture of the leeks and sorrel intact or puree it and make it smooth. It's good both ways.

4 to 6 thin leeks or scallions

2½ tablespoons unsalted butter

4-ounce bunch sorrel

1 teaspoon sea salt

1 cup half-and-half or whole milk

3 market eggs

freshly ground pepper

2 ounces fresh goat cheese

1. Preheat the oven to 350°F. Thinly slice, then chop the white parts of the leeks, going into the pale part of the greens a short way. You should have about 1 cup. Rinse them well. Melt the butter in an 8-inch skillet. Use some of it to brush four ½-cup ramekins, then add the leeks to the skillet. Add ¼ cup water or white wine and cook gently over medium-low heat until softened, about 12 minutes.

2. Strip the sorrel leaves off the stems; wash and finely chop them. Add them to the pan with the leeks, sprinkle with salt, and cook until wilted, about 2 minutes. Add the half-and-half and heat until warm but not boiling.

3. Beat the eggs well, then stir in the sorrel mixture. Season with pepper and crumble in the cheese. If you want smooth custard, puree in short pulses. Don't overmix, or it will be too foamy on top.

4. Divide among the ramekins; place in a baking pan and surround with a hot water bath. Bake until the custards are set and a knife inserted comes out clean, 30 to 35 minutes. Set the ramekins on small plates and serve with buttered toast.

Savory Custard with Caramelized Onions and Smoked Cheese | MAKES SIX ½-CUP RAMEKINS

This savory custard is just the thing to serve on a crisp October evening with roasted winter squash, sautéed black kale, and baked apples for dessert. You can bake the custard in a tart shell, but if you wish to avoid the trouble and calories involved in a crust, then try these flans. They are light, yet rich with flavor. The onions can be caramelized a day or more in advance, then reheated just before using.

1 tablespoon unsalted butter, plus
    extra for the ramekins
3 large yellow onions cut into
    medium dice
sea salt and freshly ground pepper
3 large market eggs
1½ cups milk (2 percent will taste
    fine) or light cream
pinch nutmeg
1 tablespoon all-purpose flour
1 cup finely grated smoked Cheddar
    cheese
minced parsley for garnish

1. Heat a wide nonstick pan with the butter. Add the onions, stir well to coat, then season with ½ teaspoon salt. Cover and cook over medium heat until the onions are very soft, occasionally giving them a stir as they cook. They should generate enough moisture so that they won't stick. After an hour, remove the lid and continue cooking, stirring occasionally, until the onions are pale to medium gold. Taste for salt and season with pepper.

2. Preheat the oven to 375°F. Boil water for the baking dish. Lightly butter the ramekins.

3. Crack the eggs in a bowl, then whisk in the milk, nutmeg, flour, ¾ teaspoon salt, and a grating of pepper.

4. Divide the onions and cheese among the ramekins, then pour in the custard. Stir each with a fork to evenly distribute the contents, then put the ramekins in a baking dish, add the boiling water to come at least an inch up the sides, and bake in the middle of the oven until golden and well set, about 50 minutes. Serve the flans in their dishes, or turn them out onto a plate. The tops will look rather naked since they won't be browned, so plan to garnish them with some minced parsley.

Goat's Milk Yogurt with Cilantro and Mint | MAKES 1 CUP

Goat's milk yogurt is starting to appear at more and more farmers' markets. Sometimes on the thin side, it can be mixed with thicker cow's milk yogurt or goat cheese to make this tangy sauce. Use it on grilled vegetables, on cucumber salads, or as a sauce for grilled chicken or lamb.

1 teaspoon coriander seeds
1 teaspoon cumin seeds
1 garlic clove
sea salt and freshly ground pepper
1 cup goat's or cow's milk yogurt
1½ tablespoons olive oil
⅓ cup chopped cilantro
2 tablespoons chopped mint
1 teaspoon minced jalapeño

1. Toast the coriander and cumin seeds in a dry pan until fragrant, then turn them out onto a plate to cool. Grind them to a powder.
2. Mash the garlic with ½ teaspoon salt until mushy, then work in the spices. Stir them into the yogurt, then add the oil, fresh herbs, and jalapeño. Season with pepper. Let stand for 30 minutes or more before serving.

Lamb Kebabs Marinated in Yogurt | SERVES 4

Forouz Jowkar, a friend and neighbor of the Manzanares family who raises lamb for the Santa Fe farmers' market, often makes the samples. A favorite is her marinated lamb, which I've interpreted in this recipe. I usually skewer it with little onions and peppers when they're in season, then grill it over a charcoal fire.

1 pound boneless leg of lamb,
    cut into bite-sized chunks
juice of 1 lemon
juice of 2 limes
2 tablespoons yogurt
3 tablespoons olive oil plus
    extra for basting
2 large garlic cloves
sea salt and freshly ground pepper
4 medium new onions, quartered

1. Rinse the lamb when you get home from the market and put it in a bowl or zipper-close plastic bag.
2. Puree the lemon and lime juices with the yogurt, olive oil, garlic, ½ teaspoon salt, and pepper. Pour this marinade over the lamb, then refrigerate anywhere from an hour, if that's all you have, to overnight. Turn the bag occasionally so that the marinade fully covers the lamb.
3. Soak 4 wooden skewers in water while you make a fire, preheat the broiler, or heat a gas grill. Then skewer the meat and onions and brush with olive oil. Grill or broil for about 15 minutes, turning the skewers occasionally so that the meat browns.

Cheese
Soufflé | SERVES 4 GENEROUSLY

Certainly there's nothing new about a cheese soufflé, but it expresses such a perfect harmony of lightness and nourishment, drama and ease, that it deserves to be recalled on a regular basis. Using the eggs and the cheese you'll find in your market, be it a light to a pungent goat cheese, a sharp aged Cheddar, a Gruyère, or a Cheddar made from goat's milk, you're bound to end up with a truly wonderful dish.

Tomatoes in the summer and other simple prepared vegetables, from sautéed spinach to sautéed oyster mushrooms to a salad, are always good with soufflés.

3 tablespoons unsalted butter, plus
    extra for the dish

⅓ cup freshly grated Parmesan

1¼ cups milk heated with a slice of
    onion and a bay leaf

3 tablespoons all-purpose flour

sea salt and freshly ground pepper

pinch cayenne

1¼ cups (5 ounces) grated or
    crumbled cheese (see headnote)

6 large market eggs, separated, or 5
    duck eggs, at room temperature

1. Preheat the oven to 375°F. Butter a 2-quart soufflé or gratin dish, then dust it with the Parmesan cheese, turning out the excess to use later.

2. While the milk is warming with the onion and bay leaf, melt the 3 tablespoons butter in a 3-quart saucepan, whisk in the flour, then cook over low heat for about 3 minutes, without letting it brown. Remove the onion and bay leaf from the milk, and whisk it all at once into the flour-butter mixture. Raise the heat to medium and cook, stirring more or less continuously, for 8 minutes. Season with ½ teaspoon salt, some pepper, and a pinch or two of cayenne.

3. Remove the sauce from the heat, let it cool for 10 minutes, then stir in the cheese, including the excess Parmesan, if any, followed by the egg yolks, two at a time.

4. Beat the egg whites with a pinch of salt until stiff but not dry. Stir a quarter of them into the base to lighten it, then, working quickly, fold in the rest. Turn the batter into the prepared dish. To help get that dramatic hat, smooth the top, then run your finger around the edge, leaving a border of about an inch. Bake until the soufflé is golden brown and has risen high in its dish, about 50 minutes. Serve immediately to your seated guests so you can all enjoy that brief moment of held breath.

Spinach and Green Garlic Soufflé | SERVES 4

You'll want to make this soufflé when the garlic is most tender and subtle, which is when the leaves are still green. Examine the heads before chopping them. If the outer layer is fibrous, like moist parchment, remove it, then quarter the head. If cloves or a stem have formed, remove the parts that are tough, then finely chop the rest. This is perfect for Sunday brunch, following a Saturday's trip to the market.

THE GARLIC INFUSION

¾ to 1 cup minced green garlic, about 5 small heads

1 cup cream or half-and-half

1 thyme sprig

THE SOUFFLÉ

4 tablespoons unsalted butter, plus extra for the dish

½ cup freshly grated Parmesan cheese

1 bunch spinach, stems removed, or 12 to 16 ounces loose, young spinach leaves

4 tablespoons all-purpose flour

1⅓ cups milk

sea salt and freshly ground pepper

1 scant cup (about 4 ounces) mild goat cheese

4 egg yolks

6 egg whites

1. Preheat the oven to 375°F. Butter a 6-cup soufflé dish or gratin dish and dust it with a few tablespoons of the Parmesan cheese.

2. Put the garlic, cream, and thyme in a small saucepan over low heat. Bring slowly to a boil, then turn off the heat, cover, and let steep for 15 minutes.

3. Wash the spinach well, then wilt it in a skillet with the water clinging to the leaves. Tip it into a colander, press out the moisture, then finely chop.

4. Melt the 4 tablespoons butter in a saucepan, stir in the flour, and cook for 1 minute while stirring. Whisk in the milk and stir until it thickens. Add 1 teaspoon salt, then stir in the goat cheese and remaining Parmesan. Turn off the heat and stir in the egg yolks, spinach, and the garlic-cream mixture. Season with pepper.

5. Whisk the egg whites with a pinch of salt until they form firm peaks that are just a bit on the soft side. Fold the whites and base together. Scrape the batter into the prepared dish and bake until golden brown and set, about 25 minutes for a gratin dish, 30 minutes if using a soufflé dish.

Giant Popover
with Chanterelles | SERVES 4

This dramatic popover makes a fine companion for the woodsy flavors of mushrooms, wild or otherwise. So would a Yorkshire pudding, or regular popovers. Use chanterelles, morels, oyster mushrooms of any hue, sliced fresh porcini, or even plain little market mushrooms.

1 pound chanterelles or other
   mushrooms (see headnote)
4 tablespoons unsalted butter
4 large market eggs
1 cup milk
sea salt and freshly ground pepper
¾ cup all-purpose flour
2 to 3 tablespoons freshly grated
   Dry Monterey Jack or Parmesan
   cheese
2 tablespoons cream, optional
1 scant teaspoon minced thyme
   leaves
1 tablespoon minced parsley leaves

1. First clean the mushrooms: Pick out any pine needles and brush off any forest dirt. If using morels, slice them in halve lengthwise so you can brush out the centers. Only if they're really quite dirty should you dunk them in water, but you can wipe them with a damp cloth. Slice into attractive pieces that nicely reveal the shapes of the mushrooms. Set them aside.

2. Preheat the oven to 400°F. Put a 10-inch cast-iron skillet in the oven with half the butter while you whisk the eggs, milk, and ½ teaspoon salt together. Add the flour and whisk until smooth. When the butter has melted, brush it around the rim of the skillet, then stir it into the batter. Add the cheese, then pour the batter back into the hot skillet. Set in the center of the oven to bake. In 20 minutes it will have risen dramatically around the edges and be puffed in the center as if it's trying to lift itself out of the skillet.

3. While it's cooking, melt the remaining butter in a sauté pan. When it's hot, add the mushrooms, salt lightly, and sauté over high heat. Once they begin to give up their juices, reduce the heat to medium and cook the mushrooms until they're tender, about 5 minutes, possibly longer for wild mushrooms. If, as is sometimes true with fresh chanterelles, there is a huge amount of juice, raise the heat to let it reduce, but don't let it cook away completely. Stir the cream into the juices and allow them to mingle and thicken slightly. Season with pepper, then toss with the thyme and parsley.

4. Remove the popover from the oven and spoon the mushrooms into the center. Or slice the popover into wedges and spoon the mushrooms over each serving.

Quiche with Smoked Fish, Scallions, and Crème Fraîche | SERVES 4 TO 6

The smoked albacore I've found in several farmers' markets is what originally inspired this quiche, but any smoked fish that can be flaked is bound to be good—bluefish, whitefish, salmon, and so forth. Serve with a tossed green salad for supper, lunch, or brunch.

THE CRUST

1 cup plus 2 tablespoons all-purpose flour

¼ teaspoon sea salt

6 tablespoons cold unsalted butter, cut into pieces

3 tablespoons ice water, plus extra if needed

1. Using a food processor, pulse the flour and salt with the butter until it forms a coarse meal, then dribble in enough water for damp crumbs to form. Gather the crumbs, shape them into a disk, wrap in plastic, and refrigerate for at least 15 minutes. Roll the dough into a 13-inch circle (save any trimmings), drape it into a 9-inch tart pan, fold the excess into the shell, and press firmly. Use the dull side of a knife to make a pattern of diagonal lines across the rim. Prick in a few places and freeze for 25 minutes.

2. Preheat the oven to 425°F, set the frozen shell on a sheet pan, and bake until lightly colored and set, about 25 minutes. Check during the baking and pierce the base if it swells. When done, be sure to mend any holes that might have been made with a bit of the dough trimmings.

THE FILLING

2 small market eggs, or 1 giant one

½ cup crème fraîche

½ teaspoon sea salt and freshly ground pepper

½ cup milk, as needed

1 teaspoon unsalted butter

¾ cup thinly sliced scallions, including some of the greens (about 2 bunches)

5 ounces boneless and skinless smoked fish

1. Preheat the oven to 400°F. Have your prebaked tart shell on a sheet pan to make it easy to handle. Beat the eggs in a 2-cup measuring cup with the crème fraîche, salt, and pepper until fairly smooth. Don't worry about small lumps. Add enough milk to bring the total volume to 1¾ cups.

2. Melt the butter in a small nonstick skillet. When hot, add the scallions and cook for about 1 minute. Distribute them in the tart shell. Break the fish into small pieces and set it over the scallions. Pour in the custard and bake until the custard is set and pale gold in places, about 35 minutes. Let cool for a few minutes, then loosen the tart from the rim and ease it onto a serving plate.

Savory Goat Cheese Tart with Leeks | SERVES 6 TO 8

When I first worked at Chez Panisse in 1978, Alice Waters frequently made a goat cheese tart for lunch, which, at that time, was the most amazing food I had ever eaten. The dish has not lost its appeal. This one comes right from the fall market, a time when slender new leeks and eggs are still in supply, though the eggs are beginning to dwindle along with the daylight. For the goat cheese, we have a choice between fresh and one that's more aged, which I prefer, but either will be good and so will both used together. Serve modest slices with a mound of lightly dressed lettuce leaves or frisée for supper, lunch, or a first course.

1 (9-inch) prebaked Tart Shell, page 388

6 slender leeks (an inch or less across)

1 tablespoon unsalted butter

6 ounces goat cheese

1 large market egg

½ cup crème fraîche

½ cup milk

sea salt and freshly ground white pepper

2 teaspoons chopped thyme leaves

1. Preheat the oven to 400°F. Keep the prebaked tart shell on its baking pan.

2. Slice the leeks into thin rounds, separate them, and wash them well in a bowl of water. Lift them into a strainer. Melt the butter in a medium skillet, add the leeks with any water clinging to them, and cook over medium heat until tender, 10 to 12 minutes. Season with salt and pepper to taste.

3. Beat the goat cheese with the egg until fairly smooth, then stir in the milk, crème fraîche, pinch of salt, and a little white pepper. Pour the custard into the shell and bake until golden and puffed, about 30 minutes. Scatter the thyme leaves over the top. Remove the tart from the pan and transfer to a round serving platter. Serve warm.

A little street with wide, grassy borders runs through the center of Shaker Square, and this is where the North Union farmers' market is held. In contrast to other midwestern markets, such as Madison's with its 300 farmers, or St. Paul's with its 160 farmers and continuous existence for nearly as many years, this market was little and just a few years old when I first visited it. But it was inspiring. I came away from my visits there with the sense that the family farm was very much alive. Many of the farmers were families working their stands together—parents, children, cousins—and several even wore T-shirts with the names of their farms printed on them.

An Amish family had a big display of varied produce; a Serbian refugee was selling tomatoes grown from seeds from his country; the Rullos, a mother and daughter who raise free-range chickens and make the most wonderful goat's milk fudge, were working side by side. And at one end of the market a couple worked with a sharpening stone. You could drop off your dull knives, do your shopping, buy some of the most delicious buttery pastry imaginable from Lucy's Sweet Surrender, an old Hungarian bakery that was enjoying a renaissance, then go back to pick up a set of gleaming blades. Chopping and slicing all these vegetables is much more pleasant and easy when a knife is sharp.

On the opening day of each season, an Episcopal priest blesses the market with branches of parsley dipped into holy water from Lourdes. He offers prayers for the farmers, prayers for the animals, prayers for everything that has to do with the market. Couples have met and married there. The market is very successful.

But it had a problem, one that's common to many new markets, and that was how to get more diversity into it. "At a certain point," Mary Holmes, one of the market's founders, told me, "everyone was selling corn and tomatoes, corn and tomatoes! That's all there was!" But Mary and cofounder and manager, Donita Anderson, had an idea: When the next farmer applied to sell at the market, they told him that he could come, but only if he could grow something new.

"Go home, look at some food magazines, and watch the TV Food Network and see what foods are popular and different," they said. And he did. And he decided that heirloom potatoes were the new vegetable. His seed potatoes were expensive, and he didn't have a proven market. But on Bastille Day, when he and his wife showed up at market with red net bags filled with red, white, and blue potatoes, they flew off the table. Customers would certainly be back for these potatoes. In September another farmer showed up with oyster and shiitake mushrooms, plus foraged greens and chanterelles. The list of the market's offerings started to expand, and now, by using hoop houses and row covers, farmers show up in May with produce that wasn't anticipated until June. Farmers grow the food, but managers grow the market.

Cleveland is fortunate to have this market, and also a chef who has long been deeply committed to using local resources. Parker Bosley, the chef-owner of Parker's restaurant, started a farmers' market in Cleveland years ago, but the time wasn't right then. But he didn't let up his search for locally grown foods. They have become the basis of his cooking, which is truly midwestern from the ground up.

Every six months or so I get a letter from Parker. In one breath he might be growling that people will drive across town to shop at Saks, but not think twice about what they put in their bodies, or that the food on our tables should not come from production systems that are harmful to anyone or anything. And in the next, he's happily describing some new organic vegetable or meat he can finally use in his restaurant.

"I can finally add local beef and pork to my menu," he writes, "which makes me quite happy. The pork is certified organic. The beef is from nonchemical farming systems. I hope within the next year to have all grass-fed beef. We also have a new dairy. I have a farmer growing 15 kinds of heirloom potatoes and am working on a pork project with a hog farmer and the American Livestock Breeds Conservancy to raise more flavorful meat from a rare, slow growing breed."

The efforts of Parker and people like him are starting to create changes in both how we raise food and the flavors of the foods we eat. He recently commented to me that it seemed as if cooks everywhere are rediscovering the obvious—that local and seasonal is where the cooking begins. "What a great time to cook here in the Midwest," Parker enthuses. "I am very fortunate to have these wonderful farmers as my partners."

Goat's Milk Panna Cotta with Warm Honey | SERVES 6 TO 8

What's so nice about this quivering tangy dessert is how well it goes with your local honey. You can also serve it with various fruits as they progress through the seasons—a warm sauce of apricots or berries in June, fresh figs in August, a silky persimmon puree in October, or poached dried cherries in December.

1½ envelopes unflavored gelatin

almond oil or a neutral vegetable oil

1½ cups goat's milk

½ cup cow's milk

¼ cup sugar

2 cups cream

honey for serving

1. Sprinkle the gelatin over ¼ cup cold water in a small bowl and set aside to soften. Lightly oil a 2-quart mold or eight ½-cup ramekins.

2. Bring both milks and the sugar to a boil. Turn off the heat and stir to dissolve the sugar. Allow the milk to cool so that it's slightly hotter than tepid, about 130°F, then add the gelatin and stir until it's completely dissolved, 2 to 3 minutes. Slowly pour in the cream, stirring. Set the mold(s) on a tray, pour in the warm cream, then refrigerate until set, about 8 hours.

3. Just before serving, warm the honey by placing the jar in a pan of simmering water. Carefully turn the panna cotta out onto dessert plates or a serving plate. Drizzle the honey over the top and/or garnish it with fruit or fruit sauce.

Warm Ricotta Custard | SERVES 6

It takes about 2 minutes to assemble this custard, which provides a velvety background for all kinds of fruits, such as a plum compote or apricot puree, sugared berries, poached quince, passion fruit, and so forth. Chilled, this tastes like cheesecake, but it must be served in its ramekins, because it won't unmold easily.

unsalted butter and sugar for six
     ½-cup ramekins

1 pound fresh whole-milk ricotta

1 cup crème fraîche or fromage blanc

2 market eggs

1 egg yolk

¼ cup sugar

1 teaspoon vanilla extract

freshly grated nutmeg

1. Preheat the oven to 325°F. Lightly butter and sugar the ramekins. Process everything but the nutmeg in a food processor until smooth and silky. Pour the custard into the ramekins, then set them in a pan with hot water to come halfway up the sides. Grate the nutmeg over the tops. Bake until the custards have puffed and begun to pull away from the sides, 50 to 55 minutes.

2. Cool until warm or tepid. Run a knife around the edge of each ramekin and turn out onto individual plates. Serve plain or with a fruit accompaniment.

Zabaglione with Fruit | SERVES 4

If it's to be served warm, zabaglione must be made at the last minute, but the clang of the whisk beating against the bowl, the escaping clouds of steam and alcohol produce an entirely pleasant mood of anticipation. Zabaglione (or sabayon) is sometimes chilled, then lightened with whipped cream, but it's magical served warm with fruit, which tempers its richness. I first had zabaglione at Vanessi's counter years ago in San Francisco, where it was served in an old-fashioned sundae glass with sliced strawberries. Old-fashioned champagne or martini glasses or a French juice glass will do fine, too.

Marsala is the traditional wine, but you can also use a Muscat, Malvasia, or another dessert wine. Even champagne. For fruit, good berries are always wonderful, but if I lived in Hawaii, I might choose a dead ripe sugar pineapple or lychee nuts. Seedless Muscat grapes would also be exquisite, as would sweet ripe figs in the fall. I think that buttery pears, fresh or poached, would be perfect in winter.

1½ to 2 cups fruit (see headnote)

4 egg yolks

¼ cup sugar

½ cup Marsala or other sweet wine

1. Have the fruit washed and cut if needed, and sugared only if very tart, ahead of time. Just before you make the zabaglione, spoon the fruit into the glasses.

2. Bring a few inches of water to a boil in a 3-quart saucepan. The water should not touch the bowl or it will cook the eggs.

3. Whisk the egg yolks and sugar in a copper or stainless-steel bowl until pale in color, then gradually whisk in the wine. Set the bowl over the pot and cook, whisking constantly, until the eggs are foamy and all of the wine has been absorbed. This will take 3 to 4 minutes. Pour immediately over the fruit and serve.

In the large village square setting with the beautiful state capitol in view, I keep feeling that we the people are in charge today, voting with our forks and our dollars for what we choose to eat. It's a great feeling! I'm in Madison, Wisconsin, at the largest farmers' market in the nation, but all morning I keep feeling as though I'm in Berkeley. It's "Food for Thought" day here, a celebration of sustainability. A street has been blocked off for farm animals, vendors, various organizations, and speakers who are taking part. Representative Mark Miller gets up to speak:

"Sustainability goes beyond food production to include how we live together now and through generations to come. This implies fair wages and keeping a local economy operating. In a time when we feel impotent—we can't do much about the price of milk, for example—we can make choices about what we eat. We can choose to buy from CSAs* and markets that maintain farmlands. The decisions you make every day impact whether sustainable food economy will survive."

These are good words to hear, and more good words follow his. After the talks I walk around. Every participating farmer or rancher has a sign that asks, "What does sustainable mean to us?" Each has written an answer below the question. The answers include such thoughts as "having and maintaining fertile soils," "having clean, clear water," "growing nutritious foods," and "being vibrant people with creative minds and strong spirits." The Gray Panthers answer the question by saying "Knowing, caring, and working together." A cheese producer writes, "Developing a food policy that saves the land while providing healthy food to consumers." His neighbor, a producer of natural beef, writes, "Environmentally sound farming that's socially just and economically viable"—one of the standard definitions of sustainability. These are sentiments that take land, animals, and people equally into account.

Ironically, the great success of the Dane County market—20,000 shoppers apparently come each Saturday—could undermine its own sustainability. "The market is too crowded and big to have the kind of relationships with our customers we've enjoyed in the past," one farmer tells me. Frustrated by the demands such a large market makes, he has since left it for a smaller market closer to his farm—a benefit to his local community as well as to himself, as it turns out.

While the Madison market has succeeded in attracting tourists, they swell the crowd but don't necessarily increase sales. "Tourists don't buy!" a farmer complains. "And it makes it hard to put that energy into explaining about your

*CSA stands for Community Supported Agriculture. Farmers set up CSAs for buyers who front money at the beginning of the year when farmers have little cash, in exchange for produce to be delivered as it comes into season. This way the customer shares the risk of farming with the farmer, along with the benefits.

varieties of potatoes or whatever, when they're probably not going to come back. Some of the farmers," he continues, "have actually seen their produce sales drop off, in spite of the crowds that come to the market." What tourists do buy are those foods that last for a while—jams and pickles, nuts, cheeses. Hopefully they take home inspiration and the desire to seek out or create farmers' markets in their own communities. But that doesn't benefit the Madison vendor. Sustainability isn't so easy to sustain, it turns out.

The financial success farmers have enjoyed selling at farmers' markets means that they can finally hire help, which is great for them. Not only do additional hands work in the field, they can also help out by going to other markets that might take place on the same day, or simply spell farmers who might like a break from the exhausting market routine. But then customers grumble because it's not the farmer selling; it's someone they don't know. Replace the farmer with a helper, and there's a reaction. Customers want that connection with the producer. But farmers can't replicate themselves, and they do need to take breaks if they're to continue farming over the long haul, especially in markets that go year-round.

A market I've visited several times offers another example of too much success. To promote its Wednesday evening market, food vendors were brought in, beer was sold, and music was provided. Shoppers could buy their dinner, then spend a few hours picnicking on the shady lawn of the park where the market is held. A great idea, it succeeded in becoming such a popular community event that it's now part of the town's social fabric. But some of the farmers are saying they feel like they're just tagging along on its coattails. Sales are down, and there's a feeling that the farmers' market has been replaced by the very event that was supposed to boost its attendance. Perhaps providing take-away food for supper isn't exactly an incentive to shop for produce.

One has to ask if the same kind of situation adheres when a market includes Kettle Corn or other food franchise vendors among its farmers. It may produce revenue for the market, but does it replace buying a piece of fruit for a snack or a baked good from a local baker? Can it replace a farmer or a local producer?

It's hard to find the right balance to make a market sustainable. The experience of community that's so often enjoyed at farmers' markets can be destroyed by the markets' very success. But hopefully the flexible structure of farmers' markets can work as a self-correcting mechanism. Those growers and producers who no longer benefit by the huge markets may leave and join smaller markets, a move that can turn out to be profitable for everyone: The smaller market gains new energy and, most likely, diversity. The farmer can sell closer to home and to the local customer who doesn't want to be jostled in a crowd or drive an hour to a big, urban market. As we've seen, a one-size market doesn't fit all.

Small Tender Fruits: Berries, Grapes, and Figs

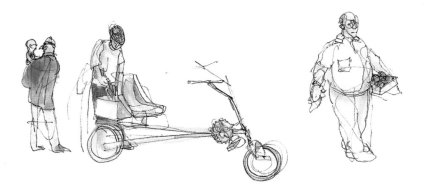

It's a breezy March day in San Diego. It's also slightly overcast, but the sun comes and goes with the moving clouds, which gives the day a moody feel. Having escaped from the pollen-bearing winds of New Mexico, where everything except the sky is brown, I feel as spirited as the breeze above. My friend, chef and cookbook author Su Mei Yu, guesses that the attendance will be down at the farmers' market because people think it's going to rain. Fair-weather customers, I'm thinking. But the rain never does come, and it turns out to be a good crowd after all.

Located in a strip mall, the two halves of the market are connected by a little breezeway. In both there is an abundance of flowers—luscious candy-color ranunculus with silken petals of yellow, orange, and cerise; tubs of large white calla lilies; and giant stock in muted old-fashioned colors—soft yellows, tender mauves, gentle violets. Every other customer is walking around with arms filled with flowers. Su Mei fills both of her arms with blooms for a wedding she's catering. I'd like to take armloads home with me, too, but flowers really won't be manageable on the plane, especially with all the fruit I end up buying.

At this transitional time of year, strawberries, guavas, and asparagus are bringing in the spring, but citrus and avocados are still present in varietal profusion. I am especially drawn to the strawberries, which are as perfumed as the stock and deep red throughout, not just on the surface. The farmer tells me that she has a seven-month season, which speaks to the stability of coastal conditions and the availability of water. She offers me a berry. I eat it, then I buy 3 quarts. At home I never buy commercial strawberries because of the pesticides used on them coupled with their lack of flavor, but these are pure fruit. My husband, who has told me for years that he dislikes strawberries, eats them with gusto, and we feast on them in all the usual ways. Combined with strawberry guavas and other fruits from the market, they make an exotic filling for a meringue shell.

A SPRING MENU FOR A COOL BREEZY DAY

Crostini with Chive-Scented Ricotta
(page 70)

Fennel Soup with Saffron Dumplings
(page 48)

Red Snapper Baked in Parchment with Pummelo and Rosemary
(page 345)

Sautéed Spinach (page 3)

Palm Sugar Meringues with Strawberry Compote (page 255)

Palm Sugar Meringues
with Strawberry Compote | SERVES 6

Strawberries, blood oranges, mangoes, and the tropical pink flesh of a few strawberry-guavas make a red and gold compote that you can nestle into a meringue shell. The palm sugar that Thai cookbook author Su Mei Yu suggested using tied the tropical nuances together into a perfect package. Palm sugar, which must be pulverized in a mortar, has a complex flavor, not unlike maple sugar. It makes a pale brown meringue. If you prefer an alabaster bowl, use white sugar.

THE MERINGUE SHELL

¾ cup palm, light brown, or white
    sugar
2 teaspoons cornstarch
4 egg whites, at room temperature
pinch sea salt
1 teaspoon white vinegar
1 teaspoon vanilla extract

1. Preheat the oven to 300°F. On a piece of baking parchment or foil, draw six 4-inch circles. Mix a tablespoon of the sugar with the cornstarch and set aside.

2. Beat the egg whites and salt until stiff, then add the sugar a little at a time and beat until thick and glossy. Add the sugar-cornstarch mixture, then fold in the vinegar and vanilla.

3. Divide the mixture among the 6 circles. Using an offset spatula, work the meringue into a bowl or nest shape with sides as high as you can make them. Bake for 1 hour, then turn off the oven and let them sit until cool. Gently pry them off the paper and set on serving plates.

THE FRUIT AND CREAM

1 pint fragrant ripe strawberries
1 small mango
2 guavas
2 passion fruit, if available
2 blood oranges
light brown sugar, if needed
½ cup cream
½ cup crème fraîche
1 teaspoon granulated sugar
½ teaspoon vanilla extract
lemon verbena, mint, or rose geranium
    leaves for garnish

1. Rinse the berries, remove the stems, and slice them into a bowl. Peel the mango and slice it into the berries. Peel the guavas, dice them into tiny pieces (scrape away the seeds if they bother you), and add them to the fruit. If you're using passion fruit, cut them in half and add them, crunchy seeds and all, to the bowl. Section the oranges and squeeze the juice from the membranes over the fruit. Gently mix the fruit. Add a teaspoon of sugar or more, to taste, if you think it needs it.

2. Whip the cream and crème fraîche with the granulated sugar until soft peaks are formed. Fold in the vanilla. Line the meringue shells with the cream, then cover with the fruit and serve immediately. Garnish with lemon verbena, mint, or rose geranium leaves.

Strawberry–Passion Fruit Cream Cake | SERVES 8

This is such a pretty cake and a delicious one, too, even without the tropical passion fruit, should that elude you. Since strawberries persist through October in some parts of the country, this could be a birthday cake for an unsuspecting Scorpio.

THE FILLING

3 cups ripe strawberries

2 to 4 passion fruit

2 tablespoons sugar, more
    or less

THE CAKE

4 tablespoons unsalted butter,
    melted, plus extra for the pan

1 cup all-purpose flour

1 teaspoon baking powder

6 eggs, separated

1 cup sugar

½ teaspoon salt

1½ teaspoons vanilla extract

grated zest of 1 blood orange

¼ cup blood orange juice

1 cup whipping cream

1. Rinse the berries, then turn them onto a towel to dry. Set aside a few perfect little berries (with leaves and stems) to garnish the top of the cake. Or, if the berries are large, set 6 aside. Remove the leafy crowns from the rest and slice them into a bowl. Cut the passion fruit in half and scrape out the pulp with the seeds. (The seeds are nice and crunchy, but you can leave them out if you prefer.) Using a rubber scraper, fold the passion fruit into the berries. Sweeten with sugar to taste. Set aside.

2. Preheat the oven to 350°F. Butter and flour an 8-inch springform pan. Sift the flour and baking powder onto a piece of wax paper.

3. Using an electric mixer, beat the egg whites on high until they're foamy, then gradually add ⅞ cup sugar and the salt. Continue beating until the whites form moist, stiff peaks. Add 1 teaspoon vanilla.

4. Beat the yolks with the zest, then fold them into the whites. Sprinkle a few tablespoons of the flour over the eggs, fold it in, then repeat until all is used. Last, fold in the juice and the melted butter. Turn the batter into the pan and bake until golden, 25 minutes. Cool, remove the rim, and slice the cake in half crosswise.

5. Coarsely mash the sliced berries. Whip the cream with the remaining 2 tablespoons sugar and ½ teaspoon vanilla until fairly stiff. Fold half of it into the berries and spread the mixture over the bottom layer of cake. If you've reserved large berries, slice them lengthwise into thirds and arrange them around the edge so that their tips are poking out. Cover with the second layer of cake and ice with the remaining whipped cream. If you have set aside small berries, arrange them in the center. And if you should have an extra passion fruit, spoon the seeds and pulp around the berries.

Strawberry Sorbet | MAKES 1 QUART

As soon as I entered the market, I picked up their scent and followed it to the table. There sat 3 baskets of small, oddly shaped strawberries. Later that day they filled the area around me on the plane to Aspen with their delicious aroma. Once in Aspen, they created some excitement among the chefs at the Food and Wine Classic, who asked where they could get some and if they could be shipped overnight to New York. But that's just the thing: they can't. Berries like these are fragile, which makes them very specific to where they are grown. They are for this time and place only.

The first time I encountered strawberries like these was many years ago at a farm stand in upstate New York, where baskets of berries stood on a table under tall white pines. A jar for the money stood next to them. I paid for 2 quarts, and on the drive back to camp their heavy scent filled the car. At that time—I was in my twenties—I wanted to understand what the word *gourmet* meant, and right then I decided that it must have to do with the perfume and flavor of foods like these berries. At least I was pretty sure that at this moment I was having a "gourmet" experience. I still think so. If strawberry sorbet seems old hat, you may be surprised at how really good it is when made with really good berries.

1 quart ripe red strawberries
grated zest and juice of 1 blood orange,
    orange, or tangerine
⅔ cup sugar

1. Reserve a few small, perfect strawberries with their stems and leaves for garnish. Combine the zest, juice, and sugar in a small saucepan. Bring to a boil and cook, stirring, until the sugar is dissolved. Set aside to cool.
2. Rinse the berries and turn them onto a clean towel. Check them carefully and discard any that are bruised or unripe. (The bad taste of the bruised part can extend to the whole berry, as can mold.) Lift out the leaves and cores with the tip of an old-fashioned vegetable scraper, then puree the berries in the food processor and stir in the syrup.
3. Freeze in your ice cream machine, according to its instructions. Serve garnished with a whole berry on each serving.

Bob Hayes grows black raspberries. He keeps beehives near the vines, so he sells some honey, too, but mostly he tends his four hundred raspberry bushes for the pleasure of it. Today the berries are lined up on his long table, a long double row of opened white cartons filled with black fruit, backed with jars of amber honey. The sun is shining through the honey, and it's a pretty sight to see. These are the only true berries we see in any quantity at our market. Mulberries don't count, in my mind, since they come from a tree.

Tall, dressed in a blue plaid shirt, jeans, and a Stetson, Bob is a very western-looking man. He shows me his hands. They're large hands, too large for such tiny fruits, you might think, and they're covered with scratches from picking. When I ask about gloves, he says no, he has to pick these delicate fruits with his fingertips. "In fact," he elaborates, "I pick them left-handed because"—he rubs the fingers of his right hand together, then pinches their tips—"I have no feeling in the tip of my forefinger of my right hand. It can't feel the ripeness of the fruit." He picks the berries right into the Styrofoam cartons so that they're handled only once. They are perfect.

At first the berries are tight and tiny. They don't have the expansive structure that red and golden raspberries do. Their taste is concentrated, dark and sweet, with an elusive fragrance, and there's a bit of a seed. Over the next few weeks the berries get larger, softer, and even more fragrant. It's a wonderful luxury having them around to sprinkle over cereal, fold into muffin batter, or add to an apricot crisp. I have lots of plans for them but start by serving them sweetened with a little maple sugar, a treasure from Vermont's Montpelier farmers' market, and crème fraîche, lightly beaten with a fork first, then slowly unwound over the top. As these are perfect for breakfast as well as lunch and dinner, other plans for them soon fade away.

Black Hawk Raspberry and Rose Geranium Sherbet | MAKES 1 QUART

Black Hawk raspberries and rose geranium are a perfect match, but if you haven't any rose geranium, you'll still end up with a wonderful sherbet.

4 cups Black Hawk raspberries
    or blackberries
1 cup sugar
4 large rose geranium leaves
1 cup cream
few drops fresh lemon juice, optional

1. Sort through the berries and remove any stems and leaves.
2. Bring the sugar and 2 cups water to a boil in a saucepan. Crush the rose geranium leaves a little with your fingers and add them to the pan. Stir to dissolve the sugar, then add the berries and turn off the heat. Let cool. Remove the leaves and pass the fruit, with the syrup, through a food mill. (If you don't have a food mill, briefly puree the berries in a food processor, then rub the pulp through a strainer to get rid of the seeds.) Stir in the cream. Taste. If the mixture seems too sweet, add a few drops of lemon juice to bring it into balance. Chill well.
3. Freeze the mixture in your ice cream maker according to its instructions. Serve with crisp little butter cookies or lemon thyme shortbreads.

Raspberry Cream Tart | SERVES 8

The plump pink and gold raspberries from the Montpelier farmers' market in Vermont inspired this luscious tart. The "crust" is really more like a cake—soft and buttery with just a little crispness at the edges. Black raspberries can be used here, too, by themselves or mixed with the others.

½ cup (1 stick) unsalted butter,
    at room temperature
½ cup plus 1 teaspoon sugar
pinch sea salt
1 teaspoon vanilla extract
3 medium eggs, at room
    temperature
⅞ cup all-purpose flour
¾ cup crème fraîche
1 heaping pint basket raspberries,
    about 2 cups
confectioners' sugar

1. Preheat the oven to 375°F. Lightly butter an 11-inch tart pan. Cream the butter with the ½ cup sugar and the salt until smooth and supple. Scrape down the sides of the bowl, then add ½ teaspoon vanilla and 2 whole eggs plus the white of the third egg. Beat until smooth. With the speed on low, add the flour and mix just until combined.

2. Scrape the batter into the tart pan. Using an offset spatula, smooth the batter over the pan, then push up enough batter to make a slightly higher rim around the edge. Even a ¼-inch rise will be sufficient. Don't worry about getting it absolutely even.

3. Mix the egg yolk with the crème fraîche and remaining ½ teaspoon vanilla. Pour this over the batter and spread it just to the raised edge.

4. Place the berries on the custard. Two cups will be enough to make a fairly close covering. You can do this randomly or start by placing the largest berries around the outer edge of the tart, then using smaller and smaller berries as you work your way in. Leftovers can be tucked into any gaps. Sprinkle the remaining teaspoon of sugar over the fruit. Bake in the center of the oven until golden brown around the edges and the custard is set, about 40 minutes.

5. Let cool for at least 30 minutes before serving. Dust with confectioners' sugar and serve barely warm.

Blueberry-Lavender Compote | MAKES 3 CUPS

I always find that lime or lemon juice does wonders for blueberries. The bit of acid makes their flavor, rather than their sweetness, come out. And lavender seems to be a natural, too. Here's a compote to spoon over vanilla ice cream, bread pudding, or an old-fashioned lemon pudding cake.

2 pints blueberries

¼ cup fresh lime or lemon juice

1 teaspoon cornstarch

½ cup sugar

pinch sea salt

1 teaspoon lavender blossoms

1. Pick over the berries, removing any stems, leaves, or rotting fruits. Give them a rinse.

2. In a saucepan large enough to accommodate the berries, mix the juice with the cornstarch, sugar, and salt. Add the berries and lavender and cook over medium heat until the fruit gives up its juice and the liquid thickens, a matter of a few minutes.

Wild Blueberry
Preserve | MAKES ABOUT 3 CUPS

There's much more excitement in the small wild blueberries than in the huge commercial ones. They're closer in nature to their cousin, the huckleberry.

I try to keep the sugar at a minimum so that the flavor isn't overridden with sweetness, even if my jam doesn't set as well. I'd rather have it more loose and flavorful than sugary sweet—and not plan to keep it as long. But if your wild berries are very tart—taste them before you start—you might want to add the other ½ cup of sugar. This quick jam keeps in your refrigerator for a month or two. In addition to putting it on toast, you can stir it into an ice cream base or spoon it over a prebaked tart shell that's been spread with mascarpone or cream cheese.

2 pints blueberries or huckleberries
¾ to 1½ cups sugar
finely grated zest and juice of 1 lime
**   or lemon**

1. Sort through the berries and remove any stems, leaves, or berries that are excessively green or overripe. Give them a rinse, then toss them in a wide pot with the sugar plus the zest and juice to taste.

2. Bring the fruit to a boil, stirring from time to time so that the sugar doesn't burn. Boil rapidly for 5 minutes, then remove from the heat. Pour a little of the juice on a plate and refrigerate for 10 minutes, or until it's cold. Run a spoon through it: It should hold together. If it doesn't, return it to the stove, boil for a few more minutes, and try again. Let cool, then spoon into clean jars or containers and refrigerate.

An old black steam engine in the market's center made a stunning background for the large sprays of flowers that were displayed around it. And the floral-print backyard umbrellas the vendors used to shade their produce gave the market a rather cheerful, let's-go-to-the-beach feel, even if it was in Missoula, Montana, and a long way from the ocean. Unlike at other farmers' markets, no crafts are allowed in the Missoula market, and they never have been. There was, however, evidence of craft: Two quilted banners hung at the entrance, one proclaiming that this is the farmers' market and the other saying "No Pets Allowed," featuring an embroidered Snoopy along with other dogs and one or two cats. Nearly all markets have some way of saying "no pets," but this was by far the most charming expression I saw.

"We have a huge contingent of Vietnamese, Laotian, and Hmong people who have enriched our area tremendously, both culinarily and culturally," my friend and guide, Greg Patent, explained as we toured the market. Their produce was much in evidence, and several women were wearing traditional dress. Greg's wife, Dorothy, the market's first treasurer, added, "When the Southeast Asians began selling at the market, they managed to produce broccoli and carrots earlier than everyone else. Before long, more and more growers were using season-extending techniques to get vegetables to market earlier and keep them going longer— a delight to buyers. I love interacting with the Southeast Asian vendors. They experiment with greens unknown to me, but give helpful tips on how to cook with them."

But I was primed for huckleberries. In fact, the promise of huckleberry pie was one of the lures that had brought me this far. Through 'Asta Bowen's passionate ode to these purple orbs in *The Huckleberry Book,* I knew that gathering wild huckleberries was a deep tradition in the Northwest. Yet it was the Hmong who were doing the picking and selling now, and they have been for the past fifteen years. "I've spoken with many huckleberry fans," Greg told me, "and they're really glad the Hmong are doing all the time-consuming work. Pretty typical human behavior, I'd say. People who've lived here most of their lives or die-hard imports still go out collecting, but on a small scale, and some of us still go out to forage on our own because it's fun being in the woods. But we know we can always buy enough for a few pies from the trusty Hmong."

And that's exactly what we did. We bought 6 pounds of berries, and Greg made a huckleberry pie and huckleberry ice cream that I will most certainly never forget. They were worth every mile traveled, every calorie consumed, and had I picked them myself, they would have been worth every scratch and sore muscle.

Huckleberries have a flavor like nothing else—wild and not too sweet and not at all watery. Intense and slightly unfamiliar, the way wild foods tend to be. It's best, of course, to taste them for yourself. If you live in Maine or some other place that has wild blueberries, you can use them as you would huckleberries. They are not dissimilar. In fact huckleberries go by other names, including bilberries, dewberries, and blueberries. But as 'Asta Bowen says, "[Although] what we call a huckleberry is in fact a type of blueberry, what we call a blueberry tastes nothing like a huckleberry." Huckleberries are sublime, but so are wild blueberries, and being a resident of neither Montana nor Maine means I don't have to say which is better.

Although this market appeared to be a huge success, Dorothy later told me about its more humble beginnings: "When we moved to Missoula in 1972, the farmer's market was just starting up. The first market wasn't very promising—a Saturday morning in early July, a day featuring the lowest high temperature for that date on record (mid-forties), and a bitter wind. A few pathetic folks sat behind card tables with a few heads of lettuce. I don't remember much else. I do remember feeling that the endeavor didn't look very promising."

And that's often how markets begin, but from a few offerings and a few brave souls they do manage to grow. And today, the Missoula farmers' market is, like markets elsewhere, the hub of the town's life throughout its season.

DINNER FROM THE MISSOULA MARKET

Elixir of Fresh Peas, garnished with flat
Chinese chives (page 41)

Shredded Salad of Many Greens (page 20)

Whole Wheat Spaghetti with Late-Summer Onions (page 73)

Greg's Huckleberry Pie (page 264)

Greg's Huckleberry Pie | SERVES 8 TO 10

Greg Patent is a consummate baker, and this is the pie he made for us. By all means, make it with blueberries or brambleberries if that's what you have.

1 recipe Pie Dough, page 387

1 cup plus 1 tablespoon granulated
    sugar

¼ cup light brown sugar,
    firmly packed

4 to 5 tablespoons quick-cooking
    tapioca

1 teaspoon ground cinnamon

½ teaspoon freshly grated nutmeg

1¾ pounds (about 5 cups)
    huckleberries, picked over

1 tablespoon fresh lemon juice

2 tablespoons unsalted butter, chilled
    and cut into small pieces

1. Divide the pastry into 2 disks, one slightly larger than the other. Refrigerate for at least an hour. Dust your work surface lightly with flour and roll the larger disk into a 13-inch circle. Fit the dough loosely into a 9-inch glass or metal pie pan, leaving the excess pastry hanging over the edge. Refrigerate until ready to fill.

2. Place one oven rack on the lowest shelf and one in the center. Place a heavy baking sheet on the lower shelf. Preheat the oven to 450°F.

3. Combine 1 cup of the granulated sugar, the brown sugar, tapioca, cinnamon, and nutmeg in a large bowl. Break up any lumps with your fingertips and mix well. Fold in the huckleberries and lemon juice and let the mixture stand for 15 minutes.

4. Remove the pie shell from the refrigerator and pour the filling into the crust, mounding it slightly in the center. Dot with butter and set aside. Roll out the second piece of dough into a 12-inch circle. Brush the edge of the lower crust lightly with water and place the top crust over the berries. Press the edges firmly to seal and trim away the excess pastry to within ½ inch of the rim of the pan. Fold the pastry back on itself to form a standing rim and flute. Make 4 or 5 slits about 1½ inches long in the top crust with the tip of a small knife. Brush the top lightly with water and sprinkle on the remaining tablespoon of sugar.

5. Place the pie on the baking sheet on the lower shelf and bake for 15 minutes. Transfer the baking sheet with the pie to the center shelf, reduce the temperature to 350°F, and bake until the juices are thickened and bubbly and the crust is a rich brown color. Cool completely before cutting. Refrigerate any leftovers.

Warm Berry Compote | SERVES 4 TO 6

This is so easy and so good, especially for those who live where berries proliferate. In fact the mix of fruits will undoubtedly reflect your region, with huckleberries, blueberries, and gooseberries predominating in the North, strawberries wherever there's water to grow them, raspberries in Washington and Vermont, and so forth. You can serve this compote with cream, ice cream, or over biscuits, making a warm fruit shortcake.

3 pints mixed berries: raspberries, strawberries, red currants, blueberries, huckleberries, gooseberries, boysenberries

⅓ cup sugar or maple syrup

1. Raspberries and other cane-grown berries needn't be rinsed. Strawberries, which grow close to the ground, should be, and blueberries, currants, and huckleberries can be. Halve larger strawberries and pluck red currants from their stems.

2. Put the fruit in a wide noncorrosive skillet or pot over medium-high heat. Sprinkle with the sugar. Cook until the berries are warm, softened, and starting to lose their juice, 1 to 2 minutes, then remove from the heat and pour them into a bowl. As they sit, their juices will come out and the flavors will open.

I try to curb my impulse and make only a few grape pies each fall, but that doesn't keep me from buying baskets of green and purple Concords, Golden Muscats, Niagaras, and other unusual varieties whenever I see them. Some grape varieties I've found at various farmers' markets include two varieties of golden, translucent Muscats, a black Muscat, dark Red Flame Tokays dusted with bloom, long, pale green Lady Fingers, and a blue-black slipskin called Venus that resembles the purple Concord. Delight is another green grape with rich fruit flavor. Clusters of tiny, purple Zinfandel grapes might also show up, or giant native muscadines if you're in St. Augustine, Florida, Birmingham, and other southern markets.

Grapes such as these have scents that are subtle, haunting, and highly aromatic. The difficulty with old varieties is that they usually have seeds, and customers, long sold on the virtue of seedless grapes, won't buy them. One farmer I spoke with grew more than a dozen of these old varieties, which he angrily pulled out after repeated seasons of watching even his most faithful market customers refuse to buy them for this reason. This is a shame. Is it that we don't know what to do with the pips? Just put them in your pocket or flick them into the grass—they're very little. In exchange for this tiny inconvenience, you get a grape with character and exquisite taste. Try a juicy Concord the next time you see one or that heavenly Golden Muscat, the same grape that makes your bubbly bottle of *moscato d'Asti*. You'll find any seeds to be of minor consequence.

Grapes with New Walnuts and Crème Fraîche

Choose one or more interesting varieties of grapes from your market. Pluck them off the stems and rinse them well. Cut them in half. If they have pips, flip them out with the point of a knife. Put them in a bowl, add a dollop of crème fraîche or sour cream, and gently stir it in. Add a bit of brown sugar or maple sugar crystals if you like. Crack a few new walnuts. Break the pieces into quarters, add them to the grapes, and serve.

Concord Grape Tart | SERVES 6 TO 8

I know I've included this recipe in various forms in other cookbooks, but Concord grape pies in any form are so extraordinary and still so unknown that I have to have one more chance to spread the word. Besides, the farmers' market is just the place to find the grapes you need. There the Concords tend to be less juicy than commercially grown grapes, which is what you want; otherwise the filling won't thicken properly.

Grape pies have all the voluptuous qualities of a blackberry pie, but I've never found a commercial one, or even one from a farmers' market, that's even half as good as homemade. The filling can also be used to make individual tarts or a lattice-covered pie. It freezes well, too, which means you can have a grape tart at Thanksgiving, if you wish.

Concords are slipskin grapes, and they have seeds. They are not difficult to work with, but you will need a food mill.

2½ pounds purple or white Concord
    grapes, washed
½ cup sugar, or more to taste
3 tablespoons all-purpose flour or
    minute tapioca
grated zest and juice of 1 lemon
1 (9-inch) prebaked Tart Shell,
    page 388

1. Squeeze the grapes with your fingers, putting the insides into a saucepan and the skins into a bowl. Bring the skinned grapes to a boil and cook until they turn white and soft, about 5 minutes.

2. Pass them through a food mill to separate the seeds, working the pulp right into the bowl with the skins. Stir in the sugar, flour, lemon zest, and juice. Simmer for 10 minutes, then taste and add more sugar if needed. Let cool.

3. Preheat the oven to 400°F. Scrape the filling into the prebaked tart shell, set on a sheet pan, and bake until the filling is set, about 35 minutes. Let cool. Serve plain or with softly whipped cream.

Concord Grape Mousse ("Grapette") | SERVES 6 TO 8

A friend who wanted me to taste something I had never eaten before served a Concord grape chiffon pie for dessert. It was covered with a soft layer of whipped cream and garnished with huge floppy mint leaves, and she was right: I'd never had such a pie. She kindly shared the recipe, which came from her mother, an Iowan. I began to play with it, and when it reached this mousse stage, a friend exclaimed, "This reminds me of Grapette!" a soda she grew up drinking in Texas. I stopped right there, short of the crust.

I make my "grapette" from the Concord or Muscat grapes that start appearing in September in farmers' markets everywhere.

2½ pounds white or blue Concord grapes or Muscat grapes

1½ packages unflavored gelatin

⅔ cup plus 1 teaspoon sugar

pinch sea salt

juice of ½ lemon

1 cup whipping cream

2 egg whites

1. Rinse the grapes well. Pluck them from their stems and put them in a heavy saucepan. Add ¼ cup water, cover the pan, and cook over high heat until the skins have separated from the pulp and the grapes are soft, about 5 minutes. Press down on them with a potato masher to break them up and to ascertain their tenderness. If they're resistant, cook them a few minutes more. Pass the grapes through a food mill to separate the skins and seeds. You should have at least 2 cups of juice. If not, add water to bring it up to the volume.

2. Sprinkle the gelatin into ¼ cup water and let stand for 5 minutes. Meanwhile, combine the ⅔ cup sugar with the grape juice and heat, stirring to dissolve the sugar. Add the salt and lemon juice to taste.

3. Add the softened gelatin to the grape juice and stir over low heat until the gelatin is dissolved, about 3 minutes. Transfer to a clean bowl and refrigerate until partially thickened, about 3 hours.

4. Beat the cream in a mixer with the remaining teaspoon of sugar until it forms soft peaks, then scrape it into a bowl. Without washing the bowl, add the grape mixture and egg whites and beat on high until thick, about 5 minutes. Return to the refrigerator for it to set.

5. You can serve the mousse three ways. One: layer it into wineglasses, alternating with layers of whipped cream and ending with cream and a garnish of mint. Two: fold the cream into the grape mixture, leaving streaks of grape and cream. Three: pile it into a graham-cracker crust and cover it with the whipped cream.

Fresh Grape Juice with Lemon Verbena | MAKES ABOUT 1 QUART

Making grape juice is very easy, but you do need a food mill. The amount of juice per pound depends on how juicy the grapes are. Big, juicy, flavorful grapes are what you want—Muscats, muscadines, Concords, etc.

3 to 4 pounds grapes
Simple Syrup, page 388
soda water
1 lemon, sliced
lemon verbena, lemon basil,
    or mint sprigs

1. Rinse the grapes well under running water, plucking them off the stems as you do so. Don't worry about getting rid of every bit of stem—the food mill will do most of the work.
2. Put all the grapes in a wide, heavy pot. Add 1 cup water, turn the heat to high, and cover the pan. Once it starts to boil, lower the heat to medium and cook for 15 minutes. Pass them through the food mill set over a bowl.
3. Taste the juice and sweeten it with the syrup if needed. When you've got it as sweet as you like, pour it into a jar and refrigerate. Serve over ice mixed with soda water, lemon slices, and herb leaves.

While most people think of California as the source of figs, and it is commercially, there are also a number of interesting figs grown in the South, especially in Texas and Georgia, that make it to the farmers' markets there. These are varieties that are too small and too fragile to ship, but they are the really good ones. Celeste, for example, is a small violet fig with berry-colored pulp, the size of a quarter, but at least dollar size in flavor. There are Italian Honey figs (Latterula), strawberry-fleshed Panachee Tiger Stripes, green-gold Adriatics, and Angelique, once grown by Thomas Jefferson, which sports yellow skin and amber flesh. Then, of course, there are the more familiar Brown Turkeys and black Mission figs.

Figs have two crops. The figs that come on in June are called *brebas;* the second, in August, are the true figs. The second crop is what's harvested for drying, but both are enjoyed fresh. Mostly, though, figs are late-summer fruits that arrive with the late peaches and second crop of raspberries, then continue through the season of grapes and, finally, persimmons. But because of the *brebas,* they actually span both ends of the long summer season.

Figs with Cheese, Pepper, and Honey

This scarcely qualifies as a recipe, but here's a wonderful way to enjoy figs. It also provides the perfect occasion to feature a delicate fresh ricotta cheese.

Choose 2 or 3 ripe luscious figs per person. Any variety will do as long as it has lots of flavor. Rinse them, remove the stems, then quarter them from top to bottom without cutting clear through the base. Press them with your fingers at the bases to open them up, then insert a spoonful of cheese. Add a little pepper and a small leaf of anise hyssop. Drizzle a spoonful of honey over each fig and serve.

Fig Tart with
Orange Flower Custard | SERVES 8

This tart beautifully showcases mixed varieties of figs. The green, golden, red, and purple hues of the skins and flesh of various figs make a soft, faded mosaic. If only one type of fig is offered at your market, make the tart anyway.

12 to 16 ripe figs, a mixture of
   varieties or just one type
1 prebaked Tart Shell, page 388
1 egg yolk
½ cup crème fraîche
2½ tablespoons light brown sugar
2 teaspoons orange flower water
confectioners' sugar

1. Preheat the oven to 375°F. Rinse the figs, cut off the stems, and slice them lengthwise in half. Set them cut side up on the tart shell, arranging them in circles, or just lay them in the shell randomly, which looks beautiful, especially with different types of figs. Fit them together as closely as you can with the number of figs you have.

2. Mix the egg yolk, crème fraîche, brown sugar, and orange flower water together, then pour carefully around, not over, the figs. Bake until the custard is lightly colored and set, about 30 minutes. Remove the tart from the pan, set on a serving plate, and serve, dusted with confectioners' sugar. Serve while still slightly warm.

Fig Focaccia with Orange-Scented Olive Oil | MAKES 1 BREAD, SERVING 6 TO 10

This lightly sweetened focaccia was inspired by both the figs and Mr. Sciabica's orange-scented olive oil from the Modesto farmers' market. Slice this long loaf crosswise and serve it, fresh or toasted, with a mild fresh goat cheese or fresh ricotta.

1 cup warm water

1¼-ounce envelope or 1 scant tablespoon active dry yeast

4 teaspoons honey

1 teaspoon anise seeds plus extra for the top

¾ teaspoon sea salt

2 tablespoons orange-scented olive oil plus extra for the top, or extra virgin olive oil plus ⅛ teaspoon Boyajian orange oil

2 teaspoons grated orange zest

2½ cups all-purpose flour, approximately

1 (1-pint) basket figs, about 10 ounces, quartered

1 teaspoon orange flower water

cornmeal

2 teaspoons turbinado sugar

1. Mix the water, yeast, and 1 teaspoon honey in a mixing bowl and set aside until foamy, about 10 minutes. Meanwhile, crush the anise seeds in a mortar and pestle.

2. Add the salt, oil, orange zest, and remaining tablespoon of the honey to the yeast. Beat in 1 cup of the flour, then continue adding more until the dough is shaggy. Turn it out onto a lightly floured counter and knead until you have a smooth but slightly tacky dough, working in more flour as necessary. Place the dough in a lightly oiled bowl, turn once, then cover with plastic wrap and set aside to rise until doubled, about 45 minutes.

3. While the dough is rising, remove the stems from the figs and cut them into quarters. Sprinkle them with the orange flower water.

4. Lightly dust the counter with flour and sprinkle a sheet pan with cornmeal. Turn out the dough and press or roll it into a 12 x 16-inch rectangle. Scatter a third of the figs down the center third of the dough. Fold one end of the dough over the figs, letter fashion, and cover with the second third of the figs. Fold the final third of the dough over the figs and gently press it down. Carefully roll the dough out to make a rectangle about 7 x 16 inches, taking care that the figs don't burst through the dough. Transfer it to a baking pan and set aside to rise until doubled, about 30 minutes.

5. Preheat the oven to 400°F. Dimple the dough with your fingers, then brush with additional oil. Add the remaining figs and sprinkle the bread with the sugar and anise seeds. Bake until golden, 25 to 30 minutes. Remove to a rack to cool.

Fig and Ginger Jam | MAKES ABOUT 1½ CUPS

When I first tasted this after making it, I found the heat of the ginger and the snap of the vinegar startling. But a week later it had calmed down, mellowing into a subtler jam that's delicious on toast with fresh ricotta or sheep's milk cheese.

⅓ cup aged red wine vinegar

1 tablespoon red wine

¼ cup honey

⅓ cup raisins

2 teaspoons slivered candied ginger
   or peeled fresh ginger

2 cups (about ¾ pound) fresh figs,
   cut into quarters if small, into
   eighths if large

½ teaspoon mustard seeds

3 cloves

¼ teaspoon tamarind

1 teaspoon fig balsamic or regular
   balsamic vinegar

1. Combine the red wine vinegar, wine, honey, raisins, and ginger in a noncorrosive saucepan. Bring to a boil, then simmer until syrupy, about 5 minutes. Add the figs, mustard seeds, cloves, and tamarind, cover, and cook over low heat until the figs are soft but still hold a little of their shape, about 10 minutes. Check once to make sure the pan isn't too dry. If it is, add a little water.

2. Remove from the heat. When cool, taste and, if you wish it to be sharper, add a little fig balsamic vinegar to taste.

As well as serving as a stage for farmers, markets have become a stage for musicians, and live music is an enjoyable part of the atmosphere of many farmers' markets. We have a constant parade of musicians moving through our market. There are the four kids who play violins together and a couple of young boys singing old Dylan songs. An extremely compelling group of college kids play wild marimba music, which practically stops the market. There's a very skillful dulcimer player and a "gypsy" singer who plays guitar and sings passionate songs in a rich, operatic voice. Occasionally an accordion player shows up, and this year we acquired a Hawaiian-style group called Poi White Trash. Blue grass bands, Dixieland bands, and mariachis get everyone moving briskly. A group always gathers around to watch the staccato clogging component of the latter band.

Except for the Hawaiian music, most of this music is lively. It makes the market feel energetic. But on one Saturday at the Bellingham farmers' market in Washington, it was the soft, mellow tone of a vibraphone that drifted through the fall sunshine. Languid notes floated out over the market, and everyone seemed to slow from a walk to a stroll, as if in a dreamy sort of slow motion. This was a mellow market. Someone was getting Rolfed; another person was getting a shoulder massage. Across from the market was a table set up for the Green Party, and next to it stood a man with a big sign proclaiming that we should get out of the UN, but no one was shouting or carrying on. It was all very peaceable. Though it was not particularly large, we easily spent several hours just enjoying this market. No doubt, the music was part of it.

Every market has some special feature that makes it unique. In addition to the vibraphone, picnic tables were set up at one end of the market, near various food vendors. Shoppers could buy lunch, then sit down and enjoy it. Strangers shared the tables and lingered over their meals. We bought some sweet potato pie and ice cream from a local dairy and struck up a conversation with a couple who had driven forty miles just to attend the market, which they did every Saturday. We watched a little girl spend about ten minutes struggling with an ear of corn, which she finally succeeded in husking. Then she ate it. Nearby was a wall covered with photographs of shoppers. A sign read, "If you see your picture here, please take it with our compliments." Maurice Jensen, the photographer, introduced himself and explained that he had been taking the pictures for the past three years and posting them for their subjects to claim. It was a popular feature. Every time we looked there was someone searching for a picture, and kids were especially thrilled to find theirs.

Although it was nearing the end of summer, you would have no problem eating extremely well, for the produce was exceptional. Greens, late tomatoes, and cool-weather crops were abundant, but what stood out were chanterelles, magnificent apples, aged Gouda cheese, brambleberry pies (wild blackberries and scratches on the baker's arm to prove it), hazelnuts, and shell beans. We had a chance to cook the chanterelles; eat the Gouda with the crisp, slightly tart Jonagold apples, and track down the hazelnut farm and learn why these nuts were long, like almonds, instead of round. The brambleberry pie was amazing, and the shell beans were gorgeous. The farmers are outnumbered by crafters and food stands, but if you visit this market (it runs from 11 to 3, unlike most Saturday markets), don't be deterred. This is a lovely place to shop for beautiful food and to linger.

Lummi Island is about an hour's drive and a ferry ride away from Bellingham. Its market had no music component and just a handful of farmers. But again, there was the most beautiful food. One farmer brought a pet piglet, which was the market's main entertainment. Given the island's small population, everyone knew everyone else and, more precisely than most, where their food came from. Again, there were pies—rhubarb, blueberry, and wild blackberry—eggs, pastured chickens, cool-weather vegetables, herbs, and the most tender salad greens. This was where I had found the succulent hickory-smoked albacore, along with big, fat asparagus and artichokes. Our friends Riley Starks and Judy Olsen, who raise chickens and eggs, grow vegetables, make pasta, *and* fish, hosted dinner. (They now run an inn as well.) Riley wanted us to taste everything—the Dungeness crabs he had caught, a Fraser River salmon he had frozen for us at the end of the season, his chickens. We wanted to taste all that plus everything Judy grew and made, especially her nettle ravioli. Their neighbors arrived with *their* produce, plus we had our haul from Bellingham, so dinner turned out to be an embarrassment of local riches, only partially recollected below.

A FARM DINNER ON LUMMI ISLAND

Dungeness crabs with lemon butter

Spaghetti Squash Gratin with Chanterelles (page 154)

Sautéed Artichokes and Potatoes with Garlic Chives
(page 39)

Grilled Fraser River salmon with Lovage Oil (page 61)

A big salad of mixed lettuces and herbs

Jonagold apples and aged Gouda cheese

Greg's Huckleberry Pie (page 264)

Stone Fruits: The Warm Heart of Summer

Cherries, apricots, plums, peaches, nectarines, and pluots have a pit, or stone, that contains the seed. To be able to "give your love a cherry that has no stone" speaks of something far more rare than a gift of a four-leaf clover. The stone fruit season begins with cherries and apricots in early summer and goes into the heart of the season with peaches, nectarines, and, finally, plums. To me the stone fruits are the quintessential fruits of summer. Others may feel that summer reserves its keenest expression for berries or melons. It matters not.

What does matter is the quality of the fruit, and with stone fruit that means tree-ripened and untraveled. Almost every person I've interviewed about his or her farmers' market has boasted about the superb peaches. While I was assisting with a tasting of stone fruits from our market one Saturday, it seemed that every other out-of-towner approached the table saying "Let's see if these peaches are as good as ours!" Fredericksburg, Texas, is known for its peaches, but a visitor from east Texas was adamant about hers. The whole state of Georgia is known for its peaches too, yet a shopper in Iowa swoons over the ones she finds at her market. Montmorency cherries reign supreme in

Michigan, but the peaches there are also superb. At the Missoula farmers' market people lined up to get their share of Lambert cherries from nearby Flathead Lake. Although California has the advantage of a superbly hospitable climate, it's the *local* aspect of these fruits that accounts for their excellent reputations. Occasionally you'll see travelers in airports carrying a basket of peaches or a box of plums that they're taking to a friend or relative somewhere—a taste of home that's unlike any other.

The stone fruit I've tasted up and down California's Central Valley has been outstanding. But it's never very good when it shows up on a grocery shelf fifteen hundred miles away. You can see why if you imagine driving down California's Highway 99 in July and August. This crowded highway is one of the bumpiest, fastest roads you can drive, and you're certain to end up driving behind a huge truck loaded with flats of peaches. As you pass, look up at the cab to see the driver being shaken in his seat by the combination of rough terrain and speed. Of course the same thing is happening to the fruit he's hauling, and for a peach or a plum to survive such a journey it would have to be as hard as a stone. And stone-hard is not the meaning of *stone fruit*.

I watch shoppers at my supermarket pick up one peach, plum, or nectarine after another and bring it to their nose, looking for a hint of promise. Finding none, they put each one down, then move away. Older shoppers do this anyway. Younger shoppers, who don't necessarily associate fruit with flavor, just drop them into bags without trying to assess their contents. Unripe stone fruits shrivel, then start to spoil from the center out. They will continue to ripen *only* if picked days short of perfection. There's a little leeway, but not a lot.

One market day in Sonoma, California, farmers were complaining that the stone fruit was not at its best. This was blamed on El Niño, that winter of violent and prolonged storms, but I found the peaches to be majestic, perfumed with fruit and hints of spice; the nectarines dotted with sugar spots that promised sweetness. The peaches compared so favorably with our small fruits that I couldn't understand the farmers' complaints. But when I returned the following summer, the summer of La Niña, the stone fruit was even better. I bought bags of Babcock peaches and white Arctic Rose nectarines from a farm stand that were nothing short of astonishing. They filled my car with clouds of perfume, dripped copiously over motel towels, and those that eventually made it to a luncheon were savored slice by slice.

Although I try to think of the best ways to use such delicious stone fruits, it's hard to imagine doing much more than eating them out of hand. But there are wonderful things that can be made—the pies, buckles, crisps, and kuchens—from individual fruits or mixtures of them. There are fruit ice creams, peaches on cereal, white peaches sliced into a glass of prosecco, plum soups, nectarine gratins, and apricot jams. You could make a salad of peaches and basil or follow the Italian custom of baking a peach but replacing its pit with a knob of *amaretti,* which mimics both the look and the flavor of a peach pit. But if the fruit is really good, you needn't go further than to place some on the table, add a stack of plates, some knives, and leave it at that.

A Cherry-Almond Loaf Cake | SERVES 8

Cherries and almonds make an ideal pairing, especially in this cake. I love the golden blush of Royal Anns, but since I can't resist any of them, I often have several kinds on hand during cherry season. They look lovely together in this cake.

This moist cake is a good keeper but is truly best when still just a little warm from the oven.

1 cup blanched almonds

1 cup plus 2 tablespoons all-purpose flour

1 teaspoon baking powder

½ teaspoon sea salt

½ cup (1 stick) unsalted butter, at room temperature

¾ cup plus 1 teaspoon sugar

3 eggs, at room temperature

¼ teaspoon almond extract

½ teaspoon vanilla extract

2½ cups pitted cherries

confectioners' sugar

1. Preheat the oven to 375°F. Butter and flour a 5x8-inch loaf pan. Coarsely chop the almonds in a food processor. Remove ¼ cup and set it aside. Add the flour, baking powder, and salt to the remaining almonds and process until the mixture is smooth. Transfer to a bowl.

2. Cream the butter with the ¾ cup sugar in the food processor, then add the eggs one at a time, incorporating each one fully as you go. Add the flavorings, then half the flour-almond mixture. Pulse several times to incorporate. Add the remainder and pulse until smooth. Scrape into the prepared pan and cover with the cherries.

3. Mix the reserved almonds with the teaspoon of sugar and sprinkle over the top of the cake. Bake the cake for 1 hour and 10 minutes or until a tester comes out clean. Let cool in the pan, then turn it out and transfer to a cake plate. Dust with confectioners' sugar just before serving.

Apricot-Cherry Crisp | SERVES 6 TO 8

Apricot and cherries lead the season for stone fruits, and apricot-cherry *anything*—pie, crisp, cobbler, or crumble—is a winning combination, especially in old-fashioned desserts like these. If any pie cherries are available, include a cup for their flavor. And, if raspberry season should coincide, you can't go wrong throwing in a handful or two as well.

2½ pounds ripe apricots

1 pound sweet cherries or
    pie cherries

2 tablespoons sugar

1½ tablespoons minute tapioca

⅛ teaspoon almond extract

THE CRISP TOPPING

6 tablespoons unsalted butter,
    cut into small chunks

¾ cup light brown sugar, loosely
    packed

⅔ cup all-purpose flour

½ cup rolled oats or finely chopped
    almonds

¼ teaspoon sea salt

½ teaspoon freshly grated nutmeg

1 teaspoon ground cinnamon, optional

1. Preheat the oven to 375°F. Lightly butter a 2½-quart gratin dish. Pit the apricots and cherries, then toss them with the sugar, tapioca, and almond extract. Lay the fruit in the prepared dish.

2. Make the topping. Pat the topping over the fruit. Set the dish on a baking pan to catch the juices and bake until the top is browned and the juices have thickened around the edge, about 45 minutes. Serve warm with vanilla or honey ice cream.

Using your fingers or the paddle attachment of a mixer, work the butter with the rest of the ingredients until the texture is coarse and crumbly.

Mixed Cherry Pie with a Double Crust | SERVES 8

Pie cherries, hard to find anywhere but at a farmers' market, are tart, nearly translucent, and cherry red. These are the fruits that give cherry desserts their distinctive flavor. Even a handful will do the trick if that's all you have.

For this pie I use a pint basket of pie cherries mixed with dark ruby Bings and pink-and-gold Royal Anns. You can use other varieties as well, or all pie cherries, adding an extra ¼ cup sugar if they're very tart. This makes a big double-crust pie. If you're going to go to the trouble to pit cherries, you might as well make a large pie—it doesn't take that many more.

Pie Dough for double-crust pie,
    page 387
1 pint pie cherries
3 pints (about 2 pounds) Bing or
    other sweet cherries
1 cup sugar
¼ cup all-purpose flour or tapioca
¼ teaspoon almond extract

1. Make the pie dough and divide into 2 disks, one slightly larger than the other. Wrap in plastic wrap or wax paper and refrigerate. While it's chilling, pit the cherries and put them in a bowl roomy enough to hold them comfortably. The pits of the pie cherries can be gently squeezed out with your fingers rather than punched out with a pitter. This creates much less spatter. Toss the cherries—you should have about 8 cups or a bit more—with ¾ cup of the sugar, the flour, and the almond extract. Preheat the oven to 450°F.

2. Roll out the larger circle of dough and ease it into a 10-inch glass pie plate. Roll out the second piece. Add the cherries, set the circle of dough on top, then crimp the edges. Brush the top with water and sprinkle generously with the remaining ¼ cup sugar.

3. Cut several slits in a star-shaped patter in the center, set the pie on a sheet pan, and bake in the lower third of the oven for 15 minutes. Reduce the temperature to 350°F, move the pie up to the center rack, and bake for 1 hour or until the crust is brown and the juices have started to run. Let cool for at least an hour before serving.

Probably only a person raised happily in California's Central Valley could feel a pull toward Modesto in July. It was that warm valley air fragrant with plant life, the gurgle of irrigation ditches, and the smell of dust in the country that lured me. Then the broad shady streets in town, the mockingbirds' chatter, and the heavy scent of jasmine confirmed it: These were the smells, sights, and sounds of the California I grew up in. It was home. No matter that I had been to Modesto only one other time.

The idea of a farmers' market in Modesto is almost an oxymoron, for Modesto lies at the heart of the nation's agribusiness, a style of farming where fields and orchards go on forever, and markets lie distant from the harvest. This latest surge of farmers' markets, which began in the 1970s, started, in part, as a way for large-scale farmers to sell excess fruit at a better price than what they could get wholesale. But this market wasn't about farmers offloading their commercial excesses. It was a true farmers' market.

Only two blocks long and holding no more than fifty vendors, the farmers' market was quiet when I arrived at seven. Later there would be a band, a chef, and a canning demonstration, but for the moment it was calm, shoppers friendly yet purposeful. As it was well into fruit season, the tables were covered with stone fruits as well as wild blackberries, raspberries, and strawberries, melons of all kinds, and figs. Although this is where much of the fruit that you find in your supermarket comes from, it tastes different here. The peaches have the scent of flowers, a frosty bloom still clings to the plums, drops of honeyed nectar bead the figs, and there's a tender ripeness that astonishes the tongue on all of these sun-warmed fruits. Fruits that travel don't get a chance to mature to their full splendor.

The Modesto farmers were very much into mixing and matching their produce, an attractive approach I hadn't seen before. At one table baskets filled with nectarines; peaches, *and* plums were presented along with baskets of single fruits. At another stand baskets were filled with eggplant, zucchini, green tomatoes, and peppers, a recipe for how to use them printed on purple paper and tucked in among them. There was something nice about being told you could mix and match to your heart's content from a jumble of undersized red, white, and yellow onions. It conveyed a friendly spirit that said, "Dig in and find the ones you want!"

Labels in this market didn't rest with the obvious. Not just peaches, but White Lady (a Modesto original), not plums, but Black Friars; Tilton apricots; Sun Rose nectarines; Redhaven and Babcock peaches. Back home, while looking up fruit varietals and their origins, I was struck by how many of these fruits had been developed in Modesto and environs. My guess is that shoppers here were looking for the variety that was their favorite. At least they knew what was what.

I was delighted to see an olive oil producer, Joseph Sciabica, from whom I used to buy vats of oil when I cooked in San Francisco. The Sciabicas, who began making olive oil in 1936, are the oldest producers of olive oil in California. The third generation is now in charge of business, but Joseph, in his eighties, is unstoppable. He is still selling his oil with the enthusiasm he had thirty years earlier. I hadn't seen him in many years, but he was immediately recognizable in his "uniform," a turquoise sweater vest and matching cap, both knitted by his wife, Gemma. His oils were distinguished by the type of olive they were made from and whether the harvest was early or late. Behind the prize blue ribbons decorating the table stood an unusual and lovely orange-scented olive oil and an oaky, barrel-aged red wine vinegar. (The oil and vinegar are available by mail order. See Resources.)

Coming from one of those markets in which chard and kale are ever abundant, I was lured by the fruits, and especially gladdened to find an abundance of voluptuous figs. The white nectarines and plums got eaten in the car, but I managed to get the oil, vinegar, and figs home, packed neatly in egg cartons.

Leaving the market, the signs that had welcomed customers in read, "Thank you for coming. Have a dandy day."

A CENTRAL VALLEY DINNER

Fig Focaccia with Orange-Scented Olive Oil (page 274)

Yellow Wax Beans with Lemon Thyme and
Yellow Tomatoes (page 123)

Penne with Green and Gold Zucchini and Ricotta
(page 142)

Black Raspberry and Rose Geranium Sherbet (page 258)

White Rose nectarines with Prosecco

Apricot Custard Tart | MAKES ONE 9-INCH TART

I've made this tart using the tiniest rose-blushed apricots from the Taos farmers' market (these as late as September) and luscious Royal Blenheims, perhaps the best of the old varieties, from the Santa Monica farmers' market. They couldn't have been more different in appearance, but both were sweet and succulent. This is a good recipe for apricots that are firm and even a touch underripe, since they're poached first in a syrup. You'll end up with a bonus—some thick apricot syrup for glazing fruit tarts or sweetening iced tea.

Tart Shell, page 388
¾ cup plus 1 tablespoon sugar
32 very small firm ripe apricots or
    12 to 15 large ones
1 egg
¾ cup cream or a mixture of cream
    and crème fraîche
1 drop almond extract

1. Press the dough into a tart shell and freeze while you preheat the oven to 425°F. Set it on a sheet pan and bake until lightly colored, about 25 minutes.

2. Combine the ¾ cup sugar and 1½ cups water in a saucepan, bring to a boil, and stir to dissolve the sugar. Halve the apricots. Crack several of the pits, remove the kernels, and add them to the syrup. Poach the apricots in 2 batches until barely tender when pierced with the tip of a knife. This may take only 1 or 2 minutes—they should hold their shape nicely and not turn into jam. Gently lift them into a colander placed over a bowl. When all are done, add the drained syrup back to the pan and continue boiling until it's reduced by about half. (Sometimes I add a few lavender blossoms to the syrup and a few apricots when I have extra or they're very ripe. The apricots turn translucent and give the syrup body and flavor.)

3. Beat the egg and cream together with the almond extract and remaining tablespoon of sugar.

4. Arrange the apricot halves in the tart shell, the cut sides facing up and slightly overlapping. Pour the custard over the fruit and bake until the cream is set and the edges of the fruit are browned, about 25 minutes. Brush a little of the reduced syrup over the fruit. When cool enough to handle, remove the tart from its rim and place it on a serving plate. It's best served when still a little warm.

Apricots Baked in Parchment | SERVES 1

A gentle heat brings out the flavor of the apricots in this easy recipe. You can form the packets in advance of their brief stay in the oven and serve the fruit within or without.

PER PACKAGE

3 large ripe apricots, halved

1 teaspoon sugar

½ teaspoon unsalted butter

1 stem of flowering English lavender, stem removed

1. Cut a piece of parchment about 12 inches square. Fold it in half diagonally and then trim to make a rough semicircle. Lay the apricots on one half, cut side up, sprinkle with the sugar, dot with the butter, and add the lavender.

2. Fold and crease the parchment tightly, working your way all around the edge and ending with a firm twist of the paper, making a little handle.

3. Preheat the oven to 275°F. Add the packet and bake for 20 minutes. Set on a plate, slit the top with a knife, and serve right away. Or, if you prefer, place the cooked apricots with their juices on a plate. But part of the fun is opening a packet and releasing a soft whoosh of fragrant heat.

VARIATION WITH RASPBERRIES: Add a handful of black or red raspberries to each packet.

VARIATION WITH VANILLA: Omit the lavender. Snip a soft vanilla bean into 1-inch lengths and cut each piece lengthwise in half. Add a piece to each package. Serve with vanilla ice cream.

Apricot Nectar | MAKES 1 QUART

Here's the perfect use for those extra-soft fruits that you might have intended for jam that you didn't get around to making. At least that's how I came to make my own apricot nectar. Nectar is for drinking, of course, but you can also set it with gelatin to make a cool dessert. No matter how sweet the fruit, it usually ends up a little tart, so plan to sweeten it with simple syrup or honey.

You can cook the fruit, stones and all, then strain it, or if you halve the apricots first and remove the stones, you don't have to strain. In either case, crack a few stones and cook the kernels with the fruit for their almond flavor.

6 cups very ripe apricots

12 or more apricot kernels

½ cup Simple Syrup, page 388, honey, or maple syrup

1. Wash the apricots well and put them in a pot with 5 cups water and the kernels. Bring to a boil and simmer, partially covered, until the fruit is so soft that it's falling away from the stones, about 30 minutes.

2. Pour the fruit into a strainer or colander and work it around with a rubber spatula to force the pulp through the holes, leaving the kernels behind. Then puree or pass through a food mill. Sweeten to taste, then chill. It may thicken as it cools.

Apricot-Lavender Refrigerator Jam |

Because this isn't nearly as sweet as commercial jams, the flavor of apricots is rich and full. This is a simple little preserve to make in small quantities, not an all-day project. The lavender makes a fine match with apricots—just make sure that you use the sweet, fragrant kind, not the variety that smells of camphor.

If you leave this a little on the thin side, you'll have a sauce to spoon over warm biscuits, to flavor a semifreddo, or to drizzle over almond ice cream and top with toasted almonds. It also makes a shiny orange pool for the Panna Cotta on page 248.

7 cups ripe apricots

12 apricot pits, cracked, the kernels removed

1 cup sugar

7 lavender blossom sprigs

juice of ½ lemon, optional

1. Halve the apricots or quarter them if very large. Large pieces will give your jam a little texture. Place the apricots in a heavy pan with the kernels, sugar, and lavender. Cook over high heat, watching closely and stirring at first until the juices are released and the sugar is dissolved. Then reduce the heat to medium and cook, stirring frequently, until the fruit is thickened, 10 to 15 minutes.

2. Taste and, if you wish, add lemon juice if it needs sharpening. With so little sugar, the natural tartness of the fruit may be sufficient. Pour into sterilized containers, cap tightly, and store in the refrigerator.

PLUMS AND PLUOTS

There are Black Friars, Elephant Hearts, Damsons, all the Gages, the Mirabelles, prune plums, wild plums, yellow Shiro plums, and plums with no names that have just been in someone's garden forever. Italian prune plums and blue Stanleys are the plums that become prunes but that are now called *dried plums*. A discernible patch of something called *bloom*—it's like a white powder—may be visible on the skin of a fresh plum. Like the bloom of youth, it's a sign that a piece of fruit has hardly been touched at all. (Bloom can also be seen on fresh apples, grapes, blueberries, and other fruits.)

Plums can be magical, but they tend to be a little more problematic than other stone fruits. Cooking enhances their flavors and increases their possibilities in the kitchen, but the skins turn sharp and tannic once cooked, increasing the amount of sweetening needed. You can blanch the plums in boiling water for 10 seconds and then slip off the skins, which renders them sweeter, but then they lose their color. Plums are harder to slice, for the flesh tends to cling to the stone, except with prune plums. It's almost impossible to get a neat slice of a dead-ripe Santa Rosa plum without mangling it. Still, a great deal can be done with plums, which is fortunate because when they come on they usually come on in glut proportions. Plums make excellent sorbets, soups, crisps, pies, tarts, jams, and fillings for crêpes.

Although much is made of the Green Gage and Damson, it's the Santa Rosa, developed by the great plant breeder Luther Burbank, that is, to my taste anyway, the most intriguing plum. With its purple-red skin russeted with fine dots of gold and its golden-to-garnet-colored juicy flesh, it's one to keep an eye out for. I find it offers a quintessential plum experience, but another variety might be the plum of choice where you live.

Ripeness is essential if plums are to live up to whatever praises they garner. Just after writing this, I tasted half a dozen kinds of plums at our market, all of them picked unripe. It seems that the farmers wanted to be the first to have them, but they were so tart and unappealing, including the Santa Rosas, that any reader tasting these same fruits would have thought I had lost my sense of taste. It's better if farmers can wait until the fruit can come to market no more than a day or two, at the most, away from perfection.

Pluots, plumcots, and, most recently, apriums, are plum-apricot crosses that are still rare, although plant breeders in California have been working on them for many years. (They have a greenish-golden plum type of skin and shape but something of an apricot flavor.) But one can nearly always find dried pluots at California farmers' markets. Their red-gold color and faintly indeterminate flavor make them an unusual fruit to include in a winter compote or to use wherever dried apricots are called for.

Sugared Plums for Tarts and a Compote | MAKES 6 SERVINGS OR FILLING FOR 1 GALETTE

I always worried about all the juice that plums give off when they're baking in pastry and how to avoid ending up with soggy crusts, but you can solve such problems if you briefly cook the plums first. The fruit ends up soft, the dough stays crisp, and you can use the juice to flavor (and color) the cream that goes on the side. Nectarines and peeled peaches can be handled this way as well.

This simple method is more than just a step, for it produces a luscious compote to serve with ice cream or panna cotta or to spoon inside a cornmeal crêpe. At breakfast the plums can go over French toast. Even the juice that collects can be reduced to syrup.

Use any plum that's slightly firm and full of fragrance. To cut smaller plums easily, stand each one upright on the cutting board, then remove 4 slices as close to the pit as possible. Slice each of the quarters into halves.

6 cups sliced plums, about 2 pounds
¾ cup sugar
1 teaspoon orange flower water

Place a wide skillet on the stove over high heat. Add the plums and sprinkle with the sugar and orange flower water. Give everything a stir. When the plums begin to give up their juice and the sugar dissolves, count 2 minutes, then turn off the heat. This should take about 4 minutes in all. As the plums sit, they'll yield even more juice. Use it to make plum cream.

PLUM CREAM

juice from the plums, above
¼ cup sugar, more or less
1 cup whipping cream
2 tablespoons confectioners' sugar,
    to taste
1 drop almond extract
1 teaspoon orange flower water or
    orange liqueur
tiny pinch ground cloves

1. Simmer the juice until syrupy and reduced by about half. Taste, and if it's too tart, stir in up to ¼ cup sugar. Cool completely.
2. Whip the cream with the confectioners' sugar until soft, billowy peaks form. Add the flavorings and cold plum syrup to taste. Continue whipping until the cream once again makes soft billowy peaks. Refrigerate until ready to serve.

Cornmeal Crêpes with Plums and Honey Ice Cream | SERVES 6

Once the plums and crêpes are cooked, assembly just takes a moment.

plum juice from the compote,
   page 293
Cornmeal Crêpes, recipe follows
Plum Compote, page 293
Honey Ice Cream, page 379, or
   another, such as vanilla or
   caramel
confectioners' sugar

1. Boil the plum juice in a small saucepan until reduced enough to become syrupy. Make the crêpes. Have the plums warm and the ice cream soft enough to scoop easily. Preheat the oven to 425°F.

2. Place the cooked crêpes, golden side down, on a perforated sheet pan, if you have one, or a regular sheet pan. (The crêpes will crisp better on the perforated type.) Put them in the oven and, when hot, after a few minutes, remove and immediately slide them onto dessert plates.

3. Spoon about ¼ cup of the fruit onto half of a crêpe, add a spoonful of ice cream, and fold the second half over. Dust with confectioners' sugar, drizzle with plum syrup, and serve.

Cornmeal Crêpes | SERVES 6

Crêpes are so easy to make, yet they make a special dessert out of the simplest of fruit fillings. Try to make your crêpe batter at least an hour ahead of time so that it can rest. Leftover crêpes can be wrapped in plastic and refrigerated.

1¾ cups milk

¼ cup instant polenta or coarse
    cornmeal

1-inch piece of vanilla bean

4 tablespoons unsalted butter, melted

⅔ cup all-purpose flour

¼ teaspoon sea salt

1 teaspoon sugar

2 large eggs

1. Warm the milk in a saucepan with the polenta, vanilla bean, and butter until the butter melts. Slice the vanilla bean in half, scrape the seeds into the milk, and remove the pod. Cool until tepid.

2. Mix together the flour, salt, and sugar. Stir in the eggs, then gradually add the tepid milk. Scrape in any cornmeal that has settled to the bottom. Beat until smooth, then set aside to rest in the refrigerator for at least an hour, longer if time allows. Let the batter come to room temperature before making the crêpes.

3. Heat an 8-inch nonstick skillet with a little butter. Add 3 tablespoons of the batter and swirl it around the pan to make a thin, even layer. Cook over medium-high heat until golden, about 1 minute, then slip a knife under the edge, lift it up, and turn the crêpe with your hands. Cook the second side for about 50 seconds—it needn't brown—then slide it onto a plate. The first crêpe tells you if the batter is too thick to make a thin crêpe. If so, thin it with a few tablespoons milk or water. For the rest of the crêpes it's not necessary to add butter to the pan. Continue making crêpes until all the batter is used.

SOME OTHER FRUIT FILLINGS FOR CRÊPES

Strawberries, sliced and drizzled with honey or passion fruit, ricotta

Blackberries, scented with rose geranium leaves, brown sugar, and sour cream

Sliced peaches or nectarines with fromage blanc

Blueberries, heated briefly, flavored with lime, with ricotta and sour cream

Caramelized apple slices with yogurt cheese

Plum
Kuchen | SERVES 6

This is a sturdy crust that will stand up under the juice that plums, apricots, peaches, and nectarines are bound to release. Italian prune plums are easy to handle since they slice easily away from their stone. On the other hand, the deep red-fleshed Elephant Hearts are stellar looking—and very good. There's no reason not to mix different varieties of plums or different kinds of stone fruits you may have gathered from your market visit. Serve with softly whipped cream flavored with a little orange flower water or crème de noyaux, a liqueur made form the kernels of stone fruits.

A honey-colored earthenware gratin dish works well and looks wonderful with this dish.

1 cup plus 2 tablespoons all-purpose
 flour

⅓ cup plus 2 tablespoons sugar

¼ teaspoon sea salt

4 tablespoons cold unsalted butter

1 egg

1 egg yolk

½ teaspoon vanilla extract

⅛ teaspoon almond extract

1 teaspoon freshly grated orange zest
 or 1 drop Boyajian orange oil

¼ cup milk

THE FRUIT AND TOPPING

10 to 12 plums

2 tablespoons unsalted butter, melted

1 tablespoon sugar

½ teaspoon ground cardamom or
 cinnamon, optional

1. Preheat the oven to 375°F. Lightly butter an 8-cup gratin dish or tart pan. Pulse the flour, sugar, and salt in a food processor, then cut in the butter to make fine crumbs. Beat the egg and egg yolk with the flavorings, then add enough milk to make ½ cup liquid. Add the liquid to the flour, mixing enough to make a thick dough. Brush your hands with flour, then pat the dough into the baking dish, pushing it up a little around the edges to make a rim.

2. Slice Italian plums in half. If they're small, leave them in halves; otherwise quarter them. If you're using round plums, such as Elephant Heart, slice them into wedges about ½ inch thick. Overlap them over the dough. You can really crowd them together, because they'll collapse while cooking.

3. Drizzle the melted butter over the fruit, then sprinkle on the sugar and cardamom, if using. Bake until the crust is golden and the fruit is soft, 35 to 45 minutes. Serve warm if possible.

In the cracked pit of any stone fruit lies a kernel that has two edges of flavor, one of bitterness and the other of almond. Their flavor stems from the heart of the fruit and perfectly meets the succulence of the flesh. A dozen or more apricot kernels added to a batch of apricot jam imparts a big, round note of flavor. A handful steeped overnight in cream or milk makes an ambrosial liquid that can then be used to make an almond-scented panna cotta, blancmange, or ice cream. Any of these is the perfect match for plum crisps, peach cobblers, apricot tarts, and cherry pies. And they are equally divine with desserts made from buttery, ripe pears.

Apricot pits work best. Peach pits are too hard; plums and cherries are too small. Open them with a nutcracker or put them in a plastic bag, then break them open with a hammer. Don't worry if you crush the soft kernels—you'll be doing that in any case. If you succeed in getting the seed out intact, you'll see how closely it resembles an almond. But inhale it and you will find that it goes far beyond almonds with its notes of bitterness and sweetness.

Noyaux or Bitter Almond Ice Cream | MAKES 1 QUART

This ice cream is the one to serve with any fruit dessert made of stone fruit. True bitter almonds can be purchased by mail order from Rusty Hall (see page 396).

⅓ cup apricot kernels or bitter
    almonds
⅔ cup sugar
2 cups cream
1 cup milk
5 egg yolks

1. Pulverize the apricot kernels with the sugar in a mortar or food processor. Add the mixture to the cream and milk in a saucepan, bring to a boil, then turn off the heat. Let stand until cool, then strain. Rinse out the strainer, place it over a bowl, and set aside.

2. Whisk the egg yolks with the infused cream and milk. Return the mixture to the saucepan and cook over medium heat, stirring constantly, just until the mixture coats the spoon. Immediately pour it through the strainer.

3. Chill, then freeze in your ice cream maker.

Peach Shortcake on Ginger Biscuits | SERVES 6

It's hard to beat this variation on that classic dessert—warm biscuits covered with cold sliced peaches and a dollop of whipped cream.

THE FRUIT AND THE TOPPING

6 large ripe and juicy peaches or enough to make about 6 cups sliced

1 tablespoon maple sugar or regular sugar

THE BISCUITS AND CREAM

2 cups all-purpose flour or 1 cup whole wheat pastry flour mixed with 1 cup all-purpose flour

1 tablespoon sugar

½ teaspoon sea salt

2 teaspoons baking powder

½ teaspoon baking soda

½ cup (1 stick) unsalted butter, sliced into 8 pieces

½ cup chopped candied ginger

1 egg

½ teaspoon vanilla extract

½ cup buttermilk, milk, or cream

1 cup whipping cream

⅛ teaspoon almond extract

confectioners' sugar, optional

1. Peel and slice the peaches into wedges about an inch wide. Sprinkle with the sugar, cover, and refrigerate while you make the biscuits.

2. Preheat the oven to 400°F. Stir the dry ingredients together in a mixing bowl. Add the butter and mix on low speed, using the paddle attachment of your mixer, until the butter is broken into pea-size chunks. Stir in the candied ginger.

3. Beat the egg with the vanilla and buttermilk. Add it to the dry ingredients and stir just to moisten. If it seems too dry, add 1 or 2 tablespoons more buttermilk. The texture will be shaggy and barely moist.

4. Turn the dough out onto a counter lightly dusted with flour. Knead with a light touch a few times, then roll or pat the dough into a circle about ¾ inch thick. Using a glass or cookie cutter, cut out four 3-inch circles, then gather the remains, shape into a disk, and cut out the last 2 biscuits. Place close together on the sheet pan and bake until golden, 12 to 15 minutes.

5. Whip the cream until it holds soft peaks, then stir in the almond extract. To serve, halve the biscuits. Spoon the fruit and its juices over the bottom half, add a dollop of the cream, and cover with the top biscuit. Dust with confectioners' sugar if desired.

White Peaches in Lemon Verbena Syrup | SERVES 6

The flowery perfume of white peaches (and nectarines) sets them apart from their yellow-fleshed cousins. They are also very delicate and bruise easily, so your only good source will be a local one if you want ripe fruit that smells like a bouquet of roses and raspberries—and tastes even better.

¾ cup sugar

12 fresh lemon verbena leaves

6 perfect white peaches or nectarines

1. Simmer the sugar, 2 cups water, and 6 lemon verbena leaves until the sugar has dissolved, about 5 minutes. Cover and set aside for a half hour or longer for the lemon verbena to infuse the syrup with its flavor. Remove the leaves from the syrup.

2. Peel the peaches, then slice them into the syrup. Add the remaining fresh verbena leaves. Serve chilled.

Peaches and Nectarines in Prosecco

This is one of the loveliest ways to finish a summer dinner when you have fragrant white peaches and nectarines, such as Babcock and Arctic Rose, on your table. Of course, you can use any delicious, fully ripe peach, but the white ones are especially flowery and fragrant.

Put out peaches and nectarines, plates, knives, and champagne glasses. Have ready a chilled bottle of Prosecco. Peel your fruit, slice some into a glass, and pour the Prosecco over it. Sip the Prosecco and eat the fruit.

Spiced Peaches | MAKES 1 PINT

Do you have a big bowl of peaches that are starting to soften faster than you can eat them? It's bound to happen at some point during the summer, and when it does, turn them into these spiced peaches. This isn't a chutney but could easily become one with the addition of chile, diced shallots, and stronger vinegar. As it is, you can serve this with pork or duck, spooned over honey ice cream, or spread on toast for breakfast. For peaches, use those with firm, meaty flesh, such as Sun Crests or Redhavens.

4 cups sliced peaches and/or
   nectarines
½ cup sugar
2 long cinnamon sticks
6 cloves
seeds of 3 cardamom pods
1 tablespoon balsamic vinegar
12 pieces candied ginger, chopped

1. Peel the peaches and slice ½ inch thick. Include any smaller odd-shaped pieces as well.

2. Pour the peaches into a wide nonstick skillet. Sprinkle on the sugar and add the remaining ingredients except the ginger. Turn the heat to high to get things bubbling, then reduce to medium and cook, stirring every few minutes, until the syrup is thick, 15 to 20 minutes. Add the ginger. Store in a clean jar and keep refrigerated.

After leaving the Modesto farmers' market and its wealth of perfect fruits, I continued up the Central Valley on Highway 99 to Stockton, to visit an entirely different market, one I had heard about for years. I didn't know Stockton or where the market was located, aside from its freeway address, which meant that it had to be under Highway 99 or I-5, which converge here in Stockton. A mailman pointed me in the right direction, and miles later a pedestrian got me to the exact spot—a section under a span of I-5, the long interstate that borders the Central Valley. I parked in front of a Chinese apartment house where an elderly gentleman stood on his balcony dribbling bread crumbs from a bag to sparrows scratching in the dusty courtyard below. It was oppressively hot out, but the market looked shady and cool.

Although it was not yet eleven, some of the vendors were already breaking down their stalls, sweeping up their debris of leaves and stems, and loading their impossibly old vans and trucks, which seemed to be held together with baling wire and bungee cords. As I walked around feeling somewhat out of place, I heard scarcely a word of English spoken. I didn't know what many of the vegetables were, nor could I find anyone who could tell me their names. I needed a guide to help me sort out the tangle of exotic vines and bundles of leaves. I could recognize bunches of bitter melon vines with fledgling fruits attached, mature bitter melons covered with their warts and knobs, green pumpkins (or so it appeared), shelling beans of some kind, and bitter eggplants for pickling. I also recognized bok choy, gai lun, Mei Qing Choy, Choi Sum, sweet potato greens, and enormous bundles of lemongrass. But for the most part, I was at sea.

In other markets where there are Hmong vendors, their teenage children speak perfect English, and their parents usually sell some foods that are very recognizable to mainstream American shoppers. But here the farmers appeared to be first-generation immigrants who were selling mainly the foods they liked to eat.

The spirit of this market was lively and chaotic, like the hurried noisy markets one sees in any Chinatown. All the farmers appeared to know one another, and there was much shouting back and forth across the aisles. Occasionally the decompressing gears of an eighteen-wheeler drowned out their shouts as it slowed into the curve of the freeway above, but once it passed, the banter resumed. Produce was casually heaped on tables that were covered with bits of flowered yardage. Nothing was labeled, and no one, apparently, felt it necessary to make enticing displays or to offer recipes. The buyers knew exactly what to do with their various shoots and vines. Entire families were shopping together, stuffing rolling carts with bags of greens and discussing their purchases. I longed to follow any of them home to find out what they were going to cook.

In the very center of this busy and sprawling Hmong market stood a small, hatted Mexican man with a little painted cart of *helados* (ice creams), which he sold to the many small children who were running around while their grandparents worked. He didn't speak English or Hmong, and they didn't speak Spanish, but he had figured out a market niche for himself where desire finds a way of being expressed. He was beaming over his brisk business.

What's exciting about a market like this one is that those of us who are onlookers can hear a different language, see people who are not like us, and discover new foods. Getting a taste is harder, though, for there do not appear to be Hmong restaurants. I drove around Stockton looking for one and found nothing. I gather, from reading done since this visit, that the older generation resists assimilation while their children are eager to take on American ways of eating, speaking, and being, so restaurants do not appear to be the cultural bridge they provide in other immigrant cultures. The traditions are kept at home instead. While there are many farmers' markets in which Hmong and other Southeast Asian farmers sell alongside Anglo farmers—and much of the same produce—this market was unusual for its lack of diversity. It was completely about making traditional foods available to those who wanted them: no music, no signs, no coffee. Just shoots and vines.

A MENU LOOSELY

INSPIRED BY THE STOCKTON MARKET

Cucumber Salad with Chile and Roasted Peanuts (page 147)

Scallion Crêpes with Stir-Fried Greens (page 70)

Shredded Daikon with Scallions and Sesame Seeds (page 52)

Tropical Melon Soup with Coconut Milk (page 164)

Mid- to Late-Season Fruits: Pomes and Persimmons

On a warm spring day, strawberries and asparagus were plentiful in the market I was visiting, so I was startled to hear a farmer ask if I wanted to taste his apples. I didn't really, for my eyes were on the strawberries. But I held out my hand for a slice of a Mutsu anyway.

You too might have expected last season's apple, about six months off the tree at this point, to be soft and mushy. But it was astonishingly crisp and full of sweet juice. I tried another variety, and it was the same. When I confessed my surprise, the grower explained that apples have their own waxy coating—it's what makes apples feel sort of greasy sometimes—and at his farm they don't wash it off until they take their apples to market. Air can pass through it, so the apple doesn't turn mushy. Without a doubt this old apple was first rate. We think of apples as fall fruits, not as fruits to eat in the spring. But here were some great wintered-over "spring" apples—perfect to mix with the rhubarb that gets an early start on the season. No wonder they're so often cooked together.

Some true summer apples, such as Yellow Transparent, an heirloom dating from 1800, come into season in late June and July. Their pale gold skins do seem to be lit from within, and in years when there are no other fruits around, these early apples are very welcome, for they make a delicious, creamy-textured applesauce. There's a bit of a gap before the late-summer and fall apples and pears come on, but they always start earlier than we expect. Pears, too, have appeared as early as the end of July in Santa Fe, but that's pushing things a bit. They're not as ripe as they could be, plus who's interested in pears when there are plums and peaches vying for attention? We see them as fruits for the end of summer and fall, along with persimmons, another fall fruit that appears when the late harvest apples do.

Apple-Rhubarb Pandowdy | SERVES 6

Rhubarb and apples are at opposite ends of their season when they meet here. The apples are from storage; the rhubarb is fresh out of the ground. They're exactly the two fruits you're likely to find at any early-season market. Pandowdies are fun to make and even better to eat. You make a perfectly beautiful dessert look dowdy by scoring the crust, then pressing it into the juices that have risen from the fruit. The crust becomes saturated and partially caramelized. It may be dowdy, but it's definitely good.

butter for the dish

Tart Shell, page 388, or ½ recipe
    Galette Pastry, page 386

4 large wintered-over apples, such as
    Galas or Mutsu

1 pound rhubarb

¾ teaspoon ground cinnamon

¼ teaspoon ground allspice

¼ teaspoon freshly grated nutmeg

⅛ teaspoon ground clove

2 tablespoons all-purpose flour

½ teaspoon sea salt

½ cup maple syrup

1 tablespoon unsalted butter

cream, yogurt, or vanilla ice cream

1. Preheat the oven to 400°F. Lightly butter a 2-quart square or oval baking dish. Wrap the dough in plastic wrap and refrigerate.

2. Slice the apples into quarters, remove the peels and cores, and slice crosswise about ¼ inch thick. Dice the rhubarb into ½-inch pieces. If the stalks are very wide, slice them lengthwise in half first. In all you should have between 7 and 8 cups of fruit. Toss the fruit with the spices, flour, and salt, then add the maple syrup and toss thoroughly. Distribute the fruit in the dish and dot with the butter.

3. Roll out the dough about ⅛ inch thick and cut it about ¾ inch wider than your dish. Lay the dough over the fruit, tucking the edges into the fruit. Bake until the crust is light gold, 30 to 35 minutes. Lower the heat to 350°F.

4. Remove the pandowdy from the oven and slice the crust into 2-inch squares in a crisscross fashion. Using a spatula, gently press down on the crust, allowing the juices to flow up and over it. Don't worry if there isn't much juice at this stage. Return the dish to the oven and continue to bake until the crust is really golden and glazed, another 20 to 30 minutes. Once or twice during the final baking, brush the juices, which should be plentiful, over the dough. Serve warm, with cream, yogurt, or vanilla ice cream.

Apple-Oat Pancakes
with Cheddar Cheese | MAKES EIGHT 4-INCH CAKES

I really like the sharp accent of an aged Cheddar cheese in these apple pancakes. You can still pour maple syrup over them.

2 large eggs, separated

1 teaspoon vanilla extract

1 cup buttermilk

3 tablespoons vegetable oil or
   melted unsalted butter

¼ cup rolled oats

½ cup all-purpose flour

½ teaspoon baking soda

½ teaspoon baking spices or ground
   cinnamon

¼ teaspoon sea salt

1 large apple

½ cup grated sharp Cheddar cheese

1. Beat the egg yolks with the vanilla, buttermilk, and oil. Stir in the rolled oats. Mix the flour, soda, spices, and salt together. Grate the apple and the cheese. Beat the egg whites until soft peaks form.

2. Stir the dry ingredients into the wet ingredients. Add the grated apple and fold in the whites.

3. Melt a little butter in a nonstick pan. When hot, drop in the batter, about ⅓ cup at a time. Sprinkle a tablespoon of the cheese on top. Cook over medium heat until the bottom is golden, then turn and cook the second side without patting it down. Serve with maple syrup or boiled apple cider.

Transparent Applesauce
with Lemon Thyme | MAKES APPROXIMATELY 1 QUART

Yellow Transparents are the earliest apples to arrive at the market, which is early July. Although other fruits may seem more appealing then than apples, these make a delicious, smooth sauce. Because summer apples are so delicate, I don't like to overwhelm the sauce with cinnamon and spice. That's for later in the season. Instead I cook them with lemon thyme or a bit of lemon zest. They may be tart enough that they don't need lemon juice and sweet enough that they don't need sugar. Make adjustments after the apples are cooked.

4 pounds summer apples

½ cup water or apple juice

6 fresh lemon thyme branches

1 teaspoon freshly grated
    lemon zest

honey, maple syrup, or sugar
    if needed

lemon juice, if needed

1. Quarter the apples and put them in a pressure cooker with ½ cup water or apple juice and the lemon thyme. Bring the pressure to high and leave it there for 10 minutes. Allow the pressure to fall slowly or release it quickly. Pass the apples through a food mill to get rid of the pips and skins. Stir in the lemon zest.

2. Taste the sauce and sweeten, if needed, with honey, maple syrup, or sugar. Or add lemon juice if it needs tarting. Return it to the stove and cook over medium heat, stirring frequently, until it has reduced to the thickness you like and the sugar has dissolved.

THE APPLE: AMERICA'S FRUIT

A passion for apples exists across the country. At every market I visited during apple season, I saw unusual varieties, many of them heirlooms, proudly being sold. Cox Orange Pippins, Baldwins, Cortlands, Golden Russets, Yorks, Pink Ladies, Macouns, and many more—apples that are no longer grown commercially because of their low yields or odd shapes. They have their avid fans, though, among both eaters and growers. Kathy Reid, who sells in the FRESHFARM Market in Washington, D.C., grows sixty-five varieties of apples, which she arranges on her table from tart to sweet. She cheerfully says that she offers a "consulting service," advising customers on which apples to use for their sauce or what mix to put in a pie, and they usually report their results when they return to market for more. Eighty-nine varieties are grown at Weston's Antique Apples in Wisconsin, which are sold at the Dane County farmers' market in Madison. Their oldest apple, the Alexander, dates back to 1700.

Apples can be confusing, for they're not all alike. There are apples that are meant for eating out of hand, apples for baking, and still others, like Black Twig and Ashmead's Kernel, that are particularly fine in a cider blend. There are apples suited to warm climates and to cold ones. And there are apples that are historically connected to regions—

Arkansas Blacks, Newtown Pippins, Rhode Island Greenings, Rome (from Ohio, not New York or Italy), and Wisconsin's Wolf River. It's the growers of these apples who are likely to know the best uses for each variety, so ask them for advice. And shoppers know, too. The first time I saw a Wolf River apple, I asked, "What do you do with these?" Four people said in unison, "Pie!" And they were right.

During a fall visit to the Union Square market in New York, I counted over twenty varieties of marvelous old apples. During the same visit, the subway cars were plastered with posters advertising Washington apples. Bringing apples from the edge of the West to the edge of the East has been going on for about a century, but why buy apples from three thousand miles away when the most glorious varieties could be bought at greenmarkets around town?

When I finally tasted apples at a Washington farmers' market, I was equally impressed with their beauty and flavor. And they tasted far better than the same Washington apples you find in the supermarket. Apples *can* be shipped and stored, but just like peaches and plums, they taste best where they grow.

Sometimes markets hold apple tastings so that shoppers can taste different varieties of apples side by side. This is something you can easily do at home, too, and a comparative tasting is worth a lot of words. Just be sure to write the name right on the fruit so you can remember what it is.

It's quieter at the market now that fall is here. The days are shorter, and the tourists are gone. The farmers look tired, and they say they're looking forward to the end of the season. Two weeks later they're saying they wish it would hurry up and freeze. Mrs. Vigil shows me her hands, which are well worked, and points to her bushels of golden-blushed apples. "I've been picking apples since June, and I'd love to stop, but I can't as long as there's a market." She shrugs off her fatigue, but she can't rest yet because since school has resumed children have been coming to the Tuesday market with their teachers.

The farmers' market is a great place for kids. There's no candy at eye level, everything smells sweet and fresh, instead of like floor cleaner, and people are generally relaxed and enjoying themselves. It puts the whole experience of procuring food in a very different light from a trip to the supermarket with Mom. A mother of two young children, who shops regularly at farm stands, told me that her children had gradually changed into good vegetable eaters. "It's the immediacy of everything that's so vital. When your children see where things actually come from, it makes them want to be a part of it all. They want to cook it, eat it, and close that circle in the whole process of things."

When whole classes come to the market, they overwhelm some of the farmers who haven't prepared for them by having some small items set out at kid level. The older kids have assignments—finding particular fruits and vegetables or interviewing farmers. The really small ones stay with their teachers, tour the market, then take part in an apple tasting. I watch some five-year-olds earnestly try to discern the differences among apples, but perhaps they're a little too young. One child, his face scrunched up in an expression of deep perplexity, finally says, "They just taste like apples to me!" Later, the teacher helps his kindergartners open their boxes of thin, pale apple juice—right in front of a farmer who is selling his own freshly pressed amber-colored cider. Next year perhaps the juice will come from the farmer, then the children can taste the deep sweetness of this cold nectar.

Following the kids' market adventures, farmers visit their classrooms and talk to the children about farming. Then the classes will make field trips to their farms. Lé Adams, who runs this Farm to School program, is committed to seeing every child in Santa Fe have contact with a farmer at least once each year, from kindergarten through high school. "It's how kids can learn about agriculture, when we're not living in an agrarian area." Or era, for that matter. "Basically, we are trying to raise a crop of food-literate youngsters who like eating real food and who have some inkling about where it comes from. Hopefully some of them will want to farm too, someday." Lé, who is a farmer herself, says, "We need new, young farmers, and soon." The average age of the farming population is fifty-four (as of 1997), and getting older. "Come to our market and see a species that's *really* endangered . . . farmers!" is how one farmer from the Portland, Oregon, market puts it.

Many markets across the country find ways to involve children. During the summer in St. Paul, kids have a chance to cook at the market. At the Lincoln Hospital Greenmarket on 149th Street in New York, the Cornell Extension Service has devised a game for children: Kids spin a brightly painted "wheel of fortune," then draw a card that poses a question about fruits and vegetables. Correct answers are rewarded with stickers, which are worn with great pride.

The market can also go to the school. Santa Monica farmers' markets have successfully created a salad bar program, which provides elementary schools with vegetables and fruits from the farmers' market, most of them organically grown. The salad bar, which was once completely ignored, is now incredibly popular with the children, and the cost to the school is actually less than what it had been. Apparently the kids *do* like vegetables—when they taste good ones—and they *love* strawberries. Of course farmers also enjoy the additional business the program brings them. Here's a collaboration that's helping everyone. And parents who want their children to enjoy eating fruits and vegetables would do well to begin by taking them to the farmers' market.

Caramelized Apple Tart with Cinnamon Custard | SERVES 6

Sweet-tart apples are caramelized in a skillet, then baked in a tender crust in cinnamon-scented cream. An easy dessert to make, it's best served warm, although leftovers won't be ignored the next morning. Braeburn, Gravenstein, Wolf River, and Liberty are all fine apples to use.

THE APPLES

3 apples (see headnote)

2 tablespoons unsalted butter

2 tablespoons sugar

THE BATTER

½ cup (1 stick) unsalted butter at
    room temperature, plus extra

½ cup sugar

3 medium eggs, at room temperature

1 teaspoon vanilla extract

pinch salt

1 cup all-purpose flour

THE CREAM

½ cup crème fraîche or heavy cream

1 teaspoon ground cinnamon

1 egg yolk

confectioners' sugar

1. Preheat the oven to 375°F. Butter a 9-inch tart pan. Peel and core the apples, then slice them into ½-inch wedges. Melt the butter in a wide nonstick skillet, add the apples, and sprinkle them with the sugar. Cook over high heat, occasionally flipping the apples, until they start to caramelize, then reduce the heat to medium. Keep a close eye on the apples, turning them frequently so that they don't burn. This will take about 15 minutes in all. Turn off the heat.

2. To make the batter, cream the butter and sugar in a mixer with the paddle attachment until light and fluffy. Add the eggs one at a time, beating until each is incorporated before adding the next. Add the vanilla and salt, then stir in the flour. Smooth the batter into the tart pan with an offset spatula, pushing it up the sides to make a rim. Lay the apples over the batter.

3. Mix the ingredients for the cream together, then pour it over the apples. Set the tart on a sheet pan and bake until the crust is golden and starting to pull away from the sides, about 35 minutes. Let cool for at least 20 minutes before serving. Remove the tart from the rim, place it on a serving plate, and sprinkle with confectioners' sugar.

Apple and Quince Mince | MAKES 6 CUPS, ENOUGH FILLING FOR TWO 9-INCH TARTS OR PIES

A good mock mincemeat can be made from an assortment of dried fruits, apples, and quince. It keeps indefinitely, and the flavor mellows with time. You can be somewhat extemporaneous with your ingredient choices. I sometimes use more dates than raisins or vice versa. Red Flame and Monukka raisins make a darker filling than Thompson Seedless. Poached quinces are more succulent than fresh, though you can use either. Regardless of the combination of fruits, the warming scent of allspice, cinnamon, and clove will fill your kitchen with great expectations.

1 orange

1 lemon

1 cup apple cider or quince poaching liquid (see page 317)

5 cups dried fruits, such as raisins, chopped dates and currants

2 large apples, peeled, cored, and diced

1½ cups chopped poached quince or 1 quince, washed and grated

1 cup brown sugar, packed

pinch sea salt

½ teaspoon ground cinnamon

¼ teaspoon ground allspice

¼ teaspoon freshly grated nutmeg

⅛ teaspoon ground cloves

¼ cup brandy

1. Remove the outermost zest from the orange and lemon using a Microplane or citrus zester, then cut away and discard the white pith. Coarsely chop the fruits, then pulse in a food processor, adding the cider or poaching liquid as needed to loosen the mixture. Scrape into a large saucepan and add the zests, fruits, sugar, salt, and spices.

2. Bring to a boil, then cook, covered, over low heat. Occasionally give the pan a stir so that nothing sticks. If the mixture does seem dry, add more cider or poaching liquid. After 20 minutes it will be quite thick and soft. Add the brandy and cook for 10 minutes more. Cool, then scrape into a container and refrigerate until ready to use.

NOTE: Chopped dates are available from various California date gardens (see Resources). They're coated with oat flour so that they don't stick, which makes them easy to work with.

Winter Mince Tart with a Lattice Crust | MAKES ONE 9-INCH TART

Pie Dough for double-crust or lattice pie, page 387

3 cups (½ recipe) Apple and Quince Mince (page 313)

2 tablespoons unsalted butter, melted

1 teaspoon sugar

2 tablespoons brandy

1. Divide the dough into 2 pieces, one slightly larger than the other. Press each into a disk, wrap in plastic wrap, and refrigerate for 45 minutes. Remove the larger piece and roll it into an 11-inch circle. Drape it over a 9-inch tart pan or pie pan, easing the dough into the pan rather than stretching it. Leave the overhang. Add the filling and smooth it out. Drizzle the butter over the top. Preheat the oven to 375°F.

2. Roll the second piece of dough into a circle ⅛ inch thick, then cut 14 strips about ½ inch wide. Moisten the lip of the tart with cold water, then lay the strips over the tart, weaving them to form a lattice. Press the ends of the lattice into the edges of the tart and fold the overhang over them to make a raised edge. Press lightly to seal.

3. Dip a pastry brush in water. Lightly moisten the strips, then sprinkle them with sugar. Bake the tart until the crust is brown, 50 minutes to an hour. Remove and spoon the brandy into the filling while the tart is still hot. Serve with the brandy-flavored cream, below.

THE WHIPPED CREAM TOPPING

½ cup whipping cream

½ cup crème fraîche

2 tablespoons honey or confectioners' sugar

2 tablespoons brandy

1 teaspoon orange flower water, optional

Whip the cream with the crème fraîche and honey until soft peaks form, then stir in the brandy and the orange flower water if desired.

The texture is chalky and dry. It's tough to slice, and there's no point in tasting it raw since it must be cooked to be enjoyed. But what makes the quince alluring enough to overcome such drawbacks is its perfume, which lingers with the fruit after cooking. I once pinpointed its notes as a combination of narcissus and oak leaves when the two scents collided in a garden. Searching for the base of the flower stem, my hand disturbed both the oak leaves and the blossom. A cloud of scent rose, and there it was, the haunting spring-fall bouquet of quince. This perfume is not an exaggeration on my part. Victorians made good use of quinces to freshen their linen drawers and closets. Put one in your car and you won't mind traffic quite as much. A few on a dresser table will fill your room as if with a bouquet of flowers.

But quinces are for eating too. An old-fashioned fruit, once valued for its pectin as well as its hardiness in the garden, it reveals hints of both apples and pears in its shape and the patterns of the seeds. It is a rustic version, though, for its shape is often ungainly and its skin is sometimes coated with a soft down. When ripe, in the fall, the fruit will be hard, aromatic, and golden. Pale fruits lacking in scent have simply been picked too soon. For a quince to win the praise it deserves, you'll want to look at the farmers' market or over someone's backyard fence and choose those that are fully ripe. Wrapped in newspaper and stored in a cool place, a ripe quince will keep for months, provided it hasn't inadvertently been bruised in picking or handling. Though hard-skinned, they do bruise more easily than you might expect.

Quinces go beautifully into dishes that contain pears and apples, but they take longer to cook than either, so if you wish to add some to a dish it's a good idea to cut them more finely than the other fruits. Grated quinces can be added directly to quick breads and pancakes. Generally, I find that poached quinces are the most useful form to have. Each fall I poach as many as I can in syrup until they turn deep pink, then keep them refrigerated in their syrup and use them over the next few months, adding them to compotes of poached pears, tartes tatins, apple galettes, pies, crisps, and so forth. Anything that's made with apples or pears is even better when quince is mixed in.

Turning Quince Poaching Syrup into Ice Cream

When you poach quinces, you end up with a thick, rose-colored syrup that is good for dribbling over ice cream and quince desserts. You can also make a quick little ice cream, which is very nice when served with something like the Rustic Tart of Quinces, Apples, and Pears on page 320.

Measure the syrup, then stir in the same amount of cream or slightly less. The syrup should be sweet enough that you don't need to add any more sugar. Freeze the mixture in your ice cream maker according to its instructions. You'll have a pale pink ice cream. A cup of liquid makes about a cup of ice cream.

Spiced Quinces in Syrup | MAKES 1 QUART

This makes a supply of rosy fruit to use in winter compotes, tarts, or pies or as an accompaniment to desserts such as Honey Ice Cream (page 379) or Goat's Milk Panna Cotta (page 248). If you add poached quinces to dishes that call for apples and pears—apple crisps, pear tarts, etc.—they only make them better.

I have had quinces from the tree that weighed as much as a pound, but most are closer to 4 or 5 ounces—so go by weight, not by size, although this is hardly a recipe where quantities need to be exact.

2½ pounds ripe, yellow-gold quinces
¾ cup sugar
1 (3-inch) cinnamon stick
5 cloves
2 wide strips orange zest (removed
    with a vegetable peeler)

1. Rub the fuzz, if any, off the quinces. Using a good sharp knife, cut away the skin in long, clean strokes, just as you would an orange, saving the skins. Remove the center with an apple corer (you may have to make the hole a bit wider than you would for an apple), saving the cores. Slice the quinces into wedges about ½ inch thick.

2. Put the skins and cores into a saucepan with 2 quarts water, bring it to a boil, then simmer, covered, for 30 minutes. Strain. Return the liquid to the pot and add the sugar, spices, and orange zest. Stir to dissolve the sugar, then add the fruit. Place parchment paper or a heavy plate directly over the fruit to keep it submerged. Lower the heat, cover the pan, and simmer until the quinces have turned pink and are slightly translucent, 2 to 2½ hours. If the syrup becomes too thick, add more water as needed. When done, store the fruit in its syrup in the refrigerator. The quinces should keep for 2 months.

Seven to one seems to be the magic ratio for juice, jams, and fruit butters. At Future Fruit Farms in Wisconsin, Ellen Lane told me that she uses 7½ pounds of fruit to make 1 quart of her apple or pear juice—and that's good organic fruit.

Ellen also makes apple, peach, and pear butters. We sat around her kitchen table one Sunday morning and sampled them, along with their host fruits and ciders made from various combinations of pears and apples. I have never tasted such pure, concentrated essence of fruit. She told me her ratio of fruit to sugar in the fruit butters was seven to one, and the same was true for her raspberry jam, which had a startling, vivid flavor. This is considerably less sugar than is usually called for, but the resulting butters and jam were sweet enough, and there were clearly detectable notes of caramel and molasses in the pear and apple butters, not just sweetness. Since tasting Future Fruit's preserves, I have noticed that those proportions work consistently well for simple fruit jams, such as the Apricot-Lavender Refrigerator Jam on page 291. If the fruit is ripe and sweet, 1 cup of sugar will preserve the flavor. Use more, and it will begin to mask the flavor, replacing it with dull sweetness. (Some tart and tannic fruits may need extra, though, such as plums and quinces.)

Odessa Piper of L'Etoile restaurant in Madison, Wisconsin, uses reductions of apple and pear juice in her winter cooking. In the fall, she and her staff go out to nearby farms, gather "farmers' fruit"—the fruit that falls to the ground—press it into cider, then reduce it in huge vats until it's syrupy and dark, not unlike maple syrup. In *Home for the Holidays,* Ken Haedrich offers a recipe for boiled cider pie, which is made from cider that has again been reduced from 7 cups to 1. The resulting syrup is wonderfully intense. With such a concentration of sugars, it's not surprising that boiled cider was used by the Shakers as a sweetener. A warm apple tart with ice cream and a drizzle of boiled cider is indeed a treat. Cider jelly, an even denser reduction, reduces 9 cups of cider to 1 cup of jelly.

Making your own boiled cider is not difficult, but it can be expensive unless you also make your own juice. When reducing the juice, be sure to include some red apple skins to give it a pink hue. A home juicer will do the job. If you wish to buy it already made, it can be bought by mail order (see Resources). The Woods also make a boiled cider jelly.

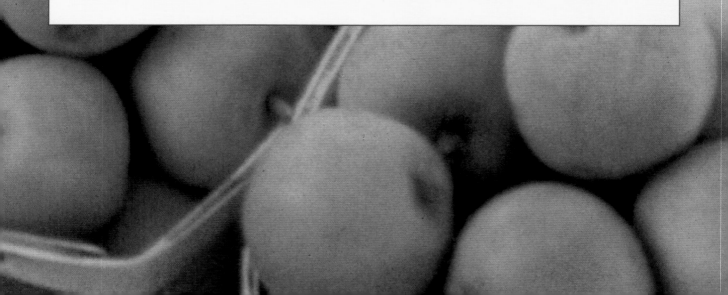

Quince Pip Tea
for a Sore Throat | MAKES 3 CUPS

When one of the Mexican cooks I was working with noticed that I was poaching quinces, he mentioned that the pectin-filled syrup was good for coughs and sore throats. (Quince is a popular fruit in Mexico.) Recently a Greek woman told me the same thing. And now I make a point of cooking the quince skins, cores, and pips in water, then sweetening the soothing liquid with honey. It keeps refrigerated for months during the winter, the time of coughs and sore throats, and it really does work.

skins, cores, and pips (seeds) of
4 quinces
honey

Put the skins, cores, and pips in a saucepan with 2 quarts water. Bring to a boil, then simmer until the liquid is syrupy and reduced to about 1 quart. Strain and sweeten to taste, while still warm, with honey. Refrigerate in a clean jar. Sip warm or cold when you feel the need for something soothing on your throat.

Quince
Butter | MAKES ABOUT 3 CUPS

Usually I make this without measuring, using fruit that's a bit old or bruised. I just trim away the bruised parts, then cut the remainder into chunks and throw them into the pressure cooker, sweetening to taste once they're cooked. But sometimes amounts are helpful, so here are some to go by.

Use this pink fruit butter for toast and biscuits, as a filling for a nut torte, as the jam in old-fashioned thumbprint cookies, or in bars, the quince replacing figs or dates. It's delicious on toast, with a very thin slice of aged Cheddar cheese.

4 cups washed and quartered quinces
wide strip orange zest
1 small piece cinnamon
1 cup light brown or white sugar, or
more to taste
additional sugar or honey

1. Put the quinces in a pressure cooker with ½ cup water, the orange zest, and cinnamon. Bring the pressure to high and maintain it for 15 minutes. Let it drop by itself. The fruit should be an intense shade of pink. Fish out the orange zest and cinnamon and discard them.
2. Pass the cooked fruit through a food mill, then return it to the stove. Turn the heat to low, add 1 cup sugar, and cook, stirring frequently, for 15 minutes or until the sauce has thickened nearly to a jamlike consistency. Taste and add additional sugar or honey if needed. Pour into sterilized jars and store in the refrigerator.

Rustic Tart of Quinces, Apples, and Pears | SERVES 6

The three pome fruits meet in this delectable pastry. I especially like this tart when made with puff pastry, which our local bakery makes far better than I do. If you can arrange to buy a 16-ounce piece of fine puff pastry from a bakery, obtain frozen made by Dufour, or are willing to make your own, then use puff pastry. Otherwise, use the Galette Pastry, which is also very good. Serve either with the Quince Ice Cream on page 315.

1 pound puff pastry
2 apples, such as Gravenstein, Golden
    Delicious, or McIntosh
2 ripe but firm Bartlett or Luscious
    pears
½ teaspoon ground cinnamon
2 teaspoons sugar
2 quinces (about 16 slices), poached in
    syrup, page 317
2 tablespoons unsalted butter, melted
whipped cream or crème fraîche

1. Roll chilled puff pastry into a square ⅛ inch thick. Place it on a sheet pan and refrigerate until ready to bake.
2. Peel and core the apples and slice them into wedges ¼ inch thick. Peel and core the pears and slice them a bit thicker. Toss the fruits with the cinnamon and the sugar.
3. Preheat the oven to 400°F. Remove the pastry from the refrigerator, loosely arrange the fruit in the middle, drizzle the butter over it, then pull the opposite corners toward each other. They won't meet.
4. Bake for 15 minutes, then reduce the heat to 375°F and continue baking until the pastry is puffed and golden and the fruit is tender, 40 to 50 minutes. Serve warm with softly whipped cream or crème fraîche.

VARIATION WITH GALETTE DOUGH: Use the fruit as described, plus an additional apple and pear.

Galette Pastry, page 386
2 tablespoons unsalted butter,
    melted
2 teaspoons sugar, approximately

Preheat the oven to 450°F. Roll the dough into a wide circle and place the fruit in the center, leaving about a 3-inch band around the edge. Fold the dough over the fruit, overlapping it as you go. Brush the butter over the dough, leaving enough to drizzle over the fruit. Sprinkle the sugar over the crust, then bake at 450°F for 15 minutes. Lower the heat to 375°F and bake until the crust is browned and the fruit is tender, about 45 minutes. Turn the pan at least once so that the galette bakes evenly.

Quince and Goat Cheese Tart | MAKES ONE 9-INCH TART

I am crazy about the combination of quince with the subtle tang of the goat cheese and walnuts. This tart, which is best when it's still a little warm, is a fruit, cheese, and nut course all in one. With the crust ready to go, and the fruit poached, you can put it together just before you sit down to dinner.

THE CRUST

¼ cup freshly cracked walnuts

1 cup plus 2 tablespoons all-purpose flour

1 tablespoon light brown sugar

pinch sea salt

½ cup (1 stick) cold unsalted butter, cut into chunks

½ teaspoon vanilla extract

THE FILLING

1 cup chopped quince from Spiced Quinces in Syrup, page 317

1 egg

1 egg yolk

1 cup crème fraîche

1 cup fresh goat cheese

½ cup ricotta

1. Pulse the walnuts in a food processor with the flour, sugar, and salt until finely ground. Add the butter and pulse until it's finely chopped into the flour. Add the vanilla mixed with 2 tablespoons water and pulse just until the dough comes together. Wash out the work bowl and blade.

2. If you've used cold butter, the dough should be cool and firm enough that you can go ahead and press it into a 9-inch tart pan, making the sides about ⅓ inch thick. (If it's soft, wrap it in plastic, shape it into a disk, and refrigerate until firm.) Freeze while the oven heats to 400°F. Bake the tart shell until light golden, about 25 minutes. (See page 388.) Remove and reduce the temperature to 350°F. Scatter the quince over the crust.

3. Combine the remaining ingredients for the filling in the food processor and pulse until smooth. Pour the filling over the fruit, then bake until firm and beginning to color in spots, about 25 minutes. Remove and let cool a bit before removing the rim from the pan. Serve warm or at room temperature.

Baked Pancake with Pear and Cardamom | SERVES 2 TO 4

A sweet version of the Giant Popover with Chanterelles, this puffs dramatically, falls instantly, and is exceedingly good for breakfast or a Sunday-night supper. Two people can eat the whole thing—four if they're modest eaters and not terribly hungry. If you're serving this for dessert, splash a little pear eau-de-vie over the top.

For the popover, use the recipe on page 243. The batter goes right over the sautéed pears, or you can spoon them over the popover once it has cooked.

Giant Popover, page 243
½ teaspoon vanilla extract
⅛ teaspoon almond extract
2 buttery pears, peeled and sliced
    ½ inch thick
½ teaspoon ground cardamom
juice of ½ lemon
2 tablespoons sugar
2 teaspoons unsalted butter
confectioners' sugar

1. Preheat the oven to 400°F. Make the popover batter as described on page 243, adding the vanilla and almond extracts to the milk.
2. Toss the pears with the cardamom, lemon juice, and sugar. Melt the butter in the same skillet used for melting the butter for the batter. Add the pears, and cook over medium-high heat until they're slightly transparent in places and tender, about 3 minutes. Pour the batter over the pears and bake until golden, puffy, and risen, about 25 minutes. Dust with confectioners' sugar and serve immediately.

Pear Sauce for Gingerbread, Ice Cream, and Other Desserts | MAKES 1½ CUPS

The sauce is pristine pale gold and the essence of the pear. Serve it warm or cold, next to the Pear Upside-Down Spice Cake on page 325 in place of cream or with gingerbread. Pears adapt easily to other flavorings. Try it with amaretto in place of pear eau-de-vie, or star anise, cardamom, or vanilla bean in place of the cinnamon.

4 large ripe pears, any variety
1 tablespoon honey
2 tablespoons fresh lemon juice
1-inch piece of cinnamon stick
2 teaspoons Poire William eau-de-vie
1 tablespoon butter or cream, optional

1. Peel, core, and dice the pears. Put them in a heavy saucepan with ¼ cup water, the honey, lemon juice, and spices.
2. Bring to a boil, then lower the heat and cook, covered, until the pears are soft, about 20 minutes. Puree in a food processor, then stir in the brandy and the butter if desired.

LUSCIOUS BUT UGLY PEARS

Pears, along with their kin, apples and quinces, are pome fruits. They are also an exquisite fruit and one of the treasures of the fall and winter kitchen, but as with apples and winter squash, we're never quite ready for them when they first appear in the market, which is as early as July—peach season. Fortunately, many varieties follow the first Bartletts into the fall. You might run into such pears as Winter Nelis, Lincolns, Seckels (or Sugar Pears), and French Butter pears. And there's Moonglow—its color is that of the harvest moon shining on the pear trees, I am told by its grower. In addition to Anjou, Bosc, and Comice, you may find Harrow Delight, a pear developed by the University of Ontario, which makes the most delicious pear butter. The Forelle is an exquisite-looking pear, small, yellowish red, and covered with a fine peppering of spots. Its flavor doesn't always measure up to its looks when eaten raw, but it is a good poaching pear. Chinese pear-apples, such as the Yali—a most primitive-looking pear with crisp, juicy flesh—are found at farmers' markets, as are the more standard apple-shaped types.

I encountered Moonglow and Harrow Delight in Wisconsin, at Future Fruit Farms. Robert and Ellen Lane have been growing heirloom pears and apples for eighteen years, which they sell in the form of fruit, juices, and fruit butters at the farmers' market in Madison. Their number one pear is called a Luscious pear. These are small, roundish green fruits, mottled with large spots—not sugar spots but blemishes—which gave them their nickname, "ugly pears." Chemical sprays would remove the spots, but the Lanes decided against using them. Their customers have decided that the spots don't matter either—a rare triumph of taste and good sense over good looks.

Unlike stone fruits, pears ripen off the tree. In fact they *must* ripen off the tree. A tree-ripened pear will be unpleasantly mushy. Choose firm pears with a little give at the stem end. If they aren't ripe, let them sit at room temperature until the skin lightens in color and their perfume becomes noticeable. If you can't use them right away, store ripe pears in the refrigerator. While they make wonderful desserts, pears are also fine in salads. Since they're a fall fruit, you might mix them with nuts from your region—hazelnuts, walnuts, pecans, hickory nuts, butternuts—and their corresponding oils, if possible, such as in a salad of pears with arugula, walnuts, and walnut oil. And they are also a fine fruit to serve with cheeses, from a voluptuous Gorgonzola to a creamy goat Camembert to a pungent sheep's milk cheese.

Pear Upside-Down Spice Cake with Molasses Cream | MAKES ONE 10-INCH CAKE

The molasses—an unusual find—and pears both came from the farmers' market in Colorado Springs. The idea of a gingery molasses cake covering caramelized pears seemed like a good one, and this is now a favorite fall cake. Serve it warm, with whipped cream tinted with coffee and molasses.

3 ripe but firm Bartlett or
    other pears
3 tablespoons unsalted butter
¾ cup light brown sugar, packed

THE CAKE

5 tablespoons unsalted butter,
    at room temperature
¼ cup dark brown sugar, packed
⅓ cup molasses
3 tablespoons espresso or
    strong coffee
1 teaspoon vanilla extract
1 heaping tablespoon finely grated
    ginger
1 large egg, at room temperature
½ cup buttermilk
1½ cups all-purpose flour
1 teaspoon baking soda
1 teaspoon ground ginger
1 teaspoon ground cinnamon
½ teaspoon ground cardamom
½ teaspoon dry mustard

THE MOLASSES CREAM

½ cup cold whipping cream
½ cup crème fraîche
1 to 2 tablespoons molasses
2 tablespoons chilled espresso

1. Peel the pears, quarter them, and remove the cores. Cut each quarter lengthwise in half. Melt the butter in a 10-inch cast-iron skillet, then add the sugar. Stir until it has dissolved, then turn off the heat and let it settle evenly over the pan. Reserve 4 of the shortest pear pieces and arrange the rest around the edge. Use the short pieces to fill in the center.

2. Preheat the oven to 375°F. Cream the 5 tablespoons butter with the sugar, then add the molasses. If the coffee is hot, use it to rinse out the molasses measure, adding it to the bowl along with the vanilla and grated ginger. Add the egg and beat until smooth, then add the buttermilk.

3. Mix the dry ingredients, then add them to the butter mixture, beating on low just until combined. Remove the bowl and give the batter several turns with a rubber scraper to make sure it is well mixed, then spread the batter evenly over the pears. Bake in the center of the oven until the cake has risen, browned, and begun to pull away from the sides of the pan, about 35 minutes. Remove, let cool for a few minutes, then place a serving plate over the pan, grasp the pan and plate firmly, and reverse. Remove the pan. Serve with the molasses cream.

Whip the cream and crème fraîche until they're soft and billowy and then stir in the molasses and coffee. Use a rubber scraper to mix the molasses up from the bottom of the bowl, then scrape into a serving dish.

Pear-Hazelnut Torte | SERVES 6 TO 8

Any pear that's ripe and ready to eat can be used, but the smooth-textured varieties (Bartlett, Comice, Harrow Delight, and French Butter pears) are best. As for the nuts, I can't imagine one that isn't good with pears—pecans, walnuts, almonds, hickory nuts, and hazelnuts. You can use hazelnut meal, which is left over from oil pressing in place of the whole hazelnuts. It's available from Holmquist Hazelnut Orchards in Washington (see Resources).

If you bake this in an 11-inch tart pan, you'll have a thin, fruit-covered cake with a fair amount of crispy crust. Bake it in a 9- or 8-inch springform pan, and you'll end up with more cake in proportion to fruit.

THE TOPPING

3 tablespoons hazelnuts

2 tablespoons sugar

3 ripe pears

THE CAKE

¾ cup hazelnuts or hazelnut meal

¾ cup all-purpose flour

½ teaspoon sea salt

1 teaspoon baking powder

½ cup unsalted butter, softened

⅔ cup sugar

3 eggs, at room temperature

1 teaspoon vanilla extract

1. Preheat the oven to 375°F. Lightly butter an 11-inch tart pan or a 9-inch springform pan. Roast all the hazelnuts on a sheet pan for 15 minutes. Let cool, then rub them in a towel to loosen the skins. (Not all will come off—don't worry about it.) Pulse 3 tablespoons of the hazelnuts with 2 tablespoons sugar in a food processor until sand textured, then remove and set aside. Peel and quarter the pears, remove the cores, and slice about ⅜ inch thick.

2. Combine the remaining ¾ cup hazelnuts in the food processor with the flour, salt, and baking powder. Pulse until the nuts are finely ground. If using hazelnut meal, mix it with the flour, salt, and baking powder.

3. Cream the butter with the sugar until light and fluffy. Add the eggs, one at a time, and beat until smooth. Scrape down the sides of the bowl. Add the vanilla, then the dry ingredients. Mix slowly until combined. Give the batter a few turns with a rubber scraper and scrape it into the pan. Smooth it out, arrange the pears on top, and sprinkle the ground hazelnuts and sugar over them. Bake until risen and browned, 30 to 35 minutes if you've used a tart pan, 45 to 55 minutes in a springform. Let cool briefly, then remove the rim.

PEAR-HAZELNUT TORTE WITH CUSTARD: Beat ¾ cup crème fraîche until smooth, then pour it over the fruit before adding the ground nuts and sugar.

PERSIMMONS

At a California farmers' market one November day, my glance fell to the sidewalk: There lay a gorgeous branch of glossy orange persimmons. It made a cheerful addition to the farmer's booth on this chilly, overcast day. Persimmons always light up the gloom of winter, whether you see them hanging from their trees or filling a bowl on the counter.

Available when apples, quinces, and pears are, persimmons are fall-winter fruits where the climate is moderate. They hail from Japan, although there is also the small, plum-sized native persimmon, which thrives from East Texas to Indiana and from Kansas to Florida. These small fruits have a luscious, almost tropical scent, unlike the Japanese varieties. Cultivars have extended the region for this fruit as far north as Canada, though I've yet to see a persimmon in northern New Mexico.

Most who are familiar with persimmons know only the squat, crisp Fuyu, the big heart-shaped Hachiya, and the natives. But in his columns for the *Los Angeles Times,* David Karp writes about some of the more unusual persimmons found at southern California farmers' markets, fruits that are most likely to come from people's backyards, favorite varieties brought from the home country. (I imagine these would be well worth trying.) And although the native trees produce prolifically, you won't find their fruits at the grocery, either. For eating, they have to be ripe enough to fall to the ground, and that means they're too soft to ship or hold. Our native fruits are full of seeds, whereas the Japanese varieties sometimes have seeds but usually don't.

A very special fruit to look for is the Japanese dried persimmon, hoshi gaki. These aren't fruits that have been dried in a dehydrator, but big, moist succulent fruits that are dried by means of a laborious process that involves massaging the peeled persimmons over a period of weeks. There are still a few Japanese people left who make this delectable treat, which can be found, of course, at some farmers' markets. Dried persimmons are sweetmeats, to be enjoyed a slice at a time. (See Resources, or slowfoodusa.org/ark)

Steamed Persimmon Pudding | SERVES 6

Here's a pudding that's as dark as chocolate, as light as a feather, but dense with deep fruit flavor. It is also very easy to make. It's served warm with brandied whipped cream and a silky orange persimmon puree. This recipe was given to Joanne Neft by a friend of hers who had enjoyed it in *her* family for over 40 years. Joanne gave it to me, and it may well become a favorite of yours, a treasured recipe to pass on to friends.

Hachiya persimmons are the ones usually used for cooking, but you can also use the smaller Fuyus and native persimmons, as long as they're dead ripe. The flesh from a ripe Hachiya can be very dark, while the flesh of the Fuyu is bright orange. If you're fortunate enough to have both, use the former for the pudding and the latter for the sauce.

For steaming, you will need a bowl or pudding mold with a 6- to 8-cup capacity.

THE PUDDING

½ cup (1 stick) unsalted butter

2 to 3 ripe Hachiya persimmons,
    enough for 1 cup puree

1 cup sugar

1 egg, beaten

1 teaspoon vanilla extract

½ cup milk

½ teaspoon sea salt

1 cup all-purpose flour

2 teaspoons baking soda

1 teaspoon ground cinnamon

1. Select a bowl for your pudding. It can be made of crockery, metal, or glass, or it can be a proper pudding mold with a lid. Place a small inverted bowl in a pan for your mold to sit on and make sure it fits into a second pan when covered with a lid.

2. Melt the butter. Generously brush some of it over the pudding dish and set aside the rest. Bring a kettle of water to a boil.

3. Halve the persimmons, pick out any seeds, then scrape the soft fruit from the skins. Puree, then measure 1 cup. Mix with the remaining butter, sugar, egg, vanilla, milk, and salt. Stir the dry ingredients together, then whisk them into the wet ingredients.

4. Pour the batter into the mold and set it in the pan. Add boiling water to the outer pan to come two-thirds of the way up the mold, then cover and cook gently for 1½ hours. When the pudding is done, a cake tester will come out clean. Invert it onto a serving plate. If you're not ready to serve, leave the mold resting on the pudding so that it will retain its heat. Meanwhile, whip the cream and make the persimmon puree, if using.

5. To serve, spoon a little of the whipped cream around the base of the pudding, along with a ribbon of the persimmon puree. Or you can spoon drops of the puree into the cream, then fan them out with the tip of a knife. If you like, garnish the plate with pine or holly.

1 egg, beaten

1 cup confectioners' sugar

2 tablespoons unsalted butter, melted

¼ cup brandy

1 cup whipping cream

Beat the egg with the sugar, butter, and brandy. Whip the cream into soft peaks, then fold it into the egg mixture. If it separates before serving, a few strokes of the whisk will bring it back to a smooth ivory sauce.

4 very ripe Fuyu persimmons or 2 Hachiya persimmons

1 tablespoon sugar or honey, or more to taste

1 teaspoon fresh lemon juice, or more to taste

pinch sea salt

Halve the persimmons, remove the seeds, then puree the flesh until smooth. Stir in the sugar, lemon juice, and salt. Taste and add more sugar or lemon juice if desired. Makes about 1 cup.

Persimmons with Cream | SERVES 1

The texture of ripe persimmons is unbelievably silky and sensual. It's enough to dip into one with a spoon. However, you can add cream. It's this simple. Quarter ripe Hachiya persimmons—they can be chilled or at room temperature—with a sharp knife from top to base but without cutting all the way through. Gently press the base to open the quarters like a flower, then pour in some cold cream and serve.

Persimmon Tea Cake | MAKES ONE 8-INCH CAKE

Persimmons, dates, Red Flame raisins, walnuts, and even your own candied grapefruit peel—all from any California farmers' market in late fall—meet in this dense, moist cake, another treasured recipe from Joanne Neft. Mixing the baking soda into the persimmon puree transforms the pulp into a gelatinous mass, but it also means your bread will have a crumb when done. Persimmon pulp is full of enzymes, which will go to work on the flour if not neutralized first by the soda.

This doesn't need a frosting or whipped cream, though you can add either if you wish. It slices well, and you can make fine cream cheese sandwiches with this cake.

2 large dead-ripe Hachiya persimmons, enough for 1 cup puree

2 teaspoons baking soda

1½ cups all-purpose flour

½ teaspoon sea salt

1 teaspoon ground cinnamon

¼ teaspoon ground allspice

⅛ teaspoon ground cloves

½ cup (1 stick) unsalted butter, at room temperature

1 cup light brown sugar, packed

1 egg, at room temperature

1 teaspoon vanilla extract

1 cup walnuts, chopped

grated zest of 1 lemon or ⅓ cup chopped Candied Grapefruit Peel, page 342

½ cup raisins

½ cup chopped dates

1. Preheat the oven to 350°F. Butter and flour an 8-inch springform pan.

2. Open the persimmons lengthwise, pick out any seeds, then scrape the pulp into a measuring cup. Puree, measure out 1 cup, and stir in the baking soda. Combine the flour, salt, and spices in a bowl.

3. Cream the butter and sugar until smooth, then beat in the egg, followed by the vanilla and the persimmon puree. Add the flour mixture, then fold in the walnuts, lemon zest, raisins, and dates.

4. Scrape the batter into the pan and put it in the middle of the oven. Reduce the heat to 325°F, and bake for 1 hour and 15 minutes. Let cool in the pan for 10 minutes before removing the rim.

Fall Fruit Salad with Pomegranate Vinaigrette | SERVES 4

Fall offers the most interesting range of ripe fruits, from berries to figs, persimmons to prickly pears and, of course, grapes. And fruit salads needn't only be sweet. Oils and vinegars go with fruits as well as syrups, and this salad is sweet, peppery, and tart.

If some of these specific fruits aren't available, then use others that are, such as crisp Asian pears or a Bartlett. The walnuts are just coming in when these fruits are at their peak.

8 figs, different varieties if possible

3 Fuyu persimmons

2 prickly pears (page 351)

small bunch muscat grapes

1 pomegranate

1½ teaspoons olive oil

1½ teaspoons walnut oil

sea salt and freshly ground pepper

balsamic or fig balsamic vinegar

½ pint raspberries

1 dried persimmon, if available

6 freshly cracked walnuts

1. Rinse the figs and quarter them. Peel the Fuyu persimmons with a paring knife and cut them crosswise into rounds or into wedges. Wearing rubber gloves or holding the prickly pears with tongs, neatly peel them, then slice them thinly. Separate the grapes, rinse them well, then halve them lengthwise. Flick out the pips with the tip of a knife.

2. Halve the pomegranate. Dislodge the seeds from one half and set them aside. Squeeze the other half to extract the juice. Measure out ¼ cup, then whisk in the oils and season with a pinch of fine sea salt. Taste. If you want a little more tartness, whisk in a few drops of vinegar.

3. Arrange the fruits attractively on plates, including the raspberries and the dried persimmon, thinly sliced. Spoon the dressing over the fruit, then season with pepper. Add the walnut pieces and serve.

It's before dawn, and I'm gazing out over the Dane County Farmers' Market from the second-story window of Odessa Piper's restaurant, L'Etoile. Farmers are arriving and assembling their EZ-Ups around Wisconsin's capitol. It's so early that the stoplights are still flashing, and it's chilly enough to borrow a jacket when I leave to accompany Matthew Laux, L'Etoile's chef, to the market, where he'll shop for tonight's dinner.

Matthew is nervous. Succotash is on the menu, and he's short on corn. Plus the chill in the air makes him worry that this might be the last of it. Taking a big wagon, he pulls it uphill to the top of the market, then begins shopping. A gunnysack of Jackpot, a bicolor sweet corn, is heaved onto the wagon bed. It must weigh 100 pounds. The farmer isn't worried about the weather, so now Matthew can stop worrying too and start to relax. He takes a moment to survey the market. The square is the equivalent of eight city blocks, and we can see only one side of it, but it is full of farm stands. By the time the market officially opens there will be three hundred farmers selling on the surrounding sidewalk. This is the largest farmers' market in the United States.

We work our way down the street and around the corner, piling herbs, honey, pear cider, leeks, fingerling potatoes, Black Twig apples, Moonglow pears, a flat of Concord grapes, and bunches of gladiolas onto the cart. Along the way Matthew chats with the farmers, telling one that his kitchen compost is ready to be picked up, asking another how much longer he'll have potatoes, arranging for a delivery of buffalo with a third. When the cart is full, we unload it at the restaurant, then go back to the market for more. By

9:00 Matthew is done shopping and he heads back to L'Etoile for the day while I continue on by myself. These early hours turn out to be the only good time to talk with the growers, for later in the morning the market is so packed one can hardly move, and the farmers are clearly overwhelmed. Twenty thousand customers will have moved through the market this morning. By noon, everyone is eager to pack up and get home, and it's T-shirt weather again.

Everything here is farmer grown and produced. There is a great profusion of vegetables, fruits, and meats, some of which I've never seen before. "If it grows in Wisconsin, you'll find it here," one farmer tells me. I spend the morning looking, tasting, talking, buying. At the end of the day I look at my list of what I've seen. It's the longest inventory I've made so far. I am eagerly anticipating dinner at L'Etoile, where some of this food will be served.

L'Etoile is one of those rare restaurants that are intimately and essentially linked to the farm. Odessa Piper is a passionate woman, and her menu philosophy is squarely centered on cooking locally and seasonally. "L'Etoile, Cooking for the Seasons" is the restaurant's full name, and locally grown food in its season is what drives the restaurant, shapes its menu, and underlies its very reason for being. The menu is a sensitive one that shifts constantly in small movements, rather than big ones, to express the nuances of the seasons. Today Odessa has written on the menu a sentiment that I well understand:

This season presents our biggest menu-writing challenge. It's not from lack of creativity and excitement—rather, the opposite. We just don't know when to stop celebrating the exceptional ingredients we get to work with and the farmers who produce them.

The food at L'Etoile sparkles with the brightness that only food this fresh has, especially when it's in the hands of cooks who respect the materials they're working with. Odessa and Matthew know it's not only their kitchen skills but also the ingredients themselves that account for the magic in their food. They let them shine and acknowledge their provenance. The menu copy continues:

To give credit where credit is due, we've chosen an outstanding producer to highlight on each preparation. Some of the finest foods to be found anywhere in the world are available in our own backyard. We thank you for supporting all the local growers who supply L'Etoile, and for valuing their commitment to these patient arts.

The quality of the food at L'Etoile compares to what you might expect to find in Europe. But Odessa is right when she says, "The finest foods in the world can be found in our own backyards."

The Dane County market was not only the largest market I visited but also one of the most plentiful and varied. I could have easily cooked just about everything in this book from this one market alone. But here are some particular dishes the beautiful Wisconsin produce inspired. The hickory nuts and black walnuts I took home were used in cakes and confections and other nut-based recipes in place of walnuts, hazelnuts, or almonds.

SOME DISHES INSPIRED BY THE

DANE COUNTY FARMERS' MARKET

Leek and Sorrel Custards (page 238)

Parsnip Galette with Greens (page 210)

Late-Season Tomato-Vegetable Soup (page 183)

Concord Grape Tart (page 267)

Succotash (page 129)

Hickory Nut Torte with Espresso Cream (page 365)

Rustic Almond Truffles with Fruit Centers,
made with a portion of black walnuts, (page 370)

Winter Fruits: Citrus and Subtropicals

CITRUS AND SUB-TROPICALS

Florida, Texas, Arizona, southern California, and Hawaii are the source of our most exotic foods, the citrus and subtropical fruits that suggest warmth, sunshine, and tropical atmospheres. Lucky indeed are those who can pick up a sugar pineapple, a quart of blood orange juice, or a bag of passion fruit at the farmers' market. If you vacation in Hawaii, a visit to a market there may yield some rare treasures. But some citrus, and kiwifruit, don't depend on having a tropical climate. They thrive farther north in California as long as their growing area is free of prolonged, hard frost. Markets in the California foothills, in Placer County, for example, are sources of feijoa, mandarins, lemons, and oranges. But many of the softer exotic fruits—the guavas, cherimoyas, avocados, and lychee nuts dwell more safely southwards where freezes are less of a threat, or on the lush sides of Hawaii's islands.

A CITRUS LUNCH

Blood orange juice

Blood Orange Jelly | SERVES 6

One vendor at the market in La Jolla was selling quarts of pure blood orange juice. If you've never had blood orange juice, expect a beverage unlike any other. If made from Moros, the color will be the startling dark red that the name should prepare you for. From Taroccos it will be less so. But what also sets blood orange juice apart from that made with Valencias is the flavor, which holds hints of raspberries, the perfume of roses, and a more elusive note that is very nearly tropical.

I used the juice to make a jelly, but an unfiltered one that was dense with the bits of pulp. If you want one as clear as stained glass, strain the pulp through a fine-mesh strainer. This shimmering, cool dessert makes the truly perfect ending to a substantial winter meal. If you don't want to or can't get all those blood oranges, adding even a half dozen to the mix will alter the color and even the flavor of regular orange juice.

2 envelopes unflavored gelatin

1 quart freshly squeezed blood
    orange juice (about 24 oranges)

3 tablespoons sugar

THE WHIPPED CREAM

1 cup whipping cream

2 tablespoons confectioners' sugar

1 tablespoon framboise or kirsch

1 teaspoon finely grated blood
    orange zest

1. Sprinkle the gelatin over ½ cup cold water and set aside to soften. Strain the juice, if desired. Bring 1 cup of the juice to a boil. Pour the juice over the gelatin, add the sugar, and stir to dissolve. Add the rest of the juice, then let the mixture cool to room temperature. Give it a final stir so that the pulp, if present, is distributed evenly, then pour it into a shallow 1-quart mold. Refrigerate until set, about 8 hours.

2. Close to serving time, whip the cream and sugar into soft clouds, then stir in the framboise and zest. Chill your serving plate in the freezer for 20 minutes.

3. To serve, dip the mold into hot water for just a few seconds. Set the chilled serving plate over the mold, grasp both tightly in your hands, and invert. Refrigerate if you're not serving immediately. Garnish, if you wish, with orange segments or flowers, particularly orange blossoms and their shiny leaves. Serve the softly whipped cream on the side.

Blood Orange Salad
with Ricotta and Watercress | SERVES 4

The small bit of rosemary here is almost piney and somehow right with the sweet oranges, soft ricotta, and peppery cress.

8 blood oranges or navel oranges
    (12 if they're very small)
¾ cup ricotta
½ teaspoon finely chopped rosemary
2 teaspoons finely chopped parsley
extra virgin olive oil
freshly ground black pepper
12 watercress sprigs or another
    cresslike green (see page 8)

1. Neatly peel the oranges with a knife as described on page 389, removing all of the white pith. Slice them into rounds and arrange them on 4 plates or a platter.
2. Place spoonfuls of ricotta on each plate, sprinkle the herbs on top, and drizzle some olive oil over the oranges. Grind a little pepper over all, add the watercress, and serve.

CITRUS IN THE MARKET

Happily, the cheerful orange and yellow citrus fruits are winter fare, even though we see them year-round. The succession of citrus begins before Christmas with Satsuma mandarins and unfolds over the following four months, extending into early summer. The world of citrus is nothing if not confusing, however. Like apples, there seem to be a countless number of varieties and hybrids, including some very peculiar ones that are more rarely encountered.

Here are a few citrus you're likely to come across at a farmers' market:

LEMONS: Eureka and Lisbon lemons are both very acidic, with thick yellow, pebbly skins. The flesh is pale yellow-green, they're juicy when ripe, and they have few seeds.

Meyer lemons are highly perfumed, flower-fragrant with low acidity and thin, yellow-orange skins. They have long been a California favorite, and for good reason, because they make everything they season especially delicious.

LIMES: Persian limes are the lime America knows. These would ripen to yellow if left on the tree. Persian lemons are sweet, low-acid fruits that you can actually eat without wincing. Tiny yellow Mexican limes have a sweet perfume and lower acid than Persian limes, while orange Rangpur limes resemble small mandarins and are, in fact, a mandarin hybrid. They're juicy and very tart. Small yellow limes called calamansi are especially popular with Filipinos. Chef Su Mei Yu says, "The zest smells wonderful, especially when you throw it on top of roasted fish. Very aromatic!" They make a superb gin and tonic, too.

MANDARINS (TANGERINES): Satsumas are the first mandarins of the season. They appear in northern California markets as early as early November. Fairchilds, which are darker orange, seedy, juicy, and sweet, closely follow them. Some other varieties you may encounter are Kinnow, Dancy, and Page. Honey tangerines are encased in a tight, fine skin that's mottled with bits of green. They're very seedy, and their juice is plentiful and so intense that the obvious way to use them is in sorbets and gelatins—and for juice. Clementines (Algerian tangerines) are beautiful, small, red-orange mandarins that have been enjoying recent popularity. Although they deserve to stand entirely on their own merits, I suspect it's packaging that's done the trick, for the Spanish imports are packed in little crates that make them especially attractive. However, they are grown in the United States, and they can be found at farmers' markets.

ORANGES: Various cultivars of Valencia and navel oranges can be found, along with some exotics. One Valencia that shows up in southern California farmers' markets has skin that's striped with green, orange, and yellow—at least in its immature form. A cook seeking to make a true marmalade may encounter the traditional sour Seville oranges. A real treasure is the scented Bergamot orange, whose zest flavors Earl Grey tea. But the favorite exotic is the blood orange, which is increasingly more available. Not all are alike. Moros are really dark, blood red, a bit overwhelming, perhaps. Taroccos, on the other hand, look more like stained glass when cut open, and they possess a more intriguing perfume. There are many other varieties of blood oranges as well. They tend to have a much more complex, floral aroma and berrylike flavor than Valencias and navels.

PUMMELOS AND GRAPEFRUITS: Ancestors of the grapefruit, pummelos are the largest of the citrus. You may have seen them stacked on altars around Chinese New Year. The green or yellow skins and pith are enormously thick—the peels can be candied, and they can go into marmalades. The flesh is a bit dryish and not as sugary as the popular Rio Red grapefruits, but it is sweet and delicate. Each segment is encased in a substantial membrane, which needs to be removed. Cook the segments with fish (see page 345) or use them in a salad with fennel and endive. Pummelo segments are also very attractive alternated with kiwifruit on a platter. Chandler pummelos have pink flesh; most other varieties are white or even slightly greenish, such as Sarawaks.

There are many grapefruit varieties, but the most popular tend to be the sweet red-fleshed types—Rio Red and Ruby Red. Marsh Ruby, an older variety, is more kindly balanced to my taste. Regardless of the variety, color, shape, or size, I'm always surprised at how really very good freshly picked grapefruit are.

Cocktail grapefruits, a pummelo-mandarin hybrid, are smaller than grapefruits, and the flavor expresses its mixed parentage with a nice balance of fruit and acid. To me they have a lovely, somewhat exotic, hard-to-place flavor that always makes me think "pine." Cocktail grapefruits have lots of crescent-shaped seeds but also a great deal of juice. They make a fine citrus sorbet (see page 340). The Oro Blanco is a cross between a white grapefruit and a pummelo; this too is an enormous fruit. The skin is yellow and the flesh nearly white, hence its name, "gold and white." Like the pummelo, the fruit is sweet, but not overly so, and it is low in acid.

OTHER CITRUS: Kumquats and limequats are the smallest of the citrus. The skin is sweet, while the fruit within is sour. Kumquats that are crossed with Key limes produce limequats, a fruit that still bears a sweetish skin but a lively, sour pulp. Used sparingly, they make a good addition to a citrus fruit salad or compote. They can also be candied or used in a marmalade (see page 344).

Tutti-Frutti
Citrus Sorbet | MAKES 1 QUART

Any single citrus variety makes a wonderful sorbet. Tangerine is shockingly sweet and exploding with flavor; blood orange not only is a gorgeous deep pink but floods the mouth with hints of berries. Grapefruit sorbets are bright and sparkling, while sorbet made from cocktail grapefruit is slightly more perfumed and more subtle.

I discovered, however, when using up a lot of citrus fruits that had overspent their stay in my refrigerator, that making a sorbet from a mixture of fruits is like creating an exotic hybrid whose myriad notes come to life as it melts over your tongue. In this instance I had Honey tangerines, blood oranges, cocktail grapefruits, ruby grapefruit, a few Valencia oranges, Persian sweet limes, one Oro Blanco, and a few Meyer lemons. I juiced them all and loved the results. Here is the method, which works for single-fruit varieties as well as whatever mixture you might come up with. If you have less than 1 quart of juice, use 3 tablespoons sugar for each cup of juice.

2 tablespoons finely grated zest
from a variety of citrus fruits
¾ cup sugar
1 quart freshly squeezed citrus juice

1. Remove the zest from some of the fruits and put it in a small saucepan with the sugar.

2. Flip the pips from the fruits with the tip of a knife, then juice the fruit. Include as much pulp in the juice as you can. Remove any seeds that you missed before squeezing with a spoon.

3. Pour ½ cup of the juice over the sugar. Boil until the sugar is completely dissolved. You can tell by rubbing a drop between your fingers—there should be no graininess. Pour the syrup into the juice and chill until cold, then freeze according to your ice cream maker's instructions.

Meyer Lemon Sauce
with Tarragon | MAKES ⅓ TO ½ CUP

Spoon this simple, vibrant sauce over the first asparagus, an avocado and pummelo salad, shaved fennel, leeks—really any simply cooked vegetable or fish. And if you're planning to serve this over fish, consider adding a small avocado, finely diced, to make a lemony avocado salsa.

1 large Meyer lemon

1 shallot, finely diced

sea salt and freshly ground pepper

2 tablespoons extra virgin olive oil

2 tablespoons tarragon leaves,
     lightly chopped

Remove the zest and juice the lemon and put both in a bowl with the shallot and ¼ teaspoon salt. Let stand for 10 minutes, then whisk in the oil and add the tarragon. Season with a little pepper. If the lemon is more acidic than you like, whisk in more oil, to taste.

Candied
Kumquats | MAKES ABOUT ¾ CUP

These make a pretty garnish to use on winter desserts or in winter compotes. They'll keep for weeks in their syrup in the refrigerator.

½ cup sugar

16 plump kumquats

1. Combine 1 cup water and the sugar in a saucepan and bring to a boil. Stir to dissolve the sugar.
2. While it's heating, slice half the kumquats into rounds and halves; quarter the remainder lengthwise. This will give you a variety of shapes to use. Add them to the syrup and simmer until clear and soft, about 25 minutes. Store in the syrup.

Candied Citrus Peels
for Busy People | MAKES ABOUT 1 POUND

I'm not much on canning, jamming, and jellying except in modest quantities, but candied grapefruit peels are such a joy to use in cooking, so easy to make, and so much fun to give away that I make them every year. While I've made many batches in my life, the best were those that I just couldn't seem to find time for. I'd start simmering them in water, then have to turn off the heat and leave them until I got back from a meeting. Later, another obligation would mean I had to set them aside in the middle of the candying until I could resume. It seemed to take days to make this simple recipe, but I think that all the stopping and starting is what made these peels especially moist and succulent. And they stayed that way for weeks. Although you can go from A to B without pause, I'd suggest taking time to let the peels soak at various stages so they can absorb more moisture.

Ruby-fleshed grapefruits, such as Rio Red or Marsh Ruby, make big plump citrus candies with a rosy hue. You can also use white grapefruits, thick-skinned oranges, lemons, even the enormous Oro Blancos.

2 organic red grapefruits, 3 Cocktail grapefruits, 1 Oro Blanco, or 1 pummelo

1½ cups sugar

¼ cup light corn syrup

1 cup superfine sugar for coating

1. Score the fruits into quarters and pull off the peels. Put them in a saucepan, cover with cold water, and bring to a boil for 1 minute. Drain the fruit, then cover it again with cold water, this time placing a heavy plate on top of the fruit to keep it submerged. Bring to a boil, then lower the heat and simmer for 30 minutes. Leave the peels in the water until it has cooled to room temperature or overnight. Scrape away the white pith, then snip the skin strips with a pair of scissors, making them as wide or narrow as you like. I usually make them about ⅓ inch wide.

2. Combine the sugar, 1½ cups water, and the corn syrup in a 3-quart saucepan and bring to a boil. When the syrup is clear, add the fruit and lower the heat. Cook slowly until the peels have taken on a translucent appearance and the syrup has nearly boiled away, about 1 hour. (At any time, you can turn off the heat and allow the fruit to stand for several hours or, again, overnight.) Transfer the peels to a rack set over a tray to catch the drips.

3. Place the superfine sugar on a plate. Toss a few pieces of peel at a time to coat them with the sugar, then return them to the rack to dry for an hour. Pack in a lidded container between layers of sugar and store in the refrigerator.

CHOCOLATE-DIPPED CITRUS PEELS: Melt ¼ pound semisweet chocolate with 1 tablespoon unsalted butter in a double boiler over simmering water. Stir to blend the butter and chocolate, then dip the ends of the candied peels into the chocolate, coating just one side. Set them on wax paper and place in a cool place to harden.

Limequat and Pummelo Marmalade | MAKES APPROXIMATELY 7 CUPS

Limequats and pummelos produce a delicate marmalade with a copious amount of clear, golden jelly. This is made in several steps but is not serious all-weekend production. Oro Blancos, Cocktail grapefruits, and other grapefruits can be used in place of the pummelo.

1 pummelo
1½ pounds limequats
5 cups sugar, approximately

1. Quarter the pummelo and pull off the skins. Slice away the thick white pulp, but don't worry about getting all of it; just remove the bulk of it. Slice the peel into thin slivers. Gently tease the fruit segments from the membranes, then coarsely chop them. Slice the limequats thinly into rounds, halves, or a combination of both. Save the pips from both fruits.

2. Bring the rinds, pulp, pips and 6 cups water to a boil. After 10 minutes, turn off the heat. Set aside in a cool place for the rest of the day if you've started in the morning, or leave overnight if you started later in the day. Bring the fruit once again to a boil and cook briskly until the peels are soft. This should take only 20 minutes, but taste to make sure.

3. Measure the fruit and water, then multiply by ¾ to determine the number of cups of sugar you'll need. Combine the sugar and fruit, stir to dissolve, then again bring to a rapid boil. Boil until it reaches the jelly stage, about 40 minutes. You can determine this by dribbling a spoonful of the marmalade onto a plate and placing it in the freezer. It should jell up by the time it's cool, after 5 minutes or so. If not, continue cooking until it does.

4. Decant into sterilized jars, cap and cover, and boil for 15 minutes. (At 7,000 feet, I boil my jars for 25 minutes since the water temperature is so much lower.)

Red Snapper Baked in Parchment with Pummelo and Rosemary | SERVES 4

The delicate, not overly sweet flesh of the pummelo (or Oro Blanco) is lovely with fish.

Parchment paper, or aluminum foil

2 to 3 tablespoons unsalted butter

4 red snapper fillets, 4 to 6 ounces each

sea salt and freshly ground pepper

2 pummelos or Oro Blancos, peeled and sectioned, page 389

2 teaspoons minced rosemary

1. Preheat the oven to 450°F. Tear off 4 pieces of parchment paper, each about 1 square foot. Rub the center of each piece lightly with butter.

2. Rinse the fish, pat dry, and season with salt and pepper. Place a fillet on each piece of foil and divide the fruit among them. Sprinkle with the rosemary and dot with the remaining butter.

3. Fold each piece of parchment paper to make a loose but tightly sealed packet. Bake for 30 minutes. Serve the fish in the packets.

Citrus Compote with Star Fruit | SERVES 6

A young boy at the market told me, "Star fruit tastes like a really sour orange that's crisp." He wasn't far off. They're crisp, they're sour, and you can even get the flavor of a ripe orange in there. Sliced crosswise, carambola fall into a row of golden stars—hence their other name. If you simmer them in syrup for a few minutes, they taste much better. Try them in a compote or rice pudding, the flavor-infused syrup drizzled over the top.

The colors of the fruits in this compote look like Shirley poppies.

2 pummelos or Oro Blancos

3 blood oranges

3 navel oranges

4 Satsumas, clementines, or other mandarins

1 small star fruit

3 tablespoons sugar

3 large kumquats, sliced into rounds

2 kiwifruit

fresh mint sprigs or orange blossoms and leaves

1. Remove several strands of zest from one of each of the citrus fruits, taking just a little from the pummelos, with a citrus zester (not a Microplane) and set aside.

2. Peel the pummelos, oranges, and mandarins, then section them over a bowl to catch the juice (see page 389). Slice the star fruit into ¼-inch slices. Measure ½ cup of the juice and put it in a saucepan with the sugar. Bring it to a boil, add the citrus zest, kumquats, and star fruit, then simmer for 10 minutes. Cool, then add to the rest of the fruit.

3. Neatly peel, then thinly slice the kiwifruit. Add to the compote. Refrigerate. Serve garnished with sprigs of mint or orange blossoms.

"Don't buy those!" my friend warned as I reached toward a huge Reed avocado. "It will be watery!" But I couldn't resist it—it was so big and green and tempting. And he was right; it was insipid. Yet Steven Facciola, in *Cornucopia,* describes the Reed as "buttery, with a rich, faintly nutty flavor. Quality excellent." The Fuerte, that Floridian fruit which is usually dismissed as being watery, is also described in flattering terms. What was wrong? I wondered.

I called Michael Abelman of Fairview Gardens, in Goleta, California. He grows quite a few avocado varieties on his urban farm, and I had just eaten my way through the Bacon, Fuerte, Hass, Rincon, and Pinkerton avocados that he had sent me to photograph. The first surprise was how absolutely wonderful the Fuertes were.

"Why were they so good?" I wanted to know. It's the same old answer: "Because, what you've had was a Fuerte that was picked when it was ready. Fuertes are watery only when they're picked too young," Michael explained. And the reason they're picked young is that commercial growers use them to close the market gap that appears before the Hass comes in.

Once again, it's the market, not flavor, that's driving things here. But business as usual means that we were all missing out on a really good avocado. It's the Hass that's touted as the number one variety, and it *is* good—buttery, creamy, rich, and all of that. Sellers like it because it's easy to tell when it's ready to eat—the pebbly skin turns black—and growers like it because it's a good shipper.

"The problem with the Hass, though," says Michael, "is that it tends to obscure lesser-known varieties. It's like the Red Delicious apple. There are a hundred wonderful varieties, but this one dominates." And that, I think, is one of the main problems with produce in America: We allow one or two varieties, be they peaches, avocados, or potatoes, to pose as the *only* varieties, while all others are obscured. Fortunately, I think we're starting to wake up from our slumber and see how much is out there and how much we've been missing.

The lesser-known varieties I've tasted from various farmers' markets have all been truly wonderful. And the Reed *is* one of the more nutty and interesting avocados around—when ripe. The flavor differences from one fruit to another are a bit subtle, but avocados do differ greatly in appearance. Some are enormous (up to 36 ounces!), others tiny (weighing only 3 to 5 ounces), but there's a use for every size. Small avocados make a perfect little nibble; slightly larger and you have the makings of a sandwich; while the giant ones are easy to turn into a bowl of guacamole. An enormous avocado Michael showed me was unsalable except at his farm stand or a farmers' market. Even though it was organic and delicious, no natural foods store would buy it because of its size: They didn't have a way to price it. The tail seemed to be wagging the dog!

Other differences to note: Skins can be thin, thick, or leathery; pale green to nearly black; uniform green to flecked with golden spots. Shapes vary from oval to pear shaped to oblong to round. They can be easy to peel or as hard as the dickens. Pits might rattle in some varieties but not in others. But all avocados are watery before they're really at their peak, which is why we're told that early-season avocados are less caloric than those that come later. Wait for later is my advice.

My Standard
Avocado Sandwich

These are equally well suited for breakfast, lunch, and dinner: Toast whole wheat bread. Halve, peel, and slice an avocado. Gently arrange the slices over the toast and then lightly mash them. Drizzle fresh Meyer lemon, calamansi, or Key lime juice over the top, and add a pinch of sea salt and some black pepper. If you don't mind the calories, add a little olive oil, too. Repeat as often as needed.

Avocado and Grapefruit Salad with
Pomegranates and Pistachios | SERVES 6

It's the acid tang of the citrus next to the creaminess of the avocado that makes this combination such a classic, but there's no need to be limited to grapefruit. Give other citrus a try as well.

1 very small red onion, sliced into thin rounds, about ⅓ cup

2 tablespoons white wine vinegar

1 bunch watercress

1 small pomegranate

3 red grapefruits or a mixture of citrus fruits

2 kiwifruit

1 large avocado, such as a Pinkerton or Reed

grated zest and juice of 1 tangelo or Satsuma mandarin

sea salt and freshly ground pepper

2 tablespoons extra virgin olive oil

¼ cup roasted pistachio nuts, coarsely chopped

1. Toss the onion rings with the vinegar and set them aside in the refrigerator. Sort through the watercress and discard the large, heavy stems. Rinse under cool running water, spin dry, then wrap in a towel and refrigerate until ready to use.

2. Cut the pomegranate into quarters, then break out about ½ cup of the seeds. Working in the sink, gently squeeze a tablespoon or so of juice from the remaining pomegranate and set it aside. Peel and section the grapefruits. Neatly peel and thinly slice the kiwi. Peel and cut the avocados into neat chunks.

3. To make the dressing, combine the zest, ¼ cup tangelo juice plus 1 tablespoon pomegranate juice, and ¼ teaspoon salt, then whisk in the oil.

4. Loosely arrange the watercress on a plate with the grapefruit sections (minus their juice). Add the kiwi, avocado, and onions, which will be pickled by now, then pour the dressing over all. Season with pepper and garnish with the pistachio nuts.

Avocado and Jícama Salad with Lime Vinaigrette | SERVES 4 GENEROUSLY

This salad looks and tastes best when the lettuce and jícama are very finely sliced. It should end up a tangle of greens and whites, very cool looking and tasting.

Try different limes—Rangpur, calamansi, etc.—if your market has them. They vary in acidity, so taste the vinaigrette and adjust the balance of juice to oil as needed.

1 head butter lettuce, leaves
    separated
1 head romaine, the heart leaves only,
    or several handfuls small spinach
    leaves and arugula leaves
1 small jícama, about ½ pound
2 large avocados, ripe but firm
zest of 1 lime, plus 1 tablespoon juice
5 tablespoons extra virgin olive oil
sea salt and freshly ground pepper
2 scallions, including an inch of the
    greens
15 mint leaves, torn into small pieces

1. Wash and dry the greens. Slice them into narrow ribbons and set aside. Peel the jícama and sliver it into very thin matchsticks. Peel and slice the avocados into wedges. Whisk the lime zest, juice, and olive oil together with a few pinches of salt. Slice the scallions into long, thin slivers.

2. Toss the greens with the jícama, avocado, scallions, mint, and a few pinches of salt. Then dress the salad with enough of the vinaigrette to coat lightly but thoroughly. Season with pepper and serve.

Pummelo and Avocado Salad with Endive and Fennel | SERVES 4

Try a Pinkerton avocado if you can. It's large, buttery, easy to peel, and available at farmers' markets before the citrus go out.

3 pummelos or Oro Blancos, peeled
   and sectioned, page 389

2 Belgian endives

1 small fennel bulb

1 tablespoon white wine vinegar

1 shallot, finely diced

sea salt and freshly ground pepper

4 to 5 tablespoons olive oil

1 large avocado

1. Peel and section the pummelos. You'll have to slice very deeply into the thick, pithy covering to get to the flesh. Separate the sections over a bowl. Sliver the endives. Slice the fennel very thinly using a sharp knife or mandoline.

2. Measure 2 tablespoons of the juice into a bowl. Add the vinegar, shallot, and a pinch of salt, then whisk in the olive oil.

3. Toss the endive and fennel with enough dressing to coat lightly and divide among 4 salad plates. Peel, then slice the avocado onto each plate. Add the pummelo sections. Spoon the remaining dressing over the fruit, season with pepper, and serve.

Feijoa Bavarian Cream | SERVES 6 TO 8

2 pounds ripe, fragrant feijoas
   (pineapple guavas)

¾ cup sugar

1 envelope unflavored gelatin

1 cup milk

1 cup whipping cream

½ vanilla bean, split in half
   lengthwise

1. Halve the feijoas lengthwise and scoop out their flesh. You should have about 2 cups.

2. Combine the sugar and ½ cup water in a saucepan, bring to a boil, and cook until the sugar is dissolved. Add the fruit, return to a boil, cook for 3 minutes, then turn off the heat. Puree. Don't worry if there's a little graininess. Feijoas tend to be that way, but get it as smooth as you can. Measure out 1¼ cups and refrigerate the rest.

3. Sprinkle the gelatin over ¼ cup cold water and set aside to soften.

4. Combine the milk, cream, vanilla bean, and puree. Add the softened gelatin, cook for 2 minutes to dissolve, stirring constantly, then turn off the heat and let stand for 15 minutes. Remove the vanilla bean and scrape the seeds into the mixture. Pour the custard into individual ramekins or a single 4-cup mold and refrigerate until firm, 6 to 8 hours. Unmold the dessert and place on individual plates or a single plate with the remaining puree spooned over or around it.

FIVE SUBTROPICAL FRUITS

FEIJOAS: Also called pineapple guavas, they are small cylindrical fruits about 3 inches long with dark green pebbly skin. They're not much to look at, but they are just as delicious as any of the showier subtropicals. A ripe feijoa is fragrant and yielding to the touch. Unripe feijoas will be tart, so allow them to soften. To eat, just slice them lengthwise and scoop out their flesh with a spoon.

GUAVAS: When stashed in the refrigerator in a plastic bag, their scent will waft out at you every time you open the door, and that alone makes them a worthy purchase. The guava group is a large one, so you'll find a lot of variations—from those that are as tiny as olives to others that are lemon-sized or pear-shaped. Their skin can be green, yellow, or some shade in between. Inside, the fruits are luscious hues of pink, salmon, and occasionally white. Seeds run through them like buckshot, and the texture is sticky and slightly grainy. Although these factors might understandably lessen their appeal, only a few pieces of the fruit have the power to transform an ordinary compote into something sensual and exotic. In fact, guavas are not as enjoyable for eating out of hand as they are to use as a flavoring. They are densely sweet, so a little acidity from a passion fruit or a lime brings their flavors into focus. A puree is perhaps the best way to go with guavas, for once you have some, you can use it in fruit compotes, smoothies, fools, or ice creams or add it to a syrup to use as a sherbet or sauce.

CHERIMOYAS, those more or less pear-shaped fruits covered with dull green scalelike skin, look as protected as armadillos. I bought a large one from a grower in California who said it would be ripe when the skin blackened and the fruit was growing increasingly soft. By the time we had driven back to New Mexico, it was ready to eat. We sliced it into wedges, admired its big glossy black seeds, then spooned out the soft white fruit. It lived up to its other name, custard apple—the custard part, not the apple. It was as smooth and silky as custard and had that soft, tropical perfume. It was good eating the cherimoya just like this, but pureed, it made a worthy addition to the Frozen Subtropical Mousse on page 352.

PASSION FRUIT: No fruit looks less promising than a ripe passion fruit. And it reveals absolutely nothing about itself until you cut into it. About the size of a small lemon, when ripe the passion fruit is purplish brown and very wrinkled. Amazingly, no perfume escapes its brittle-looking skin, even though passion fruit is so aromatic that even a small amount lends other fruits its tropical flavor. Passion fruit is also one of only a few tart tropical fruits, which makes it useful for balancing those fruits that are less so, such as guavas or very ripe pineapples. You can easily sweeten the pulp by stirring in a little simple syrup or superfine sugar.

To get at the fruit, slice a passion fruit in two or simply slice off the top, then scoop it out with a spoon. The black BB-sized seeds, which are edible, are suspended in an orange pulp. Scoop out the insides, getting every single drop. There may be not much more than a tablespoon, but it can go far. The shells are quite beautiful. You can use them as containers for a few satiny bites of passion fruit fool.

PRICKLY PEARS (TUNAS): The southern parts of Arizona, Texas, California, the drier sides of Hawaii, are where you might find cactus *tunas,* as the fruits of the prickly pear are called. Encased in their dull-looking skins is the most unbelievable magenta flesh, peppered with hundreds of tiny black seeds. When pureed you end up with a neon-colored sauce (it looks completely fake) to dress a compote of fruits (try mangoes, papayas, strawberries, and pineapple) or to spoon over ice creams or sorbets. Of course it can go into drinks, from smoothies to margaritas, or *agua fresca*. Whether the spines have been removed or not, do handle *tunas* with care: Wear gloves or hold them with tongs while you're working with them. Like the paddles, they do have spines.

Frozen Subtropical Mousse | SERVES 4 TO 6

This is the simplest way to make a fruit ice cream without making custard, using a machine, or having to scrape trays of frozen slush. It takes little time to put together, and if you forgo the freezing, you can serve this as a fool with no delay whatsoever. Poured into a single mold, it can be frozen in about 3 hours, and individual ramekins take even less time.

You'll need 1 cup pureed fruit—guavas, feijoas, pineapple, cherimoya, prickly pears, sapotes, or a mixture of fruits. It's good to have extra puree to use as a sauce.

THE GUAVA PUREE

1 pound guavas

⅓ to ½ cup sugar, depending on the tartness of the fruit

1 passion fruit, pulp and seeds, or juice of 1 lime

If the guava skins are fresh and unbruised, slice off the ends, then chop the rest into large pieces. If the fruit is not perfect, peel them first, then chop. Put the guavas in a saucepan with the sugar to taste and ½ cup water. Bring to a boil, then lower the heat, cover the pan, and cook for 20 minutes or until soft. Stir in the passion fruit pulp. Strain to remove the seeds from the pulp. (If you didn't use passion fruit, add lime juice to taste at the end.) Chill well.

THE MOUSSE

1 cup whipping cream

⅓ cup confectioners' sugar

grated zest of 1 lime

few drops vanilla extract

fresh lime juice, if needed

extra guavas or other fruits for garnish

1. Whip the cream with the sugar until stiff. Fold in the guava puree, lime zest, and vanilla. It should be well balanced, but if it seems too sweet, add a few drops of lime juice, to taste.

2. Scrape into individual ramekins and freeze for 2 hours or until firm. To serve, let the ramekins stand at room temperature for a few minutes, then dip them into hot water until the cream begins to melt around the edges. Turn onto plates. Garnish with thin slices of guava or extra guava puree.

"You won't forget Hawaii, will you?" the journalist from Hawaii asked. The edge of anxiety in her voice suggested that it was common to. But I assured her that the market in Hilo was one of my favorite farmers' markets anywhere. And I'm hardly alone, for every Saturday crowds surge at the entrance, waiting impatiently for the market to open. In fact there's enough enthusiasm in Hawaii to support more than twenty farmers' markets.

The wide ethnic diversity in Hawaii is reflected in the range of foods that show up at the market, but what are most unusual to most mainlanders are the subtropical fruits. Included are guavas of all shapes and sizes, feijoas (or pineapple guavas, which are different from true guavas), passion fruit, pineapple, breadfruit, red bananas, soursops, mangoes (Hayden and Cigar), star fruit, cherimoyas, and sapotes. And although they're treated as a vegetable, avocados are also subtropical fruits.

The centers of nearly all these fruits are soft. Sometimes the texture is gummy or sticky (as in guavas) or pulpy with large seeds (the passion fruit). Some are unbelievably silky (lychee nuts and mangoes), and not all are for eating out of hand. But all seem to be potent conveyers of the soft flowery breezes one associates with the tropics, that indeterminate blend of flowers (roses, jasmine, plumeria), berries (raspberries, strawberries), and banana—the perfume of paradise. A little passion fruit juice or the diced pink-fleshed guava can utterly transform a bowl of strawberries or a dish of melon, transporting one to the lush side of a Hawaiian island.

If you haven't seen or eaten fresh lychee nuts, then you owe yourself a trip to Hawaii (or Florida) just to do so. Under their red dimpled husks, the silky white fruits lie waiting to provide your mouth with slithery pleasures. Sugar pineapples found in the Hilo market are unlike any you'll find on the mainland. They're long, deeply gold on the outside, and the color of saffron within. They're sweet and full of big flavor, the acidity nicely in check. Exquisite! And bananas, other than the common Cavendish, have surprising nuances of flavor we've never expected to look for, and find, in a banana.

At Hawaiian markets you'll come across the smooth, fawn-colored rhizomes of ginger that have a freshness we seldom see on the mainland, and stalks of white ginger flowers, buckets of orchids, and all kinds of strange, waxy-looking flowers that tourists fly home with. Those beautifully grown vegetables that are familiar to most of us are there, but so are the more interesting-looking yard-long beans, bitter melons, gobo (burdock), fern shoots, taro, and big, buttery macadamia nuts.

The lively ethnicity of Hawaii is also reflected in some of the foods that are made to take away, from coconut pastries (and ice-cold coconuts) to tamales, Portuguese egg breads, red bean buns, mochi, fresh poi, Spanish rolls, and lumpia. To wash it all down? Hawaiian coffee and fresh fruit juices made from those luscious fruits.

Passion Fruit with Cream or Coconut Milk

This is the kind of dessert for when you want only a taste. Or it might serve as part of a more elaborate platter of fruits.

Slice off the top of a passion fruit, stir in a little sugar, then float a spoonful of cream or coconut milk on top. Set the fruit in an egg cup and serve with a small spoon. There will be just a few small bites, but they will be very good.

Passion Fruit Sauce and Syrup | MAKES ABOUT ⅓ CUP

A syrup is one way to extend the range of expensive passion fruits. Use it in compotes, spoon it over other fruits, such as strawberries, or try it with melons, pineapples, and bananas.

5 or more passion fruits
1 to 2 tablespoons Simple Syrup,
    page 388

Halve the passion fruits and scoop the pulp and its seeds into a strainer. Press the pulp against the strainer to force out as much juice as possible. It will be bright orange. Sweeten it with simple syrup to taste. It may take just a few teaspoons or a bit more if it's very tart. Keep refrigerated until ready to use.

Passion Fruit and Pineapple Fool | SERVES 6

This makes a delicious filling for a jelly roll as well as a simple dessert. If you want a dessert without cream, cut the pineapple into larger pieces, add the passion fruit juice and seeds, and garnish.

1 small pineapple
1 cup whipping cream
2 tablespoons confectioners' sugar
strained juice from 2 passion fruits
pineapple sage leaves and blossoms,
    white ginger blossoms, or the
    seeds from the passion fruit

1. Slice the skin off the pineapple, remove the eyes with the tip of a potato peeler, then cut the flesh away from the core. Coarsely chop in a food processor, then transfer to a bowl. As the fruit settles and the juice pools around it, pour off the excess juice.
2. Whip the cream with the sugar until barely stiff, then fold in the passion fruit and the pineapple. Mound the fool into parfait glasses, garnish, and serve.

Pineapple in Ginger Syrup with Pineapple Sage | SERVES 6

The fruit-scented red flowers of the pineapple sage are a bright and cheerful addition to this compote. Plus, they really do smell like pineapples. Their lack, however, should not deter you from making this compote. Lemon verbena and mints of various kinds are also good with this fruit.

⅓ cup sugar
1 (3-inch) knob fresh ginger, peeled
    and sliced into thin coins
6 pineapple sage, lemon verbena, or
    mint sprigs
1 pineapple
2 tablespoons kirsch
6 pineapple sage blossoms and extra
    leaves for garnish

1. Simmer the sugar with 1½ cups water and the ginger until the sugar is dissolved. Turn off the heat, add the pineapple sage, and set aside to steep.
2. Slice off the pineapple leaves, then, standing the pineapple upright, slice off the skin. Remove the eyes with the tip of a potato peeler. Quarter the fruit lengthwise, cut out the core, then slice it crosswise into ½-inch pieces. Put it in a bowl and pour the syrup over. Add the kirsch and chill well.
3. Serve in glass dishes, with a sprig of sage and a red blossom in each.

Prickly Pear Sauce | MAKES ABOUT 1½ CUPS

6 to 8 prickly pears (tunas)
½ cup sugar
½ cup fresh orange juice or water
fresh lime juice, if needed

1. Holding the *tunas* upright with tongs, slice off the skins. Puree, then pour through a fine-mesh strainer.
2. Simmer the sugar in the juice or water until it's completely dissolved. Combine it with the cactus puree and chill well. Taste and sharpen the flavor, if needed, with a little fresh lime juice. If it needs to be sweeter, add Simple Syrup to taste, page 388.

One-Minute Citrus and Subtropical Salad Plate | SERVES 4

When time doesn't allow for a more laborious presentation of perfectly peeled and sliced fruits, just cut them up into pieces and serve them on an ornamental plate with a knife and fork. The fruits themselves are so beautiful that you needn't do more than this. Serve such a salad as part of a brunch or light lunch.

3 blood oranges, quartered
3 kiwifruit, peeled and quartered
1 small star fruit, raw or poached, page 345
4 pineapple guavas, halved
1 avocado, quartered
1 slice fresh pineapple
1 cherimoya, sliced
lychee nuts in their husks
1 lime, halved

Rinse, then neatly cut all of the fruits. Arrange them on 4 individual plates and serve. Squeeze the lime over the avocado.

Being January, the morning was cool enough for a light jacket, but by the time Kitty Morse and I had finished shopping the Vista farmers' market, we had stripped down to T-shirts.

Kitty is from Morocco and cooks beautiful Moroccan dishes. I was with her to help with a photo shoot for her book *Cooking at the Kasbah* (Chronicle Books, 1998). The produce from this market was perfectly suited to her cooking. Here was the source for her translucent pink juice of pomegranate and lime, her preserved lemons, her baked pumpkin with caramelized onions, dates stuffed with almonds, and thick vegetable soups and tagines.

Vista, California (near San Diego), lies close to Mexico and just a mountain range away from Palm Desert and the Coachella and Imperial Valleys. Before freeways and houses defined the landscape, the hills here were covered with orchards and strawberry fields. A few citrus and avocado groves have prevailed, but the agricultural feel of the area is gone. Now only a few scattered fragments remain. Farming still takes place in pockets, though, and this January market had a staggering array of fruits and vegetables—from leeks and parsnips to citrus and cherimoyas—and all at the same time. While the possibilities such diversity suggested were exciting, they were also bewildering. What would you cook when you could make a hearty braise of root vegetables as easily as you might a Moroccan tagine with pumpkin and dates, or avocado and citrus salads, or a squash blossom quesadilla—all from local, seasonal produce and all on the same day? Where was the narrow season of winter with its roots, tubers, and cabbages? Clearly not in southern California, where eating seasonally means something very different from what it means elsewhere in the United States. The climate *is* favored, and it is Mediterranean.

Several varieties of organic dates were for sale at the first stand I approached, big Mexican pumpkins at the last. Everything you can imagine lay in between. But citrus were the fruit of the moment. Here were Eureka, Lisbon, and sweet Meyer lemons; green limes, tiny yellow Mexican limes, orange Rangpur and tiny sour Philippine limes called calamansi. On the sweeter end of the citrus scale were Satsumas, blood oranges, cocktail grapefruits, and the giants of the citrus, the Oro Blancos and pummelos—both a joy to see for their sheer size, which is nearly preposterous.

"What do you do with this?" I asked, and three shoppers answered in unison, "You eat them!" It didn't seem likely, somehow, but underneath the protective thick skin were amazingly delicate segments of flesh, softly perfumed and sweet. In contrast were piles of kumquats, the tiniest of the citrus, and calamansi limes. There were many varieties of avocados, along with the reptilian-looking cherimoyas. Most everything else at the market was familiar, but from the other months of the year: tomatoes, zucchini, baskets of squash blossoms, peas, cauliflower with perfect creamy curds, verdant bunches of broccoli rabe, clusters of jewel-like beets, and some early artichokes. Mixed in with these were more wintry offerings of cabbages and Brussels sprouts. The trunk of one farmer's car was filled with fennel bulbs, their long stalks and feathery greens intact. "Come back in the spring!" she shouted. "It will be full of fava beans!"

Seeing her mass of fennel, I recalled a man in Sicily standing by his car at the side of the road. The open trunk was crammed with artichokes on their long stalks. Bundles of them were lashed to the roof and the hood, and more jutted out of the back windows, small violet thistles in a tangle of long, winding leaves. A one-man, one-item market, he was doing a brisk business. A young woman in Lesbos offered another variation on vehicular marketing. Her motor scooter had bags of zucchini hanging from the handlebars, baskets of tomatoes striding the seat, and onions hanging off the back. And although it's no longer as common as it once was, you can still find people sitting by the side of the road, their trucks filled with produce. It's always worth taking a look. A farmer may have sent a family member out to try to get rid of that sweet corn that won't keep, those extra melons that are about to crack, or sacks of field peas. Treasures can be found if you slow down and take a look.

As we were leaving, Sui Lin Robinson, a grower of herbs and heirloom lettuce starts, remarked, "Everyone is nice here; people talk and share recipes. I learn so much from selling." I've heard this sentiment at every market I've visited. It's not only the customers who enjoy the direct exchange that occurs at the farmers' market but the growers too. They learn from their customers and love it when customers let them know that their work is appreciated. Never hold back that compliment!

A SIMPLE WINTER SUPPER

IN SOUTHERN CALIFORNIA

Date and Orange Salad
with Feta Cheese and Pistachios (page 373)

Pasta with Golden Fennel (page 47)

Feijoa Bavarian Cream (page 350)

The Foods That Keep

14

As keenly central as fresh foods are to the market, they are not the only foods from the farm, and summer is not the only season. There are also the foods that keep. Nuts, dates, and other dried fruits, maple syrup, wild rice, and dried beans have had little done to them. But there are also those foods that the farmer makes into something lasting, such as berry jams and pear butters, hazelnut cookies, pickled okra, preserved horseradish, sauerkraut, olive oil, vinegars, even candles from beeswax. Filling our pantry with such foods gives us a way to continue our relationship to where we live over the winter.

The foods that keep, sometimes more so than produce, tend to be emblematic of a region, which is one of their qualities that makes them so special. Gleaned from farmers' markets across the country and in my cupboard right now are many such regional foods. There's a jar of preserves made from the Arctic Rose white nectarine from California, a fruit that I love but taste maybe only once a year, and enough of Larry Butler's smoke-dried tomatoes from Texas to give some away to friends who covet them. A gallon of maple syrup from Highland Sugarworks in Vermont will see us through the winter, along with regional honeys and a jar of Colorado molasses. There are bags of bolita and pinto beans from Max Martinez, *posole* grown and made by Gloria and Rose Trujillo, plus a few frozen packages of their delicious tamales.

My freezer also holds all kinds of dried fruits and delicious nuts, including pluots and Red Flame raisins, hazelnut meal from the Holmquist family, hickory nuts from Wisconsin, luscious Empress and Medjool dates, native wild rice, and those delicious dry-farmed almonds of Rusty Hall's. In a cool corner of the garage are a few bottles of the Barianis' olive oil and a gallon of the Sciabicas' aged red wine vinegar. It's even possible to add a quarter of locally raised organic beef or lamb to the freezer.

With such treasures on hand, I look forward to cooking from the winter pantry, knowing that it's increasingly possible to sit down to the winter table still knowing who has produced much of the food we eat.

A WINTER MENU FROM NORTHERN CALIFORNIA

Endive on Toast with Gruyère Cheese,
appetizer portions (page 29)

Chicken Thighs Braised with
Dried Fruits, Shallots, and Bay (page 376)

Winter Squash "Pancake" with Mozzarella and
Sage made without the mozzarella (page 155)

Rustic Tart of Quinces, Apples, and Pears (page 320)

Black Walnut–Banana Cake | SERVES 10 TO 12

If you're lucky enough to find black walnuts anywhere (I found them at Wisconsin markets), use them up quickly. Even in the refrigerator, they don't last long before their oils turn. Black walnuts have a strong, distinctive taste, too assertive for some when used in full strength, so I mix them with a portion of English walnuts. Hickory nuts, or pecans are also good in this cake.

THE CAKE

¾ cup black walnuts, hickory nuts,
    or walnuts

¼ cup English walnuts

1 cup all-purpose flour

1 teaspoon baking powder

1 teaspoon baking soda

½ teaspoon freshly grated nutmeg

½ teaspoon sea salt

3 eggs, separated, at room
    temperature

6 tablespoons unsalted butter

1 cup light brown sugar, packed

1 large ripe banana, mashed

1 teaspoon vanilla extract

½ cup buttermilk

confectioners' sugar

THE CREAM CHEESE FILLING

¼ pound cream cheese

2 tablespoons unsalted butter

¾ cup confectioners' sugar, plus extra

2 tablespoons light brown sugar or
    maple sugar

½ teaspoon vanilla extract

1 large ripe banana, sliced

1. Preheat the oven to 350°F. Butter and flour an 8-inch springform pan. Toast the nuts until they smell fragrant, 10 to 12 minutes. Pulse in a food processor until finely chopped. Whisk the dry ingredients together.

2. Beat the egg whites until they hold firm peaks, then scrape them into a bowl. Wipe out the mixing bowl and return it to the mixer. Cream the butter and sugar until light and fluffy. Add the egg yolks one at a time, followed by the mashed banana, vanilla, and buttermilk. Turn the mixer to low and add the dry ingredients, then the nuts. Stir in a quarter of the whites, then fold in the rest. Turn the batter into the pan, then bake until the cake is golden and pulling away from the sides, 45 to 50 minutes. Cool in the pan 10 minutes, then remove the rim.

3. For the filling, beat the cream cheese with the butter, then add the sugars and vanilla and mix until smooth.

4. Slice the cake in half horizontally, cover the bottom layer with the filling, then thinly slice the other banana over it. Return the top layer and wrap in plastic wrap until ready to serve, then unwrap and dust with confectioners' sugar.

December in California's Central Valley can be dazzlingly bright. It can also be gray and damp, the air thick with tule fog. A December visit to the Davis farmers' market coincided with the latter weather, but even so the market was crowded and busy, as it always is. As a traveler, I was drawn to the dried fruits and nuts, which were just a little more than a month off the trees and out of their shells. Davis is my hometown, so I often visit this market, and I always stock up on nuts and dried fruits to use throughout the winter.

One farmer was selling two types of walnuts, the familiar white-fleshed English walnut, the Chandler, and a darker one, called a Hartley. At first I declined the offer to taste it, thinking it was last year's old walnut. But the farmer pointed out that this nut was, in fact, newly harvested; the coloring was part of its character. The taste was indeed fresh, with more of the rich tones of the black walnut. It's a delicious walnut and one worth keeping your eye open for.

Mission almonds always seem to be available at the Davis market, along with the more familiar Nonpareils. The two small almonds nestled pointy end to end in their shell are small, and their points and curves make them slightly tedious to blanch and peel. However, this difficulty can be overlooked in favor of their taste, which is fuller and more of what we want to find in an almond. Flavor, however, is determined by factors other than variety. Rusty Hall, architect turned farmer, dry-farms eighty-year-old almond trees in the southern part of the state, near Paso Robles. He has a number of varieties, including the Missions and Nonpareils, but it's the lack of water that accounts for the intense flavor his almonds are known for. They are highly coveted by restaurateurs and other aficionados but available by mail order too (see Resources).

Walnuts and almonds are particularly easy to crack, and they'll keep for a good year, so consider buying them in the shell, then cracking them as you need them. You'll be surprised at how long they keep their pristine flavor and how little time it takes to crack a cupful.

Pecans, a relative of the walnut and the nut of the South, including southern Texas and New Mexico, are not easy to crack and end up with nice-looking pieces. Unless you have the proper tool, it's best to pay the higher price and buy them already shelled. Hawaii has its famous macadamia nuts, another hard (impossible, nearly) nut to crack. Hickory nuts, a midwestern treat, can be found at the Dane County market in Madison, as can black walnuts. Hazelnuts are the nut of the Northwest—Washington as well as Oregon—and pine nuts can sometimes be found in the fall at southwestern markets. They are soft shelled, tiny, and insanely laborious to peel. It took a week of devoted evenings to get enough for one tart.

The dried fruits at the Davis market were similar to those I have seen elsewhere in California. They were little gems of translucency—apricots, nectarines, peaches, pears, plums, pluots, and prunes. Geri Bogdanich, whose family specializes in fruits and nuts, sells bags of mixed dried stone fruits. With a few dried cherries added to them, they cook into a stunning compote. Drained, the fruits can be used to make the upside-down cake on page 374. And if you've ever been drawn to making a raisin pie, a mince tart, or *anything* with raisins, try to get your hands on some Gold and Red Flame raisins. They dry in shades of red, plum, and gold and are exceptionally large and plump (see Resources for mail-order information).

Hickory Nut Torte with
Espresso Cream | SERVES 10 TO 12

With only a small, precious supply of cracked hickory nuts from a Wisconsin market, I was hard-pressed to figure out how best to use them. Would it be in an ice cream, served with a syrupy reduction of pear cider? Or in a melt-in-your-mouth butter cookie? The nuts would make an intriguing addition to grain dishes, but I settled on this torte to showcase their special flavor. I serve it with softly whipped cream flavored with just a little ground espresso.

Use a full measure of hickory nuts, but if you can manage only a cup, then use unroasted almonds for the half cup. Their flavor will disappear behind the oilier, richer hickory nuts.

THE TORTE

1½ cups hickory nuts or 1 cup hickory
    nuts plus ½ cup almonds

½ cup all-purpose flour

¼ teaspoon sea salt

6 eggs, separated

½ teaspoon cream of tartar

1 cup sugar

1 teaspoon vanilla extract

2 tablespoons unsalted butter, melted
    and cooled

finely chopped hickory nuts plus finely
    ground espresso for garnish

THE ESPRESSO WHIPPED CREAM

1 cup heavy cream

½ teaspoon finely ground espresso
    coffee beans or 2 tablespoons
    cold brewed espresso

½ teaspoon vanilla extract

2 teaspoons sugar

1. Preheat the oven to 325°F. Butter and flour a 9-inch springform pan. Toast the hickory nuts in the oven just until you can smell them, about 7 minutes. Grind them with the unroasted almonds in a hand-cranked grater. This takes longer than a food processor but yields a delicate powder, which results in a lighter cake. Mix with the flour and half the salt and set aside.

2. Beat the egg whites with the remaining salt and the cream of tartar until they form soft peaks. Gradually add ½ cup of the sugar and continue beating until they crest into stiff peaks. Scrape them into a large bowl. Add the yolks to the mixing bowl and beat on high speed with the remaining sugar until thick and pale. Add the vanilla.

3. Pour the egg yolks over the whites and a quarter of the nuts. Fold partially, then add another quarter of the nuts and fold partially again. Continue until all the nuts are fully incorporated, then fold in the butter. Take care not to overmix and deflate the whites. Scrape the batter into the prepared pan, even the surface, and bake in the center of the oven until browned and slightly pulling away from the sides, about 1 hour. Cool, then remove the rim.

4. Whip the cream with the remaining ingredients until it forms soft, billowy peaks to spoon along each slice of cake. Alternatively, whip it a little stiffer then smooth it over the top and down the sides of the torte. Garnish with finely chopped hickory nuts and a light dusting of espresso.

HAZELNUT TORTE: Substitute hazelnuts for the hickory nuts in the cake. You can also use the hazelnut meal available from Holmquist Hazelnut Orchards in Washington. It is a by-product of their oil production, very fine and very flavorful. Reduce the flour to ¼ cup.

TORTE WITH APRICOT FILLING AND CHOCOLATE: Slice the cool cake in half and spread ½ cup Apricot-Lavender Refrigerator Jam, page 291, over the bottom layer. Cover with the second layer. Melt 3 ounces semisweet chocolate with 2 tablespoons unsalted butter over hot water, then pour it over the top layer and smooth it out with a spatula.

Hazelnut Crisps | MAKES 2 DOZEN

Fragile, crisp, and very good, these are perfect just as they are, but you can also drizzle them with melted chocolate.

1 cup toasted hazelnuts
1 tablespoon granulated sugar
½ cup (1 stick) unsalted butter
½ cup light brown sugar, packed
¼ teaspoon sea salt
1 teaspoon vanilla extract
1 egg yolk
1¼ cups all-purpose flour

1. Preheat the oven to 350°F. Grind the hazelnuts in a food processor with the granulated sugar until fine, but leave a few chunks scattered throughout.

2. Cream the butter and brown sugar with the salt until light and fluffy, then add the vanilla and egg yolk. Stir in the hazelnuts and the flour.

3. Roughly shape the dough into a log, wrap in wax paper or plastic wrap, then run the dough through your thumb and forefinger to force it into a log about 1½ inches in diameter. Keep it round or square the sides. Refrigerate for at least an hour, preferably longer.

4. Cut the log into ¼- to ⅓-inch-thick slices and place on ungreased sheet pans, leaving at least 2 inches between them. Bake until lightly browned on top, about 15 minutes. Cool on racks and store in a tightly covered container, high on a shelf unless you want to see them disappear.

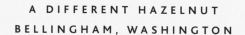

For several months now I've had three hazelnuts (also known as filberts) sitting on my desk. One is the usual-looking round hazelnut, one is the same shape only a lot larger, and the most interesting is the third, which is long rather than round, somewhat like an acorn. The first one I'd recognize anywhere, for it's the variety that's most common, the Barcelona. The second would surprise me by its sheer size if I didn't know it was an Ennis, which runs to XL. And I wouldn't even have guessed that the third was a hazelnut. But it is, and its name is Du Chilly.

I found this wonderful nut at the Bellingham, Washington, farmers' market. At the Holmquists' stand I wondered, What are these long nuts? A kind of almond? The young man who had his hands full selling bags of roasted hazelnuts dipped in Belgian chocolate explained that these were a special variety that his family grew. He was too busy to talk, but he said that we could visit the farm.

The next day Patrick and I drove up to the Canadian border. We met with the young man's uncle in the drying room, where huge vats of hazelnuts were gradually losing their moisture to 105-degree heat. We shouted at each other over the fans for a half hour, then escaped to the coolness and calm of the orchard. Long, even rows of shrubby hazelnut trees led off in all directions, a beautiful sight to view, even in the rain.

The Holmquists attribute much of their success to the Du Chilly hazelnut, which lacks the bitterness that is so often detected in the hazelnut skins. The difference was clearly detectable in side-by-side tastings of the three varieties. I have since cooked my way through a few pounds of Du Chillys and have never felt compelled to get rid of all of the skins before using them. In fact the skins tend to stay attached to the nuts, even after roasting.

Some of the Holmquists' nuts are made into a light but aromatic oil. It doesn't have the heft that oils made from roasted nuts do, but it does have the flavor. Its delicacy makes it quite nice to spoon over salads of pears, persimmons, and fennel or to drizzle into an artichoke soup. It's a lovely oil, and so is its by-product, a dark hazelnut meal. Nearly as fine as a flour and with the rich aroma of hazelnuts, this meal is perfect to use in a hazelnut torte or to add to tart crusts, crumbles, and crisp toppings.

A FALL MENU WITH A HAZELNUT THEME

Fall Fruit Salad with Pomegranate Vinaigrette, using hazelnuts and hazelnut oil (page 331)

Artichokes and Jerusalem Artichokes Braised with Black Lentils, seasoned with hazelnut oil and served with roast duck or wild rice (page 40)

Pear-Hazelnut Torte (page 326)

Chocolate-Flecked Hazelnut Rusks | MAKES 40 RUSKS

The dough will not taste sweet enough, but when the rusks have gone through their second baking, I think you'll find the sweetness is just right.

½ cup (1 stick) unsalted butter, at
    room temperature
¾ cup light brown sugar, packed
2 eggs
1 egg yolk
2 teaspoons vanilla extract
½ cup sour cream or crème fraîche
4 cups all-purpose flour
½ teaspoon sea salt
½ teaspoon baking soda
1 cup chopped roasted hazelnuts
1 cup chopped semisweet chocolate,
    such as Scharffen Berger

1. Preheat the oven to 325°F. Beat the butter and sugar until light and fluffy, then add the eggs and egg yolk one at a time, beating well after each addition. Next add the vanilla and sour cream and beat well.

2. Combine 1 cup of the flour with the salt and baking soda and add it to the batter. Add the remaining flour in 1-cup increments until the dough is stiff, then stir in the hazelnuts and chocolate. You may have to incorporate the last of the flour, nuts, and chocolate by hand.

3. Divide the dough into 6 pieces and roll into logs about 1½ inches across. Set on the sheet pans and bake until golden brown, about 40 minutes. Remove and slice each log diagonally about ½ inch thick. Place the pieces cut side down on the sheet pans and return them to the oven for another 30 minutes or until lightly browned. These will keep well for weeks, either in an airtight container or in the freezer.

Rustic Onion Tart with Market Cheese and Walnuts | MAKES 1 LARGE PAN PIZZA OR TWO 12-INCH PIZZAS

The tangier the better when it comes to the cheese, given the sweetness of the onions. The goat blue or goat's milk Brie from our market are both delicious here. Your market may have another interesting cheese. The inclusion of fresh walnuts makes this a pizza for early fall. Make the dough first so that it will be ready when the onions are.

Pizza Dough, page 386
3 tablespoons olive oil
3 pounds onions, thinly sliced
several thyme sprigs, leaves plucked
    and chopped
sea salt and freshly ground pepper
2 ounces local blue or Gorgonzola
    cheese, crumbled
4 walnuts, shelled and chopped
1 large handful small arugula leaves

1. Make the pizza dough. While it's rising, heat the oil in a Dutch oven over medium heat. Add the onions and two thirds of the thyme and toss to coat the onions with the oil. Cover and cook until lightly colored, stirring occasionally so they cook evenly, 30 to 40 minutes. Season well with salt and pepper.

2. Twenty minutes before it's time to bake the tart, preheat the oven to 450°F. Roll the dough into a thin rectangle just large enough to fill a 12x16-inch sheet pan or two 12-inch round pans. Cover it with the onions and bake for 12 minutes. Add the cheese and walnuts, and return the tart to the oven until the crust is crisp and the cheese is melted, about 10 minutes more. Remove, add the remaining thyme, and cover with the arugula. Cut into squares and serve.

Creamy Walnut Sauce | MAKES ABOUT ½ CUP

Combine walnuts with roasted walnut oil, and you'll have a silky rich sauce for foods such as giant heirloom beans, grilled eggplant and fennel, poached chicken, and fresh egg noodles. Make this just before serving since the walnut skins, even if you've removed most of them, will turn the sauce slightly pink.

1 slice sturdy white bread, crust removed

2 garlic cloves

sea salt and freshly ground pepper

½ cup freshly cracked walnuts

¼ cup walnut oil

2 tablespoons fresh lemon juice

boiling water as needed (about 1 cup)

1. Soak the bread in warm water until it's soft, then squeeze dry. Pound the garlic with ½ teaspoon salt in a mortar until smooth.

2. Using a food processor, grind the walnuts until smooth, then add the soaked bread, oil, and enough water to bring it to the consistency of thick cream.

3. Stir in the garlic, add lemon juice to taste, and season with pepper. The dressing will thicken as it sits. You can thin it by stirring in boiling water.

Rustic Almond Truffles with Fruit Centers | MAKES ABOUT THIRTY 1-INCH BALLS

These truffles get better with time, but make sure they're well wrapped so that they don't dry out.

1½ cups whole almonds, blanched

1 cup sugar, plus extra for rolling

¼ cup unsweetened cocoa powder

½ teaspoon almond extract

1 or 2 drops orange oil or

   1 tablespoon rum

30 pitted dried cherries or 30 small pieces candied citrus peel

1. Pulse the almonds with the sugar and cocoa in a food processor until the almonds are very finely ground. Transfer to a bowl and knead briefly, adding the almond extract and orange oil. Add water by teaspoons to make a stiff dough.

2. Scatter sugar over your counter, shape the dough into a disk, then coat with the sugar on both sides. (At this point you can wrap up the dough and refrigerate it until ready to use.)

3. Roll the dough into logs about an inch across, then slice into 1-inch pieces. Roll each piece into a ball. Insert a dried cherry or piece of candied citrus into the center of each. Roll the balls in the sugar and serve in paper candy cups.

Date, Dried Cherry, and Chocolate Nut Torte | MAKES ONE 9-INCH CAKE, SERVING 10 TO 12

This cake keeps so well that you can make it at least 3 days ahead. It's made with dates from the desert, dried cherries, pecans or walnuts, and chocolate. Serve it plain or garnished with softly whipped cream, Candied Kumquats (page 341), and leaves from the kumquats or mint leaves. I like to use Deglet Noor and Black Sphinx dates, which retain their shape and color, along with a few Medjools, which disappear into sweet, soft pockets.

1 cup Deglet Noor dates, pitted and
    snipped into 4 or 5 pieces each
½ cup Black Sphinx or Medjool dates
1 cup dried cherries
1 teaspoon baking soda
1 cup boiling water
¼ cup brandy
1⅓ cups all-purpose flour
¼ cup unsweetened cocoa powder
    (not Dutch process)
½ teaspoon sea salt
¾ cup (1½ sticks) unsalted butter,
    softened
¾ cup sugar
2 large eggs, at room temperature
1 teaspoon vanilla extract
1 teaspoon grated orange or
    tangerine zest
6 ounces bittersweet chocolate,
    coarsely chopped
¾ cup finely chopped pecans or
    walnuts
Brandy or orange liqueur, optional

1. Butter and flour a 9-inch springform pan. Preheat the oven to 375°F. Put the dates and cherries in a bowl with the baking soda. Pour the boiling water and brandy over them and mix together. In a separate bowl, whisk together the flour, cocoa, and salt.

2. Cream the butter with the sugar until light and smooth, then add the eggs one at a time, beating until well blended. Add the vanilla and orange zest. Add half the flour mixture and mix on low speed until combined. Add the date mixture, including the liquid. When combined, add the remaining flour mixture. Stir in the chocolate and nuts.

3. Scrape the batter into the prepared pan and smooth the top. Bake in the center of the oven until the top is firm, slightly rounded, and cracked, about 55 minutes. Let stand for 10 minutes in the pan on a rack, then run a knife around the sides to loosen the cake and remove the side. When cool, transfer the torte to a cake plate.

4. Serve with softly whipped cream flavored with brandy or orange liqueur. Or pipe rosettes of stiffer cream along the rim of the cake and place sections of Candied Kumquats and leaves between them.

Hollywood, Torrance, and San Francisco are a few of the markets where I've encountered this very seasonal treat, at least in the United States. You can find the same round, golden dates on their stems at markets all over the Mediterranean. Their moment is brief, spanning just a few weeks in late September and early October, when the date harvest is taking place in Palm Desert. At the same time, pistachio nuts are being harvested in their green stage, before they're completely dried. Both are moist and delicate and clearly of the moment only. A plate of fresh dates and green pistachio nuts make a very special fall dessert.

The dates are picked in the "rutab" stage, when they're ripe enough to no longer be astringent, but not so much that they've begun to cure. *Rutab* means "wet" in Arabic, and these dates are practically juicy. They burst in your mouth the way a liqueur-filled chocolate does, only they're far better. You can eat them when they're golden or tannish, but my own preference is to wait until these little morsels of sugar have begun to turn brown, then to eat them chilled, with a goat's or sheep's milk cheese—and a bowl of green pistachio nuts.

The green pistachio nuts are still in their husks, which are large and soft. When absolutely fresh, they are also gorgeous, blushed with pink and green. You peel off the husks, then open the cream-colored shell just as you would normally. The shells are almost soft and the nut meats are moist, with just a bit of a squeaky crunch and a delicate flavor that is reminiscent of pine. They are sold in net bags that hold about 3 pounds, which suggests feasting to me since they don't last. There's just a small window of time when green pistachios are available, so if you find some at your farmers' market, buy them as soon as you see them, and eat them sooner rather than later. Within days they'll lose their luster as the husks begin to shrivel and dry. But until then they're enchanting. Once this moment has passed, both the dates and nuts begin to dry on their trees, becoming, eventually, the nuts and fruits we're accustomed to seeing.

Farmers' markets are also where you can find, on occasion, such rarities as green walnuts and almonds, which are at the stage equivalent to that of the green pistachio nuts. As with the pistachios, the meats are soft and delicate. Both are a pleasure just to eat, and the green walnuts can be used to make the walnut liqueur called *nocino*.

Date and Orange Salad with Feta Cheese and Pistachios | SERVES 4

Deglet Noors are better known, but Medjools are among the most luscious of the moist eating dates, along with Empress and Honey dates. There are a lot of lively and contrasting elements in this salad—the cool sweetness of the orange, the salty cheese, the pickled onions, the lushness of the dates, and the crunch of pistachios.

finely grated zest of 1 orange

½ cup thinly sliced red onion

3 tablespoons white wine vinegar

6 large moist dates, such as Medjools

4 navel or blood oranges

1 head butter lettuce, trimmed

½ teaspoon sea salt

¼ teaspoon paprika

¼ teaspoon ground cumin

⅛ teaspoon ground coriander

¼ cup chopped cilantro

¼ cup olive oil

¼ cup roasted pistachio nuts or
    shelled green pistachios

2 ounces feta cheese, thinly sliced

freshly ground pepper

1. Toss the orange zest and onion with the vinegar and refrigerate while you assemble the remaining ingredients.

2. If the dates are hard, cover them with a hot damp towel for 5 minutes or longer, as needed, to soften. Remove the stones and quarter the dates lengthwise.

3. Section the oranges, working over a bowl to catch the juice (see page 389). Tear the lettuce into bite-sized pieces.

4. To make the vinaigrette, drain the vinegar from the onion into a measuring cup and add enough orange juice to make ¼ cup. (The rest of the juice is for the cook.) Stir in the salt, spices, cilantro, and oil. Taste for balance and add more vinegar if you think it needs to be sharper.

5. Toss the lettuce with the orange sections, onions, dates, pistachios, and dressing. Mound the salad on a platter, scatter the cheese over the top, season with pepper, and serve.

Adult Prune Whip | SERVES 6 TO 8

This old-fashioned dessert is upgraded to adult tastes. The prunes are simmered in red wine, then folded into whipped cream with a hint of tangerine and chopped bittersweet chocolate.

2 cups (¾ pound) pitted prunes
grated zest of 1 lemon and 1 tangerine
2 cups Zinfandel or Merlot
¼ cup light-bodied honey, such as orange or clover
1 (3-inch) cinnamon stick
1 cup whipping cream
½ cup chopped bittersweet chocolate
ground cinnamon

1. Preheat the oven to 350°F. Place the prunes in a baking dish with the lemon zest, wine, honey, and cinnamon stick. Cover with foil and bake until they're swollen and tender, about 30 minutes. Let stand, covered, until cooled, while the prunes continue to absorb the wine, then remove the cinnamon stick and coarsely puree in a food processor with any residual juices.
2. Whip the cream until fairly stiff. Fold in the prunes along with the tangerine zest and chocolate, leaving the mix a little streaky. Spoon the prune whip into parfait glasses; add a dash of cinnamon and serve.

Upside-Down Cake with Mixed Dried Fruits | SERVES 8

Geri Bogdanich, whose family specializes in fruits and nuts, sells bags of succulent mixed dried stone fruits at various markets in California. The Peacock family sells gorgeous, unsulphured Red Flame raisins that dry to sundry shades of red and gold to nearly black. Most fruit growers are likely to add dried fruits to fresh as a way of expanding their markets. Drying also allows fruit farmers to take advantage of bumper crops too large to sell fresh.

The dried apricots, nectarines, peaches, pears, plums, pluots, and prunes you'll find at farmers' markets are translucent jewels of the winter pantry. Mixed dried fruits, from the largest to the smallest, cook into stunning compotes. Drained of their juices, they can be used to make the prettiest upside-down cakes. A handful of dried cherries, Red Flame raisins, or cranberries and blueberries from northern and eastern markets perfectly fills the niches left between the larger fruits. This cake is delicious served with Bitter Almond Ice Cream (page 298).

THE FRUIT AND THE TOPPING

2⅓ cups dried fruits (see headnote)

3 tablespoons unsalted butter

¾ cup light brown sugar, packed

1. Put all the fruit in a saucepan, cover with water, and bring to a boil. Simmer, partially covered, until the fruit is plump and soft, about 30 minutes. Drain and set aside.

2. Melt the butter in a 10-inch cast-iron skillet, then whisk in the sugar. When it has softened, turn off the heat and allow the syrup to settle evenly over the bottom. Arrange the fruits attractively over the top, the cut sides facing up. If some pieces are very large, you might cut them into halves or quarters so that the cake will be easy to slice.

THE CAKE

½ cup (1 stick) unsalted butter

¾ cup sugar

1½ teaspoons vanilla extract

⅛ teaspoon almond extract

2 large eggs, at room temperature

1 cup buttermilk

1¾ cups all-purpose flour

1 teaspoon baking soda

1 teaspoon baking powder

½ teaspoon sea salt

1. Preheat the oven to 375°F. Beat the butter with the sugar until light and fluffy, then add the flavorings and the eggs, one at a time, and beat until thoroughly smooth. Scrape down the bowl between additions, then add the buttermilk.

2. In another bowl, sift or whisk the dry ingredients together so that they are combined evenly. With the mixer on low, add them to the batter in 3 or 4 separate additions.

3. Spoon the batter over the fruit, then bake in the center of the oven until the cake is golden and starting to pull away from the sides, about 35 minutes. Cool for 5 minutes, then place a serving plate over the skillet, grasp both together, and flip them over. Remove the skillet. Serve while still a bit warm or when fully cooled.

Chicken Thighs Braised with Dried Fruits, Shallots, and Bay | SERVES 4

Dried figs, apricots, pluots, dates, and raisins are all good fruits to use with moist chicken thighs. Here, the jeweled colors and tartness of dried pluots, a plum-apricot cross, balance the sweetness and soft texture of the dates.

8 plump chicken thighs

sea salt and freshly ground pepper

3 tablespoons olive oil

10 bay leaves

4 large shallots, cut into ¼-inch rounds

⅔ cup red wine

3 tablespoons aged red wine vinegar

4 dates, halved

8 dried apricots, plums, or pluots, halved or quartered

1. Trim the fat from the chicken and remove the skins if you wish. Rinse and pat them dry. Season well with salt and pepper.

2. Place a Dutch oven or wide skillet over medium-high heat. Add 2 tablespoons of the oil and, when hot, add the chicken and the bay leaves. Cook until browned, 7 to 10 minutes per side. Add ½ cup water, reduce the heat to low, and cover the pan. Cook for 30 minutes for small thighs, up to 45 minutes for larger ones.

3. Transfer the chicken thighs to a platter. Reserve any juices.

4. Return the pan to the stove and turn the heat to medium-high. Add the remaining 1 tablespoon oil to the pan along with the shallots. Cook, stirring frequently, until they begin to soften and color a little, about 2 minutes, then add the wine and vinegar. Scrape the pot to bring up the delicious dark bits, then return the chicken to the pan, add the fruit, and return the reserved liquid. Simmer for 12 to 15 minutes. Serve with rice, couscous, or egg noodles.

Chicken Braised in Red Wine Vinegar | SERVES 4 TO 6

When I found Mr. Sciabica's aged red wine vinegar at the Modesto farmers' market, I didn't hesitate to buy a gallon. A gallon may seem like a lot, but this recipe uses an entire cup, and you may find this is a recipe you'll want to make often—it's a great winter dish. If you can make it at least a few hours ahead of time—even a day—the vinegar and tomato settle into a harmonious companionship. Delicious with egg noodles or polenta.

1 large chicken, cut up, back
    and neck reserved
1 slice onion
2 bay leaves
sea salt and freshly ground pepper
2 tablespoons olive oil
1 cup aged red wine vinegar
1½ tablespoons honey
1½ cups Fresh Tomato Sauce, page 391,
    or canned crushed tomatoes
2 tablespoons unsalted butter
2 tablespoons chopped parsley

1. Put the chicken back and neck in a saucepan and add water to cover, the onion, and a bay leaf. Bring to a boil, then lower the heat and simmer to make a little stock while you prepare the dish. Rinse the chicken, pat dry, and season well with salt and pepper.

2. Heat the oil in a Dutch oven over medium-high heat. Add the chicken and brown, turning the pieces so that both sides color well. Transfer the chicken to a plate and pour off the fat.

3. Return the pan to the heat and gradually pour in the vinegar. Scrape the bottom, then add the other bay leaf and the honey. Return the chicken to the pot and simmer until the vinegar has reduced enough that there are fine bubbles pebbling the surface, about 20 minutes. Turn the chicken once or twice as it's cooking.

4. Strain the stock and measure 1 cup. Add it to the pan with the tomato sauce, then lower the heat to a simmer, cover the pan, and cook until the chicken is tender, about 25 minutes. Transfer the chicken to a platter and whisk the butter into the simmering sauce. Taste for salt. Pour the sauce over the chicken or return the chicken to the pot and serve, the parsley scattered over the top.

Rusty Hall is so well known for the high quality of his dry-farmed almonds that he has been profiled in *Gourmet*. "But I could never make it on my almonds alone," Rusty tells me, "so we make brittle, almond butter, and other products." Doing so allows him to use what would be culls, the broken pieces that won't sell at the market, which are perfectly fine for the brittle and butters. "Customers buy some brittle, take it home and eat it, then call and order more."

Rusty may sell his almond brittle all over the world, but the farmers' market is where customers encounter a product for the first time. A farmer who can sell through the mail as well as at the market can begin to work toward having year-round income. Maintaining any kind of cash flow is a big problem for seasonal farmers, which is why, like poets and painters, so many of our small family farmers have second jobs.

"Having value-added foods," says apple grower Kathy Reid, "enables us to extend our season. We can show up at the market with our apple butter long before our apples are ready. By the time the apples come on, people know who we are." Like Rusty, having value-added products gives Kathy a way to use those fruits that aren't perfect enough to sell fresh at the market. The hole made in an apple by a bird's beak, a scar made by hail, or checkering on the skin of a date is a blemish that can disqualify fruits and vegetables for many customers, even though the food is far from ruined.

Having products to sell not only puts the farmer in the market early in the season but puts the market itself at the beginning of the distribution chain, instead of at the end of it. "Farmers arrive with full trucks and, if all goes well, go home with empty ones," says Rusty. "So I try to take advantage of the situation to buy the foods I need for my produc-tion, such as honey, from other vendors at the market." His truck goes home full, and he supports his fellow farmers.

All those apple butters, jams and jellies, almond brittle, and other food products have to be produced in certified kitchens, a requirement that can present a serious financial obstacle to many farmers. But there are various creative ways to satisfy the state. "You know, another endangered business is the small, family-owned café," Rusty points out, something I've noticed, too, as I've crisscrossed the country by car. "So instead of building our own kitchen, we've teamed up with a café that we can use during their slow hours. That way, we both benefit."

Value-added products help make a market more diverse and dynamic, and they also give tourists, who increasingly are visiting farmers' markets when they travel, something they can carry home—a bag of almonds, a jar of goat's milk caramel, a cheese, some special dried fruits, or preserves. They can enjoy them later, a souvenir of a place they enjoyed being for a morning, or give them to friends—gifts from places they've been. These are gestures that help return America to a place of regional distinctions, instead of a place of dreary sameness. And they help the farmer stay in business.

"Small family farming will survive only if there's hope for young farmers." Rusty is fervent about this. "Having something to sell—other than perishable produce—is essential for creating farm income. Adding value to what you grow brings what would be off-farm income back to the farm, and it gets the farm family out of the dirt-working conditions into other skills. Value added is the last best hope for the family farm."

Honey Ice Cream | MAKES ABOUT 3½ CUPS

I find I like honey best when it's really featured, as it is in this ice cream, so there's no vanilla or spice to interfere with its flavor. But all kinds of fruits are wonderful served alongside, such as ripe figs, white peaches and nectarines, the plum compote on page 293, fresh berries, or the Warm Berry Compote on page 265. If your market has milk, cream, and eggs as well as honey, this ice cream will brim with over-the-top goodness.

1½ cups whole milk

⅔ cup honey, your favorite

4 egg yolks

pinch sea salt

1 cup cream

1. Heat the milk with the honey until nearly boiling, then turn off the heat. Stir to make sure the honey has dissolved.

2. Beat the egg yolks with the salt vigorously for 30 seconds, then slowly whisk in the hot milk and honey. Scrape everything back into the pot in which the milk was heated. Rinse out the bowl, place a strainer over it, and set it near the stove.

3. Cook the eggs and milk over medium heat, stirring constantly, until the mixture thickens enough to coat the back of a wooden spoon, after several minutes. Don't let it boil, or the eggs will curdle. As soon as it has thickened, pour the custard through the strainer. Stir in the cream and refrigerate until cold. Freeze according to the instructions of your ice cream maker.

HONEY-NUT SUNDAE: Drizzle warm honey over the ice cream and top with roasted nuts—almonds, hickory nuts, pecans, or chopped hazelnuts.

Rice Pudding with Honey Meringues | SERVES 6 TO 8

A creamy, stove-top rice pudding is an excellent showcase for honey, maple syrup, and molasses. To me it's sweet enough with just the honey, but one tester suggested that might be a bit austere for others. Add the sugar if you wish. If your honey is very dense or crystallized, return it to its liquid state by heating the jar in a pan of simmering water. I especially like this made with lavender honey, then garnished with lavender blossoms.

1 cup Arborio or other short-grain rice

3 cups whole milk or 2 percent milk

¼ teaspoon sea salt

2 to 4 tablespoons sugar, optional

1 (3-inch) cinnamon stick

1 tablespoon grated orange zest

1 vanilla bean, slit in half lengthwise

2 eggs, separated

½ cup honey or maple syrup

ground cinnamon

1. Simmer the rice in 2½ cups water for 15 minutes. Add the milk, salt, sugar to taste if using, cinnamon stick, zest, and vanilla bean. Bring to a boil, then simmer, stirring occasionally, for 30 minutes, by which time most of the milk will be absorbed. Remove the vanilla bean, scrape the seeds into the pudding, and stir in the egg yolks.

2. Whip the egg whites until they form soft peaks. Pour in the honey with the machine on medium speed, then raise the speed to high and whisk until a creamy, dense meringue is formed. Fold the meringue into the hot rice until it's broken up into little clouds. Serve with a dusting of cinnamon and extra honey drizzled over the top.

Roasted Chestnuts

The American chestnut is back! Fans should be happy to know that a few farmers around the country are growing them. But we should also be happy, because buying fresh chestnuts eliminates the inevitable disappointment that comes from buying expensive, poor-quality imports. In fairness, they may not have started out as poor-quality nuts, but poor storage makes them end up that way.

"A chestnut is not a true nut," explained Tim Broughton, a grower of chestnuts in Auburn, California. On a cold January morning we stood close to the burning piles of chestnut leaves in his orchard. Every so often a stray chestnut would explode, and Tim would fish it out of the fire, peel it, and offer it to me. They were shockingly good. "Unlike nuts," he continued, "chestnuts should not be kept in a dry atmosphere. In a store, they should be kept right next to the lettuce and sprayed just as often. And at home," Tim advises, "wrap them in a damp towel, then put them in a plastic bag in the refrigerator. This way they'll stay moist and soft inside." This one piece of information makes all the difference between ending up with a nutmeat that's moist and succulent and one that's desiccated.

On any Sunday winter morning, Tim can be found at Sacramento's W Street market, tossing his chestnuts in a big, perforated pan. Back and forth they slide over the flames of his gas burner. The smoky smell entices the customers. They pop open and he passes them around. Then the chestnuts fly out of the bins into shopping bags. Once you've got the chestnuts, you need a method. Here's Tim's.

1. Cut an X on one side of the chestnut so it won't explode once it heats up. Put ¼ cup water in a small saucepan and as many chestnuts as desired. Bring to a boil, then cover and steam for approximately 3 minutes.

2. Put the steamed chestnuts in an *old* pan with a screen (or a perforated woklike pan) and heat it over a gas or wood fire until the chestnuts are blackened. This gives them a roasted flavor and will make your house smell good.

3. Remove the shell and the skin while the chestnuts are still hot. If you wait too long, the skin will start to stick to the meat, making it very hard to peel. If you have any problem peeling the chestnuts, you can cut them in half and scoop them out with a spoon or reheat them and try again.

Florida, Arizona, California, and Texas are obvious places to find winter markets. But Maine? There are two farmers who are growing beautiful organic produce on what I've heard referred to as "the back side of the season," which they sell in local stores.

When October 1 arrives and those farmers who worked hard all summer are cleaning up and looking forward to letting down for the winter, Eliot Coleman and Barbara Damrosch are just starting their six-month season. These two are dedicated winter farmers, and their stellar produce is every bit as delicious and fetching as summer produce. And it's in great demand. They don't have asparagus and artichokes in March like every supermarket, but it's amazing what they do have. "And," Eliot says, "we're just scratching the surface of what we plan to do next year."

They have greens: turnip, arugula, spinach, chard, mâche, watercress, Belgian endive. And they have roots: turnips, beets, *scorzonera* (a black-skinned oyster plant), parsley root, and scallions. Slides I've seen of their winter harvest from other years depict luscious red radishes, carrots, and celery root. Their carrots are apparently so sweet that kids in town carry on active lunchtime trading for them. I've eaten one of Eliot's winter-harvested parsnips, and it was, hands down, one of the best vegetables I've eaten, ever.

Even though their list is relatively small, it suggests a lot of possibilities in the kitchen. I can see a beet salad with mâche or arugula (both are excellent with beets); a fortifying winter soup made with the chard, turnip greens, radish greens, scallions, and that clean-tasting parsley root; while the *scorzonera* would make a comforting chowder. The turnips might be cooked, tossed with butter, and served on a bed of wilted turnip greens. Or you could use all the roots to make a vegetable ragout or borscht. A mound of watercress showered with slivered endive makes a beautiful winter salad. The possibilities are less limiting than we might have thought at first.

Eliot likes to say that you're eating locally when you can eat from your landscape. The average distance supermarket produce travels is fifteen hundred miles, "but we sell to stores and restaurants in a fifteen-mile radius of our farm," Eliot says. "It's our way of guaranteeing that it is fresh." Barbara and Eliot's mottoes are "From field to shelf in under twelve" and "From farm to store in twenty-four." "It depends on whether we're delivering the same day or the next," Eliot explains.

As hard as it is to imagine winter gardening in Maine, it might be even harder to imagine a thriving winter market in Chicago with its winter storms and arctic winds. But there is one, a brave new market started two years ago by cookbook author Abby Mandel, with Sara Stegner, chef of the Ritz Carlton, and other Chicago chefs (members of the Chefs' Collaborative) who wanted to see a real farmers' market in their city. "This has been the most difficult and most rewarding project I've ever undertaken" is how Abby describes the experience, a sentiment firmly echoed by Sara.

While their summer success is understandable, their willingness to continue into winter raises the questions of how and why. "I just hated to lose that momentum," Abby says, "plus we wanted to give Chicagoans a real taste of our true seasonality." And on one January day, this farmers' market had just what you might expect for winter—food that's been cellared, coddled in greenhouses, baked, smoked, or otherwise preserved—but much more variety than you might have expected.

Baby lettuce and arugula were there along with heirloom potatoes, dried wild mushrooms, carrots, two kinds of beets, and honey. From nearby Wisconsin came several kinds of turnips and rutabagas, black radishes, red and yellow onions, winter squash, and those sturdy reliables, parsnips, celeriac, and burdock. Another Wisconsin farmer brought a German beer radish, garlic, and Jerusalem artichokes.

Then there was the meat: venison, elk, veal, chicken, and rabbit. One farm offered bacon, smoked hams, pork chops, roasts, and smoked ham hocks. There were eggs for your breakfast and Michigan maple syrup for your pancakes. There were eight kinds of rustic hearth breads made with organic flour. Eleven kinds of cheeses showed up from, not surprisingly, Wisconsin. So, when you imagine all the different meals that could be made from this one market, you can see that even in winter it's possible to eat locally—and well.

AN ALL-VEGETABLE MEAL FOR WINTER

Radish Sandwiches with Radish Butter (page 51)

Green Herb Soup with Sorrel and Lovage (page 7)

Priest Stranglers (Strozzapreti) with Black Kale, Sage, and Potatoes (page 101)

Grated carrots, celery root, and beets with mâche and Shallot Vinaigrette (page 392)

Date, Dried Cherry, and Chocolate Nut Torte (page 371)

A Basic Vegetable Stock | MAKES ABOUT 6 CUPS

In previous books I've gone into vegetable stock making in great detail, so I won't do it again here. (See *The Greens Cookbook, The Savory Way,* or *Vegetarian Cooking for Everyone*.) Here is a basic approach to making a light vegetable stock that can be made while you're gathering other ingredients for your dish.

1 onion and/or 1 to 2 cups leeks
   trimmings (roots and inner leaves)

2 carrots

2 celery ribs with leaves

2 bay leaves

8 parsley stems

a few thyme sprigs or pinches leaves

4 garlic cloves

1½ teaspoons sea salt

1. Chop everything roughly into large, bite-sized pieces. In addition to the basic ingredients, include clean trimmings from the vegetables you're using in your soup, risotto, or whatever you're making, such as celery root skins, mushrooms stems, squash seeds, corncobs, zucchini ends, tomato cores, chard stems, or bell pepper cores. (Avoid strong, aggressive vegetables such as mustard greens, turnips, and parsnips.) Add these trimmings to the stock as you do your cutting and slicing. If the recipe calls for an herb, add a few sprigs to the stock as well. The more vegetable matter you use, the more flavor.

2. For a light stock, bring the vegetables, 2 quarts cold water, and the salt to a boil. Reduce the heat and simmer for 25 to 40 minutes. For a slightly more robust stock, sauté the vegetables in a tablespoon of olive or vegetable oil first to brown them, which gives color as well as flavor to the stock, then add the water and salt. When the stock is done, strain it immediately. If you want to reduce it further, do so after straining.

Pizza Dough | MAKES TWO 12-INCH ROUND PIZZAS OR ONE 12 X 16-INCH PIZZA

1¼ cups warm water
1 scant tablespoon active dry yeast
pinch sugar
3 cups all-purpose flour, or more as needed
1 teaspoon sea salt
1 tablespoon olive oil

1. Put the warm water in a mixing bowl and stir in the yeast, sugar, and 1 cup of the flour. Set aside until foamy, 20 to 30 minutes. Lightly oil a clean bowl for the dough.

2. Stir in the salt and oil, then start stirring in the flour until the dough is fairly stiff. When too stiff to stir, turn it out onto a lightly floured counter and knead until the dough is smooth and shiny, about 10 minutes. Add more flour as needed. Put the dough in the oiled bowl, turn once to coat, cover with plastic wrap, and set aside to rise until doubled in bulk, about an hour.

3. For pizzas, divide into 2 or 4 pieces, shape loosely into balls, then roll out into thin circles. For one large rustic tart, roll into a large thin rectangle and bake it on a sheet pan.

Galette Pastry | MAKES 1 LARGE RUSTIC TART

1½ cups all-purpose flour
¼ teaspoon sea salt
2 teaspoons sugar
½ cup plus 2 tablespoons (1¼ sticks) cold unsalted butter, cut into small chunks
½ teaspoon vanilla extract
⅓ cup ice water, plus extra, if needed

Mix the flour, salt, and sugar together in a bowl. Cut in the butter by hand or use a mixer with the paddle attachment, leaving some of the butter in large pea-size chunks. Sprinkle the vanilla over the top, then the ice water by tablespoonfuls, and lightly work it with the flour mixture until you can bring the dough together into a ball. Gently press the dough into a disk, slip it into a clean plastic bag, and refrigerate for at least 15 minutes before rolling it out.

Pie
Dough | MAKES ENOUGH FOR TWO 9-INCH PIES, ONE 10-INCH PIE
WITH DOUBLE OR LATTICE CRUST, OR 1 LARGE GALETTE

After watching baker Greg Patent make pie dough for his huckleberry pie (page 264) in a food processor, I'm convinced it's the way to go. If you don't want your dough enriched with egg yolk, leave it out and replace it with water.

2¼ cups all-purpose flour
½ teaspoon sea salt
¾ cup (1½ sticks) plus 2 tablespoons
    unsalted butter
½ teaspoon vinegar
1 egg yolk
scant ½ cup ice water

1. Place the flour in a food processor with the salt and pulse. Cut the butter into 1-inch chunks and add them to the flour. Pulse 4 to 6 times to break them up.

2. Combine the vinegar and egg yolk in a measuring cup and add enough ice water to bring the volume up to ½ cup. (You may not need to use all of the liquid, unless your flour is very dry.) While pulsing, add the liquid in a steady stream until the flour looks crumbly and damp. Between 25 and 30 pulses should be enough. Don't let the dough form a ball. The crumbs should adhere when you gather them in your hand. If not, add a few more drops of ice water.

3. Turn out the dough and divide it into 2 pieces, one slightly larger than the other. Wrap each piece in plastic wrap and press it into a disk. Refrigerate for 30 minutes to an hour before rolling.

4. Roll the larger piece out first and drape it into your pie plate. Add the filling.

5. Roll out the second piece of dough. If you intend to have a solid crust top, roll the dough into a circle that will just fit over the filling, then roll the outer edge of dough over the top and crimp it firmly. If making a lattice crust, roll it out somewhat larger and then cut into strips of whatever width appeals to you. Lay half the strips over the filling in one direction; the rest in the other direction. Press the ends into the edge, then roll over the excess dough from the first piece and crimp.

Tart Shell | MAKES ONE 9-INCH TART

1 cup plus 2 tablespoons all-purpose
   flour
⅛ teaspoon sea salt
1 teaspoon sugar
½ cup (1 stick) unsalted butter, in
   chunks
½ teaspoon vanilla extract mixed with
   2 to 3 tablespoons ice water

1. Using a mixer with a paddle attachment or a food processor, blend the flour, salt, and sugar, then work in the butter until coarse crumbs are formed. Add the vanilla with just enough water for the dough to come together, then shape it into a disk. Slip it into a plastic bag and chill for 15 minutes.

2. Roll the dough into a 10-inch circle and drape it over a 9-inch tart pan with a removable rim. Work the edges with your fingers so that the dough stands about ¼ inch above the rim and is about ¼ inch thick. Prick the bottom with a fork in 6 or 7 places, then freeze for 20 minutes while you preheat the oven to 425°F. Save any scraps.

3. Place the frozen tart shell on a sheet pan and bake until it's lightly colored, about 25 minutes. Check after 15 minutes and prick any swollen pockets of dough with the tip of a knife. When the tart comes out of the oven, mend any holes by carefully pressing in small pieces of the reserved scraps.

Simple Syrup | MAKES 2 CUPS

A clear syrup of sugar and water, simple syrup is useful to have on hand for sweetening fruit drinks, such as lemonade and *agua frescas*. The advantage of using syrup over sugar is that you needn't wait for sugar to dissolve to find out if it's sweet enough—you'll know as soon as you stir it in, which means you can start with a little and work up to the right amount. It keeps indefinitely in the refrigerator.

Simple syrup is also used to sweeten very thick fruit purees intended for sorbets, for it thins the purees while sweetening them.

2 cups water
2 cups sugar

Put the water and the sugar in a clean pot and heat until the sugar is completely dissolved and the liquid is clear. Let it cool, then decant into a jar. Store in the cupboard or refrigerator.

Peeling and Sectioning Citrus Fruit

You can use this method for any citrus fruit, from a lemon to a pummelo. Cut a slice off each of the polar ends so that the fruit will stand straight on the counter. Using a sharp knife and a sawing motion, work your way down the contours of the fruit. Be sure that you're cutting deeply enough to take off the white pith that lies just over the flesh. When done, trim the peel off the base.

To cut the peeled fruit into sections, hold it in your hand over a bowl. Using a sharp knife, cut between the membranes to release the segments. When done, squeeze what's left in your hand—there's usually lots of juice in it—over the segments.

Trimming Artichokes

Whether using large ones or the "babies," remove several layers of the tough outer leaves by pulling them downward so that they snap off at the base. Stop when the inner leaves become a lighter yellowish green and have a tender appearance. Trim the end of the stem and slice off the top third of the artichoke. Smooth the rough areas around the base with a paring knife, removing any dark green parts. If the recipe calls for it, cut the trimmed artichoke into quarters, then remove the fuzzy chokes with a paring knife.

So-called baby artichokes are small because they grow in the shade of the leaves. They usually don't have a significant choke. Once trimmed, they can be cooked whole or sliced lengthwise.

While it's commonly suggested that you rub the cut surfaces of the artichoke with a lemon to keep them from oxidizing, I usually don't bother. By the time the artichoke is cooked, its color will have evened out into a uniform dull green. If you've added enough lemon to keep the artichoke pale, it will also taste lemony.

When working with artichokes, always use a stainless-steel knife and a stainless-steel or glass pot. Iron and aluminum, including aluminum foil, discolor artichokes.

Roasting and Peeling Peppers

Choose peppers with thick walls if you want to char the skins. Thin-walled peppers need to be watched very carefully and roasted only long enough to loosen the skins, not char them, or the flesh will be consumed along with the skin.

On the burner: Place whole peppers directly on a gas burner or gas or charcoal grill. Those with electric burners can use an *asador* (or its equivalent), a small-mesh grill that sits right over the element. Roast the peppers until the skin becomes wrinkled and loose, turning them frequently with tongs. For peppers that will end up soft and slightly smoky, roast them until the skins are completely charred. Put the peppers in a bowl, put a plate on top, and set aside to steam for at least 15 minutes to loosen the skins.

In the oven: If you want to peel the peppers without cooking them too much, the oven is a better way to go: Cut off the tops of the peppers, then slice them in half lengthwise, remove the seeds and veins, and press down on each half to flatten. Brush the skins with oil, then set them skin side up on a sheet pan. Bake at 400°F or broil 5 or 6 inches under the heating element until the skins are wrinkled but not charred, 10 to 20 minutes. Remove and stack the peppers on top of each other to steam for 15 minutes. (Use any of the delicious juice that collects from the steaming peppers in the finished dish or use it in vinaigrette.)

Next, slip off the skins with your hand or a paper towel. Don't worry about getting every little fleck of skin. Now they're ready to use.

Fresh Tomato
Sauce | MAKES ABOUT 2½ CUPS

At the height of tomato season, when tomatoes with cracks or other flaws are available at a discounted price, use them to make this sauce. It takes little time to make if you've got a food mill, and you'll be happy to find it in your freezer during the winter. It also makes a vibrant fresh sauce for a pound of linguine.

3 pounds ripe tomatoes, rinsed and quartered

3 tablespoons torn basil leaves or 1 tablespoon chopped marjoram, optional

sea salt and freshly ground pepper

2 tablespoons extra virgin olive oil

1. Put the tomatoes in a heavy pan with the herb, if using. Cover and cook over medium-high heat. The tomatoes should yield their juices right away, but keep an eye on the pan to make sure that they do. Add a few tablespoons of water if necessary. You don't want scorched tomatoes.

2. Once the tomatoes have broken down, after 15 to 25 minutes, pass them through a food mill. If you want the final sauce to be thicker, return it to the pot and cook over low heat, stirring frequently, until it's as thick as you want. Depending on the juiciness of the tomatoes, this could take 20 minutes or as long as an hour. When done, season with salt and pepper to taste and stir in the oil.

3. To freeze, ladle the sauce into freezer bags in 1- or 2-cup portions. Lay the bags on the freezer floor until they harden. This makes slim packages that are easy to store upright. When you reheat the sauce, you can season it with crushed garlic, pepper flakes, shallots, or whatever herb goes with the dish you're making.

Two Vinaigrettes: Shallot and Garlic

Although it's not difficult to play around with vinaigrettes, I find that I've settled on 2 favorite standards, one that's studded with vinegary shallots and the other made pungent with garlic. When it comes to oil and vinegar, there isn't any absolute proportion since different vinegars (and lemon) vary in acidity and one's personal taste has as much to do with the right proportion as anything else. I never like to choke on a too-tart dressing, while others crave a heavy dousing of vinegar. If you like the 3-to-1 concept, you can start with that, but you'll have to taste it, preferably on a lettuce leaf or piece of fruit that's to be dressed, to be sure it's right for you.

SHALLOT VINAIGRETTE

1 shallot, peeled and finely diced

2 tablespoons red wine vinegar or
    champagne vinegar

½ teaspoon sea salt

6 tablespoons or more extra virgin
    olive oil

Finely dice the shallot by slicing it first lengthwise, then crosswise. It should fall into a fine dice without your having to mash it through rough chopping. Put it into a bowl with the vinegar and salt. Let stand for 10 minutes, then whisk in the oil to taste.

GARLIC VINAIGRETTE

1 crisp new garlic clove

sea salt and freshly ground pepper

2 tablespoons aged red wine vinegar

1 teaspoon balsamic vinegar

6 to 8 tablespoons extra virgin
    olive oil

Peel and coarsely chop the garlic. Pound it in a mortar with a scant ½ teaspoon salt until puree-smooth. This should take about 30 seconds. Stir in the vinegars, then whisk in the oil, tasting after 6 tablespoons. Season with pepper.

Epilogue
Time Passing at the Market

November 1, and it's the last market. It is bitter cold, as it always is on this market day. The sky is a blue blaze, but it's also windy, which makes the cold even more intense. The farmers are bundled up, and the shade covers are gone. Everyone replies to "How are you?" with "Cold!" After a while it will be too commonplace to mention, but today it's a kind of acknowledgment that winter is here. Farmers and customers chat, recalling that last year at this time there was snow and sleet. Another year it was so cold that the greens froze before our eyes, while on yet other last days the market has been protected by an insulating blanket of low clouds.

Since this is the last market, good-byes are spoken. The farmers are tired and glad that it's time to stop. The few remaining customers are buying to make the season last a bit longer at home. They load up on apples, bags of pinto beans, heirloom potatoes, quarts of frozen apple juice, ground chile, honey and jams. In spite of this being the last market, one grower has arrived with a gorgeous new collection of chicories that the cold weather has nursed into their prime, and another has arrived with Chinese dates, or jujubes, of all things.

In many ways this market resembles the first markets six months ago, which featured wintered-over apples and potatoes, roots, hearty greens, and dried legumes. The goat cheese, lamb, and chicken vendors are all here, as they were in the beginning and on every other market day. The cold, coupled with the fact that it's the last market, calls for a hearty supper to celebrate another successful season. And that's what we have.

MENU FOR THE END OF THE MARKET

Borscht: The Ultimate Root Soup (page 200)

Lamb Shanks Braised with Onions and Rosemary (page 80)

Rutabaga and Potato Puree (page 216)

Salad of winter greens

Spiced Quinces in Syrup (page 317)
with Quince Ice Cream (page 315)

With coffee: Chocolate-Flecked Hazelnut Rusks (page 368)

It's perhaps only at the farmers' market or in one's own garden that we become acutely aware of the movement of the seasons and the motion of time. Less than we thought can be taken for granted. Foods that we think of as ever present, like radishes and lettuce, vanish as soon as the weather turns hot. Others, like eggs, taper off as the daylight shortens. In less than five minutes, a passing hailstorm shreds the greens we were just figuring out how to use and sets a farmer back six weeks. Birds finish the last of the cherries we were counting on for the Fourth of July, while later, frost might rob from us the pleasure of late-season tomatoes and plans for a winter supply of sauce. There's a constant ebb and flow in produce, the passage from tender newness to seasoned roughness in vegetables, from tartness to sweetness in fruits, from scarcity to plenty and scarcity again as the season moves on.

Time in the market is measured not only in fruits and vegetables but by their growers too. After over a dozen years of shopping at my market, I've become well accustomed to the faces I see twice each week. I look forward to seeing them each season. Some farmers have been selling since the market started nearly thirty years ago, but some are new to the market, young couples with a small child or two or parents with older children who are now taking an active role in running the family business. One family, who always had the biggest display of vegetables, sells much less. I've watched another farmer who started out with fairly unattractive produce grow his skills so that he now produces beautiful organic vegetables in abundance. A mother-daughter team known for their unusual varieties of eggplants and tomatoes barely came to market during the two years that it didn't warm up in time to ripen their crops. When they returned, the next hot summer, the daughter's children seemed years older already, and of course they were.

The composition of the farmers, like their produce, is fluid and changing. People who once seemed like fixtures at the market are now retired or taking a break from farming to finish that novel, or maybe they're taking some time off to make some money doing something else. After several hard drought years combined with the water politics in our state, an excellent farmer threw in the towel, citing fatigue. It's a big loss to our market. Hopefully his farm will be sold to a new farmer with a fresh vision and energy to match, but I notice in the real estate magazine an ad that reads, like too many others, "Beautiful farm for sale; can be subdivided."

Although for most Americans where food comes from is a vague concept that's not geographically set in the mind, food doesn't come from "somewhere else"; it comes from someplace. When a farm is "developed," we town and city dwellers, as well as the farmers, lose the tie to the land that nourishes us. We also lose the security that comes from knowing that we can eat from our landscape and not have to depend on large and ultimately unsustainable food systems. As American Farmland Trust says on its bumper stickers, "No Farms, No Food." It's ultimately that simple.

Changes in the market can also mean that sometimes a food you've grown to love and whose season you've always looked forward to may not be there when a farmer moves, cuts back, quits, or decides to give up on growing that variety for something more reliable. Or a state's government may proclaim the fresh eggs and pastured chicken you've come to love as "biological hazards" and banish their presence. This has happened. In this sense, supply on a local level is more fragile than it appears, for it's intimately tied to people's lives. Just as fruits and vegetables pass through their season, the farmers we have seen at the market standing at their tables year after year pass through theirs. They will not always be here, and this realization makes the experience of the market all that more immediate.

We need to use our markets deeply if farmers are to continue to farm and we are to continue to eat well in the deepest sense, being nourished by our immediate landscape and community. How fortunate that meeting this need is one of the most pleasurable obligations we can assign ourselves.

Resources
Sources for Some Foods Referred to in this Book

Nuts

ALMONDS

Rusty Hall's dry-farmed almonds and almond brittle are available at the Santa Monica and Santa Barbara farmers' markets from October until spring, or call 1-888-549-9126.

CHESTNUTS

Amber Oaks Raspberries
Auburn, CA
530-885-3420
Available at Sacramento area farmers' markets. Also U-Pick available from mid-September to mid-November.

GREEN AND DRIED PISTACHIOS

Santa Barbara Pistachio Company
1-800-896-1044
santabarbarapistachios.com

HAZELNUTS

Holmquist Hazelnut Orchards
360-988-9240 or 360-988-0171 or 1-800-720-0895
fax: 360-988-6202
Du Chilly and Barcelona hazelnuts, hazelnut meal, hazelnut oil.

Dried Fruits

Bogdanich Farms
209-892-3159
High-quality dried fruits—apricots, nectarines, pears, figs, peaches, cherries, pluots, and prunes. Plus fruit trays, jams, jellies, and shelled walnuts, almonds, pistachios.

France Ranch
2042 S. Newcomb
Porterville, CA 93257
Dried apricots, prunes, Hartley walnuts.

Peacock Family Farms
Dinuba, CA 93618
559-591-5786 (for a catalog)
Red and Gold Flame raisins.

DATES

Flying Disc Ranch
760-399-5313
Deglet Noor, Medjool, Barhi, Dayri, and Zahidi
(certified organic).

Oasis Date Gardens
1-800-827-8017
Many unusual and rare varieties (transitional and organic).

DaVall Date Gardens
619-398-4600
Honey and Empress.

Japanese Dried Persimmons (Hoshi Gaki)

Otow Orchard
Tosh Kuratomi
Granite Bay, CA 95746
916-791-1656
Will ship long distance.

Penryn Orchard Specialties
Jeffrey Rieger
Penryn, CA
916-769-5462
www.penrynorchardspecialties.com
Will ship long distance.

Brenner Ranch
Jim and Karen Brenner
Newcastle, CA 95658
916-663-4578

Also see www.slowfoodusa.org/ark.

Boiled Cider Jelly

Wood's Cider Mill
RFD 2 (1482 Weathersfield Center Road)
Springfield, VT 05156
802-263-5547

Olive Oils, Aged Red Wine Vinegar

Nick Sciabica & Sons
P.O. Box 1246
Modesto, CA 95353-1246
1-800-551-9612
Olive varietals: Mission, Manzanillo, Marsala, Sevillana (organic available); orange-olive oil; aged red wine vinegar.

Bariani Olive Oil
Phone or fax: 916-689-9059
e-mail: Bariani@aol.com
Unrefined, cold-pressed, extra virgin olive oil, full-bodied and soft. Will ship.

Smoke-Dried Tomatoes

Boggy Creek Farm
Austin, TX
e-mail: boggycrk@realtime.net
www.boggycreekfarm.com
Cold-smoked organic tomatoes, packed in oil or dry.

Wild Rice

Manitok Wild Rice
Box 97
Callaway, MN 56521
218-375-3425

Grey Owl Foods
P.O. Box 88
Grand Rapids, MN 55744
218-327-2281

Books

Beans, Greens, and Sweet Georgia Peaches by Damon Lee Fowler. New York: Broadway Books, 1998.

Cornucopia II, a Source Book of Edible Plants by Stephen Facciola. Vista, CA: Kampong Publications, 1998. This most valuable sourcebook of edible plants is one that I used constantly to verify names and track down the origins of countless fruits and vegetables.

Garden Seed Inventory, Fifth Edition. Decorah, IA: Seed Savers Exchange, 1999. Another valuable sourcebook of heirloom seeds that gives common names of edible plants, their histories, and dates of introduction. It also tracks the rise and fall of the numbers of plant varieties available since 1981.

New Cooking from the Old West by Greg Patent. Berkeley, CA: Ten Speed Press, 1996. A regional cookbook with a special emphasis on Montana and great pies.

Recipes from Paradise: Life and Food on the Italian Riviera by Fred Plotkin. Boston: Little Brown and Company, 1997. Recipes for many of the foods we find in our farmers' markets, including bean fritters.

Savoring the Seasons of the Northern Heartland by Beth Dooley and Lucia Watson. New York: Alfred A. Knopf, 2000. A regional and seasonal cookbook for the Midwest.

The Complete Meat Cookbook by Bruce Aidells and Denis Kelly. Boston: Houghton Mifflin Company, 1998. These are the authorities on meat.

The Huckleberry Book by 'Asta Bowen. Helena, MT: American Geographic Publishing, 1998. A personal little book devoted to Montana's favorite fruit.

The Herbfarm Cookbook by Jerry Traunfeld. New York: Scribner, 2000. Lots of ideas for cooking with herbs of all kinds.

The Great Citrus Book by Allen Susser. Berkeley, CA: Ten Speed Press, 1997. Sorts out the citrus family.

The Random House Book of Vegetables by Roger Phillips and Martyn Rix. New York: Random House, 1993. A very useful sourcebook for identifying edible plants. Uses a lot of photographs.

The Kitchen Garden: A Passionate Gardener's Comprehensive Guide to Growing Good Things to Eat by Sylvia Thompson. New York: Bantam, 1995. A warm and personal approach to growing and cooking vegetables.

Heirloom Vegetable Gardening by William Woys Weaver. New York: Henry Holt, 1997. An excellent illustrated sourcebook for heirloom vegetables.

Websites

Seed Savers Exchange: www.seedsavers.org
This group has played an extremely crucial role in the heirloom seed movement and is the first to have focused on the need to save seeds and to create a way in which they could be exchanged among gardeners. They can also be reached at
Seed Savers Exchange
3076 North Winn Road
Decorah, IA 52101
319-382-5990

Slow Food (International Slow Food Movement)
www.slowfood.com
Slow Food promotes the pleasures of the table hand-in-hand with the practices of sustainable farming, animal husbandry, and the artisan ways of making, preserving, and cooking food. Slow Food produces a handsome quarterly publication and a newsletter, and there are groups all over the world, including the United States. Their toll-free number is 877-756-9336.

ON FINDING CSAS:

To find a farm near you that has a CSA program (Community Supported Agriculture) go to www.csa-center.org. Participating farms are listed by state, with phone numbers and e-mail addresses. It's a useful, well-maintained, and easy-to-use site.

ON FINDING FARMERS' MARKETS:

The guide I have depended on most is the *National Directory of Farmers' Markets*, which is published biennially by the USDA. The directory is also available on the Web at www.ams.usda.gov/farmersmarkets in a more updated form. In the directory are state-by-state listings for markets, their locations, dates, and phone numbers. You may also call 1-800-384-8704.

Surfing the Web can also produce results by entering the names of a state followed by "farmers' market." Generally, you'll get a list.

Most towns and cities also know about their own farmers' markets. A call placed to the chamber of commerce or food editor of the local newspaper should produce results.

Most markets are held on Saturdays, the biggest market day for shopping. If you're entering a town cold, with no information, look for flags, signs, banners, a town square, or a park. I've been happily surprised by how easy it is to ferret out a market. And of course you can always ask people. While most Saturday markets are held in the morning, that's not always the case, which is why a guide is helpful.

If a town can support a Saturday market, it will usually have a weekday or evening market as well since plants keep producing regardless of the day. Big cities frequently have, in addition to their large principal market, smaller satellite markets located in various neighborhoods. These are frequently easier to shop at because of their small size.

Index